The SINGLE WOMAN'S VACATION GUIDE

▶ ▶

The
SINGLE WOMAN'S
VACATION GUIDE

Linda E. Ledray

Fawcett Columbine ▶ *New York*

▶ ▶

Library of Congress Catalog Card Number: 87-91559

ISBN: 0-499-90210-2

Book design by Beth Tondreau Design
Cover design by James R. Harris
Photo: FPG International

Manufactured in the United States of America
First Edition: March 1988

10 9 8 7 6 5 4 3 2 1

Please note: All foreign prices mentioned in the text are based on the exchange rates cited by the author and were accurate at the time of her research. Recent fluctuations in exchange rates will affect prices. All other information is accurate as of publication, however changes occur frequently in the tourist industry, and it is wise to confirm ahead of time.

Contents

Romance, and Sex on Vacation ▸ Traveling Healthy ▸
Keeping in Touch with Those Back Home ▸ Capturing Your
Impressions As You Go ▸ Customs, Rules, and Regulations
▸ A Moment of Freedom

Part II
VACATION DESTINATIONS

Acknowledgments

I was fortunate to grow up in a home where dreaming was encouraged and recognized not as "the impossible," but rather as the first step in planning . . . in making your dreams come true. Instead of recognizing limits, I was taught to look for a way to overcome them. Often it took persistence, hard work, and the help of friends, but there always seemed to be a way. The completion of this book is "another one of those impossible dreams . . ." turned into a plan and now a reality. It, too, took a lot of persistence, hard work, and the help of good friends. It's those friends I'd like to thank.

In particular I want to thank Linda McMahon, Operations Manager for AAA in Minneapolis, for sharing with me the vast wealth of information and expertise she has developed as a result of her many years of experience in the travel industry. Also helpful in providing me with suggestions, information, general support, and critical review of my manuscript were Barbara Chester, Patrick W. Ledray, Teresa Ledray, Tom Kiresuk, Zig Stelmachers, Mary Wichterman, and my editor, Michelle Russell. Every author needs a good critic. I'd like to thank my best critic and dearest friend and associate, Susan Voosen, who somehow found a nice way to tell me what she didn't like.

Instead of resenting my frequent absences, my friend Mark Hartsch and my staff at the Sexual Assault Resource Service in Minneapolis encouraged my work on this project and carried on valiantly in my absence. I wish to extend my sincere thanks and appreciation to them: Barbara Ahlberg, Maureen Cullen, Jenny Fransen, Chris Lewis, Michael Luxenberg, Barbara Rolland-Martinek, Debi Heiberger, Tracy Mattson, DeAnn Rice, Linda Stock, and Sharon Tucker.

Thank you all.

Introduction:
The Adventure of
Traveling Alone

*T*raveling has always been my first love. I was fortunate to grow up in a home where I heard plenty of stories of faraway places. In 1924, at the age of seventeen, my father had left the home of his youth to work as a seaman and explore the world. As a child, I often asked to see the brown-and-white picture of himself that he carried in his wallet. It showed him as a young man, standing on a crowded street in the exotic city of Shanghai. Just to hear once again the name of that city filled me with anticipation. I had to go there. I longed for the day when I, too, could travel the world as he did.

I started traveling on my own when I was fourteen years old. I visited nearly every state before graduating from high school, and it wasn't long before I decided I wanted to visit every country in the world. I've still got a long way to go before I reach that goal, but working toward it is the real fun anyway. And although I have taken exciting trips with friends and lovers, my most wonderful experiences by far have occurred during the trips I took alone. These were excursions during which I indulged my whims, took advantage of chance occurrences, and met fascinating people—without worrying how someone else might be affected.

Having taken so many trips on my own, it still surprises me how many women wouldn't even consider taking a solo vacation. My administrative assistant, Susan, is a case in point. As a frequent flyer, I received a coupon enabling me to fly free anywhere in the United

States. I gave Susan, who deserved a long-overdue vacation, my coupon. Over the next six months I periodically asked her when and where she was going. She remained noncommittal. Finally, two months before I knew the coupon was due to expire, I asked her more seriously about her plans. She confessed that she had none. She wasn't married or dating anyone at the time, and she had a list of good reasons why she couldn't or wouldn't travel with any of her current female friends. I was shocked to discover that she hadn't even thought about taking a vacation on her own. She was equally shocked to discover that I thought it was a viable option.

Perhaps, like Susan, you long to take a vacation but present circumstances do not provide a traveling companion. Like Susan, you are probably a successful, competent, assertive, and otherwise independent woman. You may have traveled alone on business but never considered traveling alone for pleasure.

Perhaps you fear it would be unsafe. We've all heard stories about the single woman traveler being prey to the con man, the gigolo, the rapist, the thief. However, staying at home certainly does not guarantee your safety. In fact, more women are raped in their own home than any other single location. Besides, there are precautions you can take (which I provide in Chapter 4) to make your travel safer, just as there are things you can do to be less vulnerable in your everyday life.

You might think that traveling alone is socially unacceptable. Maybe you're worried about what other people would think—that you're out to get a man, or that you don't have any friends. Or you fear that if you travel alone, you'll stay alone, without anyone to share your experiences, to talk to. Worst of all, you think you'll be forced to eat alone, and therefore feel self-conscious and unwanted in restaurants.

But just because you leave on your vacation by yourself doesn't mean that you'll remain alone. In fact, one of the real advantages of traveling solo is that you are much more likely to meet other people along the way or when you get to the area you're visiting. When you travel with a friend or lover, most of your interaction is restricted to that one person. When you're on your own, you have more opportunities to meet new people.

If these fears and concerns have been keeping you at home, help is on the way. The information in *The Single Woman's Vacation Guide* will help you to arrange a fabulous vacation, as it helped Susan when she had the means but not the plans. For Susan, I mapped out a trip, made her travel arrangements, and told her what she needed to pack. She escaped the Minnesota cold, visited the then recently opened Epcot Center in Orlando, Florida, and had a wonderful time. Best of all, she learned that she could travel safely and happily on her own. Since that time, she has gone on to visit New York, Chicago, Maine, and Paris by herself.

The first part of this book provides the specific, practical information you need, gained from my own personal experience, to safely step out and meet the challenges and experience the excitement of traveling on your own, from advice on working with a travel agent to packing and getting there. Plus, there's helpful advice on areas of special concern to you as a woman on your own, such as how to deal with a stranger's advances, how to go about meeting someone to have dinner or spend some time with, even information on safe sex and your safety in general. The rest of the book is devoted to fully describing twenty-two fabulous vacations that are ideally suited to the single woman. I know because I've gone to each spot on my own. Some are areas I have visited over and over again. All are places to which I'd like to return.

This is not a bargain guide, although it does address ways you can travel well without going to great expense. The vacation suggestions in this book are meant to inspire you. Each trip has been carefully chosen with your special needs in mind. And since the time of year you decide to take your vacation plays a very significant role in your choice of destination, I have organized the trips by season. Winter vacation suggestions are presented under the headings of "For Those Who Like It Hot," and "For Those Who Like It Cold." Summer vacation suggestions are presented under three option headings: "In Pursuit of Adventure," for those who want an unusual challenge; "Rest and Relaxation in the Summertime," for those who want to really relax; and "Special Interest Trips," for those who want to focus their vacation around an activity or interest they especially enjoy and share with others.

To help you evaluate the vacation destinations, I have rated each trip according to three criteria: the general ambiance of the setting, the social climate, and the activities available. In addition, information is provided about the area and side trips of interest, special items from the area you may wish to purchase, and preparatory and travel tips specific to each location. Places to stay, restaurants, and special points of interest have been highlighted throughout the text.

If you are somewhat reserved and have difficulty meeting people but want to, one of the special interest or adventure trips may be for you. These trips facilitate interaction without necessitating group activity. (You'll also find lots of suggestions on how and where to meet people with whom to dine or sightsee in Chapter 4.)

If you're inspired to try one of these vacations on your own but are still having a difficult time taking the first step, you may want to ease into it a little. Try traveling to an area where you know someone, perhaps a friend with whom you went to school or used to work. Be sure to arrange for your hotel before you call and tell the person you're coming. That way he or she will not feel obligated to take you in and you can maintain some independence. Plan to meet your friend for lunch and shopping or dinner and a show. Staying on your own will allow you freedom, yet you will have the security of knowing someone in the area who can provide companionship if you feel hesitant about meeting new people.

If you'd still rather postpone your vacation until the perfect traveling companion comes along, you might keep looking and working while life—and your vacation time—passes you by. And that isn't being fair to yourself; you deserve a whole life independent of anyone else. Deciding to vacation alone is not a final decision to exclude other people from your life. Just because you decide on a solo vacation this year does not mean that you have to—or will—do it for the rest of your life. You may even meet someone interesting while you're away. Your decision is simply to take control of your private life, and go where you want to go now. It could be a decision that changes your life. Consider what a reader of one of my local newspapers wrote in response to the paper's request for descriptions of the turning points in readers' lives:

"My turning point came in autumn, when I took my first-ever solo vacation, a three-day weekend trip to a state park. I attended a close-up nature photography workshop. There, in the morning dew and quiet, I rediscovered a packed-away dream of becoming a children's book illustrator. My pace and path have changed. I listen to my heartbeat, dream some more and sing my own song."

▸ ▸

Part I

TIPS FOR A TRAVELING WOMAN

▸ ▸

► ► ►

CHAPTER 1

Destination Yet Unknown: Deciding Where to Go

---

*D*eciding where to go, planning your trip, and anticipating the time away should be an exciting part of your vacation. Make the most of this planning time. Enjoy yourself, broaden your horizon, look around before making the final decision. The reports of your sister's or your best friend's last trip may certainly add to your list of options, but when it comes time to decide where to go on vacation, consider other alternatives as well. Explore new areas and other types of trips. Don't keep going back to the same place each year even though it has become familiar and comfortable. Consider what you really need from a vacation right now, the climate and time of year you will be away, the activities you enjoy, the social climate and the general ambiance you are looking for.

WHAT DO YOU NEED FROM A VACATION?

►────────────────────────────────►

Probably the most important consideration in deciding where to go is determining why you want to go away. What do you need from a vacation at this point in time? Has your life seemed dull and boring lately? Do you need a little excitement and adventure? Or perhaps you have had a hectic business schedule and you need to get away to relax and slow down.

It is important to be honest with yourself about what you really want from your vacation. The wonderful ski trip your friend took might not be the best choice for you when you are exhausted. If you do not really like roughing it, you might want to skip the bike trip through Peru or the river-raft ride through the Grand Canyon, even though it is "the thing to do" in your circle of friends. The real advantage of traveling alone is being able to do just what you want. You do not need to meet the expectations of anyone else.

HOW WELL DO YOU ADAPT TO CHANGE?

The more different the area, inhabitants, and local customs are from what I am used to at home, the more I enjoy a trip. I find that I learn more about myself when I am in a uniquely different culture than at any other time. I can define who I am best when I can see how different I am from someone else. It is exciting for me to discover how the things I take for granted can be so different in another part of the world—something as small as the shape of a piece of butter or as complex as the way people interact.

I have found that the things I always believed to be "truth" are often a totally different "truth" to people of another culture. In Tahiti, for instance, many of the inhabitants believe that the days are actually shorter now than they were ten or fifteen years ago. They believe this because, as we all know, time seems to pass so much more quickly for us now than it did when we were children.

I have found that I can do fine without many of the things I once considered essential, such as a daily shower, eggs for breakfast, a television set, or even a toilet seat. I enjoy the sound of another language even when I cannot understand it. I find listening less distracting when I can forget about words and, instead, concentrate on the musiclike quality of the sounds. I also gain a certain sense of privacy speaking English to another person when most of the people around us cannot understand what we are saying. I enjoy struggling to make myself understood and to understand someone else using a combination of sign language, or a phrase or two I have managed to pick up from the native language. I generally find that if I make an effort to speak the language of the country I am visiting, and speak English slowly, the natives will try to understand me.

I enjoy trying new foods. I even got used to soup for breakfast in Japan. I often do not ask what it is I am eating, however, until after I have formed an opinion based on its taste. I prefer not to let my cultural biases about what is and what is not okay to eat interfere with how much I enjoy the flavor.

An important part of deciding where you want to go on vacation is deciding how well you adapt to a change of routine. Is change something you find an exciting opportunity or is it something you tolerate only if you must? Not everyone enjoys different cultures. You may not be one of those individuals who does. Perhaps going to the Southern states if you live in the north, or to the West Coast if you are from the east is as much of a change as you are ready to encounter.

If you choose to visit another culture, it is especially important for you to understand that a primitive culture is not necessarily an under-privileged one. Who is to say you are better off living in a high-rise in Manhattan than in a grass hut with a thatched roof in Polynesia? Different is just that, different. Better and worse are value judgments that we make based on our sociocultural ideals. And they are very likely different from our next-door neighbors', let alone those of someone raised in another culture.

A CHANGE OF CLIMATE

In considering a change of climate, consider the weather you are leaving as well as the weather to which you will be traveling. Living in Minnesota, I do most of my traveling in January, February, and March. While some people deal well with the cold, I find long, cold winters almost unbearable and need an escape. However, I no longer go south in January. When I vacation in January or February I often go skiing because, as wonderful as it is to arrive at an area that is 80 degrees when I left 20 degrees below zero, eventually I must go back. I also may then have no escape from the cold weather for months to come— an extremely depressing situation to face. If I want to take a warm weather winter vacation, I now wait until late February or March to do so.

When choosing the type of climate you want to vacation in, it is a good idea not to limit your choice to the peak season of an area. In some locations, such as Hawaii, the climate is still quite pleasant during the off season and off-season rates are much lower. You will also find that the islanders are more welcoming to visitors after the crowds have thinned. You will, however, want to miss the rainy season.

It is important to do a little research on off-season climate before deciding when to beat the crowds and avoid paying premium prices. In many areas, the off-season rain, temperature, or humidity levels preclude the likelihood of an enjoyable trip. This, too, is often a matter of personal preference and tolerance. By all means, check the off-season climate and rates first, then decide if the savings are worth the price you may pay in personal discomfort.

This book provides a variety of destinations for travel during all seasons of the year. In addition to times preferable for most persons, information is provided about off-season climate and special rates available. Special attention is paid to identifying areas that do have comfortable climates during the off-season and thus may provide an especially interesting choice for a vacation during more than one time of year.

TAX-DEDUCTIBLE TRAVEL

You may decide that you'd like to take a vacation that will be deductible at tax time. While the 1986 tax laws changed the number and amount of allowable deductions, it is still possible to deduct travel expenses. There are two types that are still deductible: trips that relate to your career, and trips in which you participate in scientific research or provide a service under the auspices of a qualifying charitable organization.

Earthwatch and University Research Expeditions Program (UREP), which is run by the University of California at Berkeley, are, for example, qualifying charitable organizations. What this means is that even if the money you give to the group goes to cover your expedition costs, it is tax deductible. In addition, travel expenses (such as airfare to the site) that are directly related to your research trip with them are also considered tax deductible by the IRS. Don't assume that all nonprofit organizations are qualifying charitable organizations, at least for tax purposes. They must have filed under the public charity section—501(c)(3)—of the Internal Revenue Code to qualify.

While you can still deduct career-related leisure travel, the rules are more stringent here, too. Now you can take the deduction only if the trip is necessary in order for you to keep up with your existing job and you're not being reimbursed by your employer. For instance, if you are a registered nurse, in most states you must obtain a certain number of continuing education credits to maintain your license. If you go on a cruise that has daily lectures and where the bulk of your time is spent in educational activities, this trip would likely qualify as tax deductible. If it makes you eligible for a promotion it will *not* be deductible unless it is also necessary to maintain your present job. Because the IRS is especially leery of foreign travel, you may need to justify why you had to go to France, for instance, for a seminar. If you were interested in research conducted by a particular French research team, or you were attending an international convention, then you will likely have no problems in justifying the trip to France.

According to the new tax code (Section 170(k)), "No deduction shall be allowed . . . for traveling expenses (including amounts expended for meals and lodging) while away from home, whether paid directly or by reimbursement, unless there is no significant element of personal pleasure, recreation or vacation in such travel." That doesn't mean, however, that to deduct your Earthwatch trip, for instance, you can't have a good time. What it means is that the travel must be genuinely work-oriented. You must be able to document that the majority of your time was spent on work-related activities. A daily log in which you indicate the amount of time allocated to work is probably the best documentation you can provide. You can also no longer deduct 50 percent of the cost if you spent half the time working and the other half visiting relatives or vacationing. The entire trip will likely be disallowed.

The bottom line appears to be that it's still okay to combine business and pleasure as long as the primary purpose is business and you can document it. If you're considering a trip and are uncertain if it meets the criteria, contact your tax consultant or your local IRS office.

For information on available UREP write: UREP, University of California, Desk NR, Berkeley, CA 94720; or call (415) 642-6586. For information on Earthwatch trips write: Earthwatch, 10 Juniper Road, Box 127, Belmont, MA 02178. *Working Holidays* is a guide listing short-term jobs around the world. For $7.50 you can obtain a copy by writing: Central Bureau for Educational Visits, 141 Laurier Avenue, Ottawa, Ontario, Canada K1P 5J3.

RATING CRITERIA

As a quick guide to help you sort through all the options and make your vacation choice, each destination included in this book has been rated according to three criteria described below: general ambiance, activities, and social climate. Each criterion has been given one to three stars. One star is equivalent to a "good" or "adequate" rating: As a single woman your needs will be met. This is a minimum requirement for inclusion in this book. A destination was not considered acceptable for inclusion if it did not receive at least one star in each of the three areas rated. Two stars is equivalent to well above the norm; and three stars, the highest rating, indicates the destination is exceptional in that particular aspect for a woman traveling alone.

Each section also includes a brief description of the general ambiance, social climate, and activities of the area. You may thus decide for yourself, depending on your vacation needs, how you might rate each particular area.

General Ambiance

One of the most important determinants of your enjoyment on a vacation is the general ambiance of the area—that special charm and warmth that some areas exude and others lack. The ambiance may result from the resort or hotel; from the surrounding area; from the staff, guests, local residents; or from the way everything fits together. The general ambiance is more than the beauty of the setting, it is the feeling you get while in the setting. It does not necessarily result from luxurious surroundings. Sometimes the most charming areas are rather simple by comparison. Because this is to a great extent a matter of personal preference, the general ambiance is rated and described. While the description is, of course, from one point of view, I have tried to provide enough information so that you can critique the area with your own particular likes and dislikes in mind.

Social Climate

Preference is given to an area that provides a number of options in its social climate. Even those of us who prefer being with other people sometimes enjoy quiet times alone, especially on a vacation, I believe it is important to be able to maintain control over when you are with others and when you are by yourself. I like to do things with other people, but I dislike feeling pressured to join a group or play a game. Thus, a location that facilitates interaction with other men and women in pairs and groups and provides ample space to be alone when you so choose receives the higher rating.

The staff at a hotel or resort play a special role in setting the social tone. They may be warm and friendly, providing you with considerable information about the area and adding to your feeling of comfort during your stay, or they may simply do their job. While staff may come and go, for the most part the management sets the tone, and much more consistency exists in any one location than most travelers expect. This, too, will be taken into consideration when each area is rated on its social climate.

Eating can be an important part of your social activity. People normally eat three meals a day, and on a vacation they may eat more often. Many women consider the thought of dining alone as the most disconcerting part of vacationing alone. You may or may not feel this way. If you want to eat alone, possibly over a good book, it is nice to have that option. Some vacation settings have tables where you can either eat alone or with your private party; others may also have a few large tables where joining a group is encouraged, or a special table where single diners are seated together. These options are reflected in a higher rating for social climate.

Some settings allow for more contact with the local residents. When this is the case, you soon get a feel for how comfortable the locals are with tourists. As a guest in their area, your own friendliness will greatly affect how they respond to you. The local men in some parts of the world, however, are less likely to let a single woman enjoy her visit without constant comment or attempts at flirtation. While this behavior may be intended as a compliment, I prefer to avoid it. It is not the kind of attention I like from men. As a result, while general friendliness on the part of the local residents will certainly add to the rating, consistent harassment from the men will lower it.

Remember, these criteria are provided only as a guide for you to use in making your own determination based on your own preferences and needs. They are meant as a point of reference for you to use in evaluating your options.

Activity Rating

The activity rating was determined by the number of activity options, equipment available, and staff for resort areas.

Although you may prefer a vacation spot that gives you a limited choice of activities, I give a higher rating to those places that offer a greater variety of activities because I believe it is a good idea to keep your options open. Even if you decide you are only interested in tennis, for instance, it may be nice to have alternatives if you find your arm muscles are not as well developed as you thought and you want to take a day off.

Areas that provide high-quality equipment for your use, free or at a reasonable rental rate, also receive a higher rating. While you may prefer to take your own equipment, as I often do, it is sometimes nice not to have to lug extra baggage in and out of airports.

Resort staff who are proficient in a sport, who are available to give you tips or lessons, or who will arrange for a partner if they do not play themselves also improve an area's activity rating.

► ► ►

CHAPTER 2

Getting Ready to Go: Final Preparations

Once you have made up your mind where you want to go, the next step is to decide on the specifics of your trip. Do you want to go with a group, purchase an individual package, or put a trip together on your own?

Obtaining the proper documents and making decisions such as your mode of transportation are essential components of the trip's preparation. This planning, as well as the actual traveling to your destination, should also be part of your vacation. With the proper information and a little preparation you can avoid letting these necessary arrangements become burdensome tasks. This chapter provides you with suggestions and the information you need to keep your vacation preparation simple, manageable, and fun.

WORKING WITH A TRAVEL AGENT

►———————————————————————————►

Travel today is a complex industry. With all the options that are available and the frequent changes in regulations, a travel agent can prove to be a valuable resource for obtaining the information you need in order to make educated choices.

The services of a travel agent are free to you. Agents are paid a commission by the airlines and travel companies. This commission is already built into the price and will be charged whether or not you use their services.

While travel agents do not work for any particular tour operator, it is naive to believe that they are totally unbiased. Often they will get a higher commission or other incentives from a preferred list of companies. Since their commission is a percentage of the tour price or airfare, they make more when they sell the high-priced packages. That's why it's important to find a travel agent you know and trust, someone with whom you can develop a rapport. A good agent depends on repeat business. The best way to get you back for your next trip is to provide you with good service on this one.

You'll get the best help from your travel agent if you provide him or her with a complete picture of what you want. How much do you really want to spend? Do you want to join a group or plan a trip on your own? Do you prefer a big resort or an out-of-the-way bed and breakfast? Is the cost of the transportation or the convenience of the schedule your most important consideration? Briefly describing a favorite trip you took in the past may help him or her understand the type of vacation you want now.

Maybe you have already decided on the trip you want. Perhaps you'll be taking one of the trips described in this book. All you want the agent to do is make the necessary reservations, answer a few remaining questions, provide you with visa forms, and issue you your tickets. Know, and clearly communicate, what you want and do not want, and you will be in a much better position to get the service you desire. Remember, you are the only one who can make the final decision. While you may listen to someone else's opinion, you should pick the trip that's right for you.

Selecting a Travel Agent

You should use the same care in selecting a travel agent as you would in choosing a doctor, lawyer, or therapist. You can start by asking friends to recommend a travel agent with whom they have been pleased. If there is a travel agency located near your home or office, you may want to check it out. Look at the ads in your local newspaper or phone book. Remember, just because you talk with an agent, and he or she sends you some information does not mean you are obligated to book your vacation through him or her. If you are not totally satisfied with the information provided, or you feel the agent is pushing too hard, look for one with whom you'll feel more comfortable. You'll find a wide range of professionalism, experience, expertise, and sensitivity to your needs and desires. You might want to look for an agency that has the following:

Certified Travel Counselors

An agent with CTC (Certified Travel Counselor) after his or her name has completed a rigorous travel course. While CTCs are usually eight- to ten-year veterans, they are required to have a minimum of five years' experience by the time they have completed the program.

Area Specialists

The more sophisticated offices will have individuals available who have expertise in specific areas or countries of the world. They will have traveled there themselves, usually many times, and thus are especially familiar with what's available. These specialists can help you book a trip to that particular area, tailoring it to your specific needs.

Computerized Office

Agents who work in computerized offices will have much greater immediate access to information. For instance, they will be able to inform you of flight options over the phone simply by checking their computer, and you will be able to select the flight you want immediately.

TOURS AND PACKAGES

▶ ──────────────────────────────── ▶

Depending on your personal preference, the part of the world you will be traveling to, and the time of the year you want to go, you may want to look into tour and package options.

Independent Travel Packages

Package options range from adventure trips with a guide to those that are "on your own." Some include air fare and hotel, others a rental car or boat trip, and still others everything down to tips and a limousine to take you from your home to the airport. The most important option, which most people do not realize, is that you do not need to join a group to take advantage of the savings and convenience of a package price. Many companies offer "package" trips that include transportation, transfers, accommodations, meals, and sightseeing that you can purchase and use as an individual. These packages usually offer you a moderate to significant savings over what it would cost you to book the trip for yourself. Most importantly, they offer you the experience of a trip operator who is familiar with the area and knows which hotels, airlines, and local tour operators are the most reliable and, therefore, offer the best value. These packages may, however, only be available during limited time periods, with even more limited departure dates. They may or may not take you to the specific hotels or locations you have in mind, and they may or may not allow for extensions so that you can include another area or city.

Group Travel Packages

You may prefer to join a group. Group travel was first developed in the Victorian era by Thomas Cook as a convenience for his friends. The idea was so successful that an entire industry resulted. What a great way to see an exotic, isolated part of the world without the hassle of trying to find a place to stay or order a meal in a language you don't understand. Everything is prearranged. Group travel with a guide familiar with the area and language has opened many remote parts of the world to those who long to see new areas but tremble at the thought of venturing out on their own.

While you may book by yourself, joining a group tour can be an excellent way to travel independently yet with other people. I find an advantage to this form of travel is the loose association with the group. You can always find someone in your group to join for a meal if you so choose. Not having come with anyone, you are, however, free to go off on your own if and when you so desire. You can either join the planned activity or not depending on how the spirit moves you.

The quality of the group tour or package is dependent not only on price but also to a great extent upon the experience and expertise of the company who puts the tour together. Your service, rooms, and meals in an area will vary as a result of their clout and the quality of their relationship with local tour representatives and hotels.

I have included a number of tours in this book, partially because the tours are great ones for a woman traveling alone and partially because the company organizing the trip is first rate. These companies include Mr. Australia Experiences, Outdoor Adventure River Specialists (OARS), Society Expeditions, and Wilderness Travel. Other companies I would recommend include Lindblad, Mountain Travel, and Sobek. If you want to visit a particular area or country not included in this book, I would suggest you check with these companies to see if they offer a trip meeting your needs. My experience and that of many other people I have checked with is that the same high-quality value and expertise in travel is found consistently on trips these companies organize. Their staffs are enthusiastic, qualified, and personable. These companies can be trusted to do everything possible to make your trip a rewarding vacation.

Before booking, it's also important to have an idea of the type of people who typically take tours. Ask the tour operator. A general rule of thumb is that the more expensive the tour, the older and wealthier the clientele will be. For instance, people who book through Lindblad and Society Expeditions are usually in their fifties, sixties, and seventies. They are often retired professionals and businesspeople. As a result, the trips are usually less strenuous and offer alternatives to the more arduous activities. Wilderness Travel, Mountain Travel, and Sobek cater to a younger professional and blue-collar group. Most people on these trips will be in their thirties and forties, with a few in their twenties and fifties. The OARS trips attract a still-younger group. I found most travelers to be in their twenties and thirties, although a few were much older and managed well.

Know Before You Book

Before you book a tour be sure you are clear what is and is not included. How much time will you spend in the areas you visit and is that adequate for you to see the sights you want? What hotels are used, what meals will be included, and what sightseeing tours will you take? You'll also want to check to see if the tour price is guaranteed, and if there is a cancellation policy. If the tour operator is not well known, check with your travel agent or your local Better Business Bureau before making your final decision. Remember, you get what you pay for on any trip.

You can always find a less expensive tour to an area; however, when meals, transfers, and sightseeing are not included, they can greatly add to your expenses. You also may be very unhappy when you wind up thirty minutes from the beach or in a poorly maintained hotel when you could have stayed in the best facility for only a moderate increase in the total price. Check the fine print to see if the tour operator can move you to another hotel if the one listed is fully booked. Unless you are very flexible and can deal with less than the best, don't purchase the least expensive tour—it may not be a bargain in the long run. I'd recommend paying a little more and going with a reputable company.

Bargain or Rip-off?

If the price looks too good to be true, it probably is. Be cautious, especially if the trip is to Mexico or the company is new and unknown. Just recently there have been a number of tours set up to parts of Mexico and elsewhere in the world that have never taken place. Small travel companies, sometimes even airlines, struggling to survive in an era of deregulation and stiff competition, are not always able to fulfill their obligations.

If you book your flight with an ASTA (American Society of Travel Agents) agent and the operator is covered under the ASTA Payment Protection Plan, you will get a full refund if the trip is canceled. The United States Tour Operations Association (USTOA) also has a Payment Protection Plan for its member operators. Otherwise, your advanced payment is only as good as the company with whom you book.

PLANNING YOUR OWN TRIP

If you decide you want to put a trip together on your own, I'd suggest you begin by writing the tourist bureau in the city, state, or country you want to visit. Tell them as much as you can about what you want to see and when you want to go, and ask them to send you any available information.

You might want to pick up a few brochures to see what the more reputable travel companies include in their tours to your area of choice. You'll certainly want to purchase one or more travel books.

Your travel agent can be helpful in suggesting hotels. Many agencies now charge a small fee for booking hotel rooms out of the country. Many overseas hotels do not pay the agents their commission, so the agents need to cover the expense of their time and telexes. You can, of course, make the necessary arrangements on your own. Allow plenty of time if you plan on writing to the hotel. Remember, if you're going to a foreign country, the small hotels may not have any English-speaking staff. If you don't speak the language, you may be able to find someone at a local university who can translate your letter for you. This will prevent even longer delays in your receiving a response. Also, while all mail in the United States goes by air, that is not the case in foreign countries. Letters sent to and from Europe, South America, Australia, and Asia that are not marked "Air Mail" will go by boat. I'd suggest sending a self-addressed envelope marked "Air Mail" for your reply.

Choosing an Airline

I usually prefer to fly on the major national carrier of the country to which I am flying. There are a number of advantages to this. First, from the moment I step on the plane, I usually feel as though I am in that country. The flight attendants will speak the national language in addition to English, and the food will usually be more typical of the destination country. In addition, should I need to change my return flight, I can count on finding a number of ticket offices and airline representatives within the country. You cannot expect one airline to change a reservation on another carrier. The better-established carriers, and the national carriers also, often get preferred landing schedules and fly to more cities within the country more often.

Even when you purchase a package or tour with a group, you should make a separate decision about the airline and flight you take. I strongly recommend you carefully consider the airline carrier and the flight schedule before you book your trip. Not only should you ask your travel agent or tour operator about your time of departure and the time of arrival at your final destination, but you should ask about the number and length of stopovers. If you find that your flight is not direct but involves many or long stops en route, you should ask about alternative flights and alternative air carriers.

If you are booking a package or group tour, your tour operator may put pressure on you to take the group flight however inconvenient it is to you. Tour operators often need to sell a minimum number of seats in order to get the group rate or a free flight for the escort. Also, a more convenient flight may cost you more because you won't get the group discount rate. If this is the case, you will have to decide if the cost difference is worth the inconvenience of the flight. It may be, however, that you can take a more convenient flight with fewer transfers on another carrier for the same price or just a little more.

When booking a flight I generally allow two hours for going through customs. International flights can always be delayed and customs usually takes longer than expected. I also make note of earlier flights; if I clear customs faster than I expected I can try to get on one of these as a standby. About 50 percent of the time I'm able to take the earlier flight. Even with discount tickets that are not transferable, I have never had a problem switching to an earlier flight at no extra charge with the major U.S. carriers.

Flight Prices

Airline prices are subject to unannounced changes. Booking a flight will not guarantee you the quoted price. Your price is only guaranteed when you have actually paid for your ticket. If there are no cancellation or change penalties, I would recommend charging a ticket to your credit card as soon as you find a flight and price with which you are satisfied. If you find a lower fare later, you can cancel the flight, and usually you will get a full refund. Be aware, however, that today more and more airlines are imposing stiff penalties for cancellations or changes in the time or day you wish to fly. Penalties vary according to fare category. Typically, the more you pay for your flight, the more flexible your ticket will be. If you purchase a full-fare ticket, there will less likely be penalties for changes. Penalties for bargain fares may be as high as 100 percent. That means that if you book and pay for your flight and then are unable to make that particular flight, you will probably lose the full price of your ticket and receive no refund.

Finally, as it gets closer to the vacation or holiday season, flight prices will very likely go up. By planning and paying for your trip early, you may save hundreds of dollars.

There are a lot of bargains on flights. Airlines will usually allocate a certain number of seats as "Q fares," the lowest; others as "M fares," an intermediate price; and then the remainder as "Y fares," the standard coach price. This means that the person sitting next to you on any flight could have paid much more or much less than you did.

In order to qualify for a lower fare, you must generally meet the airline's restrictions. This may mean that you must book twenty-one or thirty days before your scheduled departure and stay a certain length of time, usually seven to thirty days, or over a Friday night or Saturday. Sometimes you must fly midweek, at night, or through the carrier's hub city.

It's important to know what the restrictions and options are before you decide if the inconvenience is worth the difference in the cost of the flight.

Charter Flights

Travel companies and local businesses will often charter a plane for a special group. Most of the cut-rate package vacations use chartered flights. Sometimes the planes used are chartered from the major airlines and sometimes they are planes belonging to a small company and used exclusively for charter. If you're interested, you can always ask the tour operator what type of plane will be used before you book the flight. You should also ask what their policies are about delays.

One of the major disadvantages to taking a charter is that, unlike the major airlines, charter companies have very limited access to equipment. If your plane has mechanical problems, it is unlikely that they can simply substitute another plane the way a major airline can. Instead, you will most likely wait hours while they fly in the part needed and make the necessary repairs. You will also have a limited choice of flights to and from an area, and may be unable to extend your trip for a day or two.

Airline Terminology

To know what you are getting, you should understand the terminology the airlines use.

Nonstop. A nonstop flight will fly between the city of origin and the destination without stopping along the way.

Direct. Most people confuse this with nonstop service. A direct flight may stop any number of times along the way to drop off or take on more passengers. You may have long layovers. You can usually get off the plane if the stop is long enough. You will not, however, need to change to another plane.

Connecting. If you have a connecting flight you will need to change to another airplane. A real disadvantage of this type of schedule is the possibility that your flights will not connect. If your first flight is late, for instance, the flight you were scheduled to connect with may already have gone. If that happens, I'd suggest you immediately check for the next available flight, on all carriers, and try to get on standby. If at all possible, it is helpful to use only one carrier when you must connect to another flight. Out of courtesy and good business sense, an airline will often hold a flight if another of their planes is coming in a few minutes late with passengers who are connecting to the flight.

Standby. When a plane is booked, meaning all the seats have been reserved, you can still get on a standby list for the flight. You must, however, be at the airport "standing by" in order to do this. Many people book a flight, even pay for the ticket—which is, of course, refundable under most circumstances—but they don't show up. I have flown standby on many occasions. Only once was I unsuccessful when I tried to get on a flight standby.

No Show. Someone who booked a flight, then didn't call to cancel when his or her plans changed.

Waiting List. You can buy a ticket at a higher price and still get on the waiting list for one of the lower special fare tickets. If you do get on at the lower fare, you will be refunded the difference. You may also get on a waiting list for a flight that is fully booked. Unlike standby, you don't need to go to the airport to be put on the waiting list.

Overbooking. When more tickets have been sold than there are seats, the plane is overbooked. Airlines routinely do this because so many people make reservations but then don't show up for the flight. Airlines may overbook 16 percent or even more in an attempt to avoid flying with empty seats and losing revenue. This is why, except during the holidays, it's usually possible to get on a fully booked plane as a standby.

Choosing Your Hotel

In addition to price and location you will want to consider available services when you select a hotel. You will find you have a wide range of options—from a bed and breakfast, which provides simply that, a bed and breakfast, to a resort center, where all your vacation needs can be met on the premises. There are a number of organizations that rate hotels and cruise ships. Cleanliness, services, and facilities are factors considered in the rating, which will vary somewhat from place to place and country to country. The hotels and shops that get the highest rating, five stars, are also likely to be the most expensive. This is most often because they provide a multitude of services (such as swimming pools, tennis courts with an on-site pro, and even their own golf course). If you are not interested in using these facilities, you may want to choose a hotel without them, and thus reduce the price of your room.

When I am visiting a foreign country whose language I do not speak,

I usually stay at a large hotel that gets a lot of foreign visitors. At such hotels I am confident that most of the staff will speak English. I still try to speak the language, but when I get stuck or lazy, they can help me out. I can also get information and directions from the front desk in English. In addition, when traveling alone, I'm more likely to meet other English-speaking guests here, even if English is their second language.

When traveling in a developing country, I stick with the better hotels. While in the United States, I would feel comfortable staying in most two- or three-star hotels, in Morocco, for instance, I would not.

Nonsmoking Rooms

In response to consumer requests, some major hotel chains now offer special rooms to nonsmokers only. You can order a "catalog" of nonsmoking hotel rooms from Down Home Computer Services, 5713 Sam Houston Circle, Austin, TX 78731; (512) 345-5188.

Hotels That Cater to Women

Today, women make up 30 to 40 percent of the customers in hotels, and hotels that are interested in attracting women's business are attempting to better meet their needs. Since women tend to be more security conscious, these hotels are installing better lighting and closed-circuit television monitors in garages, pool areas, and other public rooms. They are also providing dead-bolt locks and electronic locking systems with numberless credit card–style keys. Nonsecurity special touches include skirt hangers, shower caps, hand lotion, and hair dryers. If you book directly, you may want to ask the hotel if they have implemented any of these security precautions and if they provide the special amenities in your room.

Renting a Car

If you think you may want a rental car while you're on vacation, it's best to reserve one when you book your trip. Shop around or ask your travel agent to do so. Some companies offer lower rates when the car is reserved early. A car with a standard transmission is usually less. If you want an automatic transmission you'll need to specify this. If you wait, they may not have an economy car available when you arrive and you will need to pay a higher rate.

Unlimited Mileage

I now always choose to pay a little more for a car with unlimited mileage. When I haven't, I've ended up paying more in the end, because I drove more than I anticipated. After a one-week trip I once paid $350 more than the initial price because of mileage alone.

Discounts

Find out if you're eligible for a discount. Many universities, corporations, automobile clubs, or frequent-flyer programs have discount agreements. The larger car rental companies are more likely to give a discount than the small, local ones.

Foreign Countries

Consider the service available in the country in which you'll be traveling. The larger companies—Hertz, Avis, National, and Budget—may charge a little more, but they are more likely to have service available should you have a problem on the road. They also have more equipment and can provide another car on the spot if there is a problem. A friend of mine had a problem with a Hertz rental car on the way to dinner while in Germany. She called Hertz and explained the situation to them before ordering her dinner. When she left the restaurant, it was in the new car a Hertz representative had delivered to her there. That's the type of service for which you may be paying a little extra.

Drop Charge

You should always check the "drop charge" if you are considering leaving the car in another city. It can get expensive, depending on the company's policy.

Before Renting

Get a confirmation number for the car rental from your travel agent before leaving. When you pick up your rental car be certain they include your confirmation number on your contract. That is the only way your travel agent will get paid. A common practice of some rental car companies is to honor your reservation and give you a car at the rate your travel agent negotiated, but to draw up a new contract. In this way they avoid paying the agent's fee. You don't save money, but they do. When you pick up your rental car, you'll need to show your driver's license and a major credit card, even if you plan to pay in cash. While not impossible, it's hard to rent a car these days without a major credit card. If you don't have one be sure to make arrangements ahead of time. You should also ask for maps, directions to your destination, and, if in a foreign country, road signs and road rules. You can also get these from your travel agent ahead of time so you will be more familiar with them upon arrival.

Some Tips

Some companies have reputations for pushing too hard to get you to take a more expensive car. If you have a reservation for an economy car and that's what you want, insist on it. If one is not available, they should give you a more expensive car at the predetermined rate. Insist on that, too.

Before driving away, have the agent note dents, damage, or a missing spare tire on your agreement so you are not charged when you return the car. Also find out what you should do if you have any car trouble. If you do have trouble, report it immediately. If you should have an accident, call the police and the car company.

When you return your car you'll likely save money if you return it with a full tank. If the rental company fills it up they will usually charge you much more per gallon than you would pay yourself on the street. Check their policy before you take the car.

Car Insurance

You'll also need to decide if you want to pay for extra "personal accident insurance" or "collision damage waiver insurance." The collision insurance will cover the deductible. Some rental car companies now have a $500 to $1,500 deductible. Check your own car insurance before you pay for the extra insurance, which can be very costly. Most car insurance will cover you if you're driving a rental in the United States but not overseas. If you are covered by your own company, you probably do not need to buy the extra coverage. Check with your insurance agent. If your insurance does not cover you, you will need to decide if the additional insurance from the rental car company is worth the price to you.

SINGLE SUPPLEMENTS

Prices on travel ads can be misleading when you plan to travel alone. Prices quoted are usually based on double occupancy. The same trip, if you do not want to share a room, could cost you an additional 25 to 50 percent. For instance, if the price of a tour is quoted at $1,000 per person based on double occupancy, it would then be $2,000 for two people. Let's say there is a 25 percent single occupancy charge; that means it will cost $1,250 if you wanted to go on this tour on your own and have your own room.

More and more pressure is being put on the travel industry to reduce the single supplement charge because more and more people are traveling alone. Unfortunately, most hotels and cruise ships still charge the single traveler more than half the price of a double room.

Hotel and cruise industry spokespersons argue that if a single person stays in a room that two people could occupy without the single supplement, the hotel would lose money. This argument makes sense during the busy season, when the hotel is full, but it does not make sense during the off season when many rooms are empty.

Guaranteed Share Program

Companies such as Sun Line Cruises have responded to this pressure with a reasonable compromise. They have implemented a "Guaranteed Share Program." Under this program, if you ask to have a roommate and they do not find you one, or the ship is not fully booked, you will sail in a single cabin at no extra charge. This compromise is much fairer to everyone. In addition, while they usually charge an additional 50 percent single supplement, during the slow months they have reduced their single supplement on selected cruises to 25 percent.

Singles Plan

Hotels in Tokyo and Osaka, Japan, have even come further in an attempt to bring more single travelers to the area. Many of their local hotels of excellent quality have cut their usual rates in half for the single traveler. Singles can now obtain a clean, attractive room here for $20 to $40 a night. Any Japan National Tourist Office can help you locate one of the participating hotels.

Singles Travel Clubs

There are a number of travel clubs for singles that will find you a roommate for a trip. It usually costs $15 to $60 for a one-year membership. Members range in age from the early twenties to the eighties. Travel clubs work much like dating services: once you've paid your membership you complete a questionnaire describing yourself and your travel interests, and the type of person, male or female, with whom you would prefer to travel. Some clubs also plan their own trips for members only. Singleworld—444 Madison Avenue, New York, NY 10022; (212) 758-2433—is one of the oldest clubs of this nature.

OBTAINING THE PROPER DOCUMENTS

▶──◀

Passport

While the rules may vary as to the type of documentation required to enter a foreign country, most countries require a valid passport. I am one of those people who consider a current passport just as important as a current driver's license. If you are not, you may want to begin the process and apply for a passport early. Passports are now good for ten years.

Your travel agent can provide you with up-to-date information on obtaining a passport in your area. You will most likely need to go to your main post office or a government service center to obtain an application. You can find a listing in your phone book under United States Government Offices (Passports). If this is your first passport, you must apply in person. You will need a certified copy of your birth certificate, personal identification such as a driver's license, two identical 2-inch full-face photos, and $42. The passport will be mailed to you. It normally takes four to six weeks to get a passport, during the busiest season. For an additional $20 "rush charge," you can get your ,passport in one week, or less, even if it's your first passport. You can also, of course, go directly to a passport office if one is located in your area.

In an emergency, you can get your passport in one day. You must arrive at the passport office by 10:00 A.M. and you must show either a ticket for a flight departing within seventy-two hours or a letter from your company or physician stating that there is an emergency. You should then have your passport by 3:00 P.M. the same day.

You can obtain a certified birth certificate by contacting the Department of Vital Statistics in the community in which you were born. There is usually a small cost, likely $5. If your birth certificate is unavailable, you will need a "letter of no record" and a secondary record of citizenship, such as a baptism record, early school records, or affidavits from your parents.

You can often get the passport photo taken at the same place you pick up and file your application. I'd suggest you start the application process early, however, and give yourself sufficient time to have a picture taken that you'll want to carry around with you for the next ten years.

It would be unfortunate to wait until the last minute, when it is too late to get a more flattering photo, and when you will have to pay the extra rush charge. If you wait too long to apply, you will likely end up anxiously checking your mailbox each day wondering if you will have to postpone your trip because you need your passport in order to apply for a visa.

For more information you can write to: U.S. Passport Services, 1425 K Street, NW, Room 62, Wahington, D.C. 20524; (202) 783–8200.

Visas

A visa is official government approval for you to enter a country, and over half the countries in the world require them. Visas are issued for a specific length of time, typically fifteen days, thirty days, or six months. Some countries will issue a temporary visa at the border, but most require that you obtain one prior to entry.

Your travel agent, tour operator, or airline will be able to supply up-to-date information about visa requirements for the countries you plan to visit. Though they will be most helpful, it is your responsibility, not theirs, to obtain the proper visas for your trip. If your agent isn't sure what's needed, you can obtain a copy of "Visa Requirements of Foreign Governments" from a U.S. Passport Office or by writing the Bureau of Consular Affairs, Room 5807, Department of State, Washington, DC 20520. Or, you can contact the consulates of the countries you will be visiting. The latter is the most official since visa requirements change frequently—and it's to the consulate that you'll have to send your application.

Some visas are issued free; for others you'll be charged a fee, usually about $20. You'll need to send in a completed application form, a valid passport, and possibly one or more passport-style photos. Allow two weeks to obtain each visa. Since you must send your passport along with each application you can only apply for one visa at a time. If you need three visas, for instance, you will need to start early.

Express Visa Services

Another option is to utilize a visa service, such as Express Visa Service, Inc.—2150 Wisconsin Avenue, Suite 20, P.O. Box 32048, Washington, DC 20007; (202) 337-2442. For a charge of $20 per visa plus the visa fees, they will obtain all the visas you require from the various consulates in a short period of time. On one occasion, when I had to leave town on short notice, I sent them my passport via

Federal Express and included enough money for them to return it Federal Express. I had the three visas I needed and my passport back in three days. While it's not advisable to be on such a tight schedule, it's wonderful to have such fast, reliable service available when you need it.

International Driving Permit

Many car rental companies, especially the smaller, less expensive ones, will require that you show a valid international driving permit. You must obtain this before leaving the U.S.—it cannot be acquired abroad. You will need a visa-style photo and $5. You do not need to take a written or driving test, but you will need to show a valid U.S. driver's license. Your license is valid for one year from the date of issue. You can get an international driving permit from the American Automobile Association (AAA).

While you will not need to demonstrate any proficiency in interpreting international road signs, I strongly recommend obtaining a list of them. Know what they mean before you go. While some are obvious, not all are easily interpreted.

TRAVEL INSURANCE

A number of different travel insurance options are available through your travel agent or tour operator.

Baggage Insurance

Airlines will typically reimburse you only a limited amount for lost baggage. Before you buy any additional insurance for your personal articles, however, you should check your homeowner's policy to see exactly what coverage you have already. Is your camera, jewelry, clothing, and luggage covered? Be sure to determine if the coverage extends outside of your home to a foreign country. You can purchase extra baggage insurance for a specific trip. For about $10 you can purchase $500 worth of insurance, and for $30 you will be covered for up to $2,000 of lost or stolen baggage. Insurance costs will, of course, vary according to the length of your trip and the company through which the policy is obtained.

Trip Cancellation Insurance

Trip cancellation or trip interruption insurance will guarantee a full refund if you become physically ill, are injured, hospitalized, or if there is a death in your family, just prior to or during your trip. Most policies, however, exclude any preexisting condition for which you have been treated in the previous ninety days. It may also cover you if your tour operator defaults or there is an unforeseen emergency that prevents your departure or continuation on the trip. The cost will vary according to the cost of the trip and may be about $5.50 for each $100 you want covered. If you will be traveling to Europe, for instance, you may want to purchase insurance to cover more than the price of the tour. Airfare home purchased at the last minute will likely cost you much more than your initial fare. Trip cancellation insurance for a $1,000 trip will be around $55. Before you buy, check the fine print of your trip contract. If, for instance, you will only lose $500 if you cancel within forty-eight hours of departure, there is probably no need for you to pay to insure the entire cost of the trip.

Medical Insurance

You should also check your medical insurance to see what the limitations or restrictions are and what coverage you have outside of the country. Some health insurance companies require that you notify them within forty-eight hours of an injury or hospitalization in order to insure coverage. Others require that you pay the bill, for which they will later reimburse you. If you do not feel your present health insurance is adequate, you can also obtain additional travel accident and sickness insurance. You can even purchase extra medical insurance that will cover the additional costs of air transportation should a physician determine that you need to return home early, as well as the cost of a family member's flight to come and fly home with you.

DECIDING HOW MUCH MONEY TO TAKE

Even when you've paid for your hotels and transportation ahead of time, you'll need to take extra money for tips, meals not included, beverages (these are often not included in meal plans), and, of course, sightseeing, cabs, and souvenirs. These things always seem to cost more than one expects. How much money you take will depend on your habits and comfort level. If you have a major credit card, you will need less of a cushion. In most parts of the world, you can borrow money against a major credit card at a local bank.

I strongly recommend getting a major credit card if you don't have one, even if you don't plan to use it. It may come in handy in an emergency. I also suggest taking extra traveler's checks so you don't run short of funds. You can use them when you get home or put the money back in the bank. In addition, I also take a few personal checks. I'm always surprised at how readily they are accepted in small villages in remote parts of the world. I even found it easier to make a purchase with a personal check in Kusadasi, Turkey, than New York City!

Traveler's Checks

Don't take more cash than you can afford to lose. Take traveler's checks. The best are MasterCard, American Express, VISA, Citicorp, and Bank of America. If you get traveler's checks from obscure sources, you may have difficulty getting reimbursed if they're lost or stolen, and they may even be difficult to cash overseas. American

Express and MasterCard have many more refund locations than the others.

In most foreign countries, you will have to show your passport when cashing traveler's checks. You can cash them in banks, hotels, restaurants, and stores. Since you will only get foreign currency in return, you may want a few traveler's checks in small denominations. Larger denominations, $50 or $100, are useful if you'll be paying for hotels as you go. Be sure to keep a list of the code numbers of your traveler's checks separate from the checks. It is much more time consuming to replace lost or stolen checks without these numbers.

Traveler's checks are available in Australian dollars, British pounds, Canadian dollars, Dutch guilders, French francs, German marks, Hong Kong dollars, and Spanish pesetas as well as American dollars. The advantage of buying the foreign currency is that you will not have to pay a conversion fee, if there is one, and you will be locked into an exchange rate should the dollar go down in value.

REQUIRED AND RECOMMENDED IMMUNIZATIONS

▶────────────────────────────────◀

Some countries require you to have certain immunizations to protect you against diseases that are prevalent within their borders. You will need an "International Certificate of Vaccination," a "yellow card," as proof that you have been immunized. In addition, there are recommended immunizations that you may choose to get for your protection but are not required to enter the country.

For each vacation destination recommended in this book, I have specifically addressed both the required and suggested immunizations. You should check with your local community or state health department to see what immunizations are required for any additional countries you may enter. If you are traveling in developing countries, you may need immunizations against polio, yellow fever, typhoid, or cholera. You may also want protection against malaria and hepatitis.

A vaccination stimulates your body to produce protective antibodies that will protect you against a specific disease or infection. Sometimes there are mild side effects, perhaps soreness at the injection site or a mild fever, so you should get your necessary vaccinations as early as possible.

It's also important to remember a vaccination is not an alternative to good hygiene. You should still be careful not to drink contaminated water, use ice cubes made with contaminated water, or eat fresh vegetables or fresh fruits washed in contaminated water. You should also wash your hands frequently and use a repellant to protect yourself from insect bites.

Yellow Fever

Yellow fever is still a problem in parts of South America, Central America, and Central Africa. Some countries require proof of immunization from all entering travelers. Others require proof of vaccination only if you have recently been in an infected area. Only certain clinics are authorized to give yellow fever immunizations. Check with your health department.

Cholera

The vaccine available, unfortunately, is only about 50 percent effective and provides immunization for only three to six months. It is, however, no longer required for travel.

The major cause of cholera is contaminated food and water, so your best protection is good hygiene and careful choice of food and beverage. You are very unlikely to be exposed if you stick to the major hotels and tourist restaurants. Never eat at street stands in infected areas.

Malaria

While you cannot be immunized against malaria, you can take pills, which provide some protection. Chloroquine is the most commonly used drug both as prevention against infection and as treatment. It interferes with the reproductive stage of the organism. Unfortunately, many areas have developed chloroquine-resistant strains of malaria. Fansidar is usually the drug of choice in these areas. Persons allergic to sulfa must *not* take Fansidar.

For protection against malaria, you should begin taking the medication at the time of departure, and continue to take one pill each week for six weeks after you return home. The pills must be taken on the same day of the week in order to be effective.

Malaria is caused by a parasite carried by several species of the female anopheles mosquito. This insect is not out during the day, only at dusk, and mosquito repellent is an effective deterrent. Staying indoors during the evening hours is also a good preventive measure. A Federal Drug Administration (FDA) panel has suggested vitamin B_1, thiamine, taken internally as an effective insect repellent, although studies have been inconclusive in supporting this claim.

The parasite attacks the oxygen-carrying red blood cells of its victim. Three to eight days after being bitten by an infected mosquito, victims begin to vomit and run high temperatures (102 to 104 degrees). They sweat profusely and shake uncontrollably. The fever subsides in a day or so; at this time, the parasite is metamorphosing into a gamete or nonpathogenic phase, multiplying and spreading.

The fever, chills, and sweating will come and go. Symptoms may last more than a year after the disease has been contracted. Only in the worst cases is the disease life threatening. You should definitely get treatment as soon as possible. Do not consider yourself safe just because the initial symptoms have subsided.

Polio

Most people living in the United States today have been immunized in school, but some older adults may not be protected. If you're in doubt, and you'll be traveling to an area of the world where polio is still an active disease, you should probably be immunized. You may need two doses, four weeks apart, so begin the process early.

Immune Serum Globulin (ISG) or Gamma Globulin

Primarily used to provide protection against hepatitis A virus, ISG is an effective defense against most nonspecific traveler's illnesses.

Some physicians recommend this type of vaccination as a general protection for their patients whenever they are traveling to a developing country, and especially when traveling away from the usual tourist routes.

Smallpox

In 1980, the World Health Organization declared smallpox eradicated. Therefore you no longer need to be vaccinated.

An Important Reminder

Should you become ill after returning home from a trip, whatever your symptoms, be sure to tell your physician where you have been. He or she will evaluate your symptoms differently, and be more likely to correctly diagnose your illness.

GETTING INTO SHAPE

▶───▶

Maintaining your health is always important. Fortunately, today more and more women are recognizing how essential physical fitness is to their general health. And for many, exercise has become a regular part of their lives. Practicing a balanced life-style with proper nutrition, exercise, and rest results in a general sense of well-being—allowing us to accomplish more in our careers and on our vacations.

If you're not one of the new breed of women who have recognized the importance of good physical fitness, now is the time to evaluate your life-style more closely. Few people walk nearly as much at home as they do when on vacation, even when the objective of the vacation is relaxation. Most of us get little exercise at our usual jobs. Some of us even drive around for "hours" looking for the closest parking space so we can avoid a short walk to the store. How often have you driven to lunch even though the restaurant to which you're going is only a few blocks away?

I guarantee that if you begin an exercise program and improve your general physical fitness before your trip, you'll have a much better time. You'll see more, do more, and feel better about yourself and your vacation when you return home.

There are some very simple steps you can take that will help you get into shape for your next trip. These are things you can easily incorporate into your everyday life. While I jog during warm weather, the Minnesota winters are much too cold for me to go out for a run. I have, however, found that I can keep in good enough physical condition to begin running three miles a day in the spring, without stress, by doing these few things.

First, I try never to ride an elevator. While in some buildings the stairs are not conveniently located—and I don't search forever—I always try to find them and walk up and down. I save time, burn extra calories, and do myself and my body a great favor. This is such an easy way to stay in shape, that I feel as if I'm cheating myself whenever I must ride an elevator.

I also take the first parking spot I find, often on the edge of the parking lot. Not only is this a benefit to me, it usually saves time as well. Most of my friends now walk to lunch, as I usually do, unless we really want to go a great distance.

Most importantly, I now ask what "too far to walk" and "a long ways away" really means. For some people it's five or six blocks, for others it's a half mile or a mile. Even if you walk slowly, you can walk a mile in about twenty minutes, and walking is probably the best exercise you can get. If I have the time, that's certainly not too far for me to walk. I enjoy the exercise and feel much better after having gone the short distance.

You may decide you want to begin a specific exercise routine or join a health club. I think that's a great idea. If you're older or have any reason to believe you might have a medical problem, first check out your proposed exercise program with your physician.

PACKING FOR YOUR TRIP

▶───▶

Nothing separates the experienced traveler from the novice more quickly then excess baggage. Remember, you want to make your whole trip a vacation, including the time you spend coming and going. What you leave at home can be as important in making your trip enjoyable as what you decide to take along.

Luggage Options

If you're still using Grandma's discarded suitcase, this may be the time to purchase your own. You usually "get what you pay for" when you buy luggage. If you buy good quality, durable luggage, it can last a lifetime. If you go cheap, not only won't the luggage last very long, but it will show wear and tear more quickly. When you are traveling or "arriving," your luggage—just like your wardrobe—is part of the first impression you make on people. When you check into an elegant resort, or run into an especially attractive stranger, you want that first impression to be a good one.

Whatever style or brand name you select, first and foremost, you want luggage that you can manage alone, because there will be times that you'll need to do so. You also want it to be strong, durable, and waterproof. It used to be that everyone embarking on a long trip packed a steamer trunk, but you'll seldom see one nowadays. While they certainly provide protection for fragile items, they're much too bulky, heavy, and unmanageable.

Hard-sided luggage provides more protection for fragile items and can be locked, but it's also heavy. Some luggage now comes with built-in wheels so you don't need to lift it. If you choose this type of luggage, be sure the wheel mounts are sturdy. If they are countersunk into the bottom of the suitcase they will have a better chance of surviving today's luggage handlers—human and mechanical.

Soft-sided luggage options include everything from a duffel bag to expensive leather hanging bags with lots of pockets. When I plan to be on the move, I find a hanging bag with side pockets ideal. I don't have to unpack to keep my clothes from wrinkling or to find what I want. I can hang my clothes, in my bag, and still get at everything in the conveniently located pockets. It has the option of a handle as well as a shoulder strap and there are no outside buckles or sharp corners to catch and tear my clothing. If I'm late to catch a plane, I can even carry it on and hang it in the plane.

A disadvantage of this type of luggage is that there are really too many pockets to lock. I also figure one locked pocket would invite thieves to cut it open. My solution is not to take anything of real value. I also generally pack my tennis shoes and dirty clothes in the outside pockets. My expensive sweaters, hair dryer, and any item I think may be more tempting to a thief, I pack in the less accessible and better protected inside pockets. I also always remove the shoulder strap and tuck it into a pocket just before I check my bag. That way it's less likely to get caught on a conveyor belt.

Some people will take along a collapsible cart on which they wheel their luggage. If you decide on this option, be sure to get a well-built, sturdy model. Carrying these around can sometimes be more of a nuisance than a help, however, especially if you must negotiate stairways. Most airports have large carts you can rent for $1. I prefer to take fewer things with me and then rent a cart if I get carried away and bring too much back.

I also generally pack a collapsible bag, which I can use to carry souvenirs home. You'll find a variety for sale that fold up to about 3 by 7 by ½ inches. Even when I'm sure I won't need it, I stick it in. It seldom comes home empty. A small collapsible backpack and a "fanny pack" can also come in handy.

Label Your Bags Properly

Every piece of luggage you take with you should be properly labeled. A number of airlines provide you with a hard plastic label on which to put your name, address, and phone number; it then closes so the information does not show when you attach it to your luggage and is not easily visible to a passerby or thief. However, the label can be opened and your luggage returned if it gets lost.

If you label your luggage with the more common tags in which your name and address are visible, I'd suggest that you use your business address and phone number. Be sure to put "USA" on your address and the area code on your phone number.

It's also important to put a business card or a slip of paper with your name, address, and phone number *inside* each bag. Tags can come off, and this gives you a second chance of having your luggage returned safely.

Your Carry-on Bags

Most airlines allow one carry-on bag limited in size to approximately 21 by 16 by 8 inches. It must fit under the seat in front of you or in the enclosed overhead compartments. A soft-sided carry-on bag is more flexible and can usually be squeezed into a tight corner, and it's also much lighter to carry. Most soft-sided carry-on bags have a shoulder strap, which allows you to keep your hands free to deal with tickets and other luggage.

I generally take a nearly empty medium-sized carry-on bag with me. That way I have extra room to carry small or fragile trinkets I purchase. I have found my ski boot bag to be ideal. It has a shoulder strap as well as handles. While large enough to stuff full, it collapses down to nothing and can easily be packed inside another suitcase when not in use. It was also inexpensive and is durable and waterproof.

What Should You Pack in a Carry-on?

There are a few items you never want to pack in your luggage regardless of what country you'll be traveling through. These are your passport, money, credit cards, traveler's checks, airline tickets, cruise tickets, railroad tickets, and valuable or fragile items. These should always be carried on your person. I generally wear a shirt with a large, buttoned front pocket and carry my passport and major credit cards there. When I'm traveling in a developing country, or any area where

I feel safety is more crucial, I wear a money belt. I keep the cash I'll need while on the road and the airline tickets more accessible, so people won't be aware that I'm wearing a money belt.

If you take prescription drugs you should hand carry your full supply, not just what you'll need while in transit. Leave them in their original containers to reduce problems taking them through customs. If you need to take anything unusual, such as insulin syringes, bring along a letter from your physician.

If you wear glasses or contact lenses, be sure to take a spare pair and plenty of wetting and cleansing solution. If you don't own a spare and don't want to go to the extra expense, at least take along the prescription for your glasses. You may want to include a record of all prescriptions on your yellow immunization card.

Some people carry a change of clothing with them in case their luggage is lost. While it's certainly a good idea, I must admit I don't. I figure if worse comes to worse, I can always buy what I need when I get to my destination, so to me it's not worth carrying bulky items "just in case." Besides, you may need to hike a long distance when changing planes, or you may have to carry your carry-on luggage around with you in an airport for hours between flights. I prefer to take only what I expect to use while traveling, although sometimes I will throw in a bathing suit and a pair of shorts on a trip south to warmer weather. These items are lightweight and don't take up much room. This way, if my luggage is delayed I can still enjoy the beach— what I came for—immediately. In my experience, a bathing suit that fits and looks good is one of the more difficult items of clothing to replace.

My boot bag usually contains a couple of books or magazines to read en route—I'll often carry a tourist guide on the area I'm traveling to, so I can plan my activities for when I arrive—a toothbrush and toothpaste, especially on overnight trips, and the sample size makeup items I'll be using on the trip.

I carry my camera equipment in a separate, well padded camera bag, which I don't have hand checked by airport security. It's not necessary. Unless the film is 1,000 ASA or faster, the X-ray machines used will not damage your film. One friend stood openmouthed and watched rolls of film being pocketed by the airport security person checking the bag. She said nothing, not believing her eyes until she recounted her film later.

If I'm taking a purse, I generally put it in my carry-on bag so I have a smaller number of separate articles to be concerned with, and less chance of leaving something behind.

Your Checked Luggage

Before you decide what to take, be sure to check the weight limits for the airline on which you'll be flying. While flights within the continental United States are seldom, if ever, concerned with excess baggage, the situation is much different on flights to Central or South America. They are very strict about enforcing their baggage limits. You'll find out why when you arrive at the airport. Even with the allowance of two bags at seventy pounds each, you'll see people paying hundreds of dollars in excess baggage charges. I've sometimes wondered how it was all going to fit on one airplane. If you need to pay an excess baggage charge in that situation, you're taking far too much for a vacation.

A Word of Caution

When in a situation such as the one described above, do not check an extra bag for the person in back of you. If you're carrying one small bag you'll stand out like a sore thumb and you may very well be asked to do so. Remember, that extra bag becomes your responsibility and you don't know what's inside. More than one person has been arrested and jailed for drug trafficking because they carried a bag for someone else.

What Should You Take?

Since each trip discussed in this book has a list of specific items that you may want to take with you, I won't go into great detail here. I'll just discuss the major considerations.

Don't take anything you can't afford to lose or replace. No matter how much you enjoy wearing Grandma's dinner ring, leave it home. Enjoy wearing it at home where you don't have to worry about losing it. If you have another dinner ring you like to wear, and can easily replace, insure it and take it if you must. However, I'd recommend not taking anything of great value. Costume jewelry can be just as much fun and lends itself to a more worry-free holiday.

Don't take more than you can carry. If you need to think twice about an item, leave it home. I *never* take something "just in case I might need it." I also never take more than one checked bag, even though sometimes my one bag is rather full. That way I figure I can fill my collapsible bag with purchases and still travel home comfortably with two checked bags. Even on the most luxurious cruises where you "dress" for dinner, I find I can do fine with one bag instead of the five many other passengers take. Choosing my clothes carefully, taking things that mix and match, and especially taking lightweight, thin materials such as wrinkle-free silk is my secret. A thin, long-sleeve silk jacket provides the same warmth with its tight weave as a bulky sweater. With few exceptions, I don't take clothes unless they pass the "crunch test." I crunch them up in my hand. If wrinkles show when I shake it out, it stays home. Or I'll fold clothes and lay them in a corner overnight to see if they hang wrinkle free in the morning. Knits and blends with some polyester are usually more wrinkle resistant than linen or 100 percent cotton. I also save room and weight by taking neutral-colored shoes and sandals I can wear with a number of outfits. For warm weather climates, sandals are more versatile and take up much less space.

I also enjoy "extending" my wardrobe with T-shirts and inexpensive dresses, blouses, or skirts from the local area. If you're going to buy something new for a trip, why not get it while you're on vacation. I find clothes and jewelry make great souvenirs when I get home. I enjoy them much more than a trinket that just sits on a shelf. They are also usually more unique and less expensive than what I could have bought at home.

For the most part, I take along clothes and shoes in which I'm comfortable. A vacation is not the time to break in a new pair of shoes, even tennis shoes. If you don't wear something at home, you'll probably not wear it on vacation either. If you don't like to wear jeans and tennis shoes, no matter how convenient your friends say they are, you probably won't wear them on vacation. Save yourself the room and leave them home.

You'll also want to think about how long you can wear an item before it needs to be cleaned. While most places do have laundry facilities, I prefer not to rely on them—overnight can often turn into three days. I take very little white, and when I do, I consider it an item I can only count on wearing once or twice, unless I'm lucky. I also prefer clothes I can rinse out in my room and hang up to dry.

Sunglasses. Whether you're going to the beach or to the mountains, it's important to take a good pair of protective sunglasses. Darker lenses alone do not mean better protection. In fact, dark glasses that don't block the ultraviolet rays can actually hurt your eyes. Because the lens is dark, your retina will open more to let in more light. Without the extra protection it will also let in more damaging ultraviolet rays. Your eyes may, as a result, get burned and be very painful. There are relatively inexpensive sunglasses on the market that filter up to 95 percent of the ultraviolet rays. Check with a reputable salesperson and get adequate eye protection.

Begin early. I begin packing a few days early by laying out everything I plan to take where I can see it. This gives me a chance to notice things I forgot and add them to the pile. As I decide on other items, I exchange them for things in my original pile. The night before I leave I put everything into my suitcase and I'm ready to go. I pack the things I'll need less often or later in the trip on the bottom or in the least accessible areas.

CHAPTER 3

Getting There (and Back Again) Should Be Part of the Fun, Too

---

*M*ore than any other single factor, your attitude about traveling determines the type of trip you have. If you plan ahead, feel comfortable that you have everything you need, know essentially what to expect, and have kept your luggage manageable, traveling can be part of the fun.

From the moment you lock your door at home behind you, you should consider yourself on vacation—ready to experience a new adventure.

Even if things go wrong—and they always can no matter how carefully you've planned—your attitude will to a great extent determine how much the mishap will affect your having a good time. If you consider it just another adventure, challenge, or learning experience, it will be. For instance, I've learned to consider getting lost as another chance to "take the scenic route." How you see something that happens to you is often much more important than the event itself.

There are a number of things you can do to make traveling more hassle free and more relaxing.

DRESSING FOR TRAVEL

The distance you'll be going, the length of your trip, and your arrival time should be important considerations in the way you'll want to dress. There are times when comfort is the primary goal and times when fun and effect might rule.

Dressing for Comfort

When you have a long flight, especially an overnight flight, you should dress in clothes in which you can sleep comfortably. Loose-fitting clothes that don't wrinkle are the rule on this type of trip. Long flights are often from one climate to another, so for these I tend to dress in layers. A jacket for a drafty airport or cool plane and a long-sleeve shirt over a sleeveless top with loose-fitting pants or a full-flowing skirt is ideal. A sporty hat, if you're taking one along, will be easier to wear than to pack. It will also dress up your outfit when you put it on at arrival time.

Dressing for Effect

Flying into Louisville for a long weekend at the Derby is a great time to dress for effect. A bright, attention-getting outfit complete with hat will set the tone for the weekend to come.

Dress to Hit the Slopes

There have been times when I wanted to be on the slopes as soon as I dropped my bags. In anticipation, I wore a pair of loose-fitting jeans, a turtleneck, and my ski jacket on the plane. I had a ski sweater, zip-on warm-up pants, and my goggles in my carry-on bag. Two days of skiing became three because I was ready to go.

Shoes

I consider comfortable shoes a must anytime but especially when I'm traveling. It's incredible how many women accept tired, sore feet as normal and unavoidable. They're not. You don't have to wear tennis shoes to avoid sore feet either. I look for shoes with a low heel and, even more important, a padded cushion for the ball of the foot. If you look around, you can even find some that are quite stylish. Buy them loose, too—perhaps a half size larger than you normally wear. This will help if you're traveling to a hot climate where your feet will probably swell a bit. If you follow no other advice in this book except for finding comfortable shoes, I guarantee you'll have a much more enjoyable trip than you would otherwise have. Be sure to get your new shoes early. If you buy them right they shouldn't hurt when you "break them in." And you don't want to find out you made the wrong selection while you're away.

The Trip Home

I always like to save one outfit to wear home. Since traveling home is another opportunity to meet people, I like to have something clean to wear so I feel and look good.

A POCKETFUL OF DOLLARS

While a bit of an exaggeration, an important part of your preparation for travel is being sure you have a number of $1 bills in an easily accessible place, such as a pocket. You don't want to be awkwardly fumbling with your purse to get a tip or money for a drink on the airplane (usually $2 or $3).

When you're in a foreign country, be sure to have the appropriate currency ready for tips there, too. Dollar bills from home are always readily accepted; in some areas, though, it would be too extravagant.

GETTING TO THE AIRPORT

▶ ─────────────────────────────────────── ▶

Sometimes it's inconvenient for friends to take you to and from the airport. And if you'll be away any length of time, it can get costly to park your car at the airport. In addition to taxis, here are two options most people don't consider.

Limousine Service

Stretch limousines aren't just for the wealthy. In most major cities, limousine companies will provide service between your home and the airport for a set fee, which may be as little as $20. In addition, if you give them your flight number and date of arrival, they will be there when your plane arrives, even if you're hours late.

What a nice way to begin and end your trip—in the luxury of a chauffeured limousine. Don't forget to tip the driver about 20 percent. If he's had to wait a long time or deal with a lot of extra bags, give him a little more.

Airport Limousine (Van) Service

Most hotels offer airport limousine service. It's important to know that what they really mean is not a limousine but a van service to the airport—which is fine, as long as you realize what you're paying for. Most hotels also have a parking lot where you can leave your car for free, or certainly for less than it would cost at the airport. While not as luxurious or convenient as limousine service, it is usually only $10 to $15 and you do not need to tip the driver.

YOUR AIRPORT ARRIVAL

Even though I'm sure you took my advice and kept the amount of luggage you're taking to a manageable minimum, it may still be easier to let someone else manage it for you. When you arrive at the airport, even if you drive yourself, don't go to the parking lot. Your first stop should be "Flight Departures" for your airline. When you drive up, find a skycap. Let him take the bags you will be checking, show him your ticket, and tell him your *final* destination to which you want your bags checked. He will take care of the rest. You should tip him $1 for one or two bags, more if you have excess luggage. You're now free to go and park your car in the lot without having to carry your luggage back with you.

Even if a friend or limousine is dropping you off, I'd recommend checking your bags with the skycap. It's worth the $2 not to have to wait inside to check your bag. Unfortunately, because of the threat of terrorism, skycaps can no longer check luggage through onto international flights. When you have an international connection to make it's best to go inside and check your bag at the counter.

The skycap won't be able to give you a seat assignment. If you check with your travel agent or directly with your airline a few days prior to your departure, you can often get your seat assignment then. If not, you still need not wait in the long lines that can develop in the airport lobby. Go directly to the departure gate, which will be listed on the TV monitor next to your flight number. You can get your seat assignment there.

I follow this procedure in reverse when I return home. I go and get my car as soon as I arrive and park it in front of the baggage claim area. By then my bags have usually arrived. I can pick them up, easily load them in my car, and I'm on my way home. You should make sure your airport allows curbside parking at the arrivals area.

WHAT TO DO IF YOUR PLANE IS DELAYED EN ROUTE

Short Delays

If your plane is delayed an hour or two, it can be a great excuse and opportunity to start a conversation with the good-looking guy you noticed earlier. Airports are a great place to meet people, much better than a singles bar. I've become friends with a number of people, men and women, I first met while waiting for a flight. Even if you decide you don't want to see this person again, talking with someone passes the time more quickly than twiddling your thumbs.

If there's no one around who looks interested in talking, it's a good time to get your book or magazine out of your carry-on bag or wander around the airport and find a good book or magazine to read. If you decide to nap, put your valuables in your carry-on bag and use it as a pillow or foot rest.

Long Delays

If you're facing a long delay, an alternative strategy is called for. One option will likely be to hang around the airport hoping the weather will clear, your plane will be repaired, or you can get on the next flight. You may or may not be lucky. Another option, one that has worked well for me, is to book another flight the next day or the last flight of the day—if you must get home.

You then have the day free to go sightseeing, go to the beach, or go skiing. While the airlines do not like to retrieve your luggage, if you insist they will do so.

The first time I skied Snowbird was when I was snowed out of Denver. I first booked a flight for the next morning. I then insisted that the airline get my luggage and skis, which they did—reluctantly. I rented a car and had a great day skiing. Because I reserved a seat on a flight the next morning as soon as I was told about the situation, I made it out the next day. Many of the passengers who had hung around the airport all day hoping to get to Denver were listed on my flight as standby. Most did not get on.

If nothing else, you can take a shuttle to town and walk around or have a nice lunch. I spent another wonderful afternoon on Bourbon Street in New Orleans while waiting for the airport to open in Minneapolis. Be creative, think of all your options. Share a cab to town with someone else from your flight. Don't just assume you're now stuck at the airport.

Your Rights

The advantage of deregulation is that air travel is cheaper. The disadvantage is that the airlines are no longer required to reimburse you for your hotel and meals if your flight is delayed. You should always ask what their policy is and what they will provide. You'll get more than those who don't ask.

AIRLINE CLUBS

Previously reserved for first-class travelers, airline clubs can be joined by anyone today for a modest fee. For $45 to $80 per year, sometimes with an addition of a $15 to $60 one-time initiation fee, you, too, can gain access. Check around the major carriers as to the policies and location of facilities. If you belong to one major airline club you can use their facilities all over the world.

Usually they will have a quiet, comfortable lounge available at most major airports. It's a much better place to wait, particularly when your flight is delayed. In addition to a number of telephones next to soft, padded chairs, you'll usually find free snacks and drinks.

WHAT IF YOUR LUGGAGE IS DAMAGED?

▶──────────────────────────────────────▶

You should be sure to check your luggage for damage when you pick it up. If there are any major dents or tears, you should file a claim with an airline representative immediately. The airline will usually repair or replace your bag or come to some settlement agreement with you. Normal wear and tear, dirt, and scratches are to be expected and will, of course, not be covered.

WHAT IF YOUR LUGGAGE IS LOST?

▶──────────────────────────────────────▶

You should file a claim with the airline as soon as you discover your luggage has not arrived. Luggage is seldom permanently lost, so don't panic. It's likely your bag will come in on a later plane, or perhaps it somehow went to another city. In most situations, the airlines will have your bag for you in a few hours or the next day. However, you must file a lost baggage claim so they will know to look for it.

If your bags do not arrive within twenty-four to forty-eight hours, you may be entitled to some reimbursement. The policies of the different airlines vary, so be sure to ask. Some airlines will reimburse your purchase of essential items, such as toothbrush, toothpaste, and makeup. Some will pay for emergency clothing. Some will do even less.

If your luggage is completely lost, you will likely be reimbursed so much per pound, often as little as $9 per pound. You will seldom be reimbursed more than $500. Jewelry and fragile items are generally not covered by the airlines. Once again, there is a wide variation in policies, and you will seldom recover an amount sufficient to replace your suitcase and its contents. I'd suggest checking your homeowner's policy or considering additional insurance before you leave home.

DEALING WITH JET LAG

Jet lag results when you travel rapidly to a new time zone and your body rhythms don't have a chance to adjust. Whenever you experience more than a three-hour time difference, you can expect to deal with some symptoms of jet lag. The most common symptom is sleep disturbance. You may have difficulty getting to sleep (your body still thinks it's daytime) or feel tired during the day (your body thinks it's nighttime). Other symptoms include a sense of exhaustion, disorientation, trouble concentrating, memory loss, and a lack of appetite. There are also a variety of idiosyncratic symptoms that you might experience while your friends may not.

Like most people you will probably find it more difficult to fly from the west to east because you lose time and usually sleep. The greater the time distance you have covered, the more likely you are to experience jet lag. If you are not feeling well before you leave, you will likely have even more trouble resolving the jet lag, so give yourself a little extra time.

Since everyone's body has its own adjustment rate, it's difficult to predict just how long recovery will take. There are, however, some things you can do to minimize your reaction and speed your recovery.

Preventive strategies include choosing a daytime flight that has you arriving in the evening, even late evening, but not in the early morning hours, when you're flying east. You'll probably sleep longer than usual the first night, but don't overdo it. If you must fly at night, try to get some sleep. Skip the movie even if it looks good and don't drink any beverage with caffeine, such as coke or coffee. You might want to have one or two glasses of wine or beer with dinner, but not more, to help you relax and sleep. If you can't sleep with a light on, take an eye cover. If possible, move to an area where you can lie down, then remove your shoes, get comfortable, and give yourself a chance to at least relax, even if you can't sleep soundly.

A few days before your trip you should cut back or eliminate all caffeine from your diet. If you do this, it will then have a greater effect on your body when you arrive. Use the caffeine to stay awake in the morning and avoid it in the evening so you can sleep.

You can also start adjusting to the new time zone before you leave home. If you'll be traveling east, you may want to start getting up a little earlier each morning and going to bed earlier at night. If you'll be traveling west, do just the opposite, stay up later at night and sleep in longer in the morning.

The most important thing is to get on the time schedule of the area you're visiting as soon as possible. Don't be tempted to keep your watch on your hometown time, and don't continually count the hours to see what time it "really" is or figure out what you'd be doing at home. That will only make your adjustment more difficult. The more you stimulate yourself visually and mentally the easier it will be for you to stay awake during the new daytime hours. So get out and see the sights, talk with other people, and be fully involved in your new location.

If you had to take a night flight, couldn't sleep, and arrived in Europe, for instance, in the morning, take a short nap if you must. But don't sleep more than a couple of hours or you won't be able to sleep that night. It will be tough, but force yourself to get up. If you can possibly stay awake until 7:00 or 8:00 P.M. without napping, you'll adjust to the new time zone much more rapidly.

If you'll be crossing a number of time zones, try to plan your trip so you get home on a Saturday night. That way you'll have a day to relax and unpack before returning to the office. I find an extra day to relax at home is more valuable toward keeping my trip a stress-free one than an extra day "on vacation."

By following these simple measures I usually experience very few symptoms of jet lag, and these are easily resolved. If jet lag is a bigger issue for you, you might want to purchase *Overcoming Jet Lag* by Dr. Charles Ehret and Lynne Waller Scanlon. They have an extensive diet preparation program that they claim will significantly reduce jet lag symptoms. I'm not very good at following specific diets, so I haven't tried it. The more time zones you'll be crossing, the earlier they suggest starting the diet. For instance, if you'll be crossing seven or eight time zones, their diet regimen begins three days before your date of departure.

Like most other aspects of travel, if you plan ahead, take a few rather simple precautions, and develop the right attitude, travel to and from your destination can be part of the fun. While you may not be able to prevent or control the mishaps you encounter, you can control how they'll affect you.

► ► ►

CHAPTER 4

Now That You Have Arrived: Checking In (and Out)

***

You've arrived. Whether you're well rested or a little tired there is still a sense of excitement about arrival. Is it what you expected? If not, how is it different? What will you explore first? Who will you meet? What exciting adventures are in store for you? All these questions will soon be answered, but first you need to check into your hotel and get settled.

CHECKING INTO YOUR HOTEL

►──►

Your initial interactions with the staff at your resort or hotel will play an important role in your general feelings about your arrival and may set the tone for your stay. This is the time to be generous when you tip the staff. It is not the time to skimp. Unfortunately, women, in general, have a reputation for being poor tippers. This is one reason porters flock toward men and doormen run to open doors for them. Generous tipping upon arrival will serve as an incentive to better service during your stay. The tip you give when you leave will help ensure better service for the next woman traveling alone whom they encounter.

Hotels in some countries require that you give them your passport when you check in. This is routine procedure and you must do so. This is for your protection as well. The passports are generally reviewed by the local police, who will check the passports against their records. They will also interview anyone coming from a country with terrorist inclinations. The hotel is responsible for your passport until it is returned, which is usually the next day. I have had a number of hotel managers tell me that Americans, as a group, are generally reluctant to part with their passports, and it can be a problem to convince them of the necessity to do so.

A Room with a View

If you'd like a room on one of the upper floors, with a view, even if you didn't make this special request with your reservation, do so now. You can also request to be on a floor set aside for women travelers if they have one or for nonsmokers or near the pool, if you prefer.

Guaranteed Reservations

With a guaranteed reservation, obtained by giving the hotel your credit card number when you made your reservation or by sending a deposit, your room will be held for you no matter what time you arrive, even if it's in the wee hours of the morning. If you've guaranteed your room, unless you cancel in time, you will, however, be charged for the room whether you show up or not. Most hotels will accept cancellations until 5:00 P.M. or 6:00 P.M. on the day of arrival.

If, as a result of the hotel's error, they are unable to provide the room you reserved, you should insist on an upgrade without additional cost to you. Most hotels will offer this upgrade without your even knowing there was a mistake. If the desk clerk is uncooperative, insist on speaking with the manager. Stand your ground. You should be reasonable but firm.

If you're convinced that they really don't have a room, insist that they locate an acceptable room for you. You should also insist they provide your transportation to the other hotel.

Your Departure

A couple of days prior to your scheduled departure, ask the concierge to call your airline and reconfirm your departure. Check on the time your flight is now scheduled to depart. Departure times may vary and flights to some parts of the world are even canceled with very short notice, so be sure to check yours. If you know ahead of time, you can reschedule.

If you'll be checking out early, ask the front desk to prepare your bill the night before your scheduled departure. Check your bill carefully. I have inadvertently been charged for an extra night as well as for restaurant charges that belonged to another room.

When you are ready to leave, call the front desk and ask to have a bellman sent up to collect your bags.

Complaints

If you have any major problems with your accommodations, let the hotel manager know before you leave. In addition, when you return home, you should send a written complaint to the Hotel and Motel Association at 888 Seventh Avenue, New York, NY 10019, or call them at (212) 265-4506. If you booked through a travel agent or tour company, be sure they are aware of the problems you encountered.

SETTLING IN

If you'll be in the same location for more than two nights, I'd suggest unpacking immediately and really moving in. Set your things out where they will be accessible. Hang your clothes so that wrinkles can come out.

Any items that look especially wrinkled should be hung in the bathroom. Then take a long, relaxing shower and keep the bathroom door closed. Your clothes will be wrinkle free before you know it. If the wrinkles are persistent, leave them in the steam-filled bathroom after you've finished your shower. You can also call hotel services for an iron, if need be.

On the desk in your room you'll likely find a brochure explaining the hotel facilities and the area sights. There may even be a map of the city. Take a few minutes to look these over.

If there are matches with the name and address of the hotel in your room, take them with you when you leave your room. Put one in your purse and another in your pocket. Especially in a country where you don't speak the language, if you get lost or tired you can always hop in a cab, show the driver the matches, and indicate that that is where you want to go. You won't need to worry about mispronouncing the name so badly he doesn't understand you.

You might want to peek into the hotel's restaurants, pool area, sauna, and shops in order to get a better idea of what is really available. If there wasn't a map in your room, stop at the front desk, or check with the concierge, and ask for one. Also ask for restaurant suggestions, the best shows to see, or for directions to the museum you don't want to miss. The hotel's staff can provide a wealth of information about the city and area. They will know what special events are in town and can recommend side trips or tours.

Flowers for Your Room

On one of your first trips out, stop at a flower stand and pick up a big bouquet of fresh flowers. When you get back to your room ask housekeeping for a vase—they always have extras. It will make your room a brighter, cheerier place to return to during your stay.

DINING OUT

If you intend to eat most of your meals at the hotel restaurant, you should get the name of the maître d' or captain. At your first meal, ask for him. Look him in the eye, smile, and introduce yourself. Tell him you've just arrived, you'll be there for a week, and hope he'll see that you're well taken care of. Then discreetly slip him a folded $20 bill that you have kept handy. From then on be sure to greet him by name each time you see him. You'll likely get a good table and extra service throughout your stay. If so, be sure to thank him your last evening. Tell him how much you enjoyed your stay and slip him another $20.

Breakfast

My favorite meal of the day is breakfast. I expect this is because it's such a treat to be able to have a leisurely breakfast. I don't need to eat a lot, it's being able to relax over my morning coffee and read the paper or a book that I find such a wonderful luxury. I've learned to love breakfast alone. Even when I'm traveling with someone, I'll get up especially early just to have breakfast alone. It's a great time to plan the day's activities, review your travel book, read a local newspaper, and see what's happening in town.

Most hotels have a small coffee shop that is open for breakfast. The large hotels will also serve breakfast in their main dining room. While you can usually order off the menu, it's here that you'll find the breakfast buffet, a real bargain. If you're watching what you eat it can often serve as brunch. Most important, for very little more, you can begin your day in a luxurious, relaxing setting rather than in a busy coffee shop. At the Palace Hotel in San Francisco, for instance, you can enjoy breakfast under a canopy of stained-glass-filtered sunlight. The service is also much better than in the busier coffee shop.

In a summer resort area, it can be fun to begin your day beside the outdoor pool or in view of the beach. Wherever you are, if you don't want to read, ask to be seated in a good area for people watching, possibly by a window. If you'd prefer company and you've met someone else you see eating alone, ask if you could join them.

Lunch

Some people prefer to make lunch the main meal of the day; others will eat very lightly, if at all. If you want to try an especially expensive restaurant that is a little beyond your budget, lunch is a good time to do it. You'll get essentially the same meal but a smaller portion, perhaps without all the extra side dishes, and you'll pay half the price. You'll usually get better service if you avoid the noon crush. Eat early or late.

Dinner

Phone ahead, or ask the hotel concierge to make a reservation for you. If possible, make your reservation early or late, to avoid the rush. You will get better service. Always "dress to kill" either formal or informal. If you feel good about the way you look, you'll command attention and good service.

When you arrive at the restaurant, introduce yourself to the maître d'. Smile and look him in the eye as you shake his hand. "Hi, I'm _____. I have an eight o'clock reservation. I'll be dining alone tonight. I'd appreciate a good table." Then discreetly slip him a $5 tip. If the restaurant has a reputation or your friends have recommended it, you might also want to tell him, "I've heard about your restaurant from friends and I've been looking forward to a chance to visit."

If you're ever seated at a table you don't like, such as next to the kitchen door, ask for another. Tell the staff you'll wait for the next table to become available, and ask how long they expect that will be. If it's too long, go elsewhere.

When you follow the captain to your table, walk with confidence, looking around you, not down. Hold your head up high. Once seated, look around you. Take command of your area before you become absorbed in the menu. Ask your waiter what the house specialties are and what he'd recommend. If he does not introduce himself, ask his name and use it during the evening.

Order a drink to sip while you peruse the menu or wait for your meal. Then order something special from the menu. Treat yourself. If you'd like, ask the wine steward to recommend a good wine to accompany your dinner. Ask his opinion about the various vintages and selections available. He'll likely relish the chance to display his vast knowledge and you'll learn something new about wines.

While I enjoy reading at breakfast or over a light, quick lunch, I generally avoid reading at dinner, especially in a nice restaurant. Instead, I concentrate fully on the ambiance and on what I am eating—the flavor, fragrance, and consistency of the foods. I also enjoy just daydreaming or watching the other people in the restaurant. It's fun to speculate on the life stories of your fellow diners. Who's here with his wife, lover, or on a secret tryst. Who looks like they'd rather be here alone, or who might you like to join?

The Unrequested Drink

You are sitting in a restaurant having a pleasant meal and the waitress brings over an unordered drink, compliments of a stranger also dining alone. There may or may not be a note. You have two choices. You can ask the waitress to thank the stranger but refuse the drink, or you can accept the drink.

If you accept the drink you now have an even greater number of options. If you're really not interested in company, you can simply smile and nod appreciatively to the sender then avoid looking in his direction. Even though you accepted the drink you are not obligated to invite him to your table, and you should not go over to his. If he looks interesting, you may decide you'd like to invite him to join you, possibly for coffee and dessert. If you do, you are not obligated to leave with him. It may be that once he starts talking you'll be anxious to be rid of him. Maybe not. What happens next should be your choice, your decision. Don't allow yourself to get pressured into an uncomfortable situation.

If You Don't Want to Eat Alone

There are times when you'd really like to eat with someone. If so, see if there is a group tour to an Elizabethan feast, or a dinner show. If you've casually met another single traveler or a couple, ask them if they'd like to join you for dinner.

This is another good time to use the services of the concierge. Ask him if there are any restaurants in the area that have a joiners table, where single diners are seated together. Perhaps he knows a Japanese restaurant where the food is cooked in the center of a table that seats eight to sixteen diners.

If you book a dinner show alone, you will usually be seated at a table with a group of people. So if you can't find a group or individual to go to dinner with, you can meet others to dine with once you arrive. If you're lucky, as I've been in the past, the host or hostess will pair you up with a charming, attractive dining companion as you arrive. Many nightclub owners pride themselves on their "matchmaking," and they're especially pleased if they see you together at a later time.

Another good option for less formal meals is to go to a restaurant that has a counter. Sit at the counter, next to someone interesting, and strike up a conversation. "Are you from this area?" "Have you been here before?" If they're reading the paper, "Is there any good news today?"

Local Specialties

To me, one of the most interesting parts of travel to far-off places is the opportunity to try the local foods. However, I don't eat at the street-side vendors or small sidewalk cafés in developing countries. While the fragrance coming from many of them is alluring, I resist. Too many of my friends and acquaintances have not resisted and have suffered severe bouts of traveler's diarrhea as a result.

I do, however, try the local specialties in the better restaurants. I still have fond memories of the Pigeon Pie in Morocco and the Liver Dumpling Soup in Munich. Don't let the names scare you off. Ask what the local specialties are and be adventuresome. Give them a try.

If you only eat steak, potatoes, and hamburgers, you miss half the fun of travel, and you'll probably be greatly disappointed. The hamburger and steaks in other countries are generally thin, tough, and have an entirely different flavor than we are used to at home. Meat, especially the beef Americans eat routinely, is hard to find and very expensive in many parts of the world. Just as you won't find a good pigeon pie in Minneapolis, you won't find a good steak in Marrakech.

TIPPING

▶ ── ◀

Women, especially, are often uncomfortable about tipping. Because they have not had a lot of experience, they are uncertain when and how much to tip. Some compensate by overtipping, others choose to ignore the situation and go on blindly without tipping, and still others significantly undertip.

Tips are important when you're traveling. A well-placed tip can buy you extra service and attention (see "Checking Into Your Hotel" and "Dining Out"). The amount of the tip you leave should, of course, be dependent upon the quality of service you have received. However, the amount will also determine to a great extent the type of service you and other single women travelers receive in the future.

You should plan ahead and have the tip ready in your hand or pocket. Offer the folded bill as you look the recipient in the eye and say "thank you."

Various factors determine the amount you tip: the service, the standards of the country, the elegance of the setting, and the length of your stay. In Japan and China, for instance, tipping is considered an insult. It's also inappropriate to tip the owner or manager of an establishment in any country, and it's inappropriate to tip the front desk clerk, even when requesting a room with a view.

Again, be sure to carry a lot of $1 bills, especially when you're traveling to and from new locations. Otherwise, you could end up tipping much more than you planned. Also, familiarize yourself with the local exchange rate so you know how much you're tipping.

If you're in doubt about what to tip, ask the tour operator, front desk, or concierge.

Doorman

You need not tip the doorman unless he helps you out of the cab with your bags ($1); gets you a cab ($1); or gets you a cab at rush hour, in the rain, or when you're late ($2).

Bellman

Tip a minimum of $1 for one or two bags. Tip 50 cents to $1 per bag for more. If one bellman helps you from the curb to the front desk and another to your room, it is customary to tip both. If the bellman or a porter shows you to your room without your bags, you are not required to tip. However, unless it's an assistant manager, whom you should absolutely not tip, I'd suggest you tip $1.

Chambermaid

Many places, especially in the United States, consider it unnecessary to tip the housekeeping personnel, particularly when a service charge is added to your room bill. If you tip, leave $1 to $3 per day in an envelope with your maid's name on it. You should also tip for special requests, such as a vase for flowers ($2), letting you in when you've locked yourself out ($1 to $2), or finding you a hair dryer or iron ($2).

Floor Valet

If your hotel has a valet assigned to your floor who tidies up whenever you step out, tip him $2 to $3 per day at the end of your stay.

Room Service Waiter

Tip $2 for delivery, $5 if he serves each course. Tip an extra $1 if you call him to retrieve the dishes, otherwise you can leave them on the table or place them outside your door.

Concierge

Because the concierge considers himself a master in the old tradition, in the finer hotels even the smallest request will necessitate a $5 tip. For theater tickets, he'll expect 10 percent of the cost; for train tickets, $5 to $10 will do. If he needs to "use his contacts," always tip more. If he gets you a reservation in the hottest restaurant in town, he'll once again expect 10 percent of the cost.

You may either tip him for each service or at the end of your stay.

Coat Check

Tip 50 cents to $1 depending on the elegance of the restaurant. More if you also leave a bag or hat.

Waiter

This is most dependent upon the custom of the country and can vary from 10 percent in a developing country to 20 percent in New York City. In most places 15 percent is expected. If you order wine, you need only tip 15 percent of the food bill, unless, of course, you intend to frequent the establishment; in that case tip 15 percent of the whole bill. Be sure to check your bill to see if a service charge has automatically been added. If it has, you need not leave an additional tip.

Maître d'

Tip him 5 percent of the bill, but only if he provided a special service. Give him your tip as you leave.

Taxi

Tip 10 percent of the fare, unless you're in New York City, then 20 percent. If you've bartered on the fare, then you need not tip beyond that, unless, of course, he took you someplace special.

DON'T TAKE A VACATION FROM SAFETY

Feeling safe is essential to feeling relaxed. If you're anxious about your safety, you won't enjoy your trip. On the other hand, you don't want to relax so totally that you lose all cautions, take unnecessary risks, and become a target for a thief or con man. Unfortunately, because vacations are supposed to be carefree and relaxing times, many travelers take risks they would not consider taking at home. You are more likely to overindulge in alcohol, for instance, when you are on a vacation, and liquor makes you more vulnerable to mishap. With poor judgment, you become an easy target. If you're going to drink, make sure to eat so you don't become easily intoxicated. Drink at your hotel bar so you're close to home and don't take your valuables with you. If you have too much to drink and you're not at your hotel, don't accept a ride with a stranger. It can be a costly mistake. Ask the bartender, waiter, or doorman to call you a cab, then wait inside until the cab arrives.

Yes, you should relax and have a good time, but you should do so without making yourself vulnerable to crime. In fact, the less vulnerable you are, the more relaxed you will likely be in the long run. There are measures you can take to lower your vulnerability when traveling alone, even in the most unlikely areas of the world. Learning to be more aware while traveling may even result in your becoming less vulnerable at home.

Lowering Your Vulnerability to Crime

You can decrease your chance of becoming a crime victim before you leave home. Don't take or wear expensive jewelry. This includes gold neck chains, large diamond engagement rings, and a good watch. It will make you a target for theft. That's why insurance companies charge you more per $1,000 when you insure more jewelry. The price goes up, not down, because you become a more visible target, inviting theft.

My rule is to never take expensive jewelry or furs that are not adequately insured and I wouldn't mind losing. That way I lower my losses as a result of theft. Energy spent worrying about property could go into enjoying the setting.

Take only the credit cards you'll use. Leave your hometown department store charge cards and bank instant cash cards at home. Again, take traveler's checks instead of a lot of cash and be sure to keep the numbers separate in case of theft or loss. When you do have cash, keep the $100 bills tucked out of sight, not on the outside of a roll of bills or on the top of your billfold. You don't want them to be visible when you take money out of your wallet.

It's also a good idea not to keep your cash, traveler's checks, checkbook, and credit cards together. If you keep your credit card and checkbook in a separate place from your cash and traveler's checks, for instance, and one is taken, you will still have the other to rely on. Whenever you use your credit card, check the bill and make sure that they return the correct card to you. Also, ask for the carbons and destroy them yourself; there have been instances where the carbons have been used to falsify charges. Keep your receipts and be sure to check your bill when you receive it: If you pay in cash, count your change.

I prefer to pay for an item with my credit card whenever the store is shipping my purchases for me. If the item has not arrived by the time the bill does, I'll notify the credit card company and ask them not to pay the bill until I have received the item. If it doesn't come, I don't pay.

If you're on a cruise ship that provides a locked drawer in your cabin, as most do, use it. Keep all your valuables locked away and take the key with you when you leave.

Hotel Security

If you can afford to do so, stay at a better hotel frequented by local business executives and tourists. Their security in general will be better, the staff will be better screened, and it will likely be in a safer part of town.

Even when you're in your room, keep the doors locked, including the door to your balcony if it is connected to the balcony next door. Use the chain and double lock your door when you're inside. If your door has a key lock, leave the key in the lock on the inside when you are in your room. That way no one will be able to insert a key from the outside.

Use your peephole if there is one. Don't let anyone you don't know or are not expecting into your room. Be aware of anyone who might be following you to your room. If you're uncomfortable, go quickly back downstairs and ask a bellman to accompany you to your room.

When you leave your room do not put the "Make This Room Up" sign on the door. It's a signal to a thief that the room is occupied but unattended. It's also a good idea to leave a light and the TV or radio on when you leave your room so it appears and sounds as if someone's there. For extra security put the "Do Not Disturb" sign on the door as you leave.

Don't think of your room as a secure place to leave your valuables. The same goes for a locked suitcase in your room. While this may be fine, why take the chance. You can lower your risk and vulnerability by locking your valuables in the hotel safe-deposit box.

Safety in Your Car

Just like at home, when you're out of town you should keep your car doors locked even when you're in the car. This is especially true when you're driving through towns with which you are unfamiliar. Carry an area map and ask for directions before setting out so you don't accidentally end up in areas that are unsafe.

Thefts from cars are common. You should never leave bags or valuables in your car that are visible from the outside. If you must leave articles in the trunk, at least put them there before you get to the area where you'll be parking your car. Thieves can pick the lock on a trunk faster than you or I can use a key. Don't let them see you leave things in the trunk.

Safety on the Streets

If you can avoid it, don't carry a purse. If you must carry one, shoulder strap purses worn over your neck and shoulder and hung in front of your body or clutched to your chest are best. You should still not keep much of value in it. Use it to carry only the money you expect to need. Leave the rest in your hotel safe-deposit box or keep it in a money belt (usually a small, flat zipper pouch worn around your waist), or in a "bra buddy" (a small bag you can tuck inside your bra).

The biggest excuse people give for not wearing a money belt or bra buddy is that they are inconvenient to get money out of when it comes time to pay a bill. However, you should not be using the money you carry there to pay a bill. Keep the money you expect to need easily accessible in a pocket. If you need to get into your money belt, go to the rest room so you will have privacy.

Another option is to wear a lightweight vest with a number of pockets of various sizes. Most will have one large zippered pocket which is a good place for most of your valuable items. Other pockets will hold maps, extra camera equipment, film, books, and paper and pencil. These are especially convenient to wear when you are traveling from one location to another. Everything you'll need is readily accessible. (Obviously, they're not exactly appropriate for evening wear.)

If you wear a small backpack, wear it backwards on your chest when you're in especially dangerous areas. This is common practice in many countries with high crime rates. It's much too easy for a thief to either cut it open or open a pocket when it's worn on your back.

When you change money or cash traveler's checks at a bank, be sure to put the money in a safe place before you leave the bank. Don't count it as you're walking out.

Always be aware of your purse, camera, and bags. Instead of setting them on a chair next to you or behind you, set them on your lap or between your feet. Take them with you if you go the bathroom. Don't trust someone you've just met to watch them for you. Why test someone's honesty?

Carry your camera with the strap over your neck and shoulder, like your purse. Clutch it to your chest in a crowd or on a subway.

Develop habits. If you always have your camera over your neck and shoulders, you're more likely to miss it and not leave it behind if it's not there. Get into the habit of never setting your glasses and keys on a table. Instead put them into a pocket when you sit down.

Dealing with Strangers

The best defense against being the target of a crime is to be aware— of your surroundings, the people around you, and of your belongings. Don't be overly trusting. Unfortunately, not everyone is honest. If someone says, "What's wrong, don't you trust me?" that should be a red flag. Tell them, "I'm the careful type. I don't choose to trust people I've only recently met."

Be aware of the possibility of pickpockets in large crowds, at festivals, in subways and train stations, or on long lines. If you're jostled, be alert. Don't open your wallet to make change for someone if the change isn't handy in your pocket. Don't put your camera or a bag down to give someone a light. Pickpockets, especially kids, often work in pairs or groups.

Don't feel as if you have to be friendly to a stranger. If someone starts walking beside you on the street and you're not interested in talking with them, ask them to leave. Cross the street, enter a store; if they follow you, ask a police officer or clerk for assistance.

Safety from Cons

The best way to avoid being overcharged is to always agree on the price of a service ahead of time. If you want to take a cab to a nearby town and do some sightseeing, ask your local tour representative or hotel concierge what you should pay. When you hire a taxi, negotiate the price before you start out and don't pay him until you return to your hotel. Unless the meter is running, don't get in a cab without having negotiated a fair price. (Paris cab drivers are notorious for overcharging.) I'll spare you the countless stories of tourists who unsuspectingly hop into a cab without a meter and do not negotiate a price. There is at least one on every trip. They end up being charged $20 or more for what should have been a $2 or $3 trip. Once you're back it's too late to argue.

The same applies when you hire a guide to show you around town. Negotiate exactly what you'll see, who will pay the entrance fees, how long you'll be gone, and the price. You should also be wary of the stores to which guides take you for shopping. Even those from reputable tour companies will often take you to shops that charge up to 20 percent more than market value. They charge more because they pay the guide a commission, usually a percentage of what you spend.

Be wary when you buy products on the "black market," as well. If you don't pay a premium price, it's unlikely you will receive premium goods. It may be an expensive lesson. Know what you're buying. If you're not absolutely certain of the goods, you're usually better off buying in a reputable store.

FRIENDSHIP, ROMANCE, AND SEX ON VACATION

Even if you like your own company, no one wants to spend a whole week without even the cat to talk to. One of the big advantages to traveling alone is the opportunity to meet other people. I've found the most rewarding part of traveling alone has been the people I've met and the long-term friendships that have resulted. Interestingly, the people I've kept in touch with have been friends rather than lovers. I expect that is because the boundaries and expectations of the relationship developed out of town were such that we could easily step back into our "real worlds." No change was necessary for our friendship to continue.

So where do you start if you're interested in meeting people with whom to spend some time or perhaps only a week-long fling?

Meeting People

The opportunities to meet other people are unlimited. I sometimes find amazing the extent to which some people will go to overlook these opportunities. For instance, I grew up with a father who, if he had to wait in a line five minutes, would be laughing and joking with the people in front of him and in back of him. If he had to wait in a line for thirty minutes, he'd know everyone in the line and it would seem more like a party than a line. He'd usually have at least one offer to join a group near the head of the line as well. What was his secret? He talked to people. Sure, once in a while he'd run into some "sourpuss" who preferred to be bored and angry that he had to wait in line, but my dad didn't take it personally. He went to the next person.

It really is as simple as that. If you want to meet people all you really need to do is not be afraid to talk to the people you find around you. It helps to smile, too. The real secret to meeting people is as simple as putting yourself in situations where there will likely be people around you to whom you can talk.

Standing in line for a buffet, to buy tickets, to check into the hotel, to get into a museum, or any other line in which you find yourself, is a great opportunity. You have a captive audience. Sitting next to someone is similar. Talk with them before, during intermission, or after a concert, movie, or lecture. You even have an event in common about which you can make some comment as trivial as "How did you like the show?" or "How did you hear about it?" Anything will do to break the ice. If you take a plane, bus, or train trip, talk to the people you're sitting next to. Don't be afraid to get on last and sit beside someone who looks interesting.

A great way to meet people is to join some group activity. If you want to meet men, go scuba diving or skiing. You'll find a plethora of single or at least solo men. If you don't ski or dive, take lessons. You'll meet them there too. Tennis lessons are also great and most resorts will match you with a partner for a couple of sets. Join a beach volleyball game. Don't wait to be asked; if one side is short, ask "Can I fill in here?"

If you don't consider yourself the athletic type, check out the resort poolside bar around lunchtime. Most serve some kind of food. Sit at the bar, not at a table by yourself. If there's an interesting guy sitting at the bar, sit next to him, not down at the other end.

Find out where people "hang out" in the evening, besides the bars. At a ski resort shortly after the lifts have closed but before dinner, it will probably be the Jacuzzi. It's a great place to meet a man, woman, or group with whom to go out to dinner, if you haven't already met someone riding up the chair lifts during the day.

In some places, the hotel lobby at tea time is *the* place to be. This was certainly true in Cairo at the Shepherd Hotel. They serve ice cream, a real treat in Cairo. In addition to numerous interesting local businessmen, I met a sheik.

What I hope you are by now aware of is that there is always the opportunity to meet people. If you're interested in companionship you can certainly find it. What's totally up to you is whether or not you take advantage of these opportunities. Life—and especially a vacation—is generally too short to sit and wait for someone to come to you. You've got absolutely nothing to lose and a lot to gain, so start talking.

If you have a hard time starting a conversation but see an interesting-looking man across the room, try this. First, be sure you're standing in a place in which you're easily accessible and approachable. Catch his eye, smile, look him straight in the eye, and count to ten. Then look down and turn away. If he's available and interested, he'll find you. If he doesn't come right over but you see him watching you, give him a second chance. Do it again.

Lust or Love

Most people seem to think single women go on a vacation in order to find romance. It's been my experience that this idea does not hold true. That's not to say that a romantic interlude is not sometimes welcomed. It can certainly make a trip more memorable.

Few travel books talk about sex on vacation, even though it can be a more important topic than what hotel you'll stay at or which sights you'll see. Probably the most important thing about sex on a vacation, or at home, is that *you* decide if you want it. Don't let someone else coerce you into having sex if you'd really rather not. Not becoming intoxicated is a good way to maintain this control. It's hard to say no or get yourself out of an uncomfortable situation when you've had too much to drink.

If you're sexually active, you'll always want to travel prepared. Take your contraceptives with you. You can't assume you'll be able to purchase contraceptives when you're away from home. You also can't assume that the man you might be interested in while away will have a condom anymore than you can assume a man at home will. Women are now purchasing 40 percent of all condoms. I'd suggest you come prepared with these too if that's what you rely on to prevent pregnancy and contracting a sexually transmitted disease. If you don't have them, it could be a costly omission. Taking contraceptives does not mean you're looking for sex any more than taking Lomotil along means you're looking for diarrhea. It means you're smart enough to travel prepared.

It's also important that you realize that romance on vacation is generally just that, with or without sex. When the vacation ends, the romance usually does too. Having worked with crews on ships and staffs at resorts, I know that many have a new romance with each group of tourists. It's beautiful while it lasts, but don't expect them to give up their life-styles to follow you home. They often already have at least one wife with children. I met one sailor with three wives in different parts of the world, each with two children.

What that also means is they are generally very sexually active, and as a result are a high risk for sexually transmitted diseases. Sailors and resort staffs deserve their "sexually rich" reputations.

If you are going to have sex make sure it's *safe sex*. Insist he wears a condom. Today there's more than gonorrhea, syphilis, chlamydia (which are all curable), and herpes to be concerned about—you also need to worry about AIDS. While in the west homosexual men, bisexual men, and IV drug users are, of course, still the highest risk, AIDS has become a general worldwide health crisis. Latex condoms have been found to prevent the transmission of the AIDS virus during intercourse. A condom will also prevent the passage of germs causing gonorrhea, syphilis, chlamydia, and hepatitis-B.

The other side of the coin is the men who are out to marry American women in order to get into the United States. This is not as unusual as you might think. A friend who recently returned from a one-week trip to Jamaica with her daughter said they each had two or three serious marriage proposals while there.

Even if you meet someone you really find yourself attracted to, don't make any serious commitments when you're under the allure of a romantic island. Come home to the "real world" before you decide what to do with the rest of your life.

Giving Clear Messages

In some parts of the world more than others, just the fact that you are a woman traveling alone makes you appear available to the local men. This can be both an advantage and a disadvantage. If you want to meet someone, especially a man, it will likely be easy for you to do so. If you're only looking for companionship, not romance, it will mean you'll need to be cautious and be sure that you are giving clear messages.

Giving clear messages is hard enough for some women to do back home where they know all the rules and customs. It's much harder when the things you do are interpreted differently than they would be at home. Smiling and batting your eyes when you tell someone you're not interested in his offer is a good example. It's also a good way to get yourself into a very uncomfortable situation if you're really not interested. Many men would interpret such a "No" as a "Yes, but I need to be convinced a little harder."

In order to avoid these double messages, it's important for you to understand why you may be unclear. First, it may be that you're really not sure what it is you want. You better make up your mind or someone else will end up deciding for you and you could be sorry. At the very least you're passive, indecisive, and deferential. Unfortunately, many women are taught to be just that from the time they start to walk, talk, and smile. Most don't even recognize when they give unclear, ambivalent signals.

Smiling when you don't really want to, or shouldn't be, is probably the next most important thing to consider. "Girls" are taught to smile. If a drunk with a drink in his hand flops down beside you and says, "A cute girl like you shouldn't be here alone. Let me get you a drink," don't smile and giggle when you tell him, "No, I'm really not interested. I think you should find someone else to drink with." And you can let him save face—and will probably have an easier time sending him on his way—if you add, "But thanks anyway." That way you won't hurt his ego and he won't feel the need to retaliate by being abusive.

But don't smile. If you do he could ignore your words and be encouraged by your smile, a nonverbal sign of welcome.

You also don't have to be polite at all costs. Just because someone says "Hi, how are you?" does not mean you must answer—only social custom and your grandmother say you have to. Those comments, especially when carried into conversations, can be very intrusive. If you're walking by someone, it's often easiest to say "Hi" back and keep walking. If you're not interested in talking with someone, it's okay not to. Be firm, clear, and, once again, don't smile when you tell them you're busy and not interested in talking at the present time.

Especially in a foreign country, what you agree to do can also give messages you may not want to give. For instance, if you are on a cruise ship, "going up on deck to look at the moon" means the likelihood of at least heavy petting to a member of the crew, so be forewarned. At a resort, "a walk along the beach" means the same thing. An invitation to go to someone's room for a drink, yours or his, can also be interpreted as consent for sex, especially if the man has bought dinner.

In the good ol' U.S.A., women's behavior is often misinterpreted by men. So just imagine how much more common misunderstandings are in countries where women would never consider traveling on their own or going out with a man they don't know well. In addition, many foreign men think American women are sexually available. The reality is that compared to many of their women, we are "loose" sexually. As liberated, independent women, we are able to make our own choices about where we travel and whom we'll sleep with and when. Our moral and social codes about what is acceptable behavior for a single woman are quite different from South American customs, for instance.

Unfortunately, the differences in cultural expectations may result in a man from another culture, such as South America, feeling as if American women have "led him on" or are "teasing him." Unless you proceed with caution, your pleasant evening may have a very unhappy ending. More important than considering what your behavior and dress may convey at home, you should think about how it might be interpreted in the country you're visiting.

TRAVELING HEALTHY

▶──▶

Traveler's Diarrhea

Diarrhea is a common problem of travelers to remote parts of the world. It's often contracted by drinking contaminated water. However, most experts agree that undercooked or poorly refrigerated foods are an even greater health risk in developing countries. While the natives seem to do fine, you need to remember that they have had years to develop a resistance to the organisms encountered. You have not. The best solution is to eat only in the better restaurants, never at street stands. Be careful where you drink the water. If in doubt, drink only bottled water and bottled drinks, and if you can't drink the water, don't use ice either. Research has shown that the organisms responsible for illness are not eliminated by freezing, even for twenty-four hours. Alcoholic beverages won't kill them either: shigella (a bacteria that causes dysentery) was found in 86-proof tequila one hour after all the ice had melted. Also be wary of vegetables and fruits washed in unsafe water.

It's a good idea to take antidiarrhea medication with you. Check with your doctor to see what he recommends. There are a number of good products on the market. Pepto-Bismol is an excellent one.

Fortunately, most traveler's diarrhea, while a nuisance, is self-limiting. The most serious problem is dehydration, especially if you're nauseated at the same time. Be sure to drink plenty of water and eat salty foods to replace what you lose.

The best fluid replacement is apple juice or orange juice (rich in potassium) with a pinch of table salt (sodium) and half a teaspoon of honey, corn syrup, or table sugar. The World Health Organization recommends drinking this until your thirst is satisfied. Your body will let you know.

If your diarrhea does not subside in a couple of days, or if you have blood in your stool or severe stomach cramps, you should consult a physician.

Sunburn

Inadequate protection from the sun is probably the most common health hazard of travel. Prevention is, of course, the solution. If you must get a tan, don't try to get your whole tan in one day. Start with brief exposures and use protective sunscreen. You may even want to go to a tanning studio to get a protective base tan before leaving home. But remember, you can still burn with a base tan. The only way to avoid a bad burn is to always use a sunscreen. You should also remember that tanning increases the aging process and the likelihood of skin cancer. If you do get burned, take a cold bath. Don't put oil on your skin that will hold the heat in. Find a soothing cream.

Insect-Borne Disease

Be sure to use mosquito repellent. It's the best preventive measure against malaria and dengue fever.

Medical Emergencies

If you need medical assistance while in a foreign country, contact your local tour operator, the hotel concierge or manager, or the nearest U.S. embassy or consulate. You can also contact the U.S. Department of State's Citizen Emergency Center at (202) 632-5225. They will help you contact the nearest embassy or consulate. They are open twenty-four hours a day. Don't buy or use over-the-counter medicines with which you're unfamiliar.

Before you leave, you can obtain information on English-speaking physicians in your destination country by writing to the International Association for Medical Assistance to Travelers, 736 Center Street, Lewistown, NY 14092; or call them at (716) 754-4883. They will also provide you with up-to-date information on sanitary conditions and suggested vaccinations.

KEEPING IN TOUCH WITH THOSE BACK HOME

The most common method of keeping in touch is to send postcards. Fewer travelers take advantage of the telex or airfone.

Mail

If you're going to send postcards to the office or to your friends, it's a good idea to write as early in your trip as possible. Otherwise, you'll beat the cards home. Also be sure to write "Air Mail" on all letters, postcards, and packages and get the proper postage. Unlike the United States, where everything goes by air these days, if you don't specify "Air Mail" your postcard from Europe will take the slow boat. Having the proper amount of postage for Air Mail delivery alone is not necessarily sufficient. You must also have "Air Mail" written out.

If you want to be more creative, send a surprise via Federal Express. Your friends can sample the wonderful pork buns you found in San Francisco's Chinatown the next day, or your best friend can wear her lei from Hawaii while you're still there.

Phoning Home

While the practice varies from hotel to hotel, many hotels will charge as much as 75¢ per call including in-house calls. They often charge much more for long-distance calls. Question their policy when you check in.

Take your AT&T calling card with you, or get one before you go, and use it. Never charge a call to your room. The best way to make a call in Europe, for instance, is to go to a post office—after you have figured out the time back home, of course. Tell them the country, area code, and phone number you wish. They will direct you to a phone booth and place your call for you.

If you're on a ship you can utilize the global maritime satellite system. Calls can be made to almost anywhere in the world as clearly as from home. An average cost for this service is $12 per minute. You may call collect, person to person, or direct. You can usually charge the call to your major credit card.

Since the fall of 1984, airfones have been available on selected flights. You must be in the U.S. airspace to use this service. You can then, however, call anywhere in the U.S., including Alaska and Hawaii.

Telex or Telegraph

Less expensive than phoning, but almost as fast, is the telex. You can telex from ship or shore. To send a telex from a ship you need simply write out your message and the name and address of the person you wish it sent to. Take it to the communications officer or the ship radio station. The operator will assist you in sending your telex.

CAPTURING YOUR IMPRESSIONS AS YOU GO

Some people take pictures, others buy souvenirs, but we all want to somehow capture the special moments of a vacation indelibly in our memories. Writing a journal about the people you meet, the things you see, and the feelings evoked is a good way to be able to relive the trip as well as to remember the name of a favorite restaurant or local dish to tell a friend. Attractive books with blank pages are available in most bookstores and make great journals.

I met a woman on a recent trip who, instead of keeping a written journal, drew a picture of a flower or bird in each place she stopped. I always felt this was a wonderful idea. Other people write poems or prose capturing their feelings.

Still others have a theme to their picture taking or souvenir collecting. They may be taking pictures of flowers, children, people's faces, or men with the intention of making them into a collage when they return home. I try to buy one piece of ceramic tile from each country I visit, which I will eventually use in my entry room floor. I also love unique local clothing and jewelry. I've met people who take a small sprig of flowers and press it between the pages of a book to take home, or buy a miniature to put in a shadow box. It requires a little thinking ahead of time, but souvenirs *can* be more than dust collectors.

CUSTOMS, RULES, AND REGULATIONS

The best strategy is to be honest when you fill out your customs declarations form. If you are, customs will likely be a breeze. It's really not something to get nervous about, as long as you have nothing to hide. Customs officials are trained to spot potential smugglers, so you don't want to look unduly nervous. They always have the option of searching your bags and having a woman do a body search; however, they seldom do this.

Allowed Exemptions

As a U.S. citizen you may bring in $400 worth of goods duty free provided you have been out of the country forty-eight hours or more and have not claimed this exemption within thirty days. The forty-eight-hour rule does not apply to the U.S. Virgin Islands. You can also bring an additional $400 worth of goods purchased in the Virgin Islands into the U.S. duty free. This is based on the price of the items in the country in which they were purchased. To avoid problems, it's best to keep all sales receipts in order to verify the purchase price. State laws vary as to the amount of liquor (usually one quart), cigarettes (usually two cases), or perfume that can be brought back.

You can usually bring back crafts from developing countries duty free. This is to encourage the development of these small industries and stimulate economic growth of these countries, which include Israel, Portugal, Brazil, India, and Hong Kong, as well as most of those in the Caribbean and Central America. Handcrafts from other countries may be included as well. Be sure to check before you visit.

Shipping Gifts Home

In order to avoid duty, gifts must be shipped separately and be under $50 in value. The same person cannot receive more than one package in the same day. The package should be marked "Unsolicited Gift" with the contents and value indicated on the package. You should get a green customs declaration tag at the post office to attach to each package.

Shipping gifts is a great way to avoid extra baggage and extra customs charges. Most stores will pack your items and ship them for a small fee. I've never had a problem with a package's arrival, although I have friends who have. I generally only have purchases shipped from reputable stores and, as I mentioned previously, I try to pay for them with a major credit card. That way, if the item has not arrived by the time I receive my bill, I contact the credit card company and ask them not to pay the bill. They have always been most agreeable.

Duty Free Shops

Duty free shops are often misleading. All "duty free" really means is that duty was not paid on the item when it came into the country. The cost "should" thus be lower. It does not mean you won't have to pay duty on it when you enter the U.S. In fact, you will if you exceed the customs limitations.

Value Added Tax

Many countries have a value added tax that is included in the price of all merchandise. It can be 10 to 25 percent. In some countries, Germany for instance, you can get this money back when you leave the country. To do so you must get a special document from the merchant when you make your purchase and keep your sales slip. Show these and the item at the border when you leave, or at the airport. The money may be given to you then or sent to you. If you have the merchant ship an item directly, you should not have to pay the extra tax. Ask them.

Forbidden Items

Unless specifically treated, it is usually illegal to import any live plant or plant material. Birds and animals must often be quarantined, depending on state law. This is to prevent the introduction of new diseases. Parts of the world that do not have rabies, for instance, will not allow you to take your pet cat or dog into the country without months of quarantine to ensure they are not infected.

Many countries have laws against killing endangered species of animal life. Unfortunately, the poachers kill them anyway. The problem is that they don't have laws against selling the products and, more unfortunate, tourists still buy them.

Whenever someone buys an item, a whalebone necklace or a leopard skin coat for instance, it produces a market for that item. It's not true that "it's already dead, so it doesn't matter if I buy it." If you buy it, another animal will be killed to make more jewelry and coats for other people to buy. So think before you act.

In an attempt to protect endangered and threatened species from extinction, Congress passed the Marine Mammal Protection Act of 1972 and the Endangered Species Act of 1973. The important points of these acts for you, the traveler, is that they have made it illegal to import any item made from any part of an endangered or threatened fish or wildlife into the United States. While we can't prevent the slaughter or sale of the items in another country, we can limit their import and, as a result, the market. Species covered by the acts include polar bear, sea otter, marine otter, walrus, dugong, whale, manatee, and monk seal. Most spotted cat skins are caught illegally as are sea turtles.

While it might be tempting to try turtle or monkey meat in a restaurant, before you do, ask yourself at what expense you want the experience. The same is true of the souvenir with the colorful bird feathers from the tropics, or the stool made from an elephant's foot, or the lynx coat, or tortoiseshell jewelry.

What you decide to do does make a difference. Don't assuage your conscience by saying it doesn't. If we're all responsible shoppers on the world market we can have an impact on the illegal slaughter of endangered and threatened species.

It's best to know what you can bring home before you go. For more information read "Know Before You Go." You can get a copy by writing to the Department of the Treasury, U.S. Customs Service, Washington, DC 20229.

A MOMENT OF FREEDOM

Now that you've arrived, you have your moment of freedom: from your usual roles and routines, from the expectations of others, from the demands of your job, from the rules of your life back home. You are in a totally new setting with new people. You can be anyone, do anything. You can experience a new part of the world.

Hopefully, as a result of your travel experience, you'll go home better able to see yourself and your culture. Perhaps you'll gain a new appreciation for your day-to-day life, or realize how really unimportant an event you once considered to be a crisis, actually is.

I usually return home with an inner sense of peace and tranquillity that I guard and try to maintain. I also return with a new perspective from which to measure future crises. Somehow from this vantage point, they seem less serious.

▶ ▶

Part II

VACATION DESTINATIONS

▶ ▶

CHAPTER 5

▶ ▶ ▶

Winter Vacations: For Those Who Like It Hot

CRUISING SOLO

▶—————————————————————————————▶

GENERAL AMBIANCE	★ ★
SOCIAL CLIMATE	★ ★
ACTIVITIES	★ ★

FOR TOUR ARRANGEMENTS CONTACT:
Sun Line Cruises
One Rockefeller Plaza, Suite 315
New York, NY 10020
(800) 445-6400

Phyllis Zeno's Merry Widows
1515 N. Westshore Boulevard
Tampa, FL 33607
(813) 872-5000

▶—————————————————————————————▶

*N*ot long ago, cruising was almost exclusively a privilege of the wealthy and usually the old. I was in my early twenties and I was on

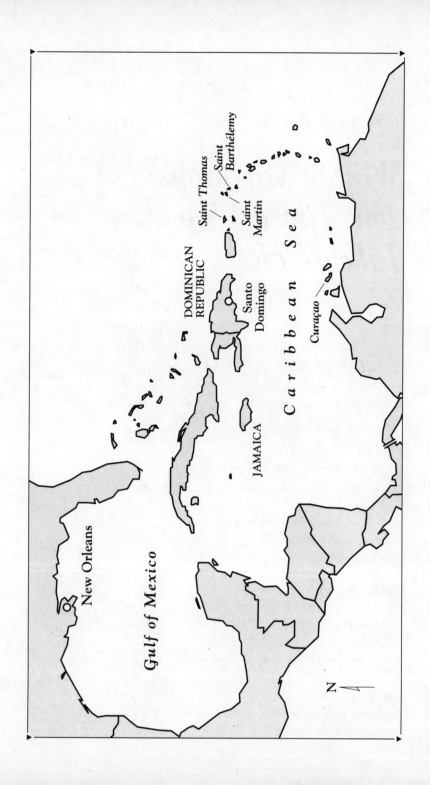

my first cruise in the Mediterranean. I was considered a child and, much to my dismay, I felt like a child compared to the other, much older passengers. Now things have changed, perhaps due to "The Love Boat" and a new image of cruising. Over 40 percent of cruise ship passengers today are under thirty-five years of age, and more than 40 percent of those going on a cruise for the first time are single.

If you've seen the movie *Love Boat II* starring Linda Evans, then you've seen the T.S.S. *Stella Solaris*, one of three Sun Line Cruise ships. While Linda Evans was not aboard on my Caribbean cruise, Billy Eckstein, the Harlem Blues and Jazz Band, Jacki Sorensen and a number of her aerobic dance instructors, and Phyllis Zeno's Merry Widows were. The "Merry Widows" aren't necessarily widows. They are single, divorced, widowed, and even married women who want to join a group of women who, like themselves, love to dance. Phyllis is their tour leader.

General Ambiance

A Greek ship, the *Stella Solaris* was in many ways an excellent choice for the filming of *Love Boat II*. A number of women, of all ages, shapes, and marital status told me they felt more appreciated on this ship than they had felt in years. "I think I should come back periodically just for an ego boost," said one woman. That is due to the staff and crew—no matter what they're doing, they always have time for a friendly smile and greeting. They really seem to enjoy their work and having you on board. Greek men genuinely appreciate a woman just for being a woman, and they don't hesitate to let you know it.

The *Stella Solaris* is rated a five-star cruise ship and she deserves this highest rating. The public areas are well appointed and consistently spotless. The rooms are freshened up, trash removed and fresh towels provided, at least three times a day. The food is some of the best I've had either on board a ship or in a restaurant. It is artistically presented as well as tasty, but it's the overall elegance of the ship and the individual service that makes dining a real pleasure. Your waiter and cabin steward will go out of their way to identify and fulfill your individual desires, be that a glass of tomato juice in your cabin with breakfast or a cup of cappuccino after dinner at night. You need only ask once or twice and after that, it seems to magically appear. If another entrée or dessert looks more tempting than the one you ordered, your waiter will gladly bring you something else . . . or both.

If you prefer a more informal meal around the pool, you may choose from the large buffets of salads, fish, meats, and oh . . . the pastries! There's even a midnight buffet after the last dance to the orchestra.

Social Climate

A floating hotel of medium size, the *Stella Solaris* has a capacity of about 600 passengers plus 300 crew. Unlike the large ships that hold 1,200 to 1,800 people, by the end of a week or two you have met many of your fellow travelers. With open seatings for breakfast and lunch, and the buffet meals in the poolside lounge, you have an opportunity to sit with a variety of people from many parts of the country and a number of countries around the world. The friendly staff will seat you with others, so you need never eat alone. Dinner is with your group, such as the Merry Widows, or with other individuals traveling alone if you're not with a group. One of the real highlights of my trip was getting to know more intimately the group of six people I ate dinner with each night.

Unlike many cruise lines, the Greeks have cabin stewards instead of stewardesses. While the single men on board did not necessarily consider this an advantage, to some extent it accounts for the incredible welcome any woman receives, especially one traveling alone. The Greek lines also allow their crew to socialize with the guests when off duty, unlike many other companies. This has both advantages and disadvantages. The advantage is that you'll have many opportunities for company, if that's what you want. The disadvantage is that all of the attention can be a little overwhelming and you'll need to set limits (see "Friendship, Romance, and Sex on Vacation," p. 71).

This is one of those times when you'll really want to be sure you're clear in your own mind—and make it clear to the people you meet—what you really are or are not interested in. Clear limits are quickly understood and respected. If for any reason you should feel uncomfortable, there are two female hostesses who are warm, friendly, understanding, and willing to help you resolve any uncomfortable situation without hurting anyone's feelings. If you're sailing with the Merry Widows, Phyllis is always available. If there is a special man you'd like to meet but haven't yet, Phyllis always has a number of delightful suggestions on how to get his attention. She's charming, a great "mother hen," and she'd make a great sleuth!

Activities

Cruising is probably one of the best ways to combine a relaxing, carefree vacation with the excitement of seeing new countries and a variety of different ports of call in a limited amount of time.

The ports of call will vary somewhat from trip to trip, even on the same ship. They may even vary from the original schedule. If the weather's bad and you've planned to stop at a small port without adequate docking facilities, you may find an unexpected change of schedule. You'll likely arrive at your next stop early and have more time there, which can be an advantage.

Shipboard Activities

Each night in the Solaris Lounge, you'll enjoy continuous dancing to two orchestras. In addition, there is a nightclub show each evening that includes a number of internationally renowned dance groups as well as a variety of performances by individuals whose names are now household words. Not only will you have a front row seat to watch them perform, but you'll have multiple opportunities to get to know them while on board.

Host Program. Sun Line now has a host program that follows in the tradition of the Merry Widows program. Men with dancing experience, some previously instructors, have been hired to act as hosts on board ship. A primary part of their function is dancing with the women traveling alone. So even if you're not able to book a Merry Widows Dance Cruise, on any Sun Line trip you'll likely have the opportunity to dance to the orchestra as you sail across the open sea. There are a limited number of hosts on board ship at a time, so you won't be guaranteed a full evening of dancing as with the Merry Widows program. It's a great alternative, however, and a good ice breaker.

If you're not interested in dancing or watching the after-dinner show, there's always a movie in the theater at night. There's one each afternoon as well. Prior to dinner you can attend a piano concert or, at tea time, enjoy a fashion show. Most afternoons also include the option of listening to a guest lecturer speak on a variety of subjects. The usual Ping-Pong, trap shooting, bingo, and bridge (with lessons) are also available. If you'd like, the *Stella Solaris* has gambling tables in the back lounge and slot machines for you to try your luck on the days you're at sea.

I especially like the *Stella Solaris* because the boat deck has a continuous outside walkway. Seven revolutions equals one mile. You can watch porpoise and sailing fish, islands on the horizon, or other ships as you walk or jog.

The Merry Widows

In the process of escorting a group on a Caribbean cruise in 1977, Phyllis Zeno noticed that while the couples enjoyed dancing to the orchestra in the evening, the single women did not. They might linger in the lounge a while after dinner, but finding no available dance partners they soon went below to their cabins.

A creative woman, Phyllis came up with an inventive solution to this dilemma. She began the Merry Widows Dance Cruises. It's not a requirement to be a widow, it's not even a requirement to know how to do ballroom dancing. I did my first tango, rumba, and samba on the cruise. Three or four times a year through the Tampa AAA she organizes cruise groups. She hires one male dancer for every five women who sign up. These guys are such incredible dancers that by the second dance they made me look as if even I knew what I was doing. Former dance teachers turned real estate brokers or restaurant owners, "the guys" were charming gentlemen and a real pleasure to dance and travel with.

Another interesting side benefit is that when the other single men on board see you dancing, they are more likely to ask you to dance, too—much to the envy of the single women not with the group. I guess this is because they can see that you like to dance and they don't need to worry that you'll say "No." Phyllis, obviously in charge, also makes an even less threatening envoy to the ship's officers, staff, and others, who will arrange to have her introduce them to you.

Sailing with the Merry Widows, you soon become a member of a close-knit smaller group within the larger group of passengers. You'll find other women with similar interests not only to eat, tour, and shop with, but also with whom to share the many aspects of life aboard the ship. A couple of women in the group confided some initial hesitation and ambivalence about cruising with the Merry Widows, but that was soon dispelled. "Boy, am I glad I decided to come. This is wonderful," I was told at dinner the second night out. One woman on my cruise was there for the seventh time. While she now uses a cane to walk, she doesn't need it to dance. A charming dance partner is much better support than a cane any day.

The Merry Widows also appreciated being able to travel with "the guys." These are men with whom you can relax and have long talks without worrying that they will misinterpret your friendliness and make sexual advances. Phyllis makes it perfectly clear that any more intimate relationship is a strict taboo. As a result, you can really let your guard down with these men. If you're interested in more intimate liaisons, there are plenty of opportunities outside the Merry Widows group.

In addition to the fun of dancing, I felt the real advantage of cruising with the Merry Widows was the delight of getting to know a unique group of women. I thoroughly enjoyed their company. Middle and upper-middle class, most were well-educated, well-traveled, fascinating women in their own right. Some had never married, others actually were recently widowed, and one had left her husband, who was too busy to travel, at home. All had a certain zest for life and were still living it to the fullest. The women were in their late fifties to eighties, the escorts their thirties to sixties.

Jackie Sorensen's Aerobics

I was also fortunate to be on board with Jackie Sorensen, the originator of aerobic dance. Each morning and afternoon all interested passengers were invited to join her and her group in aerobic workouts and aerobic dance routines. By the end of the eleven-day cruise I was in better shape than I had been all winter. She organizes a Sun Line cruise once each year. If you'd like to join a trip you can get information by calling (1-800) 22-DANCE. Jackie's program promotes a balanced life-style. The aerobics certainly helped to balance my increased food intake, but mostly it was a lot of fun. I really looked forward to the classes and I enjoyed meeting the other people who attended.

Preparing for Your Cruise

Rates

Everything except the shore tours is included in the cost of your stateroom, which will vary considerably depending on the length of the cruise and the level and size of your cabin. The lower levels have portholes, the upper levels good-size windows. You can also book an inner room without a porthole for even less. The least expensive room for an eleven-day cruise is $1,775, which includes your airfare. The most expensive two-room suite is $3,225. An outside stateroom with a large window in the superior category will cost $2,325. The prices will, of course, vary with the length of the trip. During the slow months, such as June, you can get the same trip for $250 less.

Sun Line Cruises is one of the companies who responded favorably to the tour industry's challenge to find a way to deal more fairly with the individual traveling alone. In response, they developed a "guaranteed share" program. If you request a roommate and they don't find you one, or the ship is not full at the time of sailing, you need not pay the single supplement charge. They have also reduced their single supplement charge during the slow months from the usual 50 percent additional to 25 percent.

If you book through the Merry Widows, Phyllis will arrange for you to room with another Merry Widow when possible, if you'd like to avoid the single supplement charge that way.

Documents

While you need to take a valid passport with you, I must admit I was never asked to show mine. Since the ports of call vary, be sure to check early with Sun Line or your travel agent to see if you will need a visa for any country you will be entering.

What to Take

The electricity in the cabins is 220 watts, so you'll need to take a hair dryer, curling iron, or iron that will accept European current, or take an adapter. There are no clocks or alarms in the cabins, so it's a good idea to take a travel alarm clock. Each room has a radio, but you might want to bring along a portable one with earphones for when you walk or jog around the deck or lounge in the sun.

There are three formal dinners plus a Greek night, a Spanish night, and a masquerade ball. You'll find people wearing everything from long sequined gowns to nice cotton dresses on the formal evenings. If you have anything Greek, bring it for Greek night. If not, you can find a variety of inexpensive dresses in the gift shop on board, or any dress will, of course, do. You need not bring a costume, although a few people always do. Sun Line will provide you with hats and odds and ends to put together as a costume or, as at least half of the guests usually do, you can simply watch the costume parade.

For the most part, both on the ship and on shore, informal resort wear is the rule. Cotton slacks, shorts, lightweight shirts or T-shirts with comfortable walking shoes will be the most useful. I'd also suggest taking a couple of summer dresses and, of course, your bathing suit and plenty of sunscreen.

You'll also want tennis shoes or, better yet, aerobic shoes for the aerobic workouts. If you have tights and leotards you'll fit right in with the aerobics instructors and students. I loved their bright colors and unique patterns, but my jogging shorts and T-shirt did nicely, too.

Health Concerns

While there are opportunities to eat on shore in delightful and unique restaurants, if you are concerned about exposure to food- or water-borne disease you can have all your meals on board the ship. The ports of call in the Caribbean do not usually include any areas where prior vaccination is necessary, but be sure to check with Sun Line or your travel agent when you book your trip about your particular itinerary.

While there is a doctor on board, you should not expect to obtain from him any medication you normally take. It may be available and it may not. Why take the chance of being uncomfortable because you didn't plan ahead. Bring your medication with you.

Medication for sea sickness is available from the ship's doctor, but once again, I'd suggest taking your own, especially if there is a particular kind that you know works for you. Because the *Stella Solaris* has a deeper draft than most ships her size, she rides more smoothly in the water. In addition, she has stabilizers that reduce 80 percent of the roll from side to side that you would otherwise experience. However, there are always a few people who experience some discomfort if the water is rough.

Getting There

When you arrive at the airport, in my case New Orleans, proceed toward baggage claim. Just outside of the baggage claim area, in a hard to miss location, you'll see a table with the smiling face of a Sun Line hostess and a sign indicating that you're at the right place. You should check in with her. She'll tell you where to meet the complementary bus that will take you to the boat.

If you have not already done so, you should attach the *Stella Solaris* baggage tags, with your name and cabin number written on the back, to each piece of your luggage. You need to get your own luggage to the bus (there are porters available at the baggage claim area to assist you), but once there, the *Stella Solaris* staff will see that it gets to your cabin—so, obviously, it must be properly marked. You will find your cabin number on the ticket Sun Line sent to you.

Tipping

It is customary to tip only at the end of the cruise. It is also strongly recommended that you not tip individuals; instead, place your tip in the envelope you will be given when you settle your account. Seven dollars per day is recommended. The total amount will then be distributed evenly among the entire crew. The Greek marine union has voted to handle tipping in this manner in order to be more fair. While a few individuals, usually your waiter and cabin steward, provide direct service to you, they are only able to do so because of the many other people behind the scenes. If you tip them individually, it's not really fair to those who provided essential but not so obvious services to you during your voyage.

The hairdresser and masseuse are not included in this tipping system. They should be tipped individually at the time they provide the service.

Your Shipboard Account

Whenever you use the sauna, hairdressers, get a massage, or order a drink aboard the *Stella Solaris*, you need only sign your name and cabin number. On the last day at sea you can settle your account with the purser by check or credit card.

The tours and shipboard boutique are not included in this account system. While you can still use a check or credit card to make your purchases, each item must be paid for at the time of purchase.

Ports of Call

As I mentioned earlier, the ports of call will vary from year to year and trip to trip. On my cruise we sailed from New Orleans and stopped in Jamaica, St. Thomas, St. Barthélemy, Curaçao, and returned to Fort Lauderdale. We were also scheduled to stop in the Dominican Republic and St. Martin, but as sometimes happens, rough seas made our landings impossible in these two ports.

Once you are on board the ship you'll be able to purchase tours for the various ports of call. I'd suggest deciding early which tours you'd like to take and booking them. Most tours in port have a limited capacity. If you wait too long to book, you may find you're out of luck. The tours can be charged to your credit card or you can pay by personal check.

Ocho Rios, Jamaica

Discovered by Columbus in 1494, Jamaica was occupied by the British until it became independent in 1962. Ocho Rios on the north central coast was once a banana and fishing port. Today it's most famous for its beaches and the attractive *Dunn's River Falls*.

Because of the current high rate of unemployment (35 percent), there are a great number of small shops where the locals attempt to earn money by selling a variety of handmade items—such as straw baskets and hats, wood carvings, dolls, and clothing. They will also offer to braid your hair. Remember to bargain and expect to pay half or less of the original asking price.

Motorcoach tours of Ocho Rios (US$21) or the *Plantations and Straw Market* (US$24) are bookable through the ship. The general consensus and my recommendation is that you're better off finding a friend or two with whom you can share a cab and see the sights on your own. Be sure to negotiate what you want to see and how much you'll be charged before you get into the cab.

You should be able to see the *Shaw Park Gardens*, Dunn's River Falls, and the straw market for US$20 to US$25 (about a 2- to 2½-hour tour). This includes having the driver wait or return after you walk up the 600-foot series of small rapids at Dunn's River Falls. The motorcoach tour does not include time for walking up the falls. It'll cost US$2 per person to hire a guide who knows the route. You'll need to wear a bathing suit and tennis shoes. You'll be in waist deep water at times, though most of it is only ankle deep, and you'll actually walk behind the falls on occasion.

St. Thomas, U.S. Virgin Islands

It's only a short walk to town from where the ship will dock, but if you prefer, you can take a van for US$2. At this lively Caribbean resort center, you'll find stylish boutiques, luxury hotels, and a variety of restaurants. While the shops offer a large selection of goods—watches, cameras, jewelry—don't assume you're getting a deal and do try to bargain. If you're shopping with a friend and purchase more than one item, you should definitely be able to get a price reduction. You'll also find the prices vary greatly from store to store.

Here again, I'd suggest you hire a cab on your own or with a small group, and for US$10 to US$25 you can see the main sights of the area. You'll not want to miss *Megan's Bay*, a fifteen-minute drive up the mountain and over to the other side of the island. The view is spectacular and worth the drive by itself. Megan's Bay (admission 50 cents per person) is considered one of the most beautiful bays in the world. Be sure to ask your driver to take you to *Drake's Seat*, a lookout point over the bay. Don't be surprised to see small luxury yachts anchored in the bay. Other sights include *Bluebeard's Castle* and the spectacular *Coral World*, where you can look through windows onto one of St. Thomas's coral reefs with its spectacular variety of fish.

There is a choice of tours you can book through the tour office on board ship. You can take a tour to St. John's Island nearby and go snorkeling in *Trunk Bay* (US$23) or you can take the island drive tour, which stops at *Coral World* (US$22).

The third option is snorkeling with the *U.S. Virgin Islands Diving School* (US$20) or scuba diving. If you are a certified diver and have brought your diving certificate with you, you can book the snorkeling tour on board, then pay an additional US$15 when you get to the diving school to rent your diving gear. Be sure and tell the *Stella Solaris* staff that this is what you plan to do so they can telex ahead to make the proper arrangements. To snorkel you need only know how to swim. The fee includes all of your equipment as well as transportation to the beach. For an additional US$25 you can also rent an underwater camera at the dive shop to share the experience with your friends back home. I'd suggest taking your own film instead of using the roll they provide with the camera.

St. Barthélemy, French West Indies

Columbus was the first European visitor here, too. He named the island for his brother Bartholomew. This French- and English-speaking island has somehow maintained its small fishing village flavor even though today you can buy Paris fashions in the small town of *Gustavia* where you will come ashore.

This is one of the few places in the Caribbean where you can still get away from the stress, hustle, and bustle of everyday life. On the island tour (US$15 and well worth the 1½ hours), you'll drive along the scenic coast as well as through small villages. The coast is sometimes stark and foreboding with high waves hitting coral cliffs. At other times you'll pass quiet sandy bays with peaceful, clear blue water.

Curaçao, Netherlands Antilles

The highlight of my trip was our stop at this Dutch island 40 miles off the coast of Venezuela. The floating bridge parted as we sailed up the channel past the city of *Willemstad*, with the two distinct districts of *Punda* and *Otrabanda* (the other side). This is the fifth largest harbor in the world. The language spoken here, Papiamento, is actually a mixture of six languages. Dutch and English are also spoken by most inhabitants. I'd recommend you take the shore excursion that goes through town and stops at the Curaçao liquor distillery, at one of the oldest homes on the island, and at the *Seaquarium* (US$22).

Willemstad is a delightful Dutch village with colorful pastel buildings. They even have a casino here. Be sure to allow enough time to wander through the narrow streets. You'll find lots of treasures to purchase, from clothing to watches and jewelry.

If you want to snorkel or scuba dive, this is one of the best places in the world to do so. Next to the Seaquarium, about ten minutes from the ship by cab (US$7), is the *Peter Hughes Underwater Curaçao Scuba Center*. For US$50 you can rent all your equipment for a boat dive (US$20 to snorkel from the glass-bottom boat). I have gone diving in many remote and spectacular places in the world, but Curaçao was indeed one of the best. It deserves its reputation. Dive boats leave at 10:00 A.M. and 2:00 P.M. and the trip will take about two hours. At times I was swimming through hundreds of foot-long brilliant blue fish over a massive coral ledge with a variety of species of coral and even a larger variety of fish.

While most people pick a cruise for the ports of call, you'll soon find the sights you'll see are really only one small aspect of cruising. Especially aboard the *Stella Solaris*, it's the ambiance, the quality of the service, and the friendly staff that make your cruise memorable. On my trip, the companionship of the Merry Widows, the fun of learning ballroom dancing, and Jackie Sorensen and the daily aerobics played a much more central role in my memories than the specific places we traveled to. This is one of those trips where "traveling is more important than arriving."

ANTHONY'S KEY RESORT— ROATAN ISLAND

GENERAL AMBIANCE	★ ★ ★
SOCIAL CLIMATE	★ ★ ★
ACTIVITIES	★ ★

FOR TOUR ARRANGEMENTS CONTACT:
Anthony's Key Resort
State Side Representative
1385 Coral Way, Suite 401
Miami, FL 33145
800-227-DIVE

Or *contact your travel agent*
and ask for the Anthony's Key
Resort Dive Package

I thought that the Indian Ocean off the coast of Kenya would remain unequaled as my idea of the most beautiful spot in the world, but then I stepped out onto the shore of Anthony's Key on the Island of Roatan. Although I had been told about the area, I was unprepared for the breathtaking beauty of the crystal blue waters, the soft white sand, the nearby groves of coconut palms and banana trees laden with fruit. I was even more unprepared to find myself almost immediately beginning to walk more slowly and relaxing more completely than I had in years.

The island of Roatan is the largest of three bay islands located 30 miles off the northern coast of Honduras. It is only 47 miles long and 26 miles wide. The central portion of the island has lush, green, rolling hills with periodic small mountain villages or individual thatched-roof houses along the central road. There are no paved roads on the island, and the dirt road that runs most of the length of the island is riddled with potholes and rocks, making travel slow. But once you make it to

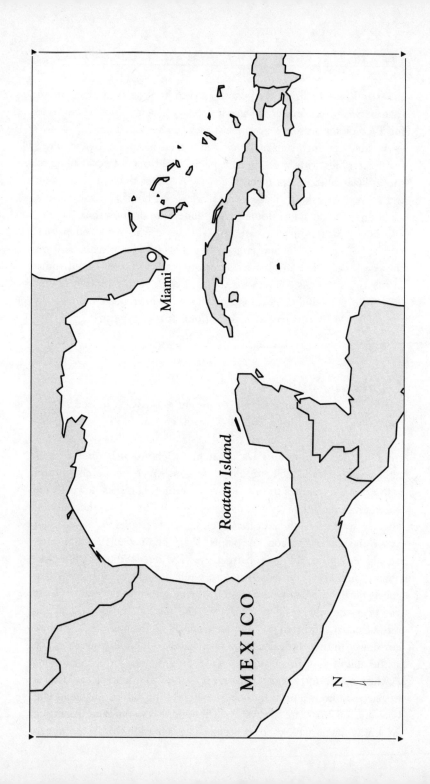

the island, you realize there is no reason to hurry anyway. Part of the road between the smaller villages is actually beach. Thus, a "cab" ride for 5 lempira a person is a wonderful way to see the area.

At times the road runs along a ridge, which allows for a view of the lush green hills with large coconut palms and banana trees leading to the brilliant blue waters of both coasts. At other times it runs along the coast, past fishing villages with rustic wood homes on stilts where children play outside, around, and under the homes, chasing the chickens and pigs in the yard. As you travel the road you pass a number of small boats and larger ships that have been marooned on the coral reefs. The locals have interesting stories to tell about some of the larger vessels, the storms that overcame them, and the rescue efforts for crew and cargo. Some of the boats have been stranded on the reefs, slowly rusting away, for as long as twenty years.

General Ambiance

Anthony's Key Resort, referred to locally as AKR, is indeed one of those areas that exudes a magical warmth, charm, and sense of luxury in the midst of an unspoiled, tropical island setting. Many of the natives still live in mud huts with thatched roofs, though wood houses built out over the water are also common. Much of the charm and sense of luxury comes from the natural setting. Hibiscus flowers with blossoms larger than any I have seen elsewhere line the curving wooden walk up to the elevated open bar and restaurant area, located above the top of the coconut palms. Walls and screens are unnecessary here, and would only obstruct the view over the bay, which frequently harbors sailboats. Boats are often brought in to house extra guests during the Christmas season, when the resort's bungalows, built out over the water, fill to capacity. The natural sense of luxury is further enhanced by the use of giant conch shells, often with a hibiscus flower in their lips, decorating your door, a table in your room, or at the end of your private deck overlooking the sea.

Most of the forty-eight Tahitian-style bungalows are located on a key accessible by a pleasant boat ride across the narrow channel. The boat and boatman are always available and are summoned by hitting an empty scuba tank used as a bell. The bungalows provide enough privacy that you can open the wooden slats that run from ceiling to floor and look out over the water while you shower or before you go to sleep. In the morning, snowy egrets often fish for their breakfast around the bungalows and a variety of other birds are visible in the coconut palms on shore.

The local inhabitants are consistently warm, friendly, and welcoming. They have always welcomed visitors, from the first-known and the most famous early visitor, Columbus. He came to the island in 1502.

The inhabitants love having their picture taken. It is not uncommon for men, women, children, and couples to pose and ask to have their picture taken when they see you with a camera of any kind. If you have a Polaroid, bring extra film. You will be the hit of the area and may provide many children with their first picture—a real treat for any child and a lot of fun for you as well.

The original inhabitants of Roatan were Raya Indians, though few of their descendants survive and quite a racial mix of people exists today. Most of the white residents are descendants of the English, who came to Roatan by way of the Cayman and St. Kitts islands in the eighteenth and nineteenth centuries. The blacks on the island today are primarily descendants of the slaves brought to the island by the Spanish and English during the seventeenth and eighteenth centuries. During the seventeenth century, Roatan was a well-known pirate base, and a few of the inhabitants today claim descent from them. Henry Morgan is perhaps the most famous of these buccaneers.

In 1850, Roatan and the other Bay Islands became a British colony. Limited sovereignty was granted to Honduras and the Bay Islands in 1861. The primary language on Roatan is still English, although the Honduran government has insisted that the schools use Spanish as the official language. Proud of their British heritage and insistent upon maintaining it, the people of Roatan have continued to speak and teach their children English. When the Prince of Wales visited in 1980, the islanders arranged with him to have interested British men and women, typically between high school and college age, spend a year on the island to teach their children proper English, usually in return for meals or housing. As a result of the pirate influence, the English spoken by many of the adults on the island can be difficult to understand. The words are run together and the final consonants dropped.

I found myself needing to listen very closely at times before deciding if the person with whom I was talking was speaking Spanish or English.

Little begging occurs here, most likely because the unemployment level on the island is low. Fishing, the primary island industry, is well established and successful. There is also no reported drug problem, although occasionally drugs are found on a plane that stops en route from South America.

Social Climate

The social climate is probably the primary factor that makes AKR an ideal vacation destination for the woman traveling alone. Not only is there ample space for private activities, but nonregimented activities are also available if you so choose. The most frequently heard response is, "No problem. Whatever you would like, we can arrange."

The food, also included in the package, is consistently good and plentiful. You have a choice of entrée, usually a traditional meat dish or fish dish—lobster, broiled or fried fish, conch salad—or you can have both meat and fish. The dining area is set up to accommodate groups of eight to ten singles at a table together, or smaller groups of two to four. The staff, from the manager on down, make a point of eating with the guests. They possess a wealth of information about Roatan and other fascinating areas of the world where they have lived and worked. Rich Honduran coffee, iced tea, and sliced fruit are available on the veranda throughout the day. This is a greatly appreciated and much used place to relax and chat with other guests, sit and read, or just look out over the Caribbean below.

Activities

While a considerable amount of time can easily be spent swinging in the hammock on your private deck or sunning on the beach, AKR is primarily a scuba diving area. Three daytime dives, one nighttime dive, and unlimited channel diving are included in the dive package.

The reefs are unmatched by any I have seen, and the fish, though not as plentiful as in other areas, are exquisite yellows, purples, and blues. Cave diving and wreck diving in shallow (20 feet) or deep (125 feet) water are available. The equipment, though old, is functional and well maintained. The buoyancy compensators unfortunately do not have an automatic fill off the tank, something I did miss. If you are going to dive and have your own equipment, I recommend taking it. The dive masters teach a short, four-hour resort course for US$60 that will prepare any reasonably good swimmer for a first dive. Safety on dives is maintained in a relaxed fashion. Unlike at many other areas, if you are a certified, experienced diver you and your dive partner may explore the reef on your own; you are not required to stay with the group. New divers should, however, stay with the dive master, a welcomed option for the inexperienced. If you like, a photographer will go along and make a video of your dive for you to show your friends back home, or you can rent an underwater camera and take your own pictures.

For those who do not dive, you can ride along on the dive boat, sun on deck, or snorkel offshore while the divers are down, then join them for lunch and a game of volleyball on the far end of the island before returning to AKR. Horseback riding on the beach, tennis, windsurfing, and sailing are available at no extra charge. While tennis balls and rackets are available, they could pass as antiques. The serious player should bring her own. If you need a partner, the staff, who know most guests by name, will find you one or play themselves.

Preparing for Your Trip to AKR

Rates

Packages that include food, lodging, all activities, and unlimited diving are available. You can indulge yourself in a week of luxury for US$226 during off-season July, or for US$688 from December 15 through April 14, the high season. A nondivers package costs US$599 per week during the peak season. Daily rates that do not include diving are US$85 a night for a single (US$75 each for double occupancy). Boat dives with air tank rentals are US$25 each under this option. You need a high tolerance for both heat and humidity during the off season. The temperature and humidity goes up as high as the rates go down. Temperatures in the nineties and 80 percent humidity are not uncommon.

Documents

You need a valid passport in order to enter Honduras, but it is not necessary to get a visa in advance. One will be issued at the La Ceiba airport in Honduras when you go through customs. There is a 20 lempira (US$10) entrance and exit tax that will be collected at the airport.

What to Take

The electrical current on Roatan is the same as in the United States, 110 volts, so you can take your hair dryer and curling iron along if you wish. You will find, however, that your hair dries fine in the air and the atmosphere is very informal, so the equipment is optional. You will want at least one swimsuit, and lots of sunscreen including some number 15. Remember, you are very close to the equator.

While you can certainly wear shorts and skimpy tops at AKR, it is inappropriate to do so on the rest of the island or on the mainland. It would offend the local residents and make you feel uncomfortable. A loose fitting, informal dress or slacks are nice to have in the evenings at AKR anyway. You may even want to take a light jacket or windbreaker for the January and early February evenings. Most of the days will be sunny, and while it may rain off and on, the rains are warm and tropical. (A bathing suit may even be a better choice than a raincoat.) Do not forget your tennis shoes if you want to play tennis and a pair of long dark slacks or blue jeans for riding the horses along the beach. You will have a difficult time finding toilet articles, such as shampoo or creme rinse, so be sure to pack a sufficient amount. The sun and salt water are hard on your hair. I ran out of creme rinse and regretted it.

Money

You will get a much better exchange rate for your dollar if you buy your lempira before leaving home. Check with your bank early, however, as it will take up to three weeks for your bank to get you the money you want. You will likely get 2.5 lempira per dollar at home, compared to 2 lempira per dollar in Honduras. Major credit cards also give a two to one exchange, so you can save by paying cash for your lodging as well. Be careful not to get more lempira than you intend to spend; the banks buy lempira back at the rate of 3 lempira per dollar. Quite a loss.

Health Concerns

You should always check with your local health department for current recommendations regarding travel abroad; the department will probably suggest the following for a trip to AKR.

Prescription drugs such as Bactrim DS, and Septra DS are helpful in preventing traveler's diarrhea. These tablets should be taken orally beginning two days before you leave and for a few days after your return home. If you do not continue with the medication after returning home, you may merely delay an attack of diarrhea. Be sure to take Lomotil or Imodium along in case you develop diarrhea. One tablet taken with each incident of diarrhea should prevent continued problems.

To prevent exposure, you should drink only bottled water, soft drinks, or beer outside of the resort area and the better restaurants. You should also resist the temptation to have ice in your drinks. Water-borne germs that cause diarrhea will survive freezing. Alcohol added to a drink, even straight 86-proof tequila, will not kill the organisms. You should abstain from eating salads or fruit that cannot be peeled, because they are usually washed in impure water. Vegetables should only be eaten when cooked. Organisms such as E. coli can enter vegetables through their root system.

Polio is still a problem in Honduras, so everyone should be immunized unless the vaccine is personally contraindicated. Check with your physician. You may already be protected. A single dose of live oral vaccine will provide a lifetime of protection.

Malaria is not a problem on the island of Roatan, thus prophylactic care is generally not recommended; however, it is endemic on the mainland. Malaria is transmitted by the bite of the female anopheles mosquito. One chloroquine pill taken on the same day of the week, beginning two weeks before you leave home and continuing for six weeks after you return home, will provide adequate protection for a mainland stay.

One of the best methods of increasing your body's general defense against all disease is to take one intramuscular dose of gamma globulin. It will provide the most reasonable protection against hepatitis B as well. This should be taken as close to the time you leave as possible because it provides only short-term protection.

Getting There

Flying out of Miami or New Orleans, the primary carrier and the one I flew is Tan-Sasha Airlines (800) 327-1225. While their airplanes are the older, propeller type seldom seen in the United States today, they are reliable and well maintained. Their bilingual flight staff was very friendly and the office personnel helpful with changes en route. They also have an office conveniently located near the Paris Hotel in La Ceiba if you decide you want to change your flight plans to or from Roatan Island.

Tan-Sasha flies out of Miami to La Ceiba daily. The flight on Sunday is direct to La Ceiba; the other days of the week you stop in San Pedro Sula, Honduras. Flights to La Ceiba out of New Orleans depart Monday, Wednesday, Friday, and Sunday afternoons. Friday is nonstop to La Ceiba; the other days of the week there is a stop in San Pedro Sula. There are two flights daily from La Ceiba to Roatan. Round-trip airfare from either Miami or New Orleans to Roatan is $390 for a three- to thirty-day stay. You can call the airline directly for reservations, or you can book through your travel agent.

Work to extend the runway on Roatan Island so that larger aircraft can be accommodated was expected to be completed in late 1987. If not yet complete, the primary access route continues to be La Ceiba, Honduras. La Ceiba is an interesting city in its own right and an important stop for those who would like to see more of Honduras than the resort area of Roatan. Once you step off the plane on Roatan and are met by your AKR driver, your week of carefree luxury will begin. If you have hand luggage, do not give it to any of the many young boys who will ask to carry it for you. They are soliciting for local cabs. Your driver from AKR will take care of your baggage for you. The ride from the airport to Anthony's Key on the northwest portion of the island is a scenic adventure.

Tipping

There is no tipping necessary nor are tips accepted at AKR. All gratuities are built into the bill. At places other than AKR I suggest you tip 10 percent of your bill, or 1 lempira when you would generally tip US$1.

Treasures to Purchase

Although three gift shops are located near AKR, the number and variety of items there are very limited. Even the T-shirts are often for sale in only one size and one of a kind. Other popular items include unique, colorful hand and beach towels from El Salvador (US$4 for a wash cloth, US$8 for a hand towel, US$15 for a bath towel, and US$25 for a large beach towel); these, too, are limited and difficult to obtain by the set. Other gift items include mahogany salad bowls and forks, carved mahogany wall hangings, cheese boards, and pink and black coral jewelry. Although they have a green stone available as jewelry and sold as Mexican jade, beware: they may be pretty, but they're worthless.

Along the Way to AKR

French Harbor

On the south side of the island is the small fishing village of French Harbor, an excellent spot to stop for lunch while touring the island. *Romero's Restaurant*, which sits out over the water, offers a varied menu.

The most expensive entrée is 22 lempira (US$11) and includes lobster, shrimp, a white fish, rice, and a green salad. Soft drinks of your choice and beer are priced at an additional 1.5 lempira each. A full bar is also available. They have a gift shop that is well supplied by island standards. It usually has T-shirts and sweatshirts in a variety of sizes and colors.

La Ceiba

The town of La Ceiba is less than a twenty-minute cab ride from the La Ceiba airport and well worth the visit. While you will probably not want to spend more than a day or two here, it is a good way to get a feel for life in Honduras, not just at a resort area. La Ceiba is more than 175 years old, and currently has a population of approximately 75,000. Carfare to town is 5 lempira (US$2.50) per person. It is common in Honduras for the cab driver to accept as many passengers as the cab can hold, unless you are willing to pay a much higher price to "charter" the cab. This gives you exclusive use, and no other passengers will be picked up.

What to See in La Ceiba. La Ceiba has a beautiful coast that is frequented by large banana boats and smaller fishing vessels. National oceanographic boats and American battleships are also seen in the harbor and welcome visitors. To board most of these boats, you need only ask a crewman to check with the officer in charge to see if a tour might be arranged. Do not be afraid to ask; they love the company and may even ask you to stay for lunch in the officers' mess.

Morning is market time. Located two blocks in back of the Grand Hotel Paris, toward the beach, the market sells everything from lobsters to rocking chairs. On Tuesdays and Fridays meat is also sold in the open air market. After wandering through the market you may want to stroll around town. Do not miss the *Mission Church*, *Atlantida Hospital*, or *the jail*, which has an ocean view.

The highlight of your trip to La Ceiba will be a cab ride out of town through the pineapple fields and up the hill to the waterfall and mountain villages. Arrange a price with your cab driver before leaving. US$20 to US$30 for a single or a group is a good price. You can expect the trip to last approximately four hours. Wear good hiking shoes and, even though it may be hot, wear a dress or long pants so as not to offend the people in the villages. The roads are made for pack animals, not cars, and may not be passable, so you may have to continue on foot. I did, and it was well worth the walk. While the waterfalls are interesting, the real experience of this trip is the mountain villages. The road runs right through the middle, and you become the novelty. Bring your camera, a Polaroid if you have one, in order to give pictures to the many children who will come up to you.

Do not be surprised or frightened by men, and even young boys, carrying machetes. The Honduran men carry them much as American men carry pocket knives (you can buy authentic machetes in beautiful leather scabbards in a small shop beside the Paris Hotel in La Ceiba for 50 lempira, US$25). They make wonderful gifts.

You are also likely to pass villagers gathering wood to take to town to sell, or making charcoal that they also then take to town on their donkeys. If you get thirsty, do not worry. Coca-Cola has made it to these villages, and for 2 lempira (US$1) you can get an ice cold bottle of Coke at a mud hut with a thatched roof.

Where to Eat in La Ceiba. Whatever you do, do not eat at the street stands and do not drink the water out of the faucets. Stomach pains and diarrhea are guaranteed if you do. La Ceiba has three especially nice restaurants where the food, including the fruit and vegetables, is safe to eat and the water, including the ice cubes, is safe to drink. These are the Palace, Ricardo's, and the Atlantida.

The *Palace* is a Chinese restaurant with a large, varied menu. The curried shrimp and sweet and sour shrimp are especially good, as is the Palace fried rice, which includes pork, chicken, shrimp, and beef. The latter is not a side dish. One order would easily suffice as an entrée. Even if you are not a fussy eater, unless you are prepared for a very unusual flavor, you may want to avoid the beef. It has a very different taste than what we are used to in the States and I found it unpleasant.

Ricardo's also has a varied menu. The specialties are, as one might expect, based on seafood. They have an especially good lobster thermidor. While I usually pass up dessert, Ricardo's is worth visiting for its dessert alone. They have one made of custard and meringue with a touch of rum called Borracho that should not be missed. The owner, a woman from the States, was kind enough to send me her recipe and it is a guaranteed hit at any party. Ask to be seated in the courtyard with its lush green plants and fountain. They have even put lights in the canopy that covers a portion of the courtyard; it's a nice touch for evening "starlight" dining. The inside area is comfortable, but more ordinary than the courtyard.

The *Atlantida* restaurant is on the beach near the pier. While the atmosphere here is interesting and comfortable, it doesn't equal the outside courtyard of Ricardo's. The food, however, I found to be better than that in the other restaurants. If you are a calamari (squid) lover, this is the place to go, and if you have never had it, try it here. There are a number of good options, all under US$8. The marinated calamari is especially good and the serving is generous. They also have a nice selection of fresh fish and lobster dishes for the less daring. Flan, a caramel custard, is a common dessert throughout Honduras, but the flan at Atlantida is the best I've had anywhere. While you can get it plain, I prefer the flan made with fresh coconut. Once again, the serving is generous. The rich, strong Honduran coffee is a welcome accompaniment. Although I usually drink my coffee strong and black and I enjoy espresso, I find milk is a must with my coffee throughout Honduras. You may want to order an accompanying pot of hot water to attain a more tolerable consistency of coffee.

If asked, the owner of the Atlantida, a warm, friendly man, will proudly bring out his parrots. He keeps them in his living quarters at the back of the restaurant with two huge Great Danes. He also has a number of stone artifacts on display, part of the atmosphere. These artifacts are usually for sale; he has more of better quality in the back and will bring them out for you. You will find his selection is better than at any store in town and his prices are competitive. These items range from US$30 to US$100. Do not hesitate to tell him what you are looking for; if he doesn't have it, he may be able to find it for you. His jewelry is of questionable quality, however. The restaurant is his primary business, so you will need to ask about the items to be purchased. They will not be mentioned otherwise.

The *Lido* is the place to go for an after-dinner drink. It is an open-air disco located on the shore just east of the pier; you can sip your drink here under a palm tree and listen to the waves break on the sandy point not more than 10 feet away. The Lido has no cover charge during the week, but it is typically 2 or 3 lempira to enter on the weekend. Soft drinks, wine, and Port Royale, a local beer, are all 3 lempira. Hard liquor, while available, is a little more costly. This is a favorite meeting place for the local Hondurans allowed to date, and for any Americans who might be in town. As in many South and Central American countries, in Honduras unmarried young women are strictly supervised by their fathers.

Where to Stay in La Ceiba. The hotels in La Ceiba are named after American or European cities. While many are available for as little as 8 to 10 lempira (US$4 to US$5), only one measures up to American standards. This is the *Grand Hotel Paris*, located in the center of town across from the city park.

The open courtyard of the hotel has the only pool in town. The coconut palms and pet rabbits running around the grass make it a very pleasant location to pass the hottest part of the day, which is from noon to 2:00 P.M. The hotel café and the bar by the pool are excellent places to meet the Americans and Europeans who live in the area. They are interesting people who are usually willing to spend some time talking with visitors. They can help you find items you may want to purchase.

Major credit cards are accepted at the hotel. Rooms, which are readily available without a reservation, are clean but not newly decorated. Old red rugs with a slightly musty smell are the rule. Rooms run US$20 to US$35 a night. Most look out onto the pool and have large patio doors and high ceilings.

The food in the hotel cafeteria is excellent. The papaya are so large that a slice hangs over both sides of a dinner plate. The coffee with milk is especially rich, though once again strong. A lunch buffet is available at noon most days for 8 to 10 lempira (US$4 to US$5) and is consistently well prepared and generous. A nice advantage to lunch at the hotel is that it can be enjoyed in the poolside courtyard. The fruit juices are fresh and the pineapple juice is especially light, frothy, and tasty.

An island paradise in a unique cultural setting, AKR offers much more to the visitor than the excitement of spectacular scuba diving. It offers much more than a relaxing, luxurious island resort. This is the place to really get away from the demands of life back home, so very far away. It is a place where you can evaluate what you want from life and the goals you are pursuing. With renewed energy and direction, you can then return home and accomplish much more.

THE AUSTRALIAN OUTBACK

▶─────────────────────────────────▶

GENERAL AMBIANCE	★ ★ ★
SOCIAL CLIMATE	★ ★ ★
ACTIVITIES	★ ★ ★

FOR TOUR ARRANGEMENTS CONTACT:
Mr. Australia Tours
35 Franmaur Street
Gladstone
Queensland, Australia 4680
Telephone: 079 79 1493

Or *State-Side Representative*:
Allstar Holidays
9841 Airport Boulevard, Suite 506
Los Angeles, CA 90045-5417
(800) 451-4440 (inside CA)
(800) 782-1600 (outside CA)

Or *contact your travel agent*
and ask for the Mr. Australia eleven-day tour

▶─────────────────────────────────▶

General Ambiance

A vast country, almost the size of the continental United States—but with only 16 million people—Australia has much to offer. On the east coast you'll find lush rain forests and isolated tropical islands with long expanses of deserted beaches just waiting for you. In the interior you'll see almost desertlike sheep stations (ranches) where 2,000 acres are needed per sheep for grazing. The flocks still number in the thousands, the stations in the tens of thousands of acres. In contrast to all

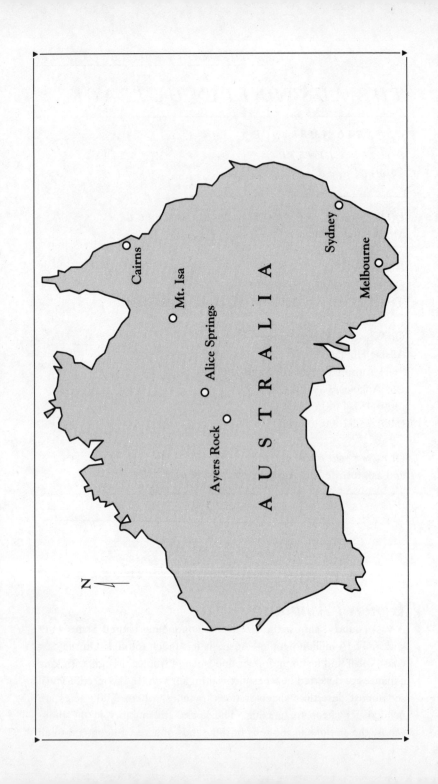

of this there's the sophisticated, bustling metropolis of Sydney, one of my favorite cities in the world. Nearby you'll find Melbourne and Phillip Island, where you can see the parade of the Fairy Penguins.

Social Climate

Even with the diverse beauty of the country there's no doubt in my mind that it's the people, the Australians themselves, that are the country's biggest asset. This is one place where it's a real advantage to be traveling alone, because that way you'll meet more Aussies, men and women. How nice that they "almost" speak English. Don't worry, you'll learn the lingo quickly. You won't wonder long what to do when someone says, "It's your shout" (your turn to buy the next round of drinks). I found the friendly, helpful, welcoming feel of the people of Australia the most charming aspect of this intriguing country. I found most of the visitors I met while in the Cairns area on the northeast coast were Australians from other parts of Australia, often the Sydney-Melbourne area. They were here escaping the cooler winter weather further south. They migrate north toward the Great Barrier Reef area in winter much as we migrate south to Florida or to Hawaii. I met a number of Australian women traveling alone who were as glad to share stories of their country as I was to hear them.

Some of the Australians you meet are so completely "country" that they seldom even visit a city and others are as sophisticated as the cities of Sydney, Perth, and Melbourne. They all exude a particular charm and allure that comes from a down-to-earth sensitivity. They let you know they really are interested in seeing that you enjoy their country. They're glad you've come and they'll go out of their way to make you feel at home. In less than twenty-four hours from the time I landed, I had an offer to sail down the east coast with three Australian blokes (guys) and a nurse originally from South Carolina—she had come for a two- to three-week visit six months earlier. I also had an offer to spend a year "or so" sailing "in the South Pacific wherever the wind takes us." Why am I here in my office now, you ask? I'm wondering that, too. I expect I'll wonder even more when the Minneapolis temperature drops below zero and it's summer down under in Australia.

Activities

This trip is designed as an introduction to this vast country, to provide an overview and give you a taste of what Australia has to offer. Since there are no scheduled daily flights to the outback stations, the best way to visit is with a small group on a chartered plane. Brian Miller, founder and managing director of Mr. Australia Tours, has put together just the trip. He doesn't like large groups any more than most of us, so he's limited his Australian Outback experience to a maximum of fifteen people. His goal is to show you the parts of Australia most people miss, the diverse parts of Australia that will bring you back once again.

Your first stop will be at a beach resort with miles of white sandy beach and lush tropical vegetation. Your stay here will ensure that you're well recovered from jet lag before your adventure into the Outback. While recuperating, you'll visit an island on the Great Barrier Reef and have the opportunity to go scuba diving or snorkeling. You'll also take a train ride through the Atherton Tablelands.

Then it's on to the Outback. While there you'll shear sheep, attend a local horse race, muster cattle on horseback, party with the locals, visit one of the largest mines in the world, and float across the landscape in a hot air balloon. You'll then ease back into civilization with dinner and a performance at the Sydney Opera House.

Preparing for Your Trip to the Outback

Rates

The Outback experience Mr. Australia Tours has packaged will cost you considerably less than if you tried to arrange the trip on your own. While there is often a savings on a package, some shrewd negotiating must have occurred to arrive at the savings on this packaged tour. Your trip will cost A\$2840 (US\$2088), which includes all of your lodgings for eleven nights, transportation within Australia, all breakfasts and lunches, and a number of dinners as well. It even includes all entrance fees, and you'll have an escort who will ensure that your trip is a worry free, relaxing vacation. It's a great value. You'll stay at the best resorts and hotels, fly on your own group chartered plane, and feel taken care of and pampered. No corners are cut on this experience.

There is a single supplement charge of A$590 for a single-room occupancy. If you'd prefer to share a room and get the lower rate, Mr. Australia Tours will try to arrange this for you.

Documents

You'll need both a valid passport and a visa to enter Australia. You can obtain a multiple entry visa good for six months by sending your passport and one passport-style photo to: Australian Consulate General, 321 North Clark Street, Chicago, IL 60610. There is no charge for this service. You should allow two weeks. You can also use an express visa service (see p. 29).

When to Go

Fall begins in Australia in April, which is a wonderful time to visit. March can be nice, but it's usually the rainy season. The winter, with daytime temperatures in the sixties and seventies, lasts through September. While it may be cool at night in Sydney at the end of your trip, it seldom gets much cooler than light jacket weather.

December, January, and February are the hot summer months you want to avoid. The heat can be blistering, even in the shade.

What to Take

The Australian Outback is very informal. The only exception is the Saturday afternoon horse races. Even in Sydney, which is sophisticated and cosmopolitan, you'll feel comfortable at the Opera House in less formal attire. It's rather like San Francisco in that respect. I'd suggest you take one dressy outfit, cool enough to wear to the races in the Outback, where the temperature will likely be in the eighties, but be sure to bring a sweater or light jacket to wear over it while in Sydney. Much like San Francisco, Sydney evenings can get chilly.

This is one place where the typical white resort wear is of limited use. You won't want to wear it in the Outback, where dust is the rule. Instead, take along loose-fitting, darker-colored long cotton pants and shirts that you can wear your first few days in Cairns and on the Great Barrier Reef, as well as in the Outback. While you will want shorts as well, long pants will be better protection from the burning rays of the sun.

Don't forget your sunscreen, especially the kind that won't wash off in the water. I'd also take or purchase a loose-fitting T-shirt to wear in the water over your bathing suit to protect your back from the sun while you're snorkeling. You will not need to take your bulky snorkeling gear. It's available free of charge in most places and the gear is in good condition.

If you must take an electrical appliance you'll need a special adapter plug. For about US$10 you can purchase one in the hardware stores in Cairns. It's always best, however, to plan ahead and pick one up prior to leaving home. The voltage is 220.

You'll want a pair of jeans and shoes with a heel (tennis shoes will do) for horseback riding. You'll also want mosquito repellent for use in the rain forest areas and on the reef islands.

A nice feature about most Australian hotels, even the really fancy ones, is that they provide clothes washers and dryers for guest use. This means you can take much less, because you'll be able to wash clothes as you go. They even provide the laundry detergent free of charge, and most will have an iron and ironing board in the laundry room as well.

If you haven't read *The Thornbirds*, by all means take it along. Meggie lives in and visits many of the cities you'll travel through on this trip. I'd also suggest you bring along *Castaway* by Lucy Irving and read about her year on an island off the northern tip of Australia. When you get to the Alice Springs airport, you'll find a number of copies of *A Town Like Alice* by Nevil Shute. I suggest you purchase one and read about life in the Outback.

Money

At the time of publication, one Australian dollar (A$1) was equal to US$1.30. The exchange rate will, of course, vary and may or may not be in your favor when you visit. Be sure to check. In Australia, you'll get the best rate of exchange at a trading bank. While most trading banks charge a fee of A$1 for the transaction, whatever the amount of money you are changing, you'll still come out ahead. Hotels, post office banks, and savings banks do not charge a fee, but they give you a significantly lower rate of exchange.

Health Concerns

Australia is a healthy country with excellent health care considering the isolation of those individuals in the Outback. Even visitors are entitled to the free services of the Flying Doctors, who provide routine and emergency health care to the isolated Outback areas.

While the Outback is infamous for its flies, I must admit I did not find them as annoying as I had expected. They don't bite like our Minnesota mosquitoes, and as long as I was in a moving vehicle or walking they were no problem at all.

Getting There

Getting to Australia has become easier and cheaper than ever. Qantas Airlines has daily flights from San Francisco, Los Angeles, and Vancouver. Most flights will make a short refueling stop in Hawaii, then on to Australia. Qantas will fly you directly into Cairns, your destination city. On the way back, Qantas has the only nonstop service from Sydney to San Francisco.

Initially, I had some misgivings about such a long flight. Much to my surprise, however, the flight turned out to be easier on me than flying to Europe, all thanks to planning on the part of Qantas. I had a leisurely dinner in San Francisco, followed by a wonderful ice cream sundae at Ghirardelli Square, so I was in the right frame of mind when I boarded my Qantas flight. The moment the first flight attendant greeted me with the soon to become familiar "G'day," I knew I was on my way to a good time. One attendant even looked a wee bit like Crocodile Dundee—if I used my imagination. He was certainly as helpful and charming.

Qantas intends to become one of the world's best air carriers, providing the best service possible, and it shows. They've gone out of their way to schedule their in-flight services to maximize your comfort, and they've been quite creative in initiating new services. Their in-flight video not only gives you up-to-date world news and insights into your destination city, but it traces your flight route and provides you with additional information about your route along the way.

To spruce up the staff's appearance, Qantas commissioned Yves St. Laurent to design new uniforms for the entire flight crew. And the streamlined kangaroo, their symbol of grace and speed, is everywhere.

The best part, however, is the schedule of service. Leaving San Francisco in the late evening, you eat dinner and see a movie prior to your arrival in Hawaii four hours later. I recommend staying awake for this portion of the flight, because you must deplane for refueling. A short nap will only prevent a good night's sleep during the longer portion of the flight. When you reboard in Honolulu it'll be night. Since you have ten hours ahead of you, this is the time to sleep, and I expect you'll be ready to do just that. Qantas seems to have figured this out. They have virtually no activity for the next five hours, when the movie begins. Sleep through this movie, if you can, to give yourself a good seven hours' rest before breakfast. Next thing you know you're in Cairns, pronounced "cans."

The only unpleasant aspect of arrival is that all arriving airplanes are required to have flight attendants walk down the aisles spraying insect spray before the passengers deplane. This is to prevent the introduction of insects that would destroy agricultural crops. They assured me the spray is not harmful and has been approved by the World Health Organization. I figured it was a small price to pay to see Australia.

Tipping

There is no tipping in Australia. Wages are considered sufficient to cover service. An Australian traveler will never tip whether in a restaurant, at a hotel, or at an airport. Unfortunately, American travelers are already beginning to spoil this situation for the locals, especially at the restaurants and big hotels frequented by tourists. No one will refuse a tip and say, "It's not our custom." Instead, they'll gladly accept it and then expect it from the next tourist.

So what do you do? I'd suggest you not tip, unless you're in a very elegant restaurant and you get service that really is exceptional. In that case, tip not more than 10 percent. In this respect, tipping is more as it was originally meant to be, a reward for especially good service. Unfortunately, that type of situation will likely not last very long. It's our own fault and the fault of those before us if the situation changes because we routinely tip even for ordinary or poor service.

Treasures to Purchase

There are a variety of Australian-made goods at reasonable prices. Sydney is the best place to shop for most clothing and jewelry. Popular now in the U.S. and considered quite chic is the Australian Stockman's coat. It makes a great raincoat and windbreaker. However, don't get the oil cloth variety; it will stain your clothing. The *Koala Bear*, in the Queen Victoria Building in Sydney, sells the newer, longer-lasting material, still brown, for A$145 with their export discount, ask about this. *Morrisons* (105 George Street, The Rocks), also in Sydney, will sell you a Stockman's hat, which is much like a cowboy hat, to go with your coat (A$60).

Fiery "black" opals are the jewelry to purchase in Australia. They are not actually black, but are of red, blue, and golden hues. In general, the more color, the better value and the higher the price. Have a reputable jeweler show you the difference and explain what you're getting if you purchase a doublet or triplet. While much less expensive, these opals are more plastic than opal and cannot be placed in water. Black opals are quite expensive. They can cost hundreds and thousands of dollars, but they are beautiful and hard to find outside of Australia.

Australia also mines diamonds in the northeast region. Some of these mines produce a particularly rare and expensive pink diamond; you should at least ask to see one of these.

You'll also find a wide variety of lovely wool sweaters. They will cost from A$180 to as much as A$250. You can purchase stuffed animals or purses made from kangaroo or sheep skin.

I found Alice Springs was the best place to purchase aboriginal art. If you're going to get a boomerang, be sure it's made from a curved branch that will provide strength. Ask someone to show you how to check the grain of the wood. Also be sure it's one that is "curved" to return, not just painted to look pretty. You'll find jewelry made from natural items, wall paintings, wood carvings, and tall, rectangular, wooden burial posts, too.

YOUR OUTBACK ADVENTURE

Your Mr. Australia Tours escort will meet you as you exit the customs area of the Cairns airport. You can find him or her under the large blue Australian flag, the company emblem. (You'll likely find a number of your flight companions are members of your group.) You just worried about your luggage, connections, and other necessary arrangements for the last time! From now on that will be taken care of for you.

Your adventure begins at the *Kewarra Beach Resort*, where you are offered a welcome drink, even though it's breakfast time, and shown to your private bungalow on a small private lagoon in the heart of a fragrant botanical garden. After a breakfast buffet you can spend the day relaxing on the immense stretch of white sandy beach and playing in the warm tropical waters of the Coral Sea. While this is scheduled as a rest day, you'll sleep better at night and get into the Australian time schedule faster if you stay up until after that night's welcoming party. You'll learn how to "talk Australian" while you relax beside the cascading swimming pool of the resort, home for the next four nights.

If you're a runner or a walker you'll find this an enticing beach at sunrise and sunset. Up the beach you'll pass men and women fishing in the surf with 10-foot-long bamboo poles. "Breakfast" one man said to me with a smile as he pulled in his catch.

If you prefer a more relaxed morning pace, you can sit on your private porch sipping coffee or tea and watching the ducks swim on the lagoon. The parrots will probably squawk at you from their perch in the coconut palms nearby.

The Great Barrier Reef

After a leisurely breakfast buffet on your second day you board a catamaran in nearby Cairns that takes you to *Green Island*, one of two true coral islands on the reef—*Heron Island* is the other. You'll have time here to walk along the beaches and on the trails through the rain forest. There is an interesting movie on the island that shows you the reef from the point of view of the fish (A$2). If you're on Green Island at low tide, be sure to take the coral walk. (You'll need tennis shoes for this.) You can actually walk out along portions of the coral reef surrounding the island, and look down onto the fish and coral.

Just before lunch you take another boat to the outer reef, which is always under water but close to the surface. The Great Barrier Reef, while extensive, is shallow, making observation of the many varieties of fish and coral a thrilling experience. Since the coral is near the surface, you get good light penetration, which shows off the golden hues, the brilliant blues, and the vibrant reds of the reef below.

You'll spend a full two hours on a stationary platform on the outer reef, where a lunch buffet is provided. Snorkeling equipment is available for your use, free of charge. If you've never gone snorkeling before, or if it's been a while, be sure to listen to the instructions by the Peter Tibbs Scuba School staff who accompany you. You can snorkel on your own or with the staff. If you're hesitant about your swimming ability, they have flotation vests that they will be happy to loan you.

If you're a NAUI or PADI certified diver, don't forget your card; for A$25 you can rent scuba equipment and go diving on the outer reef. It would be a shame to come all the way to Australia and miss seeing life below the surface on the Great Barrier Reef. So if you're not certified but would like to be, you might want to consider coming a week earlier and getting your diving certificate at a Great Barrier Reef dive school. I can think of no better place to become certified (see "Learning to Scuba Dive on the Great Barrier Reef," p. 158).

While you're resting from snorkeling or diving, you can view the reef from the semisubmersible boat. Shaped somewhat like a submarine, this boat does not actually submerge. You walk below deck where the walls on both sides are windows to the undersea world. Your host will identify the many varieties of coral and fish as you pass in the "sub." It's an exciting, informative, and yet still relaxing day on the famous Great Barrier Reef.

Atherton Tablelands

A large plateau near the top of a 5,000-foot mountain range west of Cairns, the Atherton Tablelands are indeed flat as a tabletop. They're also cool because of the altitude. Your group coach and special guide for the day departs for the Tablelands after a leisurely breakfast on your third day. You'll climb up the lush green mountains leaving the *Mulgrave River* far down in the emerald valley below. Until 1960, this steep, windy road was only one lane, which made the ride more exciting. Today, though, it's still spectacular.

Your first stop is for tea and scones (homemade biscuits with a generous portion of jam and whipped cream) at an inn beside *Lake Barrine*, a peaceful, deep blue, crater lake. Then it's up the valley to meet the Cairns-Kuranda Railway train. As you go, you'll pass more than 2,000 varieties of trees and ferns. If you look closely, you may even see scrub turkeys feeding on the forest floor. You'll also pass peanut farms on the deep red volcanic soil of the flat plateau of the Tablelands before you drive through the town of *Atherton*, settled in 1885.

At the town of *Yungaburra*, you can wander around the old wooden buildings and watch the lawn bowlers. Don't miss the pottery and wood shop. Similar pottery can be found in Cairns, but the price will be about 20 percent more. They also have a nice selection of wooden bowls made from unique native woods. If you're lucky, you'll see the local men out in their shorts and colorful knit wool knee-warmers. While once a common sight, this costume is rare today and it's really only the older men who still wear this outfit—"to keep the old joints warm," I was told.

Also along the way to the train you'll visit the 500-year-old *Curtain Fig*. This parasite, now a large tree, covered its original host tree with a curtain of aerial roots now more than 30 feet wide. Listen closely here. From deep in the forest you are likely to hear the fascinating call of the whip bird. They actually sound like the crack of a huge whip. If you're lucky, you'll see the kite hawks soaring on the thermal air currents—it's a thrilling sight.

Your last stop before the train is the *Tolga Hotel* for lunch—typical home-cooked "tucker," that's grub in Aussie. Don't take too long eating, though, you'll want time to chat with the "jackaroos," Aussie cowboys, playing pool in the bar attached to the hotel.

Kuranda Train

Next it's all aboard the Kuranda train bound for Cairns. Originally built in 1885 to serve the goldfields, the wooden cars still look much as they did in their prime. On your trip back down the mountain you'll pass through fifteen tunnels and go over thirty-seven bridges and numerous waterfalls. The highlight is the large *Stony Creek waterfalls*. But even these falls have stiff competition. The view out over the fields and the emerald valley is spectacular. What a wonderful way to end a great day in the Atherton Tablelands. What a wonderful way to return home to the Kewarra Beach Resort.

Cairns

The only disadvantage of the Kewarra Beach Resort is that it's a A$24 cab ride into Cairns. If you find others in your group with whom to share a cab, it's a more reasonable drive in for dinner and/or dancing at night. Your last day at Kewarra you will be taken into town to spend the day shopping. Don't miss a walk on the Esplanada walkway along the water or the mall.

Cairns is really a lovely town with wooden houses built on stilts to allow for the cooling circulation of air. Even during their winter months it's humid and hot, in the high seventies and eighties. You can probably imagine what it would be like on a summer day.

Lake Street is the primary shopping street. You'll find a little bit of everything here from jewelry to T-shirts. The *Shark Attack* has a good selection of T-shirts. Don't be surprised at the price. T-shirts are consistently A$18 to A$27, but they are nice and usually have the

French-cut neck most women prefer. The *Australian Craftsman Gallery*, next to the museum by the small park that blocks Lake Street, is the place to find authentic aboriginal boomerangs, wall hangings, pottery, and art. Be sure to ask for throwing instructions to go with your boomerang.

For more on Cairns, see p. 166.

Wild World

I was disappointed by Wild World, located between Cairns and the Kewarra Beach Resort. It's a small, mostly unattractive zoo. The kangaroos and the crocodiles are worth seeing, but you can do that in less than an hour. The *Cane Toad Race* was cute, but not worth the time. The snake show was more informative, but I wouldn't go out of my way to see it. I'd limit my time here, or skip this one altogether.

The Outback

While the tropical rain forests and beaches of the Cairns area are a wonderful introduction to a part of Australia most people don't expect to find, the best is yet to come in the Outback—Crocodile Dundee territory. A commercial flight takes you to Mount Isa, where you board a chartered fourteen-passenger Nomad. Everyone will have a window seat and an aisle seat on this flight. Your pilot and copilot are also your flight attendants and mechanics. It's a real treat and a very appropriate transition from the civilized tropical city of Cairns to the harsh life on an Outback sheep station. I thought of Meggie's arrival on the deep red, barren lands of Drogheda. Your Nomad will take you to a one-room "airport" seemingly in the middle of nowhere, near the Shire of Richmond, population 1,500.

The temperature here is a "cool" 80 to 85 degrees in the winter months, compared to a blistering 125 degrees in the shade during the summer. It's easy to understand why it takes 2,000 acres per sheep for grazing land. Scarcely a bush or scrub breaks the monotony of the barren downs that stretch as far as the eye can see—barren, that is, until a good rain shower changes the landscape to a sea of green grass, with turbulent rivers of water. It only lasts for a short time, however, but while it does the sheep, cattle, and kangaroos feast.

Tell Freddie, the owner of Silver Hills sheep station, that I told you to insist on a stop at the *Mud Hut* in Richmond for a beer on your way to Silver Hills. He'll probably be glad for an excuse to stop himself. If you're lucky, Sweet Pea will be there having a refreshing Fourex brew. Invite him back to the ranch for the barbecue. He will readily tell you he's a damn good cook and can dance up a storm, too. He's retired now, after thirty years as a "ringer," and he's got some good stories to tell if you get him started.

The first known white man passed by here in 1862. The area was settled by sheepmen and it's still run by them today. During the gold-strike in 1904 there were twelve hotels in town, but only a couple of these grand old wooden structures remain today. The Mud Hut is one of them.

Silver Hills Sheep Station

Silver Hills was settled by Freddie's grandfather in 1918, after World War I. He still has pictures of the original homestead in the dining room. There's an 1896 picture of a local stagecoach, too. "Bushrangers" (outlaws) were a big problem back then, but the stagecoach driver is obviously prepared with a large shotgun propped up beside him. The land is important to Freddie. He knows how to use it and he takes care of it for the generations that will follow him.

Freddie's looking for a woman to put that special touch on the place—actually, his sons are, too—so here's your chance ladies! Typical of the area, his daughters left the homestead for school, then work in the big cities. His sons stayed to run the station. There are probably ten men to every woman out here, but then there's not much for a career-oriented woman to do.

You could hardly expect the accommodations to be deluxe in the Outback, but they're clean and more than adequate. The tucker's good, too, lots of beef and lamb. I'd suggest you sleep out on the screened porch attached to the bunkhouses—you'll have a private one off your room. Even though the room is air-conditioned, you can see the stars, including the Southern Cross, better from here. Besides, the roosters and peacocks roaming around the area will wake you in the morning whether you sleep on the porch or in your room. And somehow that seems like the most appropriate way to start the day on an Outback sheep station.

You'll find George (a ranch hand, but more like a family member) has been up since sunrise and it's a good thing, too. It's his job to start the fire in the wood-burning stove at the end of the bunkhouse, and that's what heats the water for your shower.

There are some great "roads" for running across the station if that's how you prefer to begin or end your day. Don't be alarmed if you surprise a few kangaroos. They're used to having the place pretty much to themselves. As you pass the lake by the cookhouse, you'll likely disturb the flocks of thirty to forty white cockatoos and galahs (a grey-and-pink cockatoo). They'll show their contempt at your intrusion with harsh squawks.

A relaxing dip in the hot tub, filled by the natural mineral spring on the station, is the perfect end to a run, horseback ride, or simply a day of adventure on Silver Hills. I found the water temperature just right, refreshingly warm, but not too hot.

Sheep Shearing. Not only will you have an opportunity to watch the shearers at work, but if you'd like, you can actually try it yourself. In the shearing shed, five or six shearers work side by side, shearing an average of 150 sheep each in a single day. There was even one woman shearer working when I visited; she grew into the job being raised on a sheep station. After shearing, the wool is cleaned and graded prior to shipment. You'll learn about this process, too.

Outside the shearing shed thousands of sheep are either waiting to be sheared or are already "nude" waiting to be sprayed for lice and marked with the station colors for identification on the open range.

You'll also have the opportunity to watch the sheepdogs at work. Part dingo (wild dog) these animals are incredible. They work on a combination of instincts and whistle commands, moving the sheep from one paddock to another. When the sheep are all packed in tight together, the dogs will jump up on the backs of the sheep and walk across them. Once you've seen this trick a couple of times, you'll better appreciate the subway station scene in *Crocodile Dundee*. You'll be privy to the "inside" joke.

Sheep Muster. There are about 12,000 head of sheep on Silver Hills, so shearing time is a busy time of year. If you'd like to be a jackaroo (ranch hand) for a day, you can saddle a horse and help muster the animals to be shorn the next day. Sheep trucks and helicopters are also used to muster sheep.

Station Tour. While at Silver Hills you'll be driven around its 40,000 acres. You'll pass hundreds of kangaroos—big reds, blues, and grays—lying in small groups of from four to eight in the shade of the silver boore trees. But as soon as they hear you, they'll hop away at an incredible speed. You'll also pass thousands of sheep, who'll run away at a much slower pace like a sea of white bubbling foam.

At mid-morning it's time for a "smoko" (coffee break). Since there aren't any coffee shops around, Freddie will get out the "Billy can," get water from a nearby stream, and build a fire to boil water for tea. No tea bags out here, though. Leaves from a nearby gum tree supplemented by the omnipresent "vegemite" will become tea. It's difficult to describe vegemite, and once you've tried it you may wonder why the Aussies consume so much of it. It has the consistency of a thick syrup and the flavor of beef bouillon.

On the way back you'll pass an aboriginal campsite located on the slightest hill. The land below, you'll be told, was once under water. You'll also pass the now indistinguishable remains of a golf course Freddie once developed. A few years back the "roos" ate all the grass during a drought.

Horse Races. Saturday is race day in Australia. Every town of any stature has its own track and Richmond is no exception. I was told the women dress for the occasion, but I was unprepared for what I found.

Here, at a racetrack surrounded by barren downs, far from any "real" civilization, the local women were dressed in stylish silk dresses, nylons, high heels, and matching hats. Any one of them could have been transported to the Kentucky Derby and would have looked quite at home. The men, by contrast, were more often in blue jeans and a clean crisp shirt than a suit.

Not only could you bet on the local races at the betting tent, but you could also bet on the races in Sydney, Melbourne, and Perth. Before you place your bet, walk down to the paddock area and talk with the owners and trainers. One even told me not to bother betting on his horse. "It hasn't won a race yet. Really doesn't have a chance." He was right.

The refreshment tent sold patty cakes (a special type of cupcake filled with whipped cream) and Lamingtons (a square piece of sponge cake covered with chocolate and then coconut). I suggest you try both.

Bowler's Ball. If you're in town during a bowler's ball, don't mis it. The bowlers, that's lawn bowling, put on quite a party. The whole town will be there, from the youngest to the oldest. Don't get too fancy when you want to order a drink at the bar. You'll soon learn they "don't carry the fancy stuff." "We don't have no white wine, no red wine, and no blue wine. It's a beer or whiskey, thank you, ma'am." You'll meet the local mayor and the "roo shooters." It'll be the party of your life. You'll find they're as curious about you and your life as you are about them and theirs.

Your time at Silver Hills will pass quickly. But there's much more of the Outback to see and there never seems to be enough time. Perhaps that's why the nurse from South Carolina was still on her three-week visit six months later.

Mount Isa

With a population of 28,000, Mount Isa is one of the world's biggest copper, zinc, lead, and silver mines. Though there are twenty-one levels below ground, you'll see only what's on top, except through the lens of a camera. Your tour of the mine begins with a very informative movie.

The town itself doesn't have much to offer, except that it's on your way to Ayers Rock. As one local put it, "I can't get out of here, so I have to defend the town."

Ayers Rock and the Olgas

You'll arrive at Ayers Rock just in time to check into the Sheraton Yulara Resort Hotel and drive to the Olgas to watch the changing colors of Ayers Rock at sunset. I really expected this to be just another tourist area. I was surprised to experience the power of Ayers Rock and the Olgas. This is an area rich in aboriginal lore with many sacred areas. A visit here is not just a chance to see the rock, or even just to climb it. It's a chance to learn about the aboriginal culture through their myth and lore. You'll learn about Dreamtime, when giant semi-human beings roamed the earth. The rock formations, like Ayers Rock and the Olgas, rose out of the plains where these semihumans slept.

At the Olgas, a rock formation about a fifteen-minute drive from Ayers Rock, you can see the face of the black kangaroo man in the rocks. You can see the blood running down the side of his face where he was attacked by dingos in Dreamtime. You'll also visit the valley of the mice women eaten by the snake people.

A big advantage of being with a small self-contained group is that you can arrange your schedule to avoid the throngs of tourists. We did just that on our morning climbing up Ayers Rock. This, too, was one of those experiences that I found much more thrilling and moving than I had anticipated. We left the Sheraton just as the sun was beginning to rise, so we were the first group of the day to begin the ascent. Anyone in reasonably good physical condition can make the 985-foot climb even though some portions are very steep and you'll need the assistance of a permanently anchored chain. It's a challenge worth taking. You should wear tennis shoes for this; they'll provide adequate traction on the sheer rock face.

The sun was still rising as we were making our climb. It first touched the highest section of the rock cliff, then slowly washed over and down the face of the rock turning it from brown to a brilliant red, then to golden hues. The winds were so strong in portions of the climb that it felt like a reminder from the gods that this was indeed a sacred place and a climb that should not be taken lightly.

I was the first of our group—and the first of the day—to reach the top and sign the book of records. (A young Swiss man was quite disappointed to have been beaten to the top by a woman, and an American.) It was interesting to find that the top wasn't flat, but had deep groves with divided ridges worn into the rock by centuries of wind and rain.

Ayers Rock is a place where the Aborigines still come to seek guidance and to gain insight. There are areas at the base where only Aborigine men are allowed and others where only Aborigine women are allowed. There is also a birth cave where Aborigine women have come for generations to give birth. They still do today. Tourists are not allowed in any of these sacred locations.

After your climb visit the *Hunter's Cave* at the base of the Rock where the wall paintings are still visible. Also visit *Maggie Springs*, fed by the rain waters that wash down from the rock after a storm.

Sheraton Yulara Resort Center

Back at the Sheraton, there will be time before dinner to see the Visitor's Center run by the Park Department. Be sure not to miss it. It has one of the best visual displays you'll see anywhere and it provides a wealth of information about the park area.

The park rangers also offer a nice variety of walking tours during which you learn about the area vegetation, the Aborigine culture, and the constellations in the Southern Hemisphere. There's even a morning guided survival walk through the dunes where you can learn about the food and medicinal uses of local vegetation by the Aborigines. Unfortunately, once again there's just not enough time to fit everything in.

There are a number of restaurants at the Resort Center. *Giles Tavern* near the Visitor's Center is an informal tavern setting with à la carte food, where you can get turkey (A$9.50) or scallops and barramundi (A$11.50). But the best value is the dinner buffet at the Sheraton. For A$27 you can enjoy a selection of barramundi, prawns, oysters, lamb, beef, pâtés, a variety of salads, and a very tempting selection of desserts. The only problem with this buffet is the tendency to overeat. If you ask, you can order a more limited meal off the menu.

Alice Springs

In 1870, Alice Springs was a telegraph repeater station. Not long after that it became a stop on the only route from the south of Australia through to Darwin, in the north. An oasis town, it's located almost in the center of Australia, in the Northern Territory. There's a river through the center of town, but it's dry 80 percent of the year and makes a great place for a town party. After the October rains, it becomes a raging river once again for a couple of months.

Camel trains were once the primary method of transportation in the Alice Springs area. In memory, it's here that they have the yearly camel races, a major event. If you'd like, while in Alice Springs, you can take a camel ride to dinner. If you're lucky you may even get to ride on a winner.

An interesting thing about Alice is that when you arrive you set your watch back thirty minutes. That's right. I thought someone was pulling my leg at first, and while the logic totally escapes me, it seems to make perfect sense to the Australians. All of the northern and southern territories, the central one third of Australia, are thirty minutes behind Queensland and New South Wales on the east coast. Western Australia is then one hour and thirty minutes behind the central third of the country. When it's 1:30 in Perth, it's 3:00 in Alice Springs and 3:30 in Sydney. To me, the most interesting observation was how normal it seemed to the locals to divide the time zones in this manner, "Because the area is too big to divide any other way." Australia really is like no place else on earth in more ways than one.

If you're ready for a light, informal dinner, you might want to visit *Peppi's* for pizza, steak, or grilled meats (A$6 to A$10)—it's only a short cab ride from the Alice Springs Sheraton where you're staying. The *Todd Tavern*, in the same area as Peppi's and with counter meals, serves steak (A$6.50) and Wiener Schnitzel (A$7.50). It's a good place to meet locals and other visitors. I'd suggest staying away from their attached public bar; it's considered the roughest bar in town. There's also a bistro in *Lasseters Casino*, next to the Sheraton, with a large buffet (A$25) or à la carte dining (barramundi A$16, Lebanese spinach pie A$13.50).

Late at night, the casino, with its black-mirrored walls, can be an interesting spot. The disco here is open until 4:00 A.M. The dress is casual, but I'd suggest long pants or a skirt.

Royal Flying Doctor Service. While in Alice, you'll visit the regional headquarters of the Australian Flying Doctor Service, which was established here in 1934. The service is free and there are regularly scheduled clinics as well as an emergency service. Each participating sheep station or home has a cabinet with the medicines numbered. If someone becomes ill, they describe the symptoms to the doctor over the radio at the prescribed "air clinic" time. The doctor then tells the patient to take two tablets in box number six every four hours. The next day they can check in again with changes over the radio. Emergencies are evacuated by air to the nearest hospital. The government picks up 50 percent of the cost of care and 50 percent is paid through fund-raising.

There's also a *School of the Air*, by which children living on isolated sheep stations "go to school" over the radio from first through seventh grade. They meet only once a year.

Hot Air Balloon. Depending on the weather, of course, you may get to see Alice Springs and the surrounding prairie from high above in a hot air balloon. You'll ascend at sunrise, float across the sky for about an hour, then descend to a champagne breakfast.

Sydney

While it will certainly be hard to leave the life of the Outback, I can think of no better city in which to reenter civilization than Sydney. No one should go to Australia without seeing this marvelous city. It has become one of my favorite cities in the world.

The best way to describe it is as a San Francisco filled with sophisticated, unpretentious cowboys. It's a cosmopolitan city with a lot of class and style but without the pretense many cities somehow seem to develop as they expand.

Sydney is a great place for shopping. *George Street* is lined with large and small shops that carry just about anything you could want. My favorite shopping mall is the *Queen Victoria Building*, also on George Street. In this newly refurbished older building you can enjoy four floors of wonderful boutiques. It's a beautiful place to shop with a large center atrium onto which all the shops open.

Don't miss *The Rocks* area at the harbor end of George Street: during the day for shopping, in the evening for dinner or to visit the pubs. This is where Sydney had its beginnings. The area is growing quickly as more old warehouses are restored and opened as restaurants and shops. It's a spectacular part of town.

You should also be sure to visit the *Royal Botanic Gardens, Mrs. Macquaire's Point*, which overlooks the bay, and, of course, the *Sydney Opera House* complex.

Have your tour leader telex ahead for reservations at the Opera House or at one of the other theaters in the complex. There is usually a choice of performances each night—a play, a concert, ballet, or opera.

Take the tour, dinner, and performance for A$50. The tour is informative, the food good, and the atmosphere exquisite. Our table was overlooking the *Sydney Harbor Bridge*. It's also a wonderful way to spend your first night in Sydney. I strongly recommend extending your tour and spending at least two to three full days in Sydney. The tour only allows for one full day, two nights, and that just isn't long enough.

Having a few days in Sydney at the end of my trip made my departure from Australia less difficult. I knew I'd be back again.

For more on Sydney, see p. 173.

GALAPAGOS ADVENTURE

▶ ── ▶

GENERAL AMBIANCE	★ ★ ★
SOCIAL CLIMATE	★
ACTIVITIES	★ ★

FOR TOUR ARRANGEMENTS CONTACT:
Wilderness Travel
801 Allston Way
Berkeley, CA 94710
(800)247-6700 (outside California)
(415)548-0420

Or *contact your travel agent*
and ask for the Wilderness
Travel Galapagos Adventure

▶ ── ▶

*L*eading scientists were already beginning to question the mystery of evolution as young Charles Darwin set out in 1831 as the unpaid naturalist aboard the English survey ship H.M.S. *Beagle*. His five-year voyage would take him to the far reaches of the world. His journal indicates that he was most looking forward to seeing the Galapagos Islands, but little did he know that what he was to see there would so profoundly impress him and through him change the thought of the Western world.

While Charles Darwin did nothing to change the Galapagos Islands, he did much to change people's opinions of them. He discovered the magic of the Galapagos, which still remains for the adventurer of to-day.

Tourism to the Galapagos is restricted in an attempt to maintain the islands so that a million years from now visitors can experience them in the same unspoiled, natural state in which Darwin found them. As a result, this is not a place to see on your own. There are,

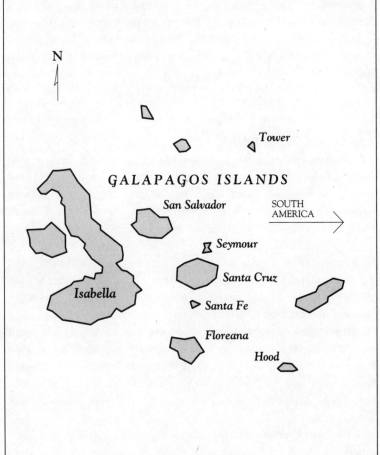

N

Tower

GALAPAGOS ISLANDS

San Salvador

SOUTH
AMERICA

Seymour

Santa Cruz

Santa Fe

Isabella

Floreana

Hood

by design, a very limited number of visitors allowed each year and limited hotel space.

Wilderness Travel of Berkeley, California, in cooperation with Metropolitan Touring in Quito, Ecuador, has organized an ideal Galapagos Adventure. In addition to your Galapagos trip, if you'd like, they can arrange for you to spend additional time on the mainland of Ecuador, or visit the surrounding countries (see "Along the Way to the Galapagos," p. 151).

General Ambiance

The Galapagos Archipelago, located 600 miles west of Ecuador, directly on the equator, consists of thirteen major islands, six smaller ones, forty-two islets with official names, and many more without names. The result of volcanic eruptions, the islands are still rough black lava peaks with sheer cliffs beaten by pounding waves. There are also hidden blue lagoons with white sandy beaches where you'd least expect them. The real fascination here comes from the sea lions, penguins, flightless cormorants, and the many other species endemic to the Galapagos Islands and found nowhere else on earth. This is the mystery unlocked by Charles Darwin.

A trip to the Galapagos Islands is an adventure for anyone interested in just seeing the islands, swimming with the sea lions in the blue lagoons, and photographing nesting blue-footed boobies or courting frigate birds up close. It is, however, also a very special adventure that awaits those who want to see what Darwin saw, and feel what Darwin felt.

What better way to see the islands than on a small sailing boat, much like the *Beagle*, with a small group of adventurers. Wilderness Travel has arranged just such a trip. While four different boats are used, all are small. My trip aboard the 63-foot wooden sailboat *Sulidae* was limited to ten passengers. Built in 1901 of solid hardwood with two tall wooden masts and outfitted with red canvas sails, the *Sulidae* comfortably took us from island to island, adventure to adventure.

Though we all had comfortable bunks below, we seldom used them, preferring instead to sleep on the deck, under the stars. While the atmosphere was relaxed and very informal, the meals were gourmet both in taste and presentation. We feasted on lobster, roast lamb, and mahimahi (dolphin) we had caught the same day while sailing.

Social Climate

The small boats, such as the *Sulidae*, attract adventurers in their twenties, thirties, and forties. The larger boats, with more conveniences, seem to be preferred by individuals in the older age groups. It takes a certain degree of agility to climb in and out of a sailboat and scramble across lava shores. It also takes a certain degree of flexibility to go for a week with your bathing accomplished primarily by swimming, then supplemented by a fresh-water rinse on deck. While this is surprisingly sufficient to feel refreshed and clean, it's not for everyone.

While at sea, especially in the evening and at night, you can join your fellow travelers for drinks and to exchange a story or two, or you can find a spot to sit alone and watch the moon and stars. Sailing through the Galapagos provides time for solitude. There's plenty of opportunity to sit totally alone on a high cliff overlooking the sea, and to watch the wildlife alone and at your leisure. You won't feel rushed or crowded. There's time to think or not think—to just be.

Activities

As we sat on lava rocks a foot or so from a Galapagos gull or reclined on the sand watching sea lions, we also learned a great deal about each species, their habitat, and how they varied from their close relatives on a neighboring island. Our captain and guide, Pepe, a native of Ecuador, freely shared his extensive knowledge about the area. Not only had he been trained at the Darwin Research Station, but he had sailed the islands for ten years observing and absorbing information. It was obvious, listening to him tell us about these creatures, that he truly loves the islands and their inhabitants. This is his home.

There is time for walking along the islands and seeing the wildlife. There is time for climbing a barren volcano and sitting on the peak to watch the brilliant colors of the sunset streaking the sky in ever-changing patterns. If you like, there is time to stop, sit, and watch the surf after the others in your group have moved on. There is no need to organize activities. With such a small group you can afford the luxury of spontaneity. You can ride the tide and go where the winds take you, remembering, as you sail, how little the islands have changed from the time of Darwin. We went to great lengths to leave only footprints in the hopes that the islands will be the same for the next visitors, and for a million years to come.

Snorkeling and Swimming

We went snorkeling and swimming at least once a day. We spent hours on deserted sandy beaches, which we shared only with the penguins, sea lions, and iguanas. The sea lions were especially inquisitive and seemed to enjoy our company. They darted around us playfully exploring their environment. Even close to shore, there were large schools of hundreds of bright yellow-, blue-, and purple-colored fish. We saw sea turtles, spotted rays, moray eels, and even a few sharks.

Scuba Diving

For certified divers, scuba diving is another option. Be sure to let Wilderness Travel know ahead of time so they can make the necessary arrangements. The *Sulidae* has a compressor aboard and will provide tanks and weights. You should bring your own equipment. In February and March, the water is usually quite warm. The rest of the year you will need a wet suit because the water can get chilly.

You won't find here the extensive coral reefs that make Caribbean diving so spectacular. Much of the coral that did exist was killed by the warm currents of El Niño in 1981. We did, however, find black coral growing in relatively shallow waters. Pacific Ocean divers are usually out looking for "the big ones," fish 6 to 8 feet long, swimming in schools. That's the real thrill of diving in these waters. You feel humbled by these creatures so much at home in the ocean depths.

Darwin's Time and Discovery

From the very beginning, the great voyagers to the New World brought back stories that had a tremendous impact on the thought of Europeans. Among those influenced were the scientists and naturalists who heard accounts of strange plants and animal life belonging to a new and mysterious world unfamiliar to them. The more they learned, the more they realized their old explanations for the order of the universe were no longer sufficient.

Many scientists contributed to the careful compilation of facts and to the evolution of thought, crystallized in Charles Darwin's theory of evolution, described in *Origin of Species*, published in 1859. Darwin's forerunners included his grandfather Erasmus Darwin, who, like Jean-Baptiste de Lamarck and George-Louis de Buffon, believed the change in the species was the result of the organisms' desire to change in order to survive the various climates. Volition rather than natural selection, was seen as the leading factor. These and other men had discovered the pieces of the puzzle that Darwin later correctly assembled.

The *Beagle* arrived in the Galapagos in September 1835. Still believing that climate was a primary factor affecting alterations in species of plants, birds, and animals, Darwin was amazed to discover distinctly different species on these islands in the same physical environment but isolated from each other by water. This was the key so important to Darwin, the key that was to change the thought of modern men and women.

Preparing for Your Trip to the Galapagos Islands

Rates

For US$2,150, you can spend eleven glorious days in the Galapagos Islands. This includes everything except your airfare to Miami (the starting point) and your Galapagos Park fee (US$40). You can also leave from Los Angeles, in which case the total cost will be US$2,380.

For those with the luxury of more free time and money, there is an eighteen-day Ultimate Galapagos Adventure for US$3,080 from Miami, US$3,310 from Los Angeles, US$3,180 from New York City.

These rates include your hotel in Quito, breakfast, welcome and farewell dinners, city tour, your boat excursion, and all meals while in the Galapagos. Wilderness Travel will also gladly arrange and book your air transportation to your departure city.

Documents

While a visa is not necessary, you will need a valid passport to enter Ecuador.

When to Go

The Galapagos are located on the equator, so the temperature does not vary greatly. January through April is the rainy season. During these months you can usually expect short, warm tropical showers. The water temperature will be in the low seventies and the air temperature seventies to eighties day and night. May to December it's a little cooler. If you want to scuba dive or do a lot of snorkeling at that time of year, you may need a wet suit as both the air and water temperature will lower appreciably.

I visited in February. The warm water allowed us to swim for hours, which I felt was a real advantage. The rains, while heavy, were warm and infrequent, and quickly passed. They did not interfere with our fun. If it rained, we simply went snorkeling or scuba diving instead of for a walk.

What to Take

Not only will you be unable to pick up the items you forgot to pack, you'll have limited space for baggage, so pack carefully and thoughtfully. Your days sailing through the Galapagos will be relaxed and very informal. I suggest taking two bathing suits—you will swim daily. Don't forget your mask, fins, and snorkel for a better view of life under the water. If you are a certified diver you should take your own scuba gear except for tanks, weights, and weight belt—and your certification card.

You will also, of course, want shorts and tops. T-shirts will do nicely. I'd suggest some lightweight, loose-fitting pants and shirts with long sleeves to protect you from the sun. Be sure your clothes are wrinkle resistant, or mostly wrinkle resistant. You won't need a nightgown. Part of the fun of life aboard a small sailboat is not needing to dress for bed at night, and waking up dressed in the morning. All you need to do at night is grab a pillow and blanket and find a comfortable, scenic spot to lay your head. There is, of course, no need for makeup. How wonderful it is to rub your eyes as often and hard as you want without having to worry about smudging your mascara. Ahhh . . . the simple pleasures!

A sunscreen is essential. Even though I had a tan when I arrived, I found the sun on the equator scorching. Number 18 sunscreen provided adequate protection, but just barely. I also found the waterproof sunscreen that won't wash off, even in salt water, a lifesaver. I wouldn't leave home without it.

There were a couple of areas we visited that had mosquitoes, so carry repellent. While you will seldom need it, it could prevent a sleepless night spent swatting bugs.

You don't need a flashlight on the ship, but if you go into the lava tube on Floreana Island you will most certainly want one. A small one is sufficient. If you scuba dive, take an underwater light that you can also use on night dives.

An underwater camera, if available to you, is an excellent way for you to share with friends back home your experiences swimming with sea turtles, sea lions, penguins, and hundreds of fish. Since there is always the possibility of a "wet landing" or rain, if your camera is not waterproof, you'll want something to protect it. In a pinch, a large Zip-lock plastic bag will provide some protection. Don't forget to take lots of film. I'd suggest taking twice as much as you usually use. You can always use it on another trip, and you won't want to run out on this one.

Thongs will be sufficient foot protection on the sun-baked boat deck and the hot sand, but you'll need tennis shoes for the lava. (Tennis shoes are better than hiking boots because they are lighter in weight and can get wet.)

You may want to take a dress and a light jacket or sweater to wear in Quito. You'll also want a hair dryer, curlers, and whatever makeup you generally use while in town, but you won't need any of this in the Galapagos. The Hotel Colon will store luggage for you. Leave as much as possible so as to avoid going over your allotted 22 pounds on your TAME flight to Baltra Island in the Galapagos. The storage is secure. If you do any shopping in Quito, I'd suggest leaving your new purchases in storage as well.

Money

The sucre is the currency used in Ecuador. One American dollar is worth about 150 sucres. It will usually be written S/.150. Though the rate of exchange fluctuates, as it does all over, you will get a better exchange rate in Ecuador than you will in the U.S. In Ecuador, you get the same rate whether you exchange your money at the hotel, bank, or airport. There is no fee for changing money. You will, however, get a little less when you change your sucres back to dollars.

Health Concerns

There are no required immunizations for travel to the Galapagos Islands or to central Ecuador. Normal precautions for tropical travel should, however, be taken, especially if you plan an extension into the Andes.

You might want to consider taking chloroquine or Fansidar for protection against malaria, as well as yellow fever immunization if you're not protected. A gamma globulin shot just prior to departure will provide good general disease protection as well as protection against hepatitis. Wilderness Travel also strongly recommends typhoid, tetanus, and poliomyelitis protection.

You should not drink tap water while in Ecuador. Bottled water will be available in your hotel room and at all restaurants. Safe drinking water will also be provided on the sailboat.

Getting There

Flights to and from Ecuador are notorious for their delays. While some airlines are worse than others, none seem to escape criticism when flying to South America. Ecuatoriana with its colorful rainbow-striped planes offers direct flights to Ecuador from New York, Miami, and Los Angeles. While they certainly have their problems with delays, Ecuatoriana is the only airline I've traveled that offered complimentary sandwiches and coffee at the airport during a two-hour delay. You are allowed to check two bags weighing up to 70 pounds each. If you have additional bags or additional weight, you have to pay extra.

There is a US$13 departure tax payable when you check in to leave the U.S. There is also a US$20 departure tax payable at the airport when you leave Quito. This is payable in dollars or in sucres. It will be approximately 3,000 sucres, depending on the exchange rate. I'd suggest using up any "extra" sucres when you depart.

Your Arrival in Quito

When you arrive at the Quito airport, a Wilderness Travel representative will meet you, collect your baggage, and take you to the *Colon International Hotel*. The Colon is the best hotel in Quito. If for some reason a trip leader is not available to meet you at the airport, take a cab to the Hotel Colon. As you exit the airport terminal you'll find a taxi stand. The ride will take about twenty minutes and cost US$3. You should contact your trip leader by calling Metropolitan Touring as soon as you arrive. They are located only two blocks from the hotel at Avenida Amazonas 239; the phone number is 235925. That night your host will return to take you and the other adventurers with whom you'll be sailing out for a welcome dinner at one of the many restaurants serving typical Ecuadoran dishes. He or she will translate the menu and offer suggestions and most likely order a number of hors d'oeuvres and local specialty drinks with which to begin your meal. This is a great way to get to know your fellow travelers.

Before you leave for the Galapagos, you'll be taken on a tour of Quito, the capital of Ecuador. A large metropolis of a million people, Quito still offers the very old and the very new. When you have more time to explore on your own, I'd recommend Avenida Amazonas, the main shopping area.

On to the Galapagos

Your Wilderness Travel representative will meet you at the hotel the next day, take you to the airport, and check you and your baggage in for your TAME flight to Baltra Island in the Galapagos. You will not need to stand in the often long and confusing lines. Everything will be taken care of for you.

When you land in Baltra three hours later, your captain and guide will meet you at the airport, collect your luggage, and load it on the bus that will take you to your boat.

It's as carefree and as well orchestrated on the way back. The only difference is that by then it will be friends who will greet you and take you out for a farewell dinner.

Tipping

At the end of your adventure, passengers generally each contribute US$20 for the crew and US$20 for the captain. Tipping is, of course, dependent upon the quality of the service you feel you received.

In Quito, I'd suggest tipping 100 sucres whenever you would normally tip US$1. Restaurants will automatically add a 10 percent service charge to your bill.

Treasures to Purchase

You can get Galapagos T-shirts on Santa Cruz near the Darwin Research Center (US$6 to US$15). Other than that, your only opportunity for shopping will be in Quito, where you'll find a great variety of local goods. You can get hand-knit wool sweaters for US$10 to US$30. Carved parrots and toucans sell for US$2 and up depending on their size and quality. Woven wall hangings are available in a variety of sizes for US$12 to over US$60. Leather suitcases and jackets of excellent quality and workmanship can be purchased for under US$200, and leather purses for much less. Wool neck scarves in a variety of colors and shapes are widely available for US$3 to US$12.

Wool capes and capes with colorful embroidery range from US$12 to US$100, depending on the workmanship. You'll find a number of

Stern's jewelry stores, including one in the Hotel Colon, with a selection of fine jewelry and stones.

Along the Way to the Galapagos Islands

Outlying Villages. For the really good prices you'll need to go to one of the markets outside of Quito. The drive through the Andes is as spectacular as the villages you'll visit. Monday is market day in *Ambato*, one hour south. Thursday you'll want to visit *Saquisili*, one and a half hours south. Friday there are a number of markets in the *Chimborazo Province* about three hours south. Saturday is one of the biggest and most famous markets in the village of *Otavalo* two hours north. If your free day is on Sunday, the market you'll want to visit is in *Pujili*.

For about 10,000 sucres you can hire a cab to take you and up to three friends to any market, except in Chimborazo, for the day. Since Chimborazo is so much farther, the price could be as high as 15,000 sucres. Ask the doorman to find you a cab driver who speaks some English, and be sure to negotiate the price before you begin your trip.

If you'd prefer, Wilderness Travel offers another tour that includes a visit to villages in the Andes and a trip to the Amazon basin before you begin your Galapagos Adventure. Yet another option would be to have Wilderness Travel arrange for you to see Peru, including the spectacular ruins of Machu Picchu before you sail in the Galapagos. Ask them for details on these trips before you make your final decision. While the Galapagos Islands are the jewel of Ecuador, the country has much, much more to offer.

Your Galapagos Adventure

The islands you visit as well as the adventures you experience on each trip will vary. There is no set itinerary and no set schedule to which you must adhere. To some extent, you go where the winds, the seas, and your captain take you. Most of the time you'll be the only group exploring the island, though occasionally you will meet another ship of adventurers anchored in a protected harbor.

Santa Cruz Island

Most of the Galapagos's 7,000 inhabitants live on Santa Cruz, the central island, home of the Darwin Biological Research Station, and our first stop.

Darwin Biological Research Station. Ecuador set aside the Galapagos Islands as a wildlife sanctuary in 1934 and made them a national park in 1959. One year before that, the Charles Darwin Foundation, an international organization, was formed. Their purpose was and still is to preserve the natural environment and promote scientific research relating to the conservation of the Galapagos. Much of the research is centered at the Darwin Research Station, which began work in 1962.

One very important project is a tortoise egg hatchery. Few Galapagos tortoises, which the islands are named after, are alive today thanks to the whalers who found them a convenient food supply. The research station hopes to regenerate the species by raising them at the station and returning them to their natural habitat at about five years of age, when they are no longer vulnerable to predators. You'll be able to pet the necks of these 400-pound beasts, who will seem to purr as you do so. Outside of the center it's important to remember you are not allowed to touch or feed the wildlife no matter how friendly they may be. Nor are you allowed to take any shells or lava home with you.

Another important function of the research station is the training of guides. Every ship sailing the Galapagos, whether private or commercial, is required to have a trained guide on board. Each September a five-week training course begins. Anyone with a degree in the natural sciences may apply; however, only thirty a year are accepted.

In addition to visiting the Darwin Research Station, we anchored off a sandy beach on an isolated portion of the island. When we came ashore we found dozens of deep depressions in the sand where giant sea turtles had laid their eggs. Their tracks could still be seen leading toward the sea. We also watched brilliant pink flamingos and great blue herons on a pond.

Just before dusk, our guide spotted frigate birds and pelicans beginning to swarm over the sand just down the beach from us. Earlier in the day we had watched them "cruise" the sand in search of newly hatched sea turtles. We chased the birds down the sand just in time to watch more than fifty sea turtles hatch through the sand and make a dash for the sea. We felt like rescuers on a special mission as we protected the sea turtles from the birds swooping down intent on a fresh morsel for dinner.

Later in the week we stopped again on Santa Cruz, at *Black Turtle Cove*. This mangrove swamp with its series of hidden coves is home to hundreds of sea turtles, and colorful green, pink, and blue parrot fish. To attest to the great strength of the delicate-looking mangrove trees with their aerial roots, chunky pelicans perched on their bows.

Tower Island

We anchored in *Darwin Bay*, a volcanic crater partially eroded by the sea. Today it is a large "protected" bay. As we walked ashore we were greeted by a masked booby feeding her baby, almost as large as herself. Not far away, two red-footed boobies, their beaks a brilliant blue, were nesting. Many more were nearby, some still building nests, others sitting on eggs. Some were within arm's reach yet seemed oblivious to the click of our cameras. They couldn't have cared less about their status as a "protected" species.

We saw great frigate birds courting their mates. The males, more than fifty of them, were impatiently awaiting the arrival of the females flying overhead. Having selected a favorite position among the bushes, they inflated the bright red balloonlike sections of their necks, creating a brilliant contrast against their black bodies. As the females neared, the males flapped their spreading wings in an attempt to attract a female with whom to mate.

This island is also the home of Galapagos doves, swallow-tailed gulls, yellow-crowned night herons, and a variety of Darwin's famed finches.

We swam in the warm waters of the bay with a lone sea lion and watched dusk fall before returning to our ship. It was a spectacular day on an island many people don't even know exists. Another adventure to remember for a lifetime.

Bartolome Island

It was here that we climbed the black volcanic sand of pinnacle rock to watch the shifting colors of the setting sun. Earlier we swam in the blue lagoon, with its brilliant white all-coral sand beach. Just a short distance up the beach we watched a lava heron trying to catch young Sally Light Foot crabs for dinner. While we watched, "Sally" proved too fast for the hungry heron. Most were also too large to be vulnerable to this black bird the size of a large robin.

Back on the boat, as we drank our rum and fruit cocktails before dinner, we saw the most spectacular shooting star I've ever seen. It was so large and bright, and its tail so long, that there was sufficient time for all aboard to witness the marvel before the large burning ball disappeared into the earth's atmosphere.

Plaza Island

The next morning we woke to the sound of sea lions and the inquisitive looks of penguins perched on the lava rocks watching us. After taking pictures to reinforce our fading memories in the years to come, we once again swam with these friendly, playful mammals. How marvelously they have mastered life on both land and sea.

After lunch we walked up the cactus-covered island and back along the picturesque cliffs. I wondered what the many land iguanas and the sea lions thought of the magnificent view or of our presence. While not tame, neither were they afraid.

Floreana Island

We anchored between *Devil's Crown* and *Point Cormorant*. Devil's Crown, a well-worn volcanic crater off Floreana Island, is a favorite stop of scuba divers. While the currents in the Galapagos can be treacherous, especially here, the rock formations are enchanting, and, once again, we saw schools of hundreds of brilliantly colored fish.

The ocean floor just beyond the crown is covered with giant starfish more than 15 inches across and bits of broken coral, killed by the warm waters of the 1981 El Niño. This area had offered some of the best coral diving prior to that time. Signs of life, while present, are minimal when compared to Caribbean coral reef formations. The 4-

and 5-foot-long red snappers and white-tipped reef shark are thrilling. I was told large hammerhead sharks are often seen here. While they may have seen me, I did not see them.

Life above the water is as spectacular here as life below the sea. The rocks of Devil's Crown are home to large numbers of regal blue-footed boobies. And we sat enchanted as about forty of the more than one hundred resident flamingos joined in an elaborately choreographed courtship dance. In unison they bowed, then gave a wing salute as they walked through the shallow waters as if in a chorus line.

Our next stop on the island was *Post Office Bay*. Ever since 1793, a barrel left on shore has been used as an informal post office. It predates the beginning of our postal service, and is still in use. It was interesting to me to be reminded that there was a time before world-wide postal service was available, something else I had taken for granted. The first and last stop from the mainland, the British whale-boats would stop here to collect fresh water that was trapped in the cones of the craters and to take aboard giant turtles for food. A large bay consistently 9 to 10 fathoms in depth, this was an ideal harbor. Upon arrival the sailors would leave mail that other boats heading home would pick up and hand deliver. The tradition is to leave a postcard and to hand deliver any that are headed for your hometown.

A short distance from the beach is the entrance into a large cavern-ous lava tube. About 5 feet in diameter, the entrance is steep and requires a rope descent. Next, there is a low area where you have to crawl on your hands and knees; then it opens into a large cavern with a shallow lake of seawater at the end. The walls hold the crystals of lava from millions of years ago. Without the flashlights and candles we used to light our way, we would not have been able to tell whether our eyes were open or closed. We were in total darkness.

Santa Fe Island

High on the cliffs, with the surf breaking on the lava rocks below, stand relatives of the prickly pear cactus. Here as nowhere on earth, how-ever, they have grown into 15-foot-tall trees. Their large trunks, some-times more than 2 feet across, have a red bark that flakes off much like birch bark. Their fruit and flowers are the favorite food of an endemic form of land iguana.

By now, isolated blue lagoons with white sandy beaches had come to be expected as a refuge from the sea. We were not disappointed on Santa Fe Island. As usual, we shared the beach with large numbers of playful and friendly sea lions who seemed to think our arrival was a great occasion for a party. They even helped carry a pair of shorts that we were attempting to launder through the water.

Later, after the hottest part of the day had gone, we climbed another cliff past a Galapagos hawk—she had likely been watching us all afternoon from her perch on top of the island—and we saw more land iguanas amid fields of cactus trees. As we returned to our ship, the hawk soared far overhead. A small school of twenty or so puffer fish surveyed our boat from below the surface of the water.

Mosquera Island

More a large, long sandbar than an island, Mosquera took the record for our "wettest landing." A deep beach front and strong waves literally swept us off our feet, soaking us head to toe. Fortunately, we were used to being wet by now and had intended to go for a swim soon anyway. A bull sea lion, not happy to see us land in his territory, added to the excitement. We found the largest number of sea lions here, well over 200. While watching them we also spotted a whale offshore.

S. Seymour Island

Our last stop before heading home. Here we sat and watched the most spectacular surf I've ever seen—more spectacular than Hawaii's pipeline, and more dangerous. Except under the best conditions, the waves break on rough lava rocks. Our guide told us that once in a while expert, dedicated surfers come here to ride the endless waves.

Within view of the surf we found another colony of frigate birds. These were magnificent frigate birds. Their red pouches were even larger and longer than those of the great frigate birds we'd seen on Tower Island. They were so large that when a male bird took to the air with its pouch still inflated, his sideways movement made his usually graceful flight look difficult and awkward.

The blue-footed boobies who usually rest here were noticeably absent this year. The effects of the present El Niño had affected their food supply and they had nested elsewhere.

At the end of our trip we all bid a sad farewell to the *Sulidae* and crew. As the bus taking us to the airport rounded a bend, she was blocked from sight. She is a grand ship that took us on a magical adventure. We all witnessed marvels we had never anticipated and made memories we will long cherish. That night in Quito, and the next morning at breakfast, we said our last farewells.

LEARNING TO SCUBA DIVE ON THE GREAT BARRIER REEF

GENERAL AMBIANCE	★ ★
SOCIAL CLIMATE	★ ★ ★
ACTIVITIES	★ ★

FOR TOUR ARRANGEMENTS CONTACT:
Hayles
P.O. Box 898
Cairns, Q. 4870
Australia

Or *contact your travel agent*

*I*f you are one of the many people who have always wanted to learn to scuba dive, who've thought about it for years, who've perhaps even taken a resort course while on vacation, I've found *the* place for you. The Great Barrier Reef, which extends for 1,200 miles off the northeast coast of Australia, is the ideal place to learn to dive. Of course, if you're an experienced diver, there's no question that you'll enjoy the reef. Most divers only dream of some day diving "the" reef, and the Great Barrier Reef is indeed "the" reef.

The reef is said to have originated over 10,000 years ago. It is the largest structure ever built by living organisms and provides the coast with almost continuous protection from the Coral Sea.

You don't need to be an expert—or even a good—swimmer to scuba dive. You just need to be an average swimmer and, most important, feel comfortable in the water. You'll find it's actually easier to swim under the water with scuba tanks, flippers, and a buoyancy compensator than it is to swim on top of the water. This chapter will highlight two Barrier Reef Island dive schools, one on Fitzroy Island, the other on Green Island. You will find either a great place to learn.

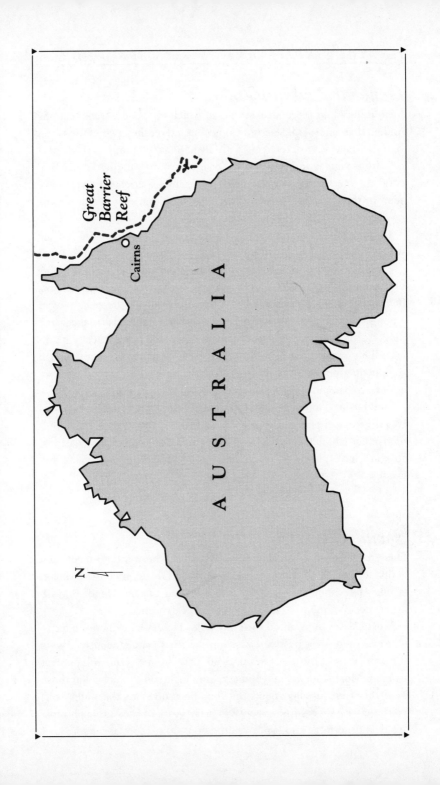

General Ambiance

I can think of no more ideal setting in which to spend a week learning to dive than on a semideserted tropical island on the edge of the Great Barrier Reef. The outer reef, with all its allure, is only a short boat ride from your island hideaway. You'll see more varieties of fish and coral on your first open water dive than many experienced divers have seen in their lifetimes. Best of all, it is all within easy reach for the novice diver.

In most areas, the reef is only a few feet below the surface of the water. As you will learn, the best light penetration occurs in 10 feet of water or less, and you need light to bring out the vibrant colors of the coral. Most of the reef is located in waters less than 30 feet below the surface, and seldom will you need to dive deeper to swim amongst the harlequin tusk fish, butterfly cod, Spanish dancer red mollusk, or giant manta rays that look menacing but are really harmless. This is the only place I've ever seen giant clams, large enough to contain a person. The starfish are large here, too, often more than a foot across, and they are deep blues and brilliant reds.

The beauty continues above the water. On land you're surrounded by lush tropical plants with blooms so fragrant that they act as a protective curtain. There is only one small resort on each of these islands, so you'll have plenty of peace and solitude after a day of diving and classes.

Social Climate

One advantage to scuba diving for a woman who wants to meet men is that at least 60 percent of divers are men. Diving, much like skiing, is one of the popular vacation trips for men to take alone, or with other men. Women are just beginning to catch on.

Most classes are limited to ten people. However, if there's a lot of interest, there may be two classes in progress simultaneously. While the mix varies, most classes are 60 percent men and 40 percent women. Most students range in age from eighteen to thirty, and those over thirty are usually men. On your boat dives to the outer reef, you'll be with divers from twenty to sixty years of age, although most are twenty to forty and, once again, about 60 percent are men.

The members of your group will be from all parts of the world. You'll be with Australians from the mainland, Europeans, Japanese, and other Americans as well. You may even find that you want to keep in touch with a few and later meet to dive some other exotic part of the world. While you have a group of people with whom to eat, study, and play during your week on the reef, you also have lots of opportunities to take off on your own and get totally away from civilization on an isolated part of the island.

Activities

The focus of this trip is, of course, scuba diving, and most of your week will be focused on water activities. Since you'll be at a resort, there are small boats and windsurfers you can rent, the beach to relax on, and the sea to dream beside.

Cairns, on the mainland of Australia, is your gateway city. There is much to see and do in this area and the rest of Australia as well, so you may want to extend your trip and tour Australia after learning to dive (see "The Australian Outback," p. 117). At the very least, you should see Cairns and Sydney before returning home.

Underwater Photography

While you're in Cairns, be sure to stop by the *School of Underwater Photography* at the Underwater Camera Center, 21 Lake Street. You can rent a Nikonos V with a strobe light for A$25 a day, if you rent it for five or more days. For A$175 you can take a two-day underwater photography course. This is for the newly certified as well as the experienced diver. You may decide to extend your diving experience for two days and take their course after you become certified.

Preparing for Your Trip to the Great Barrier Reef

Documents

You need a valid passport and a visa to enter Australia. You can obtain a visa by sending your passport and one passport-style photograph to: Australian Consulate General, 321 North Clark Street, Chicago, IL 60610. There is no fee. Allow two weeks. You can also obtain a visa through Express Visa Service, Inc., 2150 Wisconsin Avenue, Suite 20, P.O. Box 32048, Washington, DC 20007; (202) 337-2442. If necessary, they can obtain your visa within a few days. There is a US$20 fee for this service.

When to Go

The best time of year for diving is December, January, and February. The locals brag about having 600 feet visibility at that time of year. This is not, however, the best time of year *out* of the water: the temperature can be quite warm in the shade. The Christmas candles literally melt on the trees even before they're lit. The mangos are ripe in December, which is a treat, but I think you'd be better off going during their winter months, May through October, so you'll be comfortable out of the water as well as under it. October is an especially good month for visibility and weather. Cairns is like Florida during wintertime. In June and July, the coolest months, it will still be in the seventies during the day, cooler at night. May and September are probably the optimal months to visit.

What to Take

The whole of Australia is informal, especially the reef islands, so you'll need only informal resort wear. There is no need to dress up, but you may want a nice summer dress or slacks for dinner, and a light sweater for the evenings during the winter months. You'll likely spend most of your time in your bathing suit.

I'd suggest a lightweight, long-sleeved T-shirt to wear over your suit when you go diving. One-piece, Danskin bodysuits with long sleeves make great dive wear for the warm tropical waters. They provide a little protection for the cooling effect of long periods in the water, and they protect you from the coral. You'll also find lightweight diving suits available for sale at the dive shops. These are just a little heavier than the Danskin and much more expensive. You can also rent a wet suit if you prefer. Most of the year, however, a T-shirt will be sufficient.

Before you leave home, go to a reputable dive shop in your area and purchase mask, fins, and a snorkel to take with you. Try the equipment out to make sure you have a good fit. You really won't need anything else. If you'd like, buy a pair of booties to wear over your feet; however, a pair of socks will provide nearly as much foot protection. You may also want to pick up some simple dive tables and a dive logbook while you're there.

Later, you may decide to buy a regulator and perhaps a buoyancy compensator, but I'd suggest you wait. I strongly recommend that you *not* buy equipment from the dive shops on the islands. Some may pressure you to do so, but resist. Diving equipment, like any other sports equipment, is constantly being updated. It's also bulky to carry around. While you may have every intention of spending two to three weeks a year diving from now on, that's unusual. If you only make one trip a year, you'll likely find you're better off renting your equipment. I have always found rental equipment is readily available, up to date, and well maintained.

Because the islands are tropical, I suggest you take mosquito repellent along for your forest walks and a good pair of tennis shoes; you'll need these for walking along the coral. I'd also suggest you take sandals that can get wet without damage.

For those quiet moments, I recommend you take along *Castaway*, Lucy Irvine's account of her year on a deserted Australian island in the Torres Strait. It'll make great beach reading.

Money

At the time of publication, one American dollar was worth A\$1.30. The exchange rate will, of course, vary. You'll be better off changing your money at a trading bank in Cairns than at the island resort. You will also get a good exchange rate on your major bank card charges, unless, of course, the U.S. dollar is falling in value. Check just before your departure.

Health Concerns

You do not need any immunizations for travel to Australia or the reef islands, and the water is safe to drink.

Your primary health concern will be coral cuts and scratches. The coral on the reef contains organisms that can cause infection if you do not receive proper attention immediately. The dive staff have solutions with which to wash coral cuts. Use it or you will be uncomfortable and sorry later.

Getting There

Cairns is the Australian mainland gateway city to the Great Barrier Reef. Qantas Airlines has daily flights from San Francisco, Los Angeles, and Vancouver to Cairns. They offer a convenient, comfortable flight schedule that will get you to Cairns refreshed and ready for adventure on the reef (see "Australian Outback," p. 117).

Your Arrival

A cab to town will cost A$6. For A$3 you can take an airport bus that will drop you at the door of your Cairns hotel. Bus tickets can be purchased at the stand just outside the exit from the customs area at the airport.

Tipping

There is no tipping in Australia. This includes the resorts at which you will be staying. The only exception is if you visit the big tourist hotels and restaurants in Sydney, where the American tourist trade has had a major impact. You should still not tip your cab or doorman. Only tip for exceptional service in the better restaurants, and then tip

10 percent. Average-good service need not, and should not, be rewarded here.

Treasures to Purchase

With the exception of T-shirts, postcards, and a few other souvenir-type items, you'll find there's not much to purchase on the islands. Cairns and other mainland cities will be your best bet for shopping (see "Australian Outback," p. 117).

Eating Out in Australia

During your stay in Australia you'll find a number of food specialties. Cairns, in particular, is a fishing town. You'll see the trawlers off the coast daily. They'll come into port teeming with prawns and a variety of fish. The most popular, for good reason, are barramundi, John Dory, and reef fish. You'll also find lots of passion fruit, paw paw (papaya), and, if you're there in November, December, or January, mangos. You'll also find kiwi fruit imported from New Zealand. "Bugs" or Morten Bay bugs are on the menus in the better restaurants. They're like miniature lobsters, about the size of a large prawn. They're wonderful, every bit as good as a lobster, which are referred to here as crayfish. Scones, a biscuit served with lots of jam and whipped cream, is the favorite midmorning accompaniment for your coffee or tea. Sometimes you'll get "bickies" (cookies) with your tea.

Don't be surprised if you order a hamburger and they ask you if you want it "with the lot." That means with the works, and it often includes beets, which Australians seem to put on everything. Coffee and tea are ordered black or white (with milk).

Save room for dessert. The specialty is Pavlova. It's a light meringue with whipped cream and fruit that literally melts in your mouth.

Much to my surprise, Australia produces some excellent wines. You won't go wrong with a Hunter Valley wine, but don't be afraid to sample others as well.

YOUR GREAT BARRIER REEF EXPERIENCE

▶ ─────────────────────────────────────── ◀

Your entry city is Cairns (pronounced "cans," or sometimes "canes"), and it's a great place to adjust to the new climate and time zone before going to the reef. After your week—actually five days—of diving lessons on the reef, I'd suggest, if time permits, joining an outback adventure or, at the very least, seeing Sydney and Melbourne before returning home.

Remember, Australia is a big country, nearly as large as the continental United States. You can't see the whole U.S. in two, three, or even four weeks. You'll be happier when you return if you see less territory and have time to enjoy the areas you do visit.

Cairns

Since you'll soon be out on a reef island, spend your first two or three days in town rather than at a nearby beach resort. A delightful tropical city with white wooden houses built on stilts to allow for air circulation, Cairns is expanding rapidly. The past few years have brought a large influx of tourists to the area. Large hotel chains have already purchased land along the still-deserted beach areas north of the city on the way to Port Douglas. By the early 1990s, it will be large resorts instead of isolated beaches, so now is the time to visit.

Where to Stay in Cairns

Tradewinds, 137 The Esplanade (single A$80, double A$95), opened in March 1987. The entire hotel is decorated in soft, warm peach colors with tropical wicker furniture, and the high ceiling and white marble lobby are spectacular. The staff is very helpful and friendly. All rooms have a pool and bay view. Conveniently located, it's only a short walk from the center of town down the Esplanade, beside the bay. Formal and informal restaurants and shops make this hotel an excellent choice and a great value, especially with the attractively decorated spacious rooms and private balconies.

Pacific International Hotel, 43 Esplanade (single A$115 to A$135, double A$122 to A$168). Also conveniently located on the bay, almost in the center of Cairns, this, too, is an attractively decorated, although somewhat older, hotel. It was *the* place to stay before the Tradewinds opened. If you choose to stay here I'd pay the extra A$20 per night to get the significantly larger corner executive suites. They have two balconies, a spectacular view, and a number of extra amenities in the room. For A$20 they will have the limousine pick you up at the airport.

TraveLodge Cairns, corner Esplanade and Alpine Street (single A$67, double A$78). A good value although not as spectacular as the previous two properties, this conveniently located hotel has only a limited number of rooms that overlook the bay. These rent for the same rate, so request one ahead of time. While adequate, they are not spectacular.

Back Packers Hotel, 149 Esplanade (single in dorm A$7, single own room A$16, double twin share A$8). If you don't mind roughing it a little, this hotel is bright, cheerful, and clean. The dorms have bunk beds and sleep four to sixteen. While the hotel is not air-conditioned, a breeze off the bay keeps the rooms cool. There is an attractive outdoor pool where Pro Dive offers scuba lessons. There were lots of good-looking men hanging around here when I visited. While most of the guests appeared to be in their twenties, there were a few in their thirties and forties, and everyone seemed to be having a great time watching the dive lessons in the pool. Book by sending the first night's payment at least two or three days ahead. It's conveniently located, nearly in the shadow of the Tradewinds Hotel.

Where to Eat in Cairns

The better restaurants in Cairns are located in the big hotels like the Tradewinds and Pacific International. There are, however, a number of cute little cafes along the main shopping streets.

Rogues Cafe offers fast lunches from quiche (A$1.80) to a fisherman's basket (A$6) as well as a selection of deli sandwiches made to order (A$2 to A$3). Beets are, of course, a sandwich option.

The *Swagman's Rest* on Lake Street by the park mall has a nice barramunda with lemon sauce (A$8.95). You can sit outside and watch the shoppers and children in the park. It's right next to the Museum and Australian Craftsman's Gallery where you can purchase aboriginal art.

For a more formal meal, try *The Freshwater Connection* only a short cab ride out of town to Freshwater on the train route. You'll dine in a train car. If you go with a friend, ask for a private compartment in one of the three restored carriages. If you're alone, you will be dining under the ferns on the platform. A dinner here will cost A$20 to A$30.

Cairns at Night

You'll find a number of lively discos in town. The most popular is *Scandles* (Lake and Florence Streets). Each night the music is different; you'll get everything from jazz to fifties rock and roll. Casual dress but no blue jeans. The *Playpen International* (3 Lake Street), a rock disco, is a little dressier. *The Nest*, next door, is less formal and popular with the locals.

Exploring the Cairns Area

There's a lot to see in the Cairns area in addition to the town. I'd start with a ride on the *Sundancer* jet boat north to Cooktown, an all-day trip (A$79). They pick you up at your hotel in the morning and take you by bus to Port Douglas, where you board the *Sundancer*. While Port Douglas was once "the last frontier town" on the east coast, today that distinction goes to Cooktown. Captain James Cook and the crew of the *Endeavor* ran aground near here and spent time in the area repairing their ship. The *James Cook Historical Museum* holds an interesting history of the area. The town is small, so save your money and skip the driving tour; it's an easy walk. Have lunch in the downstairs public bar of the *Sovereign Hotel* and meet the "yachties" (Australian "hippies"), who've grown up and taken to living on the sea, escaping civilization. They're a little rough around the edges but a lot of fun. You'll learn their ideas and values quickly. The food's okay.

You'll also want to see the *Atherton Tablelands* west of Cairns and ride the *Cairns-Kuranda Railway Train*. This, too, is an all-day trip, but well worth the time (A$29). In addition to riding the vintage train, you'll see the famous *Curtain Fig Tree*, visit the high plateau tablelands, rain forest, crater lakes, and stop at *Lake Barrine*, where you can have coffee and scones or even take a boat ride on the lake.

To *really* see the rain forest, you may want to take an all-day trip into the *Daintree Rain Forest* (A$55). You'll see spectacular tropical beaches along the *Coral Sea*, and the sugar town of *Mossman*. You'll cross the *Daintree River* by ferry and end up in even more remote areas near *Cape Tribulation*. A delicious barbecue lunch beside a crystal clear stream and a swim in the *Mossman Gorge* or at a sea stop makes for a relaxing day.

Fitzroy Island

A forty-five-minute ride on the turquoise-tinted sea aboard the *Fitzroy Flyer* and your holiday will really begin. You'll find yourself on an isolated island paradise that feels much farther away from civilization than you actually are. The boat departs from the Hayles pier (A$24 round-trip).

You'll need your sandals for a walk along the beach. A young island by the standard of centuries, the broken coral that forms the beach won't be fine sand for another millennium. A fifteen-minute walk through the rain forest will take you to Nudie Beach, where the coral is a proper fine sand. I always had this beach to myself, which is likely why nude bathing here is so popular.

If you arrive early in the day, Wonga, the resident kangaroo, may even greet you at the pier. She was inherited from a previous light-house keeper on the island. She spends most of the day lounging around the beach houses and can often be seen looking over the diving students' shoulders while they study.

After class, you can walk through the rain forest or up to the light-house, which provides a breathtaking view of the mainland and the reef. There are great jogging trails if you still have the energy.

Fitzroy Island Resort

There are two facilities available at the resort. You can stay in one of the four spacious villas (A$79 per person twin share, A$109 sole use), or you can stay in the beach house (A$15 per person quad share,

A$52 sole use). The villas all face the Coral Sea with a sitting area, cooking space, and private bath. Each villa unit is separate and has a private porch. All are attractively decorated with tropical prints and wicker furniture.

The beach units are small rooms with two bunk beds and a shared bath facility. There's a communal kitchen and dining area attached. If you prefer, however, you can have your meals at the poolside fast-food areas or the restaurant farther down the beach.

Recently acquired by the Hayles family, the island's resort facilities have been considerably upgraded. Peg Hayles, who has an active hand in running the family business, wants to maintain a quiet relaxing resort atmosphere with first-class service without pricing the resort out of bounds for the budget traveler. That's why you have the beach house and villa options as well as the choice of fast-food or an elegant restaurant.

The restaurant is a wonderful place for an evening meal: open to the sea breeze with a thatched roof, tropical plants, and fish everywhere. The Hayles have brought the outdoors inside. The food is attractively presented and of better quality than anything I had on the mainland, even in the more expensive Sydney restaurants. An excellent selection of wines is available, too. Dinner will cost A$20 to A$30 with wine.

Pete Boundy's Dive School

The dive school on Fitzroy Island is owned by Peter Boundy. The course lasts five days and costs A$240. Your first two days will be spent becoming familiar with the equipment in the attractive pool in front of the dive shop on the edge of the sea. You'll have one or two pool sessions a day and one theory session in the classroom.

Your first dive in the open water comes on the third day. You'll do a beachside dive in the morning and, if all goes well, which it usually does, your first boat dive that afternoon. What a thrilling experience that is! Your first day to experience the wonder and beauty of the reef is always a memorable one. You'll have a second theory session that afternoon.

On your fourth day you'll do two boat dives during the day and a night dive after dark. Night diving is an even more unique experience.

This is when the coral reef really comes to life. If you're careful, you can pick up the colorful reef fish sleeping in the coral and replace them without disturbing their dreams. You may also see the large lobsters feeding on the bottom.

You must, however, earn your night dive. The exam on theory is given that afternoon. You'll be tested on your knowledge about dive planning, the use of dive tables, dangers to avoid, decompression, medical considerations, equipment, underwater hand signals, and the physics of diving. If you read the books they gave you and listened during your theory classes, you'll do fine and you'll soon have your certificate.

On your last day you do two dives on the outer reef. You'll leave the resort a certified diver with many unequalled memories and experiences of fascinating Fitzroy Island, Australia.

Green Island

A smaller and flatter island than Fitzroy, Green Island is also more developed. It was one of the first islands to be serviced regularly by the Hayles fleet of catamarans. While few people spend the night on the island, it can be quite crowded between 9:00 A.M. and 5:00 P.M. The island is surrounded by a coral beach. You can leisurely stroll the 1.6-kilometer circumference in less than an hour. At low tide you can walk out on the reef, but you'll need a pair of tennis shoes for protection.

First discovered by Captain Cook in 1770, it's a rich reservoir of marine life. A true coral cay, Green Island is composed of broken pieces of coral that have been washed up by storms to only 4 feet above sea level.

You can get to Green Island by taking the Hayles catamaran from the Hayles pier in the center of Cairns (A$24 round-trip).

Green Island Reef Resort

Also run by Hayles; the rates include dinner and breakfast. The tropical units, built of attractive red cedar, are all air-conditioned and have private baths. Their high ceilings with fans offer a pleasant tropical feel (A$89 each twin share, A$134 sole use). The lodge units, a little older, are otherwise comparable (A$79 each twin share, A$118 sole use).

Peter Tibbs Scuba School

The dive school on Green Island is run by Peter Tibbs. This school opened in 1987 and they even have a woman dive instructor, which is still, unfortunately, unusual. Other than this, the school's similar to Peter Boundy's. The course here is also for five days, and the cost is A$250. They offer NAUI certification.

Your first three days consist of an hour theory class in the morning, an hour theory class in the afternoon, and a pool lesson midday for equipment and procedure familiarization. Your written test is usually given the evening of the third day.

The last two days are devoted to open water dives, two each day from their dive boat. Most dives will only be 30 to 40 feet because that's as deep as the reef goes in most areas. That's the beauty of the Great Barrier Reef for the novice diver. You can "see it all" without doing a deep dive.

Safety

If you decide to stay in the area and do more diving, please heed this word of caution. Diving has become a competitive industry in the Cairns area. The way dive operators are trying to outdo each other is by offering more dives a day than the competition. Companies will advertise up to seven dives on a two-day trip; up to twelve dives on a three-day, two-night trip. That's a lot of bottom time and a lot of compressed air that you'll be breathing.

The problem is that all compressed air contains nitrogen. The more compressed air you breathe, the more nitrogen you breathe. The nitrogen diffuses into your blood and body tissues. The longer you are down and the deeper you go, the more nitrogen diffusion occurs. As you surface, the nitrogen diffuses out of your body tissues, which is why you need to ascend slowly. If you don't, bubbles of nitrogen can become trapped in the tissue around your joints or spinal column causing the bends or decompression sickness. Even if you are only doing shallow, repetitive dives you can get "bent."

The bends can be extremely painful and crippling. It's a serious problem. The most cautious medical advice is that once you get bent, you should really *never* dive again. Spinal column damage may lead to paralysis. The Cairns area was reported to have had nearly one dive incident requiring use of the decompression chamber each week during the 1987 season. Most cases come from companies that offered a large number of dives within a few days.

Play it safe and stay well within the limit of your dive charts. Keep close track of how deep you dive and err on the side of limiting your dives rather than risking your health. If you do that, diving is a safe sport you will be able to enjoy over a lifetime.

Coral Sea Diving Experiences

Run by a woman named Leslie, this organization operates out of Port Douglas, although they will pick you up at your Cairns hotel. They offer daily outer reef trips to the best diving sites, including *Cod Hole*. This undersea garden attracts giant cod that almost eat out of your hand. They are a reputable organization with a good safety record.

Sydney

A stop in Sydney is a must before returning home. A harbor tour is another must. *Captain Cook Cruises*, which leave from the Circular Quay Ferry Terminals, will gladly take you out around Sydney Harbour and under the Harbour Bridge. Another must is attending a performance at the world famous *Sydney Opera House* on the bay. For A$50 you get a tour, dinner, and a performance. The *Royal Botanic Gardens* and *Mrs. Macquarie's Point* are the places for pictures of the city and the opera house. For an even more spectacular view, especially the sunset, the *Sydney Tower* is *the* place.

At the harbor end of *George Street*, the main shopping street, you'll find *The Rocks*. This is the old part of town where Sydney had its beginnings and it's my favorite part of the city. You'll find wonderful colonial pubs, unique shops, and restaurants in this completely restored part of town.

The most unique shopping mall in town is in the restored *Queen Victoria Building*. It has four floors of interesting shops as well as a couple of cafes for a light snack. Thursday and Friday are late shopping nights in Sydney. The stores are open until 9:00 P.M.

Best of all are the walks along the harbor area. There's plenty of space to sit and think and dream of your next trip to Australia.

Sydney has really gone out of its way to facilitate travel for a tourist by introducing the *Sydney Explorer Bus*, which visits the city's twenty top tourist attractions. For A$7.50 you get a free guidebook and can get on or off at any stop. You purchase your Explorer ticket on the bus or at the New South Wales Travel Center. With a population of 4 million, Sydney is Australia's largest city, and this is a great way to see her.

You might also want to take a ferry to Manly, across the harbor. They leave every thirty minutes from Circle Quay jetties 2 and 3, and the ride takes about thirty minutes. Plan to have lunch harborside at the Manly Pier restaurant.

If you haven't seen a koala bear or wombat (a short, fat, furry animal with pointed ears) yet, visit *Koala Park*. It's open from 9:00 A.M. to 5:30 P.M. The best way to get there is to rent a car or take a train from any city station to the Pennant Hills station via Strathfield, then take a bus (route 184) to the park. It's near the historic city of Parramatta. The animals now roam freely in what was initially a koala bear hospital. You'll see these cuddly little bears high in the treetops as well as in an open enclosure at eye level. It's well worth the effort to get here; a trip to Australia is hardly complete without seeing a koala bear. Koala Park also has a variety of kangaroos, a wombat, dingos (wild dogs), and much more. Visit their souvenir shop; it's a good one. Because this is a wildlife preserve, I felt comfortable that the kangaroo skin goods here really were the species not endangered.

Where to Stay in Sydney

Especially in a big city, the most important consideration in picking a hotel is its location. There are two that are very different: one very old and charming, the other very new and sophisticated. What they have in common is the best location in town: on the edge of The Rocks next to the harbor.

The Regent of Sydney, 199 George Street (single A$185 to A$265, double A$200 to A$280). Somehow the Regent Hotels always seem to have the best location whatever city you visit, and the Regent of Sydney is no exception. Located on the edge of The Rocks and the business district overlooking the Sydney Opera House and Harbour, the view is spectacular. The lobby atrium of polished red granite and gleaming brass is equally spectacular. The rooms are spacious and attractively appointed with all the conveniences at your fingertips. The hotel staff are especially interested in meeting the needs and desires of the single woman traveler. If there's anything you don't find, let them know and it'll likely be there on your next visit. You'll have fresh flowers, bubble bath, and even hot chocolate in your room—the "real" indicators of luxury and thoughtfulness. Not missing a trick, at 6:30 A.M., Monday, Wednesday, and Friday, they will meet you at their front door to take you on "the most beautiful run in the world."

The Russell, 143A George Street (single A$63 to A$94, double A$69 to A$102). Also ideally located in the heart of The Rocks, near the business district, The Russell was originally built in 1887; it has been completely restored and filled with antiques. Each room is unique. You can rent an apartment, with a kitchen, that sleeps a small family for A$125 per night. The only disadvantage of The Russell is that there is no harbor view—it doesn't have the height, but it makes up for its small stature with charm.

Old Sydney Park Royal, 55 George Street (single A$156 to A$170, double A$166 to A$180). Also located in The Rocks, the building facade is historic but the interior very new. The lobby rises in an eight-story atrium that the rooms encircle. Unfortunately, only a limited number of rooms have a harbor view. The rooftop pool with whirlpool is its best attribute. While a charming hotel in many ways, the rooms are small and, for the price, not the value of the Regent or Russell.

Where to Eat in Sydney

In addition to fun shops, The Rocks area has a number of excellent places for a meal, with everything from cook-your-own barbecue to elegant dining on the water's edge.

Russell Tea Room. If you're staying in The Rocks at the Russell Hotel this is where you'll have breakfast. If not, stop by for Devonshire Tea (coffee or tea and scones, A$4) or a sandwich for a light lunch (A$6). The entrance to this bright and cheery though very small restaurant is behind the Russell Hotel.

The Cook House. Located on Greenway Lane off Argyle Street, this is a lunch stop not to be missed. None of The Rocks businessmen do—they're *all* here over the noon hour. Like most steak houses, this place is full of men, even though it's like no other steak house you'll see. For A$8 you get your choice of large 12-ounce steaks, A$4 for a salad. Then you take your meat to one of the four outdoor barbecues and cook it to your liking. While waiting, you get to know a few of the local men also cooking their steak. Seating is at large outdoor group tables under awnings and trees. It's a delightful inner courtyard as well as a great place to meet the locals.

Rock Push. For A$15.90 you'll get a four-course set menu. Wednesday through Saturday you'll hear live dinner music as you eat in the inner garden courtyard. The owner, Wolfie, assured me they'd take especially good care of any single woman and make sure she felt this was "her home away from home." Remind the maître d' of Wolfie's promise.

Italian Village. On the waterfront, almost under the Harbour Bridge, the Italian Village is a wonderful new restaurant in a restored warehouse that has become a sixteenth-century Italian village. It has antiques in strategic locations and strolling musicians to add to your dining pleasure. For A$35 you can get a four-course meal with a glass of wine. Come early and have a drink in the bar before dinner. All coins retrieved from the barside fountain go to the Cancer Foundation.

Waterfront Restaurant. You can't miss the wooden masts and sails of the Waterfront Restaurant, also in The Rocks on the wharf near the Italian Village. For lunch, you can eat outside by the water's edge overlooking the opera house. The seafood here is excellent, cooked in a variety of ways—all tasty. If you haven't tried the John Dory or barramundi yet, this is the place to do so. A complete, four-course meal is A$25.

Sydney Tower Restaurant. Located in Centerpoint, Market Street, in the heart of Sydney with the best view in town, you have your choice of three restaurants. Level one is the elegant, international restaurant. It revolves, so you'll see the many sides of Sydney as you dine. Lunch ranges from A$20 to A$26, dinner A$24 to A$32 depending on the number of courses you select. Level two is nearly as elegant, but you select your own courses from a nonrevolving counter area, A$19 to A$24. The seating area here also revolves. Both offer a selection of salads, seafood, steak, lamb, and tempting desserts. There's a nonrevolving coffee lounge on level three open from 10:00 A.M. to 5:00 P.M. You can get a light snack, A$3 to A$9, or a drink at the fully licensed (serving beer, wine and hard liquor) sky lounge.

Sydney at Night

If you stay at the Russell or the Regent you only have to step outside your door to be where the nightlife begins in the heart of Sydney. You'll find informal tavern-style entertainment with crowds on the younger side at the *Orient Hotel* and other rock establishments. If you want a little more upbeat evening, try the *Jamison Disco* on Jamison Street. The *Theatre Royal* has musical performances and, of course, there's always the opera house.

Sydney is a unique contrast to the island resorts on the Great Barrier Reef where only a few days ago you learned to scuba dive. The days must pass more quickly so far south of the equator, because all too soon you'll begin your journey literally back in time. With your passage over the international date line, you'll reach California at about the same point in time at which you left Sydney, but other than the time, not much will be the same.

CHAPTER 6

▶ ▶ ▶

Winter Vacations: For Those Who Like It Cold

DOG SLED ADVENTURE IN THE BACK COUNTRY

▶————————————————————————▶

GENERAL AMBIANCE ★ ★ ★

SOCIAL CLIMATE ★

ACTIVITIES ★ ★

FOR RESERVATIONS CONTACT:
Boundary Country Trekking
Dog Sled Adventure
Gunflint Trail 67-1
Grand Marais, MN 55604
(800) 328-3325 (outside Minnesota)
(800) 622-3583 (within Minnesota)

▶————————————————————————▶

*E*ach account I heard of Will Steiger's dogsled expedition to the north pole made me more certain that that was not the type of adventure in which I would be interested. I must admit I was pleased that

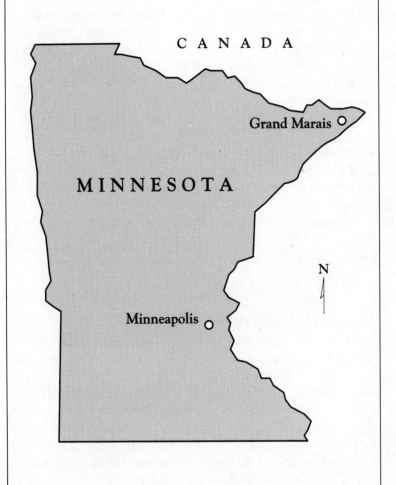

CANADA

Grand Marais ○

MINNESOTA

N

Minneapolis ○

a woman, Anne Bancroft, was a member of this first dogsled team to make the trip to the north pole. I was even more pleased to learn that she was a schoolteacher from St. Paul, near my hometown. The expedition did pique my interest in the sport, however, as I expect it did with the thousands of those who followed news of the quest.

I found I began to listen more closely to news items about other sled dog events, such as the 430-mile John Beargrease Sled Dog Marathon in northern Minnesota, and the even more famous 1,200-mile Iditarod Sled Dog Race from Anchorage to Nome, Alaska. I was excited and pleased when Susan Butcher won the 1987 race. It was her second win in a row. Another woman, Susan Riddle, had won in 1985. Women had dominated the race for three years, after never having won before—a coup. What an exciting sense of accomplishment they must feel. How nice it is to vicariously share their victories over the male mushers in the races. I hadn't previously thought of dogsledding as a sport for women to participate in, let alone excell in.

It wasn't long afterward that I heard of the Boundary Country Trekking and Dog Sled Adventure. It sounded feasible and like something I wanted to try.

General Ambiance

I must admit I experienced some initial apprehension at the idea of spending three winter nights up in the backcountry of northern Minnesota. But I soon learned that traveling with an experienced guide who knew how to live comfortably in −20-degree weather can leave you with a sense of respect and accomplishment as well as many thrilling memories of the north country's winter beauty and the excitement of driving your own team of sled dogs.

The winter weather in northern Minnesota can be harsh, but the dogs and the mushers (drivers) actually like it that way. "The dogs work best at −10 degrees," I was told by more than one musher. When I asked where they went on vacation, I was told "North. It's too warm around here for me." And after I had run up a couple of steep hills behind the dog team, and peeled off my heavy coat at the top, I began to understand why weather in the teens and low twenties was considered too warm.

At night you stay in tent camps or yurts. The tent camps, while functional, are the most rugged—and an experience to tell your friends about back home. You won't need to pitch your own tent; they are already in place when you and your dog team arrive. There are even wood-burning stoves and cots awaiting your arrival. While the kerosene lamp provides sufficient light for cooking, it's not really enough for reading, so it's stories around the camp stove between dusk, at about 5:30 P.M., and bedtime.

The yurt is backcountry luxury. Mongol tribesmen built their yurts to be easily transportable and made them out of skins. Yours, however, like your tent, will be set up when you get there. These round structures vary from 14 to 22 feet in diameter and are equipped with six bunk beds, a wood-burning stove, gas lighting, picnic table, dishes, and pots and pans. There is even a small library with a selection of books about the north country for you to browse through at night after you've feasted on trout or a Mongolian pot stew.

Social Climate

In most of my travels the biggest thrill is getting to know people who lead a life-style different from my own with values and expectations unique to their circumstances. This was true of my dogsledding adventure as well.

Since there are no TVs or radios in the Boundary Waters Wilderness Area, at night you find yourself sitting around the fire with your small group of three or four fellow adventurers. Like me, you may find that you've taken living in a home with electricity, running water, and indoor plumbing for granted, and that not everyone lives that way. By choice, many people not only heat their homes with wood-burning stoves, but also carry their water in from the lake and use kerosene or gas lamps, sometimes even candles. I was both surprised and awed to meet people who live comfortably without the many modern conveniences I've always considered necessities.

At the beginning and end of our trip, when we were privileged to visit the homes of our north country hosts, I had a sense of the merging of the past and the present. While there certainly have been changes, I expect the people who have come to the north woods and stayed live today much like the ninety-one-year-old "old-timer" down the road lived when he moved here seventy years ago. At least the night we spent at our tent camp was likely much like his winters in Minnesota. Doug, our musher, told us that, "until he was well over eighty and his rheumatism got worse," the "old-timer" moved into a tent camp in the woods each fall and spent the winter there. He apparently felt more comfortable in the woods than within the confines of a cabin.

I could tell he and Doug shared a mutual respect and value of the country they lived in as well as the life-style they had chosen. As Doug told us, to some people, dogs, like anything else, become a vehicle to be used; to others they become a way of life.

This is not a trip from which you'll bring back souvenirs. However, more valuable than souvenirs are the memories of the experience. For a few brief days, you will live as the pioneers of our country once did and as woodsmen of today still do.

Activities

A typical trip will begin at *Young's Island Bed & Breakfast*. This vertical, split-log cabin was originally built in 1932. The Young family bought the eighteen-acre island thirty-five years ago and it has been in the family ever since. The kitchen is a welcome gathering place with a wood-burning stove and a large window that looks through a stand of pine trees onto the lake.

You will travel about 15 miles a day by dogsled, which takes three to four hours, usually two before lunch and two after lunch. The food is hearty and plentiful.

Your two nights in the backcountry will be spent in one of the yurts or at a tent camp, and the last night is at the *Pin Cushion Inn* in Grand Marais. Your first hot shower in three days will be a welcome end to a wonderful adventure.

This isn't the type of trip where you just go along for the ride. There is usually only one musher and two teams of sled dogs, so you will actually be responsible for your own team. You'll trade off riding and driving. You'll learn to harness and feed your dogs, and you'll learn that "Haw" is the lead dog's cue to go left at the trail junction. "Gee" means go right. "Hike" is the signal to go faster. "Mush," from the French word *marche* (march on), is no longer used. "Let's go" or "straight ahead" are the terms that let our teams, already pulling hard against their harness, know that now they could go. The excitement of the dogs as the last of the team was hitched to the sled was infectious. It was often all we could do to hold them back once they were ready. We were all glad to be off.

In addition to driving the team and being adept at winter camping, your musher, a dog breeder by necessity, possesses a wealth of information about dog care. I learned how to tell if a dog is dehydrated by the elasticity in the skin on its back and the color of its gums, how to feel a dog's loins and determine if it is over- or underweight, what to look for and avoid in pet foods, and what types of injuries or illnesses one might expect and how to treat them. This knowledge applied to my cat will likely make her healthier.

This is a great time to learn about dog behavior. These animals aren't like the pets people keep in the cities, although they certainly love affection and a kind word. They have a social structure all their own. In the evening, while you're gathered around a fire, and at night, before you go to sleep, you'll hear a rousing chorus of howls. Starting and stopping on cue as if they had a choir director, their howls echo through the wilderness. You can sometimes even hear the faint reply of another pack of sled dogs bedded down many miles away. This behavior and the way they nuzzle and lick each other strengthens the social ties of the pack.

While the trip is centered around the dogs, in the evening or morning you can arrange time for cross-country skiing or just hiking along the ski and snowmobile trails. The trails are kept groomed for all to use, and on weekends you will likely pass an occasional snowmobiler. The winter magic of the scenery is breathtaking. The many lakes and streams are mostly snow covered, with small areas where the running water can be seen beneath the ice and snow.

Preparing for Your Dog Sled Adventure

Rates

The four-day, three-night trip including meals and camp gear costs $330 per person. If you'd like a longer trip, an additional $70 per person, per night is charged. The trips are limited to six people.

When to Go

The best snow and weather conditions will be found in January and February, although it can get extremely cold. While trips are run in March, by this time the weather will be getting too hot for the dogs, which would require more frequent stops to cool them down. The snow conditions for cross-country skiing will likely not be great either.

What to Take

When you book your trip, describe your cold weather gear in detail to your musher. He'll help you determine if it's adequate. Warm clothing is essential. If you don't have the proper clothing you'll need to find a good outfitter in your area. You won't enjoy your trip if you're cold, so listen to what the experts tell you and be prepared.

You won't need a lot of extra clothes because you won't be changing your outer clothing unless you get wet. You will want to take extra pairs of long underwear so you can let the clothing closest to your body dry well before you wear it again.

Because of the low humidity, you won't notice that you are losing fluids. So you may want to take a plastic drinking bottle for fluid replacement while you're on the road. While alcohol isn't good for fluid replacement, you may also want to take some peppermint schnapps to add to the hot chocolate your guide will provide. A flashlight will also be helpful at night.

Leave your makeup at home; you won't need it on this trip. Take lotion or moisturizer, because of the dryness. A strong sunblock to protect your exposed skin and a pair of protective sunglasses (see p. 44), are also good ideas. The glare of the sun off the snow is strong and may damage your eyes without proper protection. Even when the sun isn't out you'll need some eye cover. The dogs will kick up snow that can get in your eyes and the wind can cause eye discomfort and watering. I found a pair of ski goggles with a yellow shield to be optimal for most conditions except the brightest sunny days.

Getting in Shape

While you do trade off riding and driving, the driver usually runs up the hills behind the sled, or at least "pumps" with one foot. On the steeper hills, both people will need to get out to lighten the load for the dogs. I found jogging the hills was also a good way to keep warm even when the dogs didn't need my help.

Good physical conditioning is a key to your enjoying the trip. If you can jog a mile on level ground you should do fine on this trip (see "Getting into Shape," p. 36).

Getting There

I'd suggest flying into Minneapolis, then renting a car for the five-hour drive to Grand Marais. While you can fly from Minneapolis to Duluth, by the time you change planes and rent a car in Duluth, not only will it cost more, but it will probably take you longer.

If you drive north on Interstate 35 from Minneapolis, you'll be in *Duluth* in two and a half hours (140 miles). It's a good place for a lunch break before driving the last 110 miles to Grand Marais. The North Shore drive up Highway 62 will take you through the sleepy fishing villages of *Two Harbors*, *Gooseberry Falls*, and *Split Rock* with its lighthouse perched on the edge of a high cliff overlooking the vast open waters.

The shoreline will be covered with snow and ice that forms when the waves wash over the icy boulders along the bank. Be sure to watch for deer grazing along the edge of the road—you'll see lots of them, and possibly a few moose as well. It's an enchanting drive during the winter, well worth an extra day. Don't arrive at Young's Island after dinner, however, or you'll miss out on a great home-cooked meal.

Trail's End

You'll know each dog by name, many by their bark, by the time you reach the trail's end. It somehow seemed necessary for me to bid each one a separate farewell as we closed the kennel door. They were a very special part of my adventure, each a unique individual.

You overnight at Grand Marais prior to your drive back to Minneapolis. The hot shower will be a luxury the magnitude of which had been long forgotten during your time in the backwoods. You'll want to readjust to civilization slowly. Much of what once seemed a necessity will somehow now be superfluous, possibly even a nuisance. Life can be so much less complex.

SKI UTAH INTERCONNECT, "THE HIGHWAY TO HEAVEN"

▶ ─────────────────────────────────── ▶

GENERAL AMBIANCE ★ ★

SOCIAL CLIMATE ★ ★

ACTIVITIES ★ ★

FOR RESERVATIONS CONTACT:
Ski Utah
307 West 200 South, Suite 5005
Salt Lake City, UT 84101
(801) 534-1779

▶ ─────────────────────────────────── ▶

As we looked out over "The Highway to Heaven," the pass between Solitude and Alta, I thought of the Wasatch Walkers, the pioneers of skiing, many of whom were miners on their way to the Alta or Brighton silver mines. Skiing was a means of transportation to them. When they crossed this same pass in the early 1900s and 1920s, they wore 7- to 9-foot-long inflexible wooden skis tied to their boots with leather straps. They didn't have the quick-release bindings we wear today, nor did they get to this point by skiing from the top of the Solitude chair lift, as I just had done. They walked up the pass, their skis wrapped with ropes to keep them from slipping backward.

I felt a sense of their adventure as the wind from the approaching storm blew the snow into my face, and I wondered how many Wasatch Walkers had crossed this pass, and how many had not made it. Even with all our new equipment we weren't guaranteed success. Though the knowledge and skill of our guides and the "Piep" radio transmitters we wore certainly cut our risks to a minimum, we still had the memory of a party caught there in an avalanche the week before.

Today we would ski from Park City to Solitude, Brighton, Alta, and then Snowbird in just seven hours with the help of ski lifts. In the early 1900s, the Wasatch Walkers took three to four days just for the trip from Park City to Brighton.

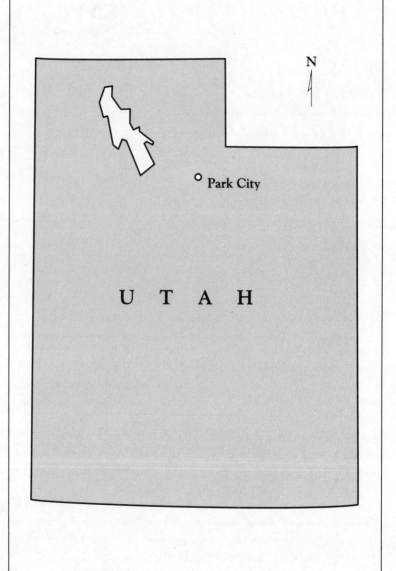

N

Park City

U T A H

The Gondola at Park City was closed when we set out. We were told the winds at the top were gusting to 70 mph. We would have to ride the ski team lift up to the Summit House, then hope the winds died down enough for the Jupiter chair to open. A few people decided to wait until a calmer day. Seven of us decided to make the trip. Our guide, Bob Bailey, has led trips in these mountains for nearly ten years, and has led the Interconnect route ever since Ski Utah first offered the excursion in 1983.

The storm was just arriving. The trips scheduled for the next two days would likely be cancelled because the new snow would make the pass too dangerous. Yet Bob assured us that the risk of an avalanche today was low. He then explained in vivid detail what we should do if we were caught in an avalanche: Swim to the top by getting rid of skis and poles, keep your mouth closed so it doesn't fill up with snow. Then "relax" (sure!) until the guides locate us by following the signal emitted by our radio transmitters. Bob assured me every guide could locate and dig out a buried transmitter within two minutes. I must admit I felt better when he told us he had never lost anyone.

We arrived at the Summit House of Park City still not certain we would be able to go. If the Jupiter chair didn't open, we couldn't get out of the next valley. We fought a strong wind with fiercely cold snow at the top, then warmed up in the shelter of Summit House while we awaited word on our trip.

We were in luck; the ski patrol was going to open Jupiter. After one final discussion, everyone decided to go. We would make the trip, and it was indeed going to be an adventure. We were keyed and ready to go regardless of the wind and cold. We had come to ski the Interconnect, and we were going to get the chance to do just that.

General Ambiance

Word of a rich silver strike in the Wasatch Mountains spread fast in the 1860s. A small mining camp soon became a boom town and was incorporated as Park City in 1884. Main Street is still lined by many of the original buildings from the silver mining days. A walk down well-maintained Main Street can easily evoke memories of times past. That special charm and sense of traditional beauty remains.

At about the same time that mineral prices were dropping in the 1930s, skiing was becoming a recreational sport. In January 1938, Utah's first ski lift, the new "up-ski device," began operating at Alta. There was a brief decline during the war years, but the postwar era saw a contagious gravitation of adventurers to the mountains and to the Park City area. The migration continues each winter as the town comes alive with the excitement of another ski season.

Park City is not just a ski area, not just a resort center. It's a charming little town nestled at the base of majestic towering peaks. But during the winter months, these peaks are covered with glistening powder snow too tempting to allow a real ski enthusiast to sleep in, even after a night on the town.

Social Climate

As at most ski areas, the men outnumber the women at least four to one. The day I skied the Interconnect, I was the only woman in a group of seven, although I was told they usually have three women to a group of ten. It's not uncommon to meet men in groups of two to eight who have come out to Utah to ski. I met fewer women.

I found the locals and visitors alike warm, charming, and friendly. Skiing single is a great way to meet people on the lifts as well as on the hill. It's a safe way, too, because you're not stuck with someone any longer than you want to be. If you enter the lift in the "singles" line, you'll never have to wait (the lines are always for doubles and triples). But best of all, you'll ride up with someone new each trip. If you're mutually attracted you can, of course, ski down and ride up again together. If not, as you get off the lift, it's easy enough to cut things off with a friendly, "Have a good run."

If you are a good skier, you'll find you're a much-sought-after companion. Men like to find women who will ski the steep runs and the bumps, women they can have fun with, but who won't hold them up or keep them on the bunny hills. If you ski well, and ski alone, they'll find you. You won't be skiing alone long if you don't want to be. It's also very easy to lose someone on a mountain if that's what you want.

You can always take a "wrong turn" and be on your own again. It's all up to you.

Preparing for Your Utah Ski Trip

When to Go

As at any ski area, Thanksgiving and Christmas are expensive and the snow conditions vary greatly. To consistently find the best snow the time to go to Park City is the month of February. Even over President's week it is unlikely that you will wait in a lift line for more than ten minutes if you learn to ski the mountain as I suggest. You could hit a storm that will dump two feet of snow on the mountain one day then offer blue sky and sunshine for spring skiing conditions the next. March and April are usually warmer, the snow a little heavier although plentiful, and there is the likelihood of good spring skiing conditions.

What to Take

Because the weather can vary within a week whenever you go, you should take your warmest ski clothes *and* your spring ski clothes. For the cold days you'll want long underwear, heavy gloves, hat, and a neck scarf to pull up over your nose. It's better to dress in layers; you'll be warmer that way. You'll also need sunglasses that will protect your eyes (see p. 44) and goggles.

For the warmer days when the sun shines, fewer layers and a powder vest will do nicely. The new Gore-tex ski suits are by far the most functional and versatile. They keep the chilly winds and moisture out, but still breathe.

You won't need to dress up in the evenings for dinner. Jeans or slacks, a sweater, and boots will take you anywhere in town. I'd suggest one nice sweater to wear to the fancier restaurants. If you have a fur coat or jacket, take it along. If you don't have one yet, you'll find a great selection in town. Be careful: while these go on sale later in the season, the prices are still not as good as the best sales back home.

Getting There

One of the nice things about skiing in the Park City area is the convenience of the slopes just outside Salt Lake City, your flight destination. Most major airlines even offer discount rates. Flying into Salt Lake, you'll look down on steep, snow-covered mountain peaks that slope down to the edge of the Great Salt Lake. Framed against a clear blue sky they are mesmerizing.

When you book your flight and room, you or your travel agent should also book your ground transportation by contacting Park City Transportation, (801) 649-8567. For $14 round-trip, they will take you from the airport to the front door of your lodging, forty-five minutes away. When you pick up your bags near carousel number three in Terminal One, you'll see a sign saying "Ground Transportation Information." That's where you'll find the Park City Transportation agent.

Getting Around

Once you're in Park City, the free shuttle bus service will get you wherever you want to go. The gray buses will stop at the gray bus stop signs and transport you to Park West, Deer Valley, or Park City Resort Center. The brown trolley car (on wheels) will stop at the brown signs to take you up and down Main Street.

From Monday to Friday, if you want to ski Snowbird or Alta, for $14 round-trip you can leave Park City at 8:00 A.M., arrive at the ski area at 9:30, then depart at 5:00 P.M. to return home. Call 649-2256 in Park City for reservations.

Treasures to Purchase

You can easily spend an afternoon or two going from shop to shop on old *Main Street*. You'll find everything from antique stores with a selection of old jukeboxes ($6,000 to $9,000) to ski clothes, New York fashions (at New York prices), furs of every variety, and Western and modern art. There's even a Mrs. Field's Mall with a cookie store (of course), a unique furniture store, an Alaskan furrier, and an art gallery.

Unfortunately, as at most resort centers, while you will find many unique items you'll likely not find elsewhere, they are not at bargain prices. Even relatively late in the season when the ski shops back home offer 40 percent to 50 percent discounts, you'll pay full price at Park City.

Utah Liquor Laws

Once you figure out the liquor laws, which are really not as difficult as I initially thought, it's easy to get a drink in Utah.

The following is a general outline:

Restaurants

You must be twenty-one years old to drink and only cash is accepted. All hard liquor must be purchased at a state licensed liquor store; however, many hotels and restaurants have licensed stores on the premises that sell mini-bottles as well as full-sized bottles. Other restaurants are licensed to sell wine and mini-bottles. You must also order food in order to drink in a restaurant.

Beer Bars

There are also a number of beer bars. In these establishments you may purchase beer and "set-ups" (drinks without the liquor). You add your own liquor, which you have brought with you. If you want a mixed drink and have forgotten your liquor, you will find that there is usually a licensed store nearby—ask the bartender to direct you.

Private Clubs

There are a number of private clubs in town that serve food and mixed drinks over the bar to members only. Anyone, however, can purchase a two-week temporary membership for $5. This will allow you and five friends to use the club.

Most clubs, beer bars, and restaurants serving liquor are open seven days a week.

Where to Stay

Park City

Washington School Inn, (800) 824-1672 (single or double $125). In 1985, the Washington School, originally built in 1889, underwent a complete restoration to become a charming bed and breakfast hotel. You'll find all the comforts of home, including a lobby fireplace, at this inn just off historic Main Street. If you book the very spacious suite at the top near the old school bell tower ($175/night), you can even have a fireplace in your room. The breakfast served just off the lobby area is a great way to start a day of skiing with the other guests. You'll also run into them in the lobby around the fire after skiing or relaxing their sore muscles in the Jacuzzi and sauna.

The Blue Church Lodge, (801) 649-8009 (single or double $75 to $150). The first Mormon Church in Park City built in 1898 now houses guests in seven elegant condominium units. In addition to a busy spa area, they have table tennis and a large lounge where guests can relax at the end of the day. While each unit has a fully equipped kitchen, a continental breakfast is served during ski season.

505 Woodside, (801) 649-4841 (single $45, double $65). The first bed and breakfast in Park City, this restored older home can only accommodate guests in two bedrooms, so it's a great place to come to relax but not to meet other people. After skiing you can enjoy wine and cheese around the fireplace in the living room, or you can relax in the Jacuzzi out back. It is a centrally located quiet retreat just a couple blocks from Main Street.

Copperbottom Inn, (800) 245-6417 (single or double $110). All single-bedroom suites have a kitchen, vaulted living room, and fireplace; each can easily accommodate four people. Breakfast (extra) is served in the lobby restaurant. After skiing you can relax with the other guests in the spacious, attractive Jacuzzi or sauna. Located halfway between the Park City Resort Center and Main Street in the new portion of town.

The Yarrow, (800) 327-2332 (single or double $99). Located in the newer part of Park City, this Dunfey Conference and Resort Center offers a variety of facilities and conveniences. The spacious, vaulted-ceiling lobby greets you with the smell of wood crackling in the brick fireplace. If you choose to partake in the skier's buffet at the Yarrow Restaurant ($6.95) you'll find an array of fruits, eggs, meats, and cereals. A crackling wood fire in the restaurant sets a cozy tone for your meal. A heated indoor pool, Jacuzzi, and sauna will greet you at the end of an exhilarating day on the slopes.

Deer Valley

Stein's Lodge (800) 453-1302 ($425 to $1,345 a night). If you want to really splurge, you can stay right on the mountain at Deer Valley Resort in the elegant and luxurious Stein's Lodge. Even the smallest two-bedroom suites have 1,660 square feet of space, three bathrooms, and can sleep six people. The lodge is named after Stein Eriksen, the director of skiing at Deer Valley, whose Olympic gold and silver medals are in the lobby display case. You will probably run into Stein with his son Bjorn in the lodge lobby or on the slopes. He can still turn those skis and so can his very young son.

If you're off the mountain between 3:00 and 5:00 P.M. you can listen to piano music over tea in the lodge lobby. Everything about this lodge exudes charm and elegance, from the well-equipped spa with a heated pool overlooking the mountain to your private deck and fireplaces in each suite (one in the living room and one in each bedroom) to the heated ice-free sidewalks and underground parking. If you wait until the last week of the season you can pamper yourself in luxury and style for only $155 a night. The smallest one-bedroom units will sleep four.

Where to Eat

Park City

If you want to avoid the crowds I suggest going to dinner by 6:30 P.M. Most restaurants take reservations, which I strongly suggest if you want to dine late. You'll find a wide range of restaurants, most in the moderate price range, on historic Main Street in Park City. If you pick up a copy of the Park City *Lodestar* ($2), you'll find a forty-seven-page menu guide at the back.

I had the best swordfish I've had anywhere at *Car 19*. Their prime rib was excellent and their desserts were much too tempting. The locals all recommend this one and I'd agree with them. For a relaxed meal you might try *Texas Red's*. Your clue to the identity of the owner will be his snakeskin boots. While the food was fine, I hope my waiter was better at skiing.

If you like pasta I'd suggest *Mileti's*, which has an excellent selection. For reasonably good Mexican food with great service and an interesting, unique setting, try *The Irish Camel*. It's located in the original Park City Telephone Company building built in the late 1800s. An Irish pub–Mexican restaurant, it's quite a combination. If you prefer to cook your own meat or fish try the *Cactus Rose*. You order by the ounce. If you like jazz, you'll hear live music while you eat each evening beginning around 7:30 at the *Jazz Pantry*.

Deer Valley

More than one person has told me to "ski the buffet" at Deer Valley. The Douglas fir timbers imported from Washington state, the fireplace, and general ambiance of the lodges at Deer Valley make them a must for lunch. If you like, you can take your food outside to "the beach," then "ski the beach" (nap or people-watch in lounge chairs) in the afternoon.

While Deer Valley, Park City, and Park West are wonderful places to come to eat, play, and relax, best of all they offer some of the best downhill backcountry powder skiing in the United States. With the addition of the Ski Utah Interconnect Trail, it's an area that will be difficult to beat, providing a unique adventure and years of memories.

Activities

While skiing is the primary activity at Park City, the skiing is varied and there's lots more to do if you can stay awake at night, or if you want to take a day off during your stay.

There are three areas around Park City, all connected by free shuttle buses. In addition, Alta, Snowbird, Solitude, and Brighton are just a short drive away. If you don't have a rental car, you can call ahead and arrange to have the Park City Transportation Company take you to one of these neighboring areas (649-8567).

Park City Ski Area

(Full day, adult lift ticket: $30.) As in most areas, if you know how to ski the mountain at Park City you can avoid standing in a line. Except in the early morning, late afternoons, and between noon and 1:30 P.M. (when most people stop for lunch) you should avoid riding the Prospect, Lost Prospector, and the King Consolidated chairs. If you stay on the runs serviced by the Motherlode, Pioneer, and Jupiter chairs, you'll have great skiing and avoid the crowds. If there's a line at the Gondola in the morning, and there often is, take the Ski Team lift, then Prospector chair to Summit House. Another good option is to take the Town lift, which starts in the middle of town. You can even buy your ticket there, and the line is usually shorter than at the ski area plaza ticket office.

I also prefer to eat early or late, after 1:30, so I can ski when the majority of people are in the midmountain lodges eating.

Park City is an exceptionally large area. You can ski hard for two days and still not see the entire mountain. You'll find wide open, groomed runs such as Climax, Sudden Splendor, Power Keg, Sunny Side, Parley's Park, and Assessment. You'll find bump runs with slopes not too steep, such as Dynamite, Double Jack, Gotcha, and other great bump runs for advanced skiers off the Ski Team chair. Best of all, in Jupiter Bowl you'll find 650 acres of open bowl powder skiing. The easiest, gentlest slopes on the West Face are on the left as you ride up Jupiter lift. A strong intermediate skier will do fine here. If you want to "catch some air" or watch others who do (I prefer watching myself), a short hike up on the right of the lift will put you on the edge of Scotts Bowl, where the brave (or foolhardy) can jump into the bowl. When you tire of watching their feats you can traverse in and safely ski down. There's something here to challenge even the most adventuresome skier. It's a great place for sightseeing on the way up to the chair as well.

The scenic trail out of the Jupiter lift area passes the Keystone and the Thaynes mines. While they have been out of operation for many years, they are a reminder of the area's past. When the price of silver gets high enough mining may resume in this area.

Deer Valley Ski Area

(Full day, adult lift tickets: $33.) The Rolls-Royce of ski resorts, Deer Valley is an area you won't want to miss. Fifty percent of the runs are groomed every night, making this area a "cruiser's paradise." Because it's the groomed runs that draw the skiers, there's good news for those of us who still prefer the bumps. They're wide open. No crowds.

Once again, if you know how to ski the mountain, you'll avoid the lines. At Deer Valley that means "skating" a few feet over the Mc-Henry run to the Wasatch chair to get to the top of Bald Mountain; avoid the Sterling chair, where the crowds will be.

The most advanced portion of the hill with the largest number of bump runs is off the Mayflower chair. If you like bumps, you'll be in paradise here. While there are a couple of more challenging runs off the Wasatch and Sultan chairs, such as Reward and Rattler, for the most part Deer Valley is designed to meet the needs of the intermediate and advanced intermediate skier who wants to kick back and cruise.

While the skiing is great, what everyone talks about—and what makes Deer Valley unique—is the food and McHenry's Beach in front of Silver Lake Lodge on the top of Bald Eagle Mountain. In the spring, you'll even find palm trees beside the barbecues.

Inside you'll find an incredible array of culinary delights. There's a deli where you can get just about any sandwich you want, a grill with roast beef and veal, and a natural food buffet that includes fresh fruit, salads, and even artichoke hearts. While it's reported to be expensive, the value is great. For $10 to $12 you can eat more than you'll wish you had and even have carrot cake, cheesecake, or an 8-inch cookie for dessert. After your first meal at Deer Valley, you'll understand why so many people decide to "ski the beach" in the afternoon. Try not to wake them as you put your skis on. Remember, if they're lounging in the sun they won't be in front of you at the lift.

The brass Kleenex holders strategically placed for your convenience as you get ready to get on the chair lift are only one advantage. Another is that the staff has time for you. You'll find friendly, smiling ski patrol in red suits at the top of each chair ready to point you where you want to go or to answer any questions about the area. At Deer Valley you won't find the ski patrol keeping to themselves, as they do at most resort areas. Not only do they make a point of skiing with you, they also make a point of riding the chairs with you. It's all part of the Deer Valley difference.

Park West

(Full day, adult lift ticket: $24.) A short ride out of Park City on the free shuttle, Park West is a great area that has not yet come into its own with the stiff area competition. Park West as a good advanced skiing area is deceiving from the road, from which you can see only about 10 percent of their runs, and the very easiest ones at that. What escapes the eye of the highway traveler heading toward Park City is Park West's four ridges. After a new snowfall, you can cut untracked powder here even later in the day.

While Park West has many gentle runs where you can get your ski legs, it also has a number that are very challenging for the more advanced skier. It's a popular place with the locals, and a great place to go if you want to avoid the crowds.

Interconnect

In addition to the individual areas around Park City, thanks to the foresight and creative planning of area ski enthusiasts, Utah has an incredible interconnect ski system. Depending on the day of the week, you can ski between four or five areas. The trips are run on alternate days. You will either ski from Park City to Solitude, Brighton, Alta, and end at Snowbird ($85) or you'll start at Snowbird then ski to Alta, Brighton, and Solitude ($70). The trip includes your guide, use of a Piep radio transmitter, a great barbecue chicken lunch, and transportation back to the starting point. This is a unique way to safely experience the adventure of backcountry skiing the way few people have the opportunity to do.

An intermediate skier in good physical condition can make the trip comfortably. I found stamina was more important than style. I had never skied the out-of-bounds areas and I had had the opportunity to ski very little powder prior to this trip. By the end of the day I was actually beginning to feel rather comfortable skiing the untracked knee-deep powder bowls, although I still wasn't leaving the perfectly sculptured tracks many of my companions left behind them on the slopes.

It was an inspiring experience. The group was out to have a great time and we all did. We traversed through some thick backcountry woods to find the deep, untracked powder bowls our guides knew so well. We even surprised a coyote who didn't expect our company. Our guides seemed to have the same love of the backcountry I expect the Wasatch Walkers had and they had special names for each part of the landscape, from The Backdoor (our exit trail from Park City Ski Area) to Grizzly Gulch (named after the Grizzly Mine) to The Highway to Heaven (the pass to Alta and Snowbird). They are a unique, very skillful, and dedicated group of modern-day Wasatch Walkers. The spirit, thank God, lives on.

Hot Air Ballooning

For $85 you can spend one to one and a half hours up in the blue sky looking out over the mountains you skied earlier in the week. From the slopes on a clear day, you'll usually see four or five brightly colored balloons soaring through the valley below.

Cross-Country Skiing

White Pine Touring on Main Street is the cross-country skiing headquarters of Park City. They offer half-day trips ($22), full-day trips ($35), and overnight trips ($60/night). For $70 you can get two lessons, a half-day tour, and one all-day tour. Equipment rental is $8 for a full day. They also rent snowshoes ($7.50).

Massage

At *Vie* on Main Street you can get a soothing, relaxing massage at the end of a hard day on the slopes. Be sure to book early (649-6363). This is a popular way to relax tense muscles.

Egyptian Theatre

This restored theater on Main Street has a new play every three months. I saw *The Pump Boys & Dinettes*, a musical comedy. It was a hit. Shows are usually performed only on Thursday, Friday, and Saturday nights at 8:00 P.M. ($7). Call and reserve a seat before show time. You can then pick up your ticket at the door.

Gamblers Tour

For $12 you can take the Gamblers Tour to the state line and Silver Smith casinos in nearby Wendover, Nevada. The trip includes transportation, a prime-rib dinner, four $1 keno tickets, two free drinks, a chance for a Hawaiian vacation, and $10 in cash back. The tour departs every Thursday at 5:00 P.M. and returns at 2:00 A.M. Call (801) 649-DICE (3423) for reservations.

There's something for everyone at one of the area ski resorts. The license plates don't lie—Utah really does have "The Greatest Snow on Earth."

YELLOWSTONE IN WINTER

▸──▸

GENERAL AMBIANCE ★ ★ ★
SOCIAL CLIMATE ★ ★
ACTIVITIES ★ ★ ★

───────────────────────

FOR TOUR ARRANGEMENTS CONTACT:
TW Services
Yellowstone National Park
Wyoming, CO 82190-0165
(307) 344-7311

Or *contact your travel agent*

▸──▸

Many are awed by the beauty of Yellowstone National Park during the summer months, but few see the enchanting solitude of Yellowstone covered in a sparkling blanket of snow. I have made many summer trips to Yellowstone. The first time was as an inquisitive small child on a family summer camping trip. On each of many later visits I found yet another area which rekindled that childhood sense of awe and amazement. It wasn't until I made my first winter visit, however, that I truly experienced the solitary beauty that is Yellowstone.

General Ambiance

When I arrived at Mammoth Hot Springs, the northernmost entrance of Yellowstone, I felt as though I had emerged into another world on another planet. This wasn't winter as I knew it. Here the river ran warm. There were ponds of boiling water with moss growing next to them beside fields of deep snow. The thermal vents were even more spectacular when their warm moisture hit the cold winter air. The nearby trees, shrouded in a heavy blanket of ice, had assumed unusual shapes, like ghosts moving across the landscape under the cover of

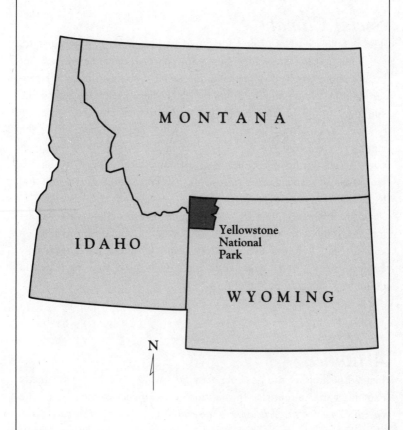

mist. This interaction of extreme hot and cold is one of the unique features of Yellowstone in the winter, creating many spectacular effects.

Social Climate

The people who work here, identified by first name and home state, are here because they love being in Yellowstone. They know her beauty and enjoy her winter solitude. Those who visit during the winter months are a unique group as well. Many prefer to escape the summer throngs of families who make the animals shy.

While Yellowstone is primarily a family vacation spot during the summer, you'll find few kids here during the winter. What makes it even better during the winter is that winter visitors seem to have a real sense of respect for nature—and the time to stop and watch and listen.

Group activities make it easy to meet other people with similar interests and with whom you may decide to spend some time on another day. I found everyone open and friendly, and I especially enjoyed meeting folks who live within a day's drive from the park and come to Yellowstone frequently.

Activities

Instead of limiting the possible activities, winter, I found, has greatly expanded the potentials. In addition to the usual excursions to the *Grand Canyon of the Yellowstone*, the *Upper* and *Lower Yellowstone Falls*, and the various geyser basins and hot springs, winter brings with it the potential for cross-country skiing, snowmobiling, and even winter camping.

Best of all, at the end of a rigorous day of exhausting and exhilarating activity, you can relax in the privacy of an enclosed outdoor hot tub. There are eight available to rent at $10 an hour. Each is enclosed by a high fence behind a small cabin with towels and a bathroom with shower for your convenience. Located under the trees and stars, it's a great place to reflect on your day and to unwind while you watch the snowflakes evaporate in the steam, or melt on your brow.

Cross-Country Skiing

There are nearly 25 miles of cross-country ski trails in the Mammoth area and another 70 miles in the *Old Faithful* area. These trails are groomed and well marked. In addition, there are more than 1,000 miles of ungroomed backcountry trails in the park, allowing skiers to easily get away from the crowds to enjoy the beauty and uninterrupted solitude of Yellowstone.

Some trails are more difficult than others. You'll find a variety from which to choose. If you prefer, you can often avoid the most difficult sections by skiing part way in and then returning to the same trailhead.

The most beautiful cross-country trail I've ever skied was in Yellowstone. I skied past rolling, snow-covered hills with bison and elk grazing. I even skied past a coyote, who quickly disappeared into the mist of a thermal area.

You'll find the staff at the Visitor Center across from Mammoth Lodge or at the ski shop next to the lodge entrance happy to provide you with current information on ski trail snow conditions and weather. Stop and discuss your trip with them.

At the ski shop, you can get your skis hot waxed for the current snow conditions for only $5. They do an excellent job and I strongly recommend you take advantage of this service. With the proper wax you'll have a much better time skiing.

If you didn't bring your own equipment, you can rent skis, boots, and poles for $12 for a full day. For $8 you can rent your equipment for half a day. If you're new to the sport, this is a great time and place to learn. A two-hour group lesson will cost $14, a private lesson $20.

If you haven't met someone to ski with, a good way to get to know your fellow travelers is to join a guided ski trip for a half day ($17.50) or a full day ($35). In addition, every other day the park rangers offer a free three- or four-hour guided ski tour. This is a great way not only to see the area, but to learn about the park and the environment. They'll provide you with a wealth of fascinating scientific information about the formation of different types of ice crystals while you catch your breath at short rest stops.

Snowmobiling

You can bring your own snowmobile or you can rent one. For $65 a day, plus $12 for insurance and $12 for a complete snowmobile suit, helmet, and boots, you can enjoy a day you will long remember. I strongly suggest you rent the proper equipment if you didn't bring your own. I for one don't like to be cold, and I wasn't. The heaters, hand warmers, and snowmobile suit kept me warm and toasty all day. A van leaves the entrance of Mammoth Lodge whenever there is someone ready to go to the snowmobile hut just above Mammoth Hot Springs. It will take two or three days if you want to see the whole park on snowmobile. The supply of snowmobiles is somewhat limited, so make a reservation when you book your trip with TW Services. Don't miss at least one day's ride. While you frequently have the trail all to yourself, if you stop long enough someone else will pass by, so safety is not a problem.

There's plenty of room for everyone in Yellowstone. Except for the northern road into Mammoth Hot Springs and the road from Mammoth to Cooke City, the park roads are not plowed. Instead, they are groomed for snowmobiles. You'll find a number of warming huts open with bathroom facilities and some even have hot food. The *Yellowstone Winter Guide,* available when you enter the park, at the Visitors Center, and from the Ranger Station will provide you with a road map that has the facilities well marked for your convenience.

You must stay on the groomed routes. The summer automobile speed regulations apply to snowmobiles during the winter—45 mph is the maximum speed limit. I was told that the rangers use radar to identify speeders and write tickets, but I didn't see any doing so. Most people respect the regulations.

Snowmobiling is probably the best way to really see the park. Even if you've never ridden before, you'll catch on fast. After 2 or 3 miles of very slow driving, you'll get a feel for the machine. By the end of your first 5 miles, you'll likely fall in love with the sense of freedom and independence.

As with the cross-country experience, you'll find the animals are used to snowmobiles. You'll pass bison grazing not 10 feet from the road. You can pass by or stop in front of them without a problem, but as soon as you get off your machine and start to walk toward them they'll likely get nervous and move away, something you want to avoid provoking.

Ice Skating

There's an outdoor ice rink that is lighted at night. Even if you don't skate, it's a great place to relax in the evening and watch those who do.

Snowcoach Rides

If you don't feel comfortable with the snowmobiles, you might want to try a snowcoach ride. For $42 to $52 you can ride round-trip from Mammoth to the Canyon or to Old Faithful. Originally built to transport the Swedish army, these vehicles are reliable (they can go through 20 feet of fresh powder), but they are also very slow. The trip from Mammoth Lodge to Old Faithful may take up to five hours one way. You'll make frequent stops to take pictures, use the rest room, or for hot coffee, which is nice. They also have large side windows to watch the scenery.

While they are a nice alternative for the less adventurous, they are slow and bumpy and they do not allow the independence that a snowmobile does. However, if you decide to stay at the Old Faithful Snow Lodge they are the best means of transportation in and out with your luggage.

Sleigh Rides

For $2.85 you can ride a horse-drawn sleigh or wagon (depending upon the snow conditions). The half-hour ride leaving the entrance of Mammoth Lodge will take you through old Fort Yellowstone, which was built between 1886 and 1916 when the army was in residence. When the National Park Service was formed in 1916, the army left and NPS took over maintenance of the park. The driver will provide you with a personal as well as historical view of the area.

Photography

Yellowstone is a photographer's paradise, especially during the winter months. Even an amateur can go home with spectacular shots that will make great Christmas cards next year. But photography in the snow can be a little tricky. You have to familiarize yourself with your camera and what it does under snow conditions *before* you come. Be sure to bring plenty of film. I had a large bull elk pose untiringly as I shot picture after picture and the same was true of the bison and the whistling swans.

You'll likely find you get your best shots from the ski trail or while sitting on your snowmobile, because you won't disturb the animals.

Observing the Wildlife

Wildlife is abundant in Yellowstone. Bison, elk, and mule deer are often drawn to the geyser basins because of the warmth from the ground. On an especially cold night they may sleep near a warm thermal area. The snow-free areas also allow animals to forage for food without expending additional energy digging through deep snow. Seen through the mist, the wildlife of Yellowstone can be especially breathtaking.

While you'll probably not see bear (they hibernate during the winter), you can expect to see hundreds of elk, bison, an occasional moose, mule deer, bighorn sheep, and coyotes. In the northern part of the park you may see herds of the graceful and elegant pronghorn antelope grazing near the road.

The Yellowstone River is home to whistling swans during the winter. Once an endangered species (man coveted their thick down for comforters), they now appear safe from extinction. What a thrill to get close enough to these majestic birds to see the depth of their glistening down, as white as the snow. These aren't the only birds in Yellowstone during the winter. You'll also see a number of friendly gray jays, more commonly known as "camp robbers," and ravens.

Large mammals survive the long cold winters at Yellowstone on stored fat—that's what the big hump on the bison's back is—which is why causing them to move will cost them precious calories vital for their survival. If you get close enough to an animal that it looks at you, you are too close. It's not uncommon to see carcasses of starved animals toward the end of a winter. Food is often scarce and what is available is hidden deep beneath the snow. But winter kills are part of the natural balance of nature. The strong live, the weak die and provide food for the coyotes and ravens.

Enjoy the wildlife without disturbing them. You'll get great pictures and can view the next one from close-up, if not this one. I doubt you really want a close-up picture at the animal's expense anyway.

Snowshoeing

If you want to get off the trails, this is the way to do it. You can rent snowshoes at the ski shop for $7 for a half day and $10 for a full day. You'll find them an asset for a day of wildlife photography.

Downhill Skiing

That's right, downhill skiing. For just $17.10 round-trip, you can leave West Yellowstone at 6:20 A.M. and be at Big Sky ski area by 7:45 A.M., with time for breakfast before the lifts open. You can then ski until 3:30 P.M., when you'll catch the bus back to West Yellowstone, arriving there at 5:00 P.M.

Ranger-Scheduled Activities

At the front desk of the hotel and at the Visitor Center you'll find a sheet listing the weekly ranger-led activities. There is usually one day activity and one evening activity. Don't miss them. They are well prepared, interesting, and free of charge. Typical activities include nature walks, cross-country ski tours, movies, and an evening lecture that is part story and part factual information.

Preparing for Your Trip to Yellowstone

Rates

Special packages for two nights ($99) or six nights ($198), which include lodging, some meals, and selected activities, are available through TW Services. Call (307) 344-7311 for information on available packages.

When to Go

The winter season begins in mid-December and runs through the first weekend in March. The weather is unpredictable and can change with little notice. West Yellowstone has the reputation for being the coldest spot in the U.S. about every other day throughout the winter. That's partly due to the elevation—Old Faithful is at an elevation of 7,370 feet—and the latitude—Yellowstone is located at about 45 degrees, halfway between the north pole and the equator. I found the Mammoth Lodge area to be the consistently warmer area because of its lower elevation. It's cold at night, which is when the records are set, and much warmer during the day when the sun is up. Nights can be below zero and the daytime temperature can reach a balmy 10 to 20 degrees Fahrenheit. I for one do not like to be cold; having grown up in Seattle, I often find the winters in Minnesota almost unbearable. However, dressed properly for the weather, 10 to 20 degrees do indeed seem balmy, even to me.

What to Take

Everyone at Yellowstone dresses informally, even for dinner, so leave your dresses and high heels at home. A nice sweater and slacks or jeans will be fine at night.

Good, warm winter clothing that you can put on and take off in layers is what you will need. Because it can get windy, you'll want a tight nylon or Gore-tex outer layer to break the wind. Check with your outdoor equipment stores. Patagonia has an excellent selection of clothing that will keep you warm when you need it, but will also breathe and prevent overheating and sweating.

You should take long underwear, gloves, a hat, and boots with a thick sole to keep your feet away from the ice and snow. You should also take a scarf or mask to protect your chin, cheeks, and nose from the wind. While it's not necessary, you may want to bring a bathing suit to wear in the hot tub.

I'd suggest taking your ice skates and cross-country ski equipment along. Don't forget your camera and plenty of film.

When the sun comes out and reflects off the snow, the glare can get very bright. You'll need a good pair of protective sunglasses (see p. 44).

Where to Stay in Yellowstone

Call TW Services (307) 344-7311 to book either of the two lodge facilities.

Mammoth Hot Springs Lodge (one or two persons with bath $43.50, one or two persons without bath $28). This is the only visitor lodging accessible by automobile during the winter season. An old stately vintage hotel, it has large, comfortable rooms. The bathrooms include the old-fashioned, deep, claw-foot bathtubs, a pleasant spot to relax after an active day. Because of the age of the hotel, there are no showers in the rooms, but there are clean and convenient showers on each floor. An excellent restaurant facility is located next to the lodge.

The large lobby has an interesting gift shop and a desk run by TW Services. It's here that you should go for information and reservations for all of your activities, from hot tub rental to snowmobiling and cross-country skiing.

Old Faithful Snow Lodge (one or two persons with bath $43, one or two persons without bath $28). Don't confuse this with the original stately Old Faithful Inn. While the snow lodge is in the same general area near Old Faithful Geyser, it is a much smaller and newer building. The lobby's wood-burning stove makes a warm welcome home from a day of activities. The same activities are available from this lodge as from Mammoth Hot Springs Lodge. An attractive dining room, offering the same menu as at Mammoth, is attached. You'll need to take a snowcoach to get here and you'll be restricted to two pieces of luggage plus your cross-country ski equipment.

Getting There

The nearest airport to Yellowstone Park is at Bozeman, Montana. Bus service is available from Bozeman to Mammoth Hot Springs Lodge through TW Services. Check with them when you book your room. The three-hour bus trip will cost $25.65 round-trip. There are three departures in each direction daily.

Along the Way to Yellowstone

If you have come by car or meet someone with a car, I strongly recommend having lunch or dinner at *The Sport* in Livingston, one hour north of Mammoth Hot Springs on Highway 89. Livingston is a delightful old western town. The Sport, with red awnings out front, is located on Old Main Street. It was originally a bar and women weren't even allowed inside until the early 1940s. Sheepherders used to entrust the owner with their summer earnings; he would then dole them out from a cigar box during the following winter, and he had a reputation for keeping each to his predetermined weekly limit.

The Sport fell into decay during the seventies, but since 1982 it has been owned and run by Suzanne Schneider, a single woman of great ability and drive. Most of the paraphernalia is from the original bar and the atmosphere is early 1900s. The food is some of the best home cooking you'll find anywhere. The half-pound Make Your Own Burgers ($2.50) are thick and juicy, and the barbecued chicken and ribs ($5.50 to $6.95) are excellent and the servings large. The old-fashioned malts are also thick and large. Save room for dessert. Suzanne's apple pie ($1.50), her grandmother's recipe, is the very best.

When she purchased the restaurant, one of Suzanne's goals was to make it a place where women would feel comfortable coming for dinner alone. While the white linen and flowered tablecloths certainly help with the overall effect, I expect it's Suzanne's charm and warmth, coupled with great inexpensive food, that brings people back.

Whether you go to Yellowstone to enjoy the beauty of the geysers and the wildlife in its natural habitat and to relax in the solitude of winter, or if you come to exert yourself and enjoy the invigoration of outdoor winter activities, I'm certain you'll find a winter trip to Yellowstone will far surpass your expectations. I did. While the golden-hued cliffs of the Grand Canyon of the Yellowstone are spectacular any time of year, they are truly breathtaking with a light coating of glistening snow. The world-famous Old Faithful Geyser and the mineral-laden Mammoth Hot Springs all take on a fresh look during the winter months. Don't miss the absolute wonder of Yellowstone in winter.

SKI NEW ZEALAND

▶ ── ▶

GENERAL AMBIANCE	★ ★ ★
SOCIAL CLIMATE	★ ★ ★
ACTIVITIES	★ ★

FOR TOUR ARRANGEMENTS CONTACT:
Mount Cook Line
Private Bag, Christchurch,
New Zealand
(800) 468-2665

Or *contact your Travel Agent*

▶ ── ▶

*D*ownhill skiing is my great passion. As a poor college student, I once missed a season of skiing because the love of my life didn't ski. He convinced me to spend all my available excess cash on a winter trip south. I vowed never again to get seriously involved with a man who did not ski or who wouldn't at least understand that that's what I would be doing whenever possible, with or without him.

I used to think that skiing was only a winter sport. Once out of graduate school, with a little more extra cash, I found that there's usually somewhere in the world the avid skier can ski any month of the year. Our summer is ski season in New Zealand. July and August are their prime ski months. What a great time to head south to winter and ski.

General Ambiance

In some respects, ski areas throughout the world are all alike. The moment you near the base area you can feel the excitement and anticipation in the air. The ski areas in New Zealand are no exception. The brightly colored ski fashions and freshly tanned faces have a fes-

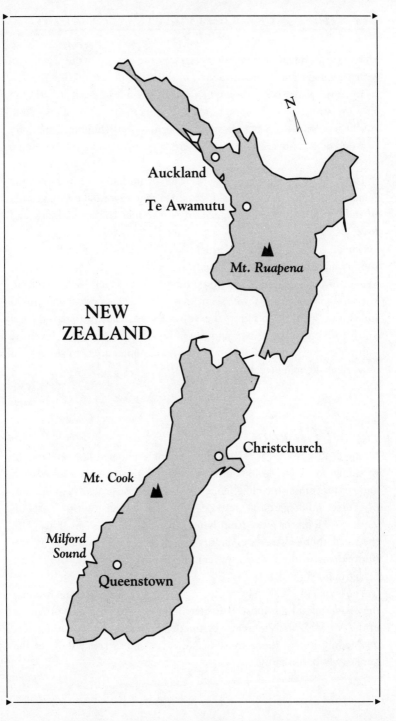

tive appeal. Regardless of their years, somehow everyone seems so much younger and more attractive in this kind of setting.

In some of the New Zealand ski areas, it's not unusual to wake up in warm spring weather conditions, then, in a matter of minutes, climb 8,000 feet into deep winter snow. You may find sublime light fluffy powder or a hard crust. As anywhere, you take what the mountain gives you.

In other ways, skiing in New Zealand is nothing like skiing at the major, established Colorado ski areas. It's much more like skiing some of the less well known European areas, the hills the locals know and love.

There are seldom any overnight accommodations actually on the mountain, and all mountain facilities are primitive by our standards. While you can certainly get something to eat, Deer Valley in Utah with its gourmet meals will seem every bit of its more than 10,000 miles away. The roads into the ski areas are usually unpaved, and you'll ride on more T-bars and poma lifts than chair lifts. However, you'll also find few lift lines and lots of wide open areas to ski as well as very challenging terrain.

Social Climate

Skiing is always a great way to meet people—either riding up a ski lift or skiing down the mountain. New Zealand also attracts a lot of men and some women traveling alone from nearby Australia, Hawaii, and, of course, other parts of New Zealand. You'll meet a lot of locals on vacation. Home or away from home, New Zealanders—or "kiwi's," as they call themselves—are, in my experience, only equalled by the Bermudians in their warm, welcoming nature. It must be the British background they share.

You'll quickly feel right at home in New Zealand. It's no wonder they have one of the most extensive home-stay or farm-stay programs in the world. This is a great way to spend a night or two as the guest in a family home. Since most of New Zealand is rural, most of the homes will be on farms.

Activities

While the focus of activity is, of course, downhill skiing, it would seem foolish to travel so many miles and not see more of what New Zealand has to offer. Without going too far astray from the ski centers on the South Island, you can take a boat on Milford Sound and drive through the sheep ranches. While New Zealand has only 3 million people, it has 70 million sheep. The rolling gold and emerald hills of the sheep ranches rise to the snow-covered mountain peaks during their winter months.

On the North Island, you'll want to visit the geyser areas around Rotorua. It's a bit like Yellowstone. Don't miss a farm stay here while in transit to or from skiing.

Preparing for Your Trip to New Zealand

Documents

You will need a valid passport but not a visa to enter New Zealand.

When to Go

While during a good year you may be able to ski by mid June, to play it safe don't plan to go skiing before early July. July and August are equivalent to January and February in Colorado. You can count on lots of good snow. September can be good, too, but it's more like late March in Colorado.

What to Take

You'll need your winter ski clothes, of course, and lots of sunscreen to protect your face from the burning rays of the sun. You'll also want goggles and a good pair of polarized sunglasses to protect your eyes.

After skiing, you'll need much lighter clothing; it will often be more like spring weather down in the valley. Evening dress is primarily casual. You might want one nice outfit for the disco and to wear when in town. You will see a lot of fur jackets and coats; however, unlike at Vail, they don't seem mandatory.

Money

US$1 is worth NZ$1.61 (at the time of publication). You'll get your best rate of exchange at a trading bank even though you pay a small fee for the transaction. The fee does not vary with the amount of money exchanged. As in most countries, you'll get a little better rate for traveler's checks than cash.

Tipping

Like Australia, New Zealand has a *no tipping* rule. You'll find no one will refuse money when offered, although I never felt as though someone had their hand out for a tip, as is so common in the U.S. New Zealanders told me repeatedly that they never tip and they wished foreigners wouldn't. Unfortunately, as tourism increases, people working in the high tourist impact areas are already beginning to like the idea of tips. Not needing to tip really reduces the cost of a meal or cab by 15 percent to 20 percent, and that's a big difference. If you are at a big, tourist-oriented hotel and you get exceptional service, you may want to consider leaving a tip of 10 percent to 15 percent, but only under these circumstances would I recommend doing so.

Language

English is the language spoken throughout New Zealand.

Getting There

Getting to New Zealand is really much easier than you might expect, given the distance. If you have the time, I suggest flying Qantas to Sydney, spending a few days there sightseeing, and then going on to Christchurch. Qantas does everything possible to make this a pleasant, relaxing flight. Most important, they have scheduled their in-flight activities to afford you optimal rest time to ensure you arrive ready to enjoy your stay. (For Qantas reservations, call 800-227-4500.)

If your time is more limited, Air New Zealand offers flights direct from Los Angeles to Auckland, where you can transfer to a Mount Cook Airlines flight to Christchurch. They, too, have an efficient operation with on-time arrivals and departures, efficient baggage handling, and courteous in-flight service. (For Air New Zealand reservations, call 800-262-1234; for Mount Cook Airlines, call 800-468-2665.)

Your Departure

There is a NZ$2 departure tax payable when you leave New Zealand.

Getting Around

While you can fly to all of the ski areas on Mount Cook Airlines, you'll miss the beauty of the landscape. I would suggest you rent a car in Christchurch on the South Island and drive first to Mount Cook and then to Queenstown. You can leave your car in Queenstown and take a Mount Cook Airlines flight to Rotorua on the North Island. I'd suggest renting a car again here for your drive to Mount Ruapehu, Te Anau, and Auckland.

National Car Rental is owned by Newmans in New Zealand and is the country's largest travel-oriented company; they seem to be everywhere. Not only did they have the lowest rates, but they brought my car to my hotel at the exact time I requested. I then had the option of dropping the car at the airport or leaving the keys with the front desk for them to pick it up at my hotel when I was done with it.

One day I discovered a flat tire as I stopped for lunch at an out-of-the-way restaurant near Christchurch. I called Newmans; by the time I finished lunch, the car had a new tire. I was ready to go without delay.

Treasures to Purchase

Since you'll drive past one sheep ranch after another, you shouldn't be surprised that woolen goods fill many stores. You'll find beautiful hand-knit sweaters in rich earth tones and bright festive colors and ski sweaters with kangaroos and koala bears on skis. You can purchase sheepskin rugs in a variety of shapes, grades, and sizes. They are graded by "stars"—three stars will usually be the lowest grade, six stars the highest. The better-quality skins will have thicker wool.

You'll also find lamb's wool and kangaroo fur slippers, vests, and purses. I was assured that the species of kangaroo used for these items is as plentiful as deer are in the U.S.

New Zealand Green, a local jade, is *the* jewelry to purchase. You'll find a wide selection of pendants, earrings, rings, and lapel pins from NZ$20 and up. You'll also find black opals imported from Australia and priced at only a little more than you'd pay there.

New Zealand has an excess opossum population. As a result, opossum coats are available in most fine leather stores. The opossum fur here is longer and softer than any I've seen, and the coats and jackets look very elegant. A hip-length jacket will cost NZ$1,000 to NZ$1,500. Longer coats are, of course, more expensive.

While I'm not a stuffed animal fan, the cats made from long white fluffy lamb's wool were irresistible (NZ$55 to NZ$75). They also sold coat hangers made from wool skin (NZ$8).

Ski Packages

Mount Cook Airlines of New Zealand has put together a number of two- to seven-day ski packages for the various New Zealand ski areas. These are not escorted or group tours. You travel on your own. They typically include lodging, lift tickets, and bus transportation to the ski area. In addition, when you purchase one of these packages you are eligible for generous discounts on sightseeing trips, at restaurants, and even air transportation to New Zealand on Air New Zealand.

The packages vary considerably according to the accommodations selected, the number of days you want to stay, and if you want to include air transportation between areas instead of driving. While they often include the better accommodations, like most packages, simpler ones are also included for a lower price.

This section reviews the primary ski areas and the better accommodations at each area. After reading it, you should write to Mount Cook Airlines for their latest "New Zealand Ski Holidays" brochure. Review what they have to offer. You may decide to include one or two of their packages and do the rest on your own. In most instances, the package prices offered are much lower than you could get by booking on your own. This is especially true when you consider the savings on the additional sightseeing you will want to include on your trip.

Where to Stay in New Zealand

The Tourist Hotel Corporation of New Zealand (THC) is the only hotel chain in the country with accommodations in all the major cities and resort areas. You'll find them at secluded beaches and bustling city centers. By contacting their main office—Private Bag, Wellington, New Zealand; (800) 421-0536—you can make all your reservations at once. Their facilities are also included in the Mount Cook Airlines ski packages.

The THC facilities are consistently of very good to outstanding quality with friendly, efficient staffs. Some of their hotels—for example, the Chateau at Mount Ruapehu—are among the finest in the world. If you are in doubt about where to stay, they are always a good choice. If you decide you want to change your itinerary en route, the staff at one hotel will gladly contact all of the others to make the necessary changes for you.

YOUR SKI ADVENTURE

Your suggested itinerary begins in Christchurch, the South Island's largest city. From there you'll drive to Mount Cook and on to Queenstown and Milford Sound prior to flying to the North Island. You'll land in Rotorua and pick up another rental car. After seeing the thermal areas, you'll drive through the Lake Taupo area to Mount Ruapehu for more skiing. You then go farther north for a farm stay prior to your flight home from Auckland.

Christchurch

With a population of more than 300,000, Christchurch is a bustling community, and the most English city you will find outside of England.

What to See in Christchurch

The *Avon River,* with willow trees along its banks, meanders through the town center, suburbs, and the enchanting *Hagley Park.* In the town square are the neo-Gothic spires of the *Cathedral,* which dominates the old part of the town. The *Botanical Gardens* nearby are a must. You can find roses still blooming in the rose garden when the ski season begins. The *McDougall Art Gallery* is located on the edge of the gardens and the *Canterbury Museum* is across the street. The museum has interesting displays on the Maori culture as well as an excellent Antarctic wing.

The *Information Center* on the corner of Worchester Street and Oxford Terrace (across from Noah's Hotel) will provide you with a detailed map for a ninety-minute walking tour.

Colombo, Cashel, and *High* streets are where you'll find the up-to-date shops and boutiques. They are open until 9:00 P.M. on Friday. *Ballantynes,* on Cashel Street, is the biggest department store.

The *Arts Center,* in the old University of Canterbury buildings (Rollenston and Worchester streets), also sells a nice selection of local crafts, including handmade pottery, rugs, and sweaters; on Saturdays you can find much more at their outdoor crafts fair. This is the largest cultural and arts center in New Zealand. You can watch ballet and theater here as well as artisans weaving, blowing glass, and making rugs.

Where to Eat in Christchurch

You'll find the food throughout New Zealand is excellent, and make sure you don't miss "Devonshire Tea," that's coffee and tea with scones (a biscuit topped with jam and lots of rich whipped cream). It's a great midmorning snack, especially welcome if you've skipped breakfast.

Most restaurants in New Zealand, even the nice ones, are BYO (bring your own liquor). Soft drinks, coffee, and tea are usually your beverage choices. One big advantage to this is that it substantially reduces the cost of dining out.

The Sign of the Takahe, Dyers Pass Road. This restaurant is not well marked, but it's hard to miss. It looks like a small stone castle and sits on a corner on the left side as you go up the pass in a residential area. Although construction on the building began in 1919, the restaurant did not open until 1949. It's well worth the drive just to see the medieval-style castle with its high carved beams and ceilings, carved stone columns, and leaded stained-glass windows overlooking town. If you don't want a large meal, come for Devonshire tea, noon to 2:00 P.M. (NZ$4.50). Lunch is an elaborate buffet (NZ$15.50) with everything including "Pavlova"—a light meringue topped with whipped cream and fruit—a must for dessert in New Zealand. Dinner is à la carte and will run around NZ$40 (7:00 to 9:00 P.M.), BYO.

Dux de Lux, Arts Center. A gourmet vegetarian cafeteria-style restaurant located in the old university buildings, it offers soup (NZ$3), salad (NZ$4), and sandwiches (NZ$4); BYO.

Garden Restaurant, Botanical Gardens. From noon to 2:00 P.M. you can get a buffet lunch here (NZ$8.80), BYO. It's simple but more than adequate.

Leinster Road, 158 Leinster Road. Located just off Papanui Road, this restaurant is in a lovely restored Edwardian home. The cuisine is continental and you can watch the fire in the fireplace while you eat by candlelight. I found it a comfortable place to dine alone. Dinner will run about NZ$40, BYO.

Grimsby's, corner of Kilmore and Montreal streets. Located in one of Christchurch's most historic buildings, a former school built in 1874. The high ceilings, exposed stone walls, and elaborate frieze work in the corners give this building the feel of a castle. The red wood ceiling is native New Zealand kauri. Ask to sit by the fire when you make your reservations; it's soothing and warm. A five-course meal will run NZ$60.

Spratts, 182 Oxford Terrace. An informal seafood restaurant with checkered tablecloths and wood spindle chairs. It's located next to Noah's Hotel in downtown. A complete meal will run you from NZ$30 to NZ$45.

Chancery Tavern, 98 Gloucester Street. Located upstairs, this cafeteria-style restaurant has good, inexpensive food. Entrées will run from NZ$3 to NZ$10.

Shakespeare, 184B Papanui Road. This gourmet restaurant, located in an elegant old English–style home—you have to go through an iron gate to find this white building—is an excellent choice. You can even get Yorkshire pudding (NZ$10.50). This is an especially good place to go with a friend.

Where to Stay in Christchurch

Cotswold Inn, 88-90 Papanui Road (single NZ$129, double NZ$140). All rooms in this attractive English Tudor–style inn are spacious, each offering a bedroom, living room, dining room, and private bath. It has a pleasant cottage appeal with rough beams, down comforters, and ruffled bedskirts. The furniture is all antique reproductions. They have two excellent restaurants. *Crofters* upstairs is more informal and comfortable for dining alone. You can even order the same chocolate truffle cake as served at *Tudors* downstairs, but at half the price.

Eliza's Manor House, 82 Bealey Avenue (single or double, shared bath NZ$45; single or double, private bath NZ$90). A charming 1860 mansion restored and converted into an antique-filled bed and breakfast with ten guest rooms. Brass beds and cozy quilts retain the old-world charm you'd expect to find in Christchurch. The heavy, carved wood staircase and leaded glass windows make this a wonderful place to return to at night. It's located on the edge of town but a comfortable walk to most sites.

Noah's Hotel, corner of Oxford Terrace and Worchester Street (single NZ$156, double NZ$180). A new, large, modern hotel well located near the town square. Most rooms have recently been redecorated. Charles and Di stayed in their royal suite, which has a marble bath, in 1983—it goes for NZ$800 a night. Because this hotel attracts local businessmen, the bar is one of the best spots to stop for a drink at night. The hotel overlooks the Avon River, so the views from the rooms are excellent.

Highway Lodge, 121 Papanui Road (single NZ$36, double NZ$50, private bath NZ$55). This lovely 1907 Tudor-style home is a leisurely twenty-minute walk from the center of town, on a main bus route. Special attention has been given to acquiring unique antique beds; one even has a lace canopy. The shared lounge has a crystal chandelier and lace pillows on the furniture.

Devon Travel Hotel, 69 Armagh Street (single NZ$30, double NZ$50). This bed and breakfast is located just a couple of blocks from the center of town. The location and price are ideal. While the rooms are clean and a room with a private bath is available, they provide only the essentials. No frills and no antiques, just good value.

Mount Hutt Ski Field

Located one hour from Christchurch, this area is usually the first ski field to open each year. An all-day ski ticket is NZ$32. They have two T-bars, one triple chair, and two platter (poma) lifts to take you up. While they have gentle slopes, they also have some of the steepest runs you'll find anywhere. After you've recovered from jet lag and have seen the town, this is a great place for a day of skiing.

Christchurch to Mount Cook

It's a beautiful 3½-to-4-hour drive from Christchurch to the Hermitage Hotel at Mount Cook. Give yourself plenty of time—remember, even though it's summer back home with long daylight hours, it's winter here and gets dark by around 5:00 P.M. Take Highway 1 out of Christchurch past the rolling emerald hills of the sheep ranches. You'll see the mountains in the distance. Go through Ashburton to snowcapped Winchester, where you should turn onto Highway 79 to Geraldine. At Fairlie, you'll turn onto Highway 8, which winds up Burkes Pass toward Twizel.

The roads are paved, well maintained, and the scenery more and more spectacular as you go. You'll pass *Lake Tekapo* with a breathtaking view of Mount Cook beyond if it's a clear day. Turn right just before Twizel and follow the signs to Mount Cook on Highway 80. This scenic winding road will take you over four one-way bridges between the base of the snowcapped foothills and *Lake Pukaki*. It's unlikely there'll be any snow on the ground even in the dead of winter until you're at the Hermitage Hotel.

Mount Cook

You should book your reservations ahead for Mount Cook's *Hermitage Hotel* (single NZ$160, double NZ$175). You book through Tourist Hotel Company (THC), Private Bag, Wellington, New Zealand, or your travel agent. This is *the* place to stay. It combines a spectacular view of Mount Cook, at 12,349 feet the highest peak in New Zealand, with excellent accommodations and great food. It's located "thousands of feet above worry level" at the base of the mountains that slope steeply down into the flat glacial valley. Both forbidding and appealing in their immensity, the mountains provide an overpowering sense of solitude as you watch them from your private balcony or as you walk on the many trails nearby.

Skiing Mount Cook

Skiing did not become popular at Mount Cook—or anywhere in the world for that matter—until the early 1920s. But the first skiers, real adventurers, were already here in 1893. They came on horseback and skied on the long wooden blades from a reaper. There weren't any ski lifts then and there still aren't any today. Mount Cook remains a ski adventure. A few things, though, have changed.

There are two primary ski areas at Mount Cook, the *Tasman Glacier* and the *Franz Joseph Glacier*. Today you can get to the Tasman Glacier on the Mount Cook Airlines fixed-wing ski plane. It's actually on skis and lands at the top of the glacier at 10,000 feet. You then get the thrill and excitement of skiing miles to the base (NZ$96). Best of all, you don't need to be an advanced skier. A good intermediate skier can handle the gentle, wide-open glacier terrain comfortably. Don't worry, you'll be with an alpine guide who'll make sure you're skiing the correct route past giant ice falls and crevasses. Mount Cook Airlines also offers sightseeing flights that stop on the Tasman Glacier, allowing you to play in the snow a little before flying you back down.

Your second option is heliskiing. If you haven't tried this before, New Zealand is a great place to do it. Not only is the scenery spectacular, but the price is lower than in most other parts of the world. The Helicopter Line will take you to the top of the Tasman Glacier, the Franz Joseph Glacier, or one of a number of favorite locations their alpine guides have found. Once again, they make sure you find long, spectacular—and safe—runs. The deep blue ice of the glacier will tower above you as you're guided through the ice flows. It's a controlled adventure. They will take you to places you wouldn't go on your own, but they will pick terrain that suits your level of ability. You need only be a good intermediate skier to meet the challenge of heliskiing at Mount Cook; however, advanced skiers will, of course, get the most out of a trip like this. Interestingly, the alpine guides told me that women intermediate skiers usually do better than men. They pay more attention to technique. Men, on the other hand, are usually more aggressive skiers.

A typical day would include a briefing on avalanche procedure and the use of the Pieps transmitter you will be issued. The alpine guides, who are fully qualified with three to five years of apprentice experience, then take you from summer weather at the lodge level to winter snow at the top—all in a matter of minutes. You may find 6 miles of untracked fluffy powder or you may find the top crusty. You make a 6-mile glacier run in the morning, then your party is met by your helicopter at a designated location and you're flown to another spot. Lunch is supplied at the top, before your first afternoon run, another 6 miles. Along the way you may have a chance to stop and explore an ice cave. You'll usually ski two runs in the afternoon for a total of around 10,000 vertical feet. That's a lot of skiing. By the end of the day you'll be exhausted, challenged, and anxious to do it again.

Sign up for heliskiing upon arrival at the alpine guides' hut near the Hermitage Hotel. A day of great skiing with lunch and a guide will cost NZ$340. These runs are open June to November, always depending on the weather. If the clouds are thick or the winds too high, the planes and helicopters, of course, won't fly.

Wanaka

From Mount Cook Hermitage Hotel, it's a two-and-a-half-hour drive on Highway 8, through Lindis Pass, then over Highway 8A to Highway 6 and Wanaka. There are two ski areas here, Trebel Cone and Cardrona. At the end of the ski season in September, when Coronet Peak in Queenstown is short on snow, these areas, because of their higher elevation, will still offer great skiing. You can get to them from Queenstown on the ski bus, but it will be a long ride. For NZ$66, you can get there by helicopter from Queenstown.

If you want to be more "out of the way," you can stay in Wanaka. While a small town, it's picturesque and there's certainly lots to do (although not as much as in Queenstown, of course). I'd suggest you stay at the *THC Wanaka* (single NZ$60 to NZ$90, double NZ$75 to NZ$105). The rooms have been attractively redecorated, the staff is friendly, and the food good. I'd also suggest you pay the extra charge for a room with a lakeside view. It's beautiful.

Cardrona Ski Field

Cardrona is primarily an intermediate ski area with a good number of runs for beginners and a few challenging runs for the advanced skier. You'll find two quad chair lifts, one double chair lift, and two beginner rope tows. A full-day lift ticket is NZ$34.

Because the area is located high in the mountains, it enjoys a long season, often far into October. This is a popular area late in the season for locals from Queenstown (only 35 miles away). If the snow is not good at the Queenstown areas, Mount Cook Airlines will provide transportation to Cardrona, about one and a half hours away.

Trebel Cone Ski Field

For NZ$30, your lift ticket will take you up the one chair lift, two T-bars, and one poma lift at Trebel Cone ski area. For NZ$44, you can take a helicopter to the summit at 2,100 feet. While much farther from Queenstown than Cardrona, this is the more challenging of the two Wanaka areas. It, too, is usually open far into October and has a number of advanced ski runs.

Mount Cook to Queenstown

If you continue along Highway 8 from Mount Cook until it intersects Highway 6, you'll soon reach Queenstown—the skiing mecca of the South Island. Once again, these roads are excellent and pleasant driving even in most winter weather conditions. You'll seldom encounter snow or ice on the roads.

Queenstown

Queenstown is the heart of skiing in New Zealand. You're within a half hour of Coronet Peak, the premier ski area of the country, and the newest area, The Remarkables. A little further away, but still accessible, are Cardrona and Trebel Cone.

Queenstown is located in the valley far below the ski facilities, and almost always below the snow line, on Lake Watatipu. The scenery here is spectacular at sunrise, as the first rays gently touch the mountain tips, and it's equally spectacular on the slopes looking back toward the lake and town. While the best action during the winter months, July through September, in my opinion, is on the slopes, you'll also find plenty going on in town. This is a real ski resort with all the excitement and nightlife you'd expect to find.

Après-ski Activities in Queenstown

If you're not totally exhausted from skiing, there's a fitness course along the water's edge you won't want to miss. It's a beautiful running trail, but the view of the lake and mountains is so breathtaking you may want to take more time and walk. You can walk back through the rose garden if you prefer, or stop and go ice skating at the rink.

Just after you exit the fitness trail near the new THC hotel, there's a pier with *Waterworld*, a below-water viewing place. It might not look like much from the outside, but it's well worth a visit. The bay here is known for its large trout. You'll see large rainbow and brown trout as well as eel and the darling "diving" ducks.

Don't miss a chance to get out on the lake during your Queenstown stay. It's much larger than you may realize. The T.S.S. *Earnslaw*, a 1912 vintage steamer, offers a number of cruises each day, including a dinner cruise. It originally carried sheep and provisions to remote sheep stations on the lake. Today it carries tourists. The visit to *Mount Nicholas Sheep Station* is especially scenic. This remote high country sheep station is the largest fully operational station on the lake. They also offer special après-ski cruises.

I usually like to take a day off midweek to rest my weary ski legs. In Queenstown, you may want to take a couple of days off to see the area around town.

One of these day trips should be to *Arrowtown*, about a twenty-minute drive up the valley. Go early enough to have Devonshire tea (NZ$3.50) at the *Stone House*, which you can't miss. You'll eat in the original living room of this 120-year-old house built of stones. You'll find many shops with excellent prices in this restored mining town. The former bank is now a museum.

Plan to see a show at the *Cattledrome* (9:15 A.M. and 2:00 P.M., NZ$4.80). It's on the way. You'll see the various breeds of cattle and learn a lot about the New Zealand farm industry; you can even milk a cow if you'd like.

Milford Sound is another area near Queenstown you should not miss. Created during the ice age, the fjords of Milford Sound provide an endless variety of scenic beauty. The easiest way to see the area is to take a Mount Cook Airlines flight to Milford Sound. Be sure to purchase the package that includes the boat ride on the sound (NZ$181). The flight over the mountains is as scenic as the boat cruise through the high cliffs of the fjords.

If the weather doesn't permit flying, you can drive to *Te Anau* in two and a half hours. If you have a couple of extra days, Te Anau is a good sightseeing base for the fjord area. The THC hotel there is a good place to spend the night (single or double NZ$176, villa NZ$220). It's just across the street from the boat launch that takes you to the *Glow Worm Caves*, another trip I highly recommend.

From Te Anau it's another two-and-a-half-hour drive to *Milford Sound* without any stops, something I do not recommend. Give yourself at least another hour so you have time to make a few stops and see the remarkable beauty of the countryside along the way. The ride on one of the "Red Boats" is NZ$20. You can purchase lunch on board (NZ$11 to NZ$20). Rain or shine, this ride is spectacular. An advantage of the rain is the spontaneous waterfalls you won't otherwise see.

When the wind is blowing up the mountain cliffs, you'll also see the water from these falls being blown back up.

If you have the time, you may want to go to *Doubtful Sound*, in the other direction from Te Anau. A less-known and less-traveled route, this is, however, equally spectacular with its mountains and water ways. Fjordland Travel offers daily trips (NZ$88). You'll be gone from 10:00 A.M. to 5:30 P.M.

Where to Eat in Queenstown

With more than fifty restaurants, Queenstown offers a wide dining selection. The BYO restaurants are usually the best value.

Sablis, 55B Arcade, Beach Street, 2nd floor. This unimposing French restaurant is where I had my best meal in New Zealand. Their daily specials and homemade ice cream are not to be missed. (Dinners NZ$15 to NZ$20).

Cobb & Co., Mountaineer Hotel. A popular après-ski stop; you can get a four-course meal here for NZ$12.25 and a light meal for NZ$6 to NZ$8. The subdued, dark wood and red velvet chairs give it that old barroom atmosphere.

Britannia, on the mall. A popular seafood restaurant with a wide selection and good food. This is the place to go if you'd like to join a group (just tell the hostess) and have a lot of fun as well as a good meal (NZ$7 to NZ$27; crayfish—that's lobster—NZ$45).

The Cow, Cow Lane. This is another favorite with the locals for spaghetti or pizza. Since there are only five tables in this old stone house, you'll be sitting with four other guests. If you don't meet someone yourself while standing around the cozy fire waiting to be seated, the hostess will find you a group to join (dinner NZ$6 to NZ$14); BYO.

Roaring Meg's, Shotover Street. Another excellent choice for homey atmosphere and good food, this cottage restaurant offers venison (NZ$20), salmon (NZ$21), and vegetarian meals (NZ$14); BYO.

Westy's on the mall. A popular après-ski stop with gourmet semi-vegetarian meals for under NZ$20.

Chico's, Eureka Inn. For a late-night dinner or drink around a cozy fire, this is it. You'll find locals and visiting skiers alike eating here; the food's great.

Skyline Restaurant, Top of Gondola. Take the gondola up the hill for the best view in town. You get dinner and the ride up as well as live entertainment and dancing at the top for NZ$30. The buffet is fine, but the view is better.

Where to Stay in Queenstown

Hulbert House, 68 Ballarat Street (single or double NZ$60 to NZ$120). A Victorian villa built in 1889, Hulbert House sits up on a hill overlooking Lake Watatipu and the town below. A short but steep two blocks down and you're in the heart of Queenstown and on the main shopping mall. Your host and the owner, Ed, will make sure that you feel right at home. He's gone out of his way to restore and maintain this home in its original grandeur. You'll even find some of the original furnishings. You can sip sherry with the other guests in the parlor in the evening, which is a good time to get tips from Ed on skiing—he was once a local ski instructor. A native of Queenstown, he knows all the best places to dine and will call ahead to see that you're well attended to, and seated with other guests if you prefer. While Hulbert House is not a listed option in the Mount Cook Airlines packages, even if you choose one of their tours, you should be able to stay here if you make a special point of asking.

Hyatt Kingsgate, near Adelaide Street and Frankton Road (single NZ$120, double NZ$145). A Swiss chaletlike building located just on the edge of town with a view over the lake. Free shuttle service is available to the center of town; you can walk it in fifteen minutes. The staff here is especially friendly and the outside Jacuzzi is a great place to meet your fellow skiers at the end of the day. If you stay here, tell the concierge, Eddie, you've come to collect the drink he owes me.

Travelodge, Beach Street (single or double NZ$175). Well situated just across from the piers near town, this modern hotel has all the conveniences and an excellent view of the lake and the Remarkables. I, however, found it lacking in warmth and the staff unfriendly.

Lakeland Regency, Lake Esplanade (single or double NZ$132). Also located on the lake, though farther from town, this is an attractive modern hotel with restaurants, bars, and a heated pool and sauna.

The Lofts, 61 Shotover Street (single NZ$150, double NZ$165). Attractively decorated in pinks and coral, this is a cheerful establishment. Located just off Main Street, it's in the center of the action. A sauna and laundry facilities are available. While there is no in-house restaurant, there are many excellent choices in town.

Queenstown THC (not open at the time of publication). Located on the edge of Lake Watatipu right in the center of town, this hotel has by far the best location. If its standards are of the traditional high THC quality, it will be a hard place to beat.

Goldfield's Motel and Breakfast Inn, 41 Frankton Road (single NZ$25 to NZ$55, double NZ$64). This is not a first-class hotel, especially the less expensive units, but if you're on a tight budget, it's clean, the staff especially friendly, and the location excellent. It also includes a full breakfast.

Coronet Peak

This is what you came for—powder snow, sunshine, unobstructed slopes, modern hillside facilities, and a remarkable view. You'll find gentle runs, well-groomed intermediate slopes, and advanced trails with steep areas and mogul fields. There's something for everyone on the 700 acres. The double chair lift is nearly half a mile long, and there's a triple chair up the other side of the mountain. They also have a poma and T-bar. This is the only ski area I would even consider driving to. It's only 11 miles from town and the road is good—it doesn't have the continous switchbacks and sheer drops so typical of the roads to other New Zealand ski areas. For convenience, however, I still recommend taking the bus.

This is *the* place to take a ski lesson. While all the major New Zealand ski areas have a ski school, this one is known for attracting the best instructors from around the world who want to keep skiing even when it's summer back home.

You can count on good snow here from early July until late September. Some years you can ski until early October. The last week in July or first week in August is Winter Festival Week. They have ski festival activities day and night on and off the slopes.

The Remarkables Ski Field

Located 17 miles from town, this area *is* remarkable, and so is the drive up the side of the mountain. Take the ski bus so you can relax and enjoy the view. You'll ski high up in the Remarkables Mountain Range in three great curving basins. It has good base facilities with cross-country as well as downhill ski schools and equipment rentals. Seventy percent of the runs are groomed for the beginner and intermediate skier, although you'll find plenty of challenging terrain and chutes if you're more advanced. Two quad chairs and a double chair will get you quickly to the top.

Heliskiing

For NZ$330 you can get a full day of heliskiing in the Queenstown area (NZ$220 for a half day; NZ$144 gets you a taste of the thrill with one ride). Flights leave daily, depending on the weather, from Coronet Peak, the Remarkables, Cardrona, and Trebel Cone ski areas. Book ahead by calling (0294) 23034. They will group you with other skiers of your ability—from hesitant intermediate to expert—and they will provide you with a guide.

If you're cautious about heliskiing here, wander over to the Cobb & Co. bar at the Mountaineer Hotel and watch the videos of that day's heliskiing (6:15 P.M.). Then, after your day on the slopes, you can watch yourself, too. They'll even sell you a copy to take home for a souvenir.

If you're interested, they provide a ski-taxi service from the Queenstown Airport to all the ski areas (NZ$66). This is the easiest and fastest way to get to Cardrona and Trebel Cone from Queenstown.

Queenstown to Rotorua

I recommend you drop your rental car in Queenstown on the South Island and fly via Mount Cook Airlines to Rotorua on the North Island. Your flight will take you over Mount Cook and the Tasman Glacier. It's a fast and beautiful route north.

Rotorua

When you make your initial rental car reservation for the South Island, you should also arrange to pick up another rental car at the airport in Rotorua. You'll need it here. While there's not much to see in town, the thermal areas nearby are fascinating. Located on a volcanic plateau, the area has been known since the 1880s for its geysers, bubbling mud pools, and numerous steam vents. It's a lot like our Yellowstone Park area. Two nights with a full day or more for sightseeing is a minimum here.

What to See in Rotorua

The Tudor Towers in town, which opened in 1908 as a luxurious spa, now houses the *Rotorua Museum* and *Art Gallery*. In the evening, the heavy carved wooden stairway leads to a nightclub open until 3:00 A.M. The building is spectacular, as are the *Government Gardens* in front of it. The *Orchid Gardens* nearby, with hundreds of beautiful orchids, ponds, and parrots, are also well worth a visit (NZ$5.50). You can have Devonshire tea (NZ$4) or a light lunch at their restaurant. After a day of sightseeing, you can relax in the soothing warm mineral waters of the *Polynesian Pools* near the Hyatt (NZ$5.50). For NZ$23.50, you can also get a massage and use the sauna.

Most of the thermal areas and sights are located off the highway circling Lake Rotorua. *Paradise Valley Springs* (NZ$6) is about ten minutes from town through the rolling hills of country farms. On their 20 acres you'll see New Zealand wildlife, trout ponds, and big cats. It's a great place for your morning Devonshire tea. If you're up early, eat outside, but don't turn your back on your scones or the peacocks and sparrows will make off with them.

Rainbow and Fairy Springs (NZ$6) is a large trout hatchery that also has New Zealand wildlife, including kiwi birds. Don't miss this one and be sure to get in on the very informal tour. It's connected by a tunnel to *Rainbow Farm*, previously a working farm, where you can watch sheepdogs at work and see sheep shearing. The *Agrodome* is another visit worth making. Here you'll learn about the various breeds of sheep in the area.

If you want to go for a ride in the country, the *Farm House* farther down the road rents horses for NZ$12 an hour. You ride across 600 acres of farmland and with sheep and beef cattle. It's best to phone ahead for reservations (dial 23771).

Hell's Gate (NZ$5). This thermal area is one of the most spectacular stops. It's a large volcanic area with boiling mud pots, steaming cliffs, sulphur springs, and much more. The *Whakarewarewa Thermal Area and Cultural Center* near town is the last stop not to be missed. Once again take a guided tour. You'll learn that the first settlers to this area were the Maori people. They still live in a village on the reserve and they still use the warm, soothing thermal waters to cook their food, cure their aches and pains, and wash in the evenings after the tourists have left. With the government's encouragement, they have done a remarkable job of maintaining their cultural identity. They are proud to introduce you to their heritage.

If you have a little extra time you should also take one of the many walks through the *Whakarewarewa State Forest* or visit the *Buried Village* destroyed by an 1866 volcano. The walk to the waterfalls is well worthwhile.

For shopping, the *Little Village* near the THC, has more unique shops than the downtown area. It also has more "olde world charm."

If you're in a hurry or want a change of pace, the *Helicopter Line* will take you sightseeing by air. For NZ$30 to NZ$275, you can see the area. The longer flights make a number of stops.

Where to Eat in Rotorua

The Landmark, 1 Meade Street, near the THC is, in my opinion, *the* place to dine in Rotorua. It's located in one of the few stately old homes remaining in the city, a large white Victorian with stained glass. They serve seafood (NZ$21 to NZ$28), steaks (NZ$21 to NZ$24), lamb (NZ$20), and more in an elegantly furnished cozy home setting. The *Steak House*, on Tutanekai Street, has a selection of steaks served cafeteria-style (NZ$9 to NZ$13) with a salad bar. It's informal and attracts lots of men—they always seem to like steaks. Downtown, you'll find a *Cobb & Co.* with an informal country atmosphere (entrées NZ$6 to NZ$11). They have live music in their bar Wednesday through Saturday. If you want something more upbeat, try *Caesars* upstairs on Arawa Street. They serve chicken, lamb, and steaks

(NZ$16 to NZ$20). For a quaint taste of German charm, *Lewisham's*, on Tutanekai Street, is a real gem. You can eat your Wiener schnitzel (NZ$16) around the blazing fireplace. *Friar Tucks*, on the corner of Tutanekai and Arawa streets, is another comfortable and informal place to dine alone. They serve burgers (NZ$6) and steaks (NZ$14 to NZ$17).

Where to Stay in Rotorua

Because the town itself has so little of interest, this is one of the few areas where an in-town location is not necessarily an advantage.

THC International Hotel (single NZ$105, double NZ$120). This full-service hotel is located on the edge of the Whakarewarewa thermal area with the only pool still filled with water from a thermal spring—the water flows down a stone waterfall into the pool. From your window you have a splendid view of the steam vents rising on the horizon. This is also the location for the most popular Maori Hangi (a Maori feast) and concert, held every night. The pork from the Hangi is actually cooked over a steam vent next to the pool. For NZ$28 you not only feast on an extensive buffet meal, but you'll learn about the native Maori customs and watch their traditional dances. Even if you don't stay here, don't miss the Hangi.

Hyatt Kingsgate Rotorua, Ervera Street (single NZ$125 to NZ$170, double NZ$140 to NZ$190). Located near the shore of Lake Rotorua, the construction is rustic modern with high ceilings and exposed wood beams. It includes highlights from the rich Maori culture. It's a full-service hotel with a pool and spa, and they even have piano music in the restaurant for breakfast.

Sheraton-Rotorua, Fenton Street (single and double NZ$130 to NZ$170). Also located on the edge of town near the thermal area, the Sheraton is warm, attractive, and welcoming. Their Gazebo coffee shop is just off the pool, where you'll find peacocks wandering by. They also have three cavelike private spas. For NZ$20 they will send their limousine to pick you up at the airport.

Eaton Hall, 39 Hinemaru Street (single NZ$29, double NZ$45). This bed and breakfast, located across the street from the Hyatt, is probably the best value in town. While the sixty-year-old Tudor-style home is not luxurious, it's clean and the owners are friendly and helpful. Some rooms have private baths. The common lounge area is a great place to meet other travelers.

Tresco Guest House, 3 Toko Street (single NZ$22 to NZ$33, double NZ$44 to NZ$66). Another excellent value and a good place to meet fellow travelers. Not elegant, but clean and friendly. They even have a mineral spa.

Princes Gate Hotel, Arawa Street (single NZ$70, double NZ$82). Conveniently located on the edge of the Government Gardens, this hotel is in one of the oldest and most unique buildings in Rotorua, dating from the late 1800s. It's built of local kauri wood and has large balconies that overlook the gardens and town. The standard rooms are in need of remodeling, but you still have to admire the high ceilings and antique furniture. The suites, though, have been redone and are an excellent value at NZ$100 to NZ$150. Their bar is one of the local "hot spots," especially on Friday night.

Rotorua to Mount Ruapehu

Your first stop twenty minutes out of Rotorua should be at the *Waimango Thermal Valley*. They open at 9:00 A.M. I suggest you get there early and do the one-hour walk to the boat for the half-hour cruise past the thermal cliffs (NZ$10.50). They'll bring you back by bus. The whole trip will take two hours. Continue to *Huka Falls*, about 5 miles before you reach Taupo. Back on the highway, six-tenths of a mile farther, on the other side of the road, you'll find the entrance to the *Craters of the Moon* thermal area. I'd also suggest a stop at the *Honey Village* on the hillside just before you reach Taupo. They have more flavors of honey than you can possibly imagine. The kiwi honey makes an especially unique gift.

It's another three hours to the Chateau of *Tongariro National Park*. Follow the signs to Turangi, then to National Park, and lastly to the Chateau.

Mount Ruapehu

One of the more scenic areas on the North Island and the primary ski field is Mount Ruapehu (pronounced "Rue-ah-pay-who."). It is located in Tongariro National Park, dominated by Mount Tongariro (nearly 6,560 feet high), and the smoking summit of Mount Ngauruhoe, 7,511 feet in height.

The Chateau—THC (single NZ$105 to NZ$150, double NZ$120 to NZ$165). Even if you don't ski, it would be worth the trip just to stay at the Chateau. Built in the grand old style seldom seen today, this hotel is often compared with the Banff Springs Hotel. It's every bit as grand and elegant and it, too, sits at the base of the mountains just a few minutes from ski fields. The rooms are spacious with a view over both the mountains and valleys. The lobby has massive chandeliers hanging from the high ceiling with an arched window that frames the mountains. You can order from the lobby bar and relax in front of a blazing fire. It's a great place to discuss your favorite run with other guests before dinner in their elegant *Ruapehu Room*, or the casual *Carvery* restaurant. The noon buffet in the Ruapehu Room (NZ$17) is a wonderful value offering both quality and quantity in a quiet relaxing atmosphere. You'll find everything you want here, including a pool and sauna, cinema, and live band in the *T-Bar*.

Whakapapa Ski Field

An all-day, all-lift ticket costs NZ$30. You can go up the express quad chair, three double chairs, six T-bars, and three poma lifts to ski down the 615-meter vertical drop to the base area. As with all the other areas, they have full equipment rental and a ski school offering private (NZ$50 per hour) and group (NZ$22 per hour) lessons.

Mount Ruapehu to Te Awamutu

It's about a three-hour drive to your next stop down on the farm. Leaving the Chateau, go through National Park, Taumaruni, and Tekuiti to Te Awamutu south of Hamilton.

Farm Stay

No trip to New Zealand is complete without a farm stay. There's no other way to get the real feel of the country. New Zealand is, above all else, farm country. You can book a farm stay in the area yourself by writing Beverly and Peter Bryant, Earl Road, Pukeatua, Te Awamutu, New Zealand, or call 082-24-812. They will treat you like family. You'll eat with them and follow them out with the sheepdogs to move the cows and sheep from one pasture to the next and to feed the deer they also raise. It's picturesque and idyllic. You'll eat passion fruit off the vine out back along with other fruit you've never heard of or seen. If you come in August or September, you'll see the new lambs just born—about 1,200 are born each year. Interestingly, usually three to four of the newborns are all black. If you're lucky, Peter Bryant's brother, who lives on the farm down the road, will let you sample his raspberry wine. If you're real lucky, you'll get to go with them to a local Lions Club meeting where you'll be the only "outsider," although you certainly won't feel like one.

You can book this and other farm stays throughout New Zealand by contacting New Zealand Farm Holidays, 177 Parnell Road, Private Bag, Auckland, New Zealand (single and double NZ$60).

Te Awamutu to Auckland

Another two-and-a-half-hour drive north through Hamilton and you'll be in Auckland. It's a good idea to go directly to your hotel and have the rental car company pick up your car there—National (Newmans) will do so without an additional charge. You really don't need a car while in Auckland. For NZ$3 you can take the bus to the airport and for NZ$12 you can get there by taxi.

Auckland

The largest city and the industrial heart of New Zealand, Auckland sits on Waitemata Harbor. It's the water that keeps the temperatures here mild all winter long.

What to See in Auckland

While here you should be sure to visit New Zealand's largest zoo, where you can see a kiwi bird if you haven't already done so. The *War Memorial Museum* includes a nice collection of Maori artifacts and carvings. The museum is in the *Auckland Domain*, so allow time to stroll through these gardens as well as visit *Underwater World*, where you'll be transported on a moving conveyor inside a transparent tunnel through the domain of the fish, kelp forests, and sandy zones. *Microworld* is a unique experience that allows you to see the world closeup through high-powered microscopes. Don't miss the terrific movie. You'll learn there are more microorganisms living on the human body than there are people on the earth! You'll see things here you never knew existed. If you'd like to see Auckland's historic wooden homes, call 545-729 for information. If you'd like an overall view of the city, stop at Mount Edam or Mount Albert.

Parnell Village, on the east edge of town, is a great place to shop; take the time to stroll through the colonial shops. *Antoines* in the village is a great dinner treat, but it's not cheap. They offer venison (NZ$35), lamb (NZ$25), and serve an excellent Pavlova (NZ$8).

Queens Street in downtown is the primary shopping center, but there are many small malls with additional shopping. Just west of town is the *Victorian Park Market*. A former factory, it was restored and is where you'll find local arts and crafts, a flea market, *Rick's Cafe American*, and a selection of honey, including honey and kiwi fruit, from the *Honey Village*. If you prefer, for NZ$14 you can join a guided shopping tour of all the local factory shops. It's a half day of worry-free shopping with a small group.

There are lots of hikes and walks around the area. You can rent bicycles to ride along the harbor or take the historic *Kestral* ferry to Devonport (NZ$15).

Where to Eat in Auckland

Like any large city, Auckland has many excellent restaurants. The following are only a few of the best.

Bronze Goat, 108 Ponsonby Road. An informal, first-class restaurant with lots of plants against the rough brick interior backdrop common in Auckland. Main courses run primarily from NZ$12 to NZ$14. They serve prawns and scallops (NZ$14), lamb and hazelnuts (NZ$14), and hot pumpkin soup (NZ$5).

Java Jive, corner of Ponsonby Road and College Hill. This popular local coffee shop is a holdout from the sixties. It's a great place to stop for a snack and to meet the local college crowd.

Carthews, 151 Ponsonby Road. For more elegant dining, try this etched-glass building for venison or pheasant and beef and fish (NZ$20 to NZ$27).

Custom House, corner Albert and Custom streets. This 1888 former custom house now has a small corner restaurant as well as a popular disco, *Brandy's*. Try their "muesli" (NZ$4) if you haven't yet. It's a popular breakfast cereal. They also serve salads and sandwiches for lunch (NZ$4 to NZ$7).

Sardi's, Queen Arcade, Queen Street. For truly elegant dining this is a terrific choice. The staff is friendly and the food excellent. They have an extremely good selection of steaks (NZ$18), lamb (NZ$26), prawns (NZ$26), and more.

Number Five. An elegant brick home across from the Sheraton, this is one of the top dining locations in Auckland. It's also among the most expensive. Dinner will be at least NZ$50.

Freeman's Afloat, Halsey Street on Freeman Bay. For a change of pace, dine aboard the S.S. *Ngoiro* floating restaurant, bar, and museum across from Microworld. You'll find a selection including salads (NZ$6 to NZ$7) and steak cooked in Scotch (NZ$16).

Catches, corner Durham and Albert streets. A selection of seafood (NZ$7 to NZ$14) in a modern open setting, served by a friendly helpful staff.

Auckland at Night

Check the events. There is an excellent orchestra as well as many touring shows. If you prefer the disco, *Brandy's* in the Customs Building is popular and convenient. *Changes* nightclub on Commerce and Gore streets is also popular. The *Exchange Tavern* in Parnell is also popular and comfortable, catering to a younger crowd. *Cheers*, 12 Wyndham Street, is upbeat with loud rock music. For a quieter stop try the *Wyndham Park Tavern* next door.

Where to Stay in Auckland

Regent of Auckland, 17 Albert Street (single or double NZ$195 to NZ$225). Once again the Regent has developed a new hotel right in the middle of all the action downtown, conveniently located near most sights. You'll be entertained with piano music when you dine on some of the best food in town in their well-appointed restaurants. You can get a light snack in the lobby bar as well. The rooms are large with all the conveniences, and the service is impeccable in typical Regent style.

Travelodge, 100 Quay Street (single and double NZ$150). While the rooms are a bit on the small side and the hotel is not elegant, every room has a harbor view. Even if you don't stay here, I'd recommend their first-floor restaurant, *Penny's*, overlooking the harbor.

Hyatt Kingsgate, Prince Street (single NZ$159 to NZ$198, double NZ$170 to NZ$209). Located up on a hill, the view from this luxurious hotel is the best in town. The rooms, recently remodeled, are flawless. Even if you don't stay here, be sure to try their fourteenth-floor restaurant, *Top of Town*. The bar here is also a great place to meet interesting people. The whole environment is plush, elegant, and inviting.

Aspen Lodge, 62 Emily Place (single NZ$36, double NZ$50). You can't miss this two-story hot-pink building located near the Hyatt. While there's not much glamour, they do provide all the necessities in a clean, friendly atmosphere. There's a comfortable lobby in front to meet the other guests and they're planning a gazebo for the backyard. It'll be used as a dining area. They even have free laundry facilities for your use.

Though skiing is your focus on this adventure away from home, your New Zealand stay won't be complete without a taste of both the farm and the big city. While a small country, especially when compared to its neighbor Australia, it, too, has a variety of options and activities for a woman traveling alone.

CHAPTER 7

In Pursuit of Adventure

MYSTERY AT MOHONK MOUNTAIN HOUSE

▸────────────────────────────────▸

GENERAL AMBIANCE	★ ★
SOCIAL CLIMATE	★ ★ ★
ACTIVITIES	★

FOR RESERVATIONS CONTACT:
Mohonk Mountain House
Lake Mohonk
New Paltz, NY 12561
(914) 255-1000
(212) 233-2244

Or *contact your travel agent and ask for the Mohonk Mystery Weekend*

▸────────────────────────────────▸

*T*his is the eleventh year a murder has occurred at Mohonk Mountain House. This year, 1872, it was Clint Hawk, a stranger to Turnip Gulch, who was killed. We were all assigned to posses Thursday night when we arrived. There were to be sixteen posses of fifteen to twenty people each. We would have until Sunday morning to decide who the murderer was.

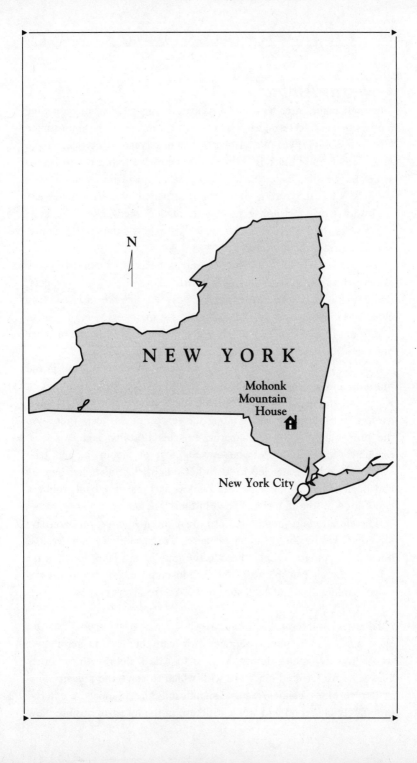

General Ambiance

That first night, after we'd had a chance to change from our traveling clothes to our Western gear, we saw a short movie of the unfortunate Clint's last day alive. We also had a chuck wagon dinner with the other members of our posse. It was an incredible buffet that included sweet potato pie, baked beans, and a selection of other wholesome victuals. Typical Western grub. The best part, however, was dessert. That was to be consistently the case throughout the weekend—dessert was always the best part of the meal. I'd suggest skipping the dinner and going right to the dessert.

There was a bounty on the murderer's head: a Mohonk Mystery Weekend bag with a mystery book written by one of the suspects, and a guaranteed spot on next year's posse. While we discussed the clues and our theories with our fellow posse members, we, of course, kept them from competing teams lest someone else solve the mystery before us.

The next day we rounded up the suspects. We had an hour in the morning and another hour in the afternoon to question the likes of Kitty Kat, the madam of the Turnip Gulch saloon, and Kane Beauregard, a "cheating gambler." Among the ten prime suspects there was the prim and proper schoolmarm, Priscilla Buttons, and two local ranchers: Travis Turnip, who owned most of the town, and Jane Plucky. Jane had struggled to keep her ranch afloat after her parents had been killed. They were the hapless victims of a bank robbery committed by the notorious Toad in the Hole Gang.

The circuit court judge rode into town and held court on Saturday. He couldn't wait until Monday because, "I'm not here to hang around but maybe you are." Right there in the middle of a land dispute case "Doc," a bit of a lush, was shot in midsentence. At that point the judge reminded us not to leave town, "You're all witnesses . . . suspects, too."

I'd always wanted to be a cowgirl when I was growing up. The Old West holds a rich cultural heritage with many heroes and heroines. I would live my fantasy during the next four days along with the other guests, as we ferreted out clues with which to solve the mystery.

Our "real life" realities changed significantly the moment we entered this stately old wood and stone structure in the forest of upstate New

York. Built on Lake Mohonk in 1879, the 300-room Mohonk Mountain House—with its 150 working fireplaces—along with the 7,500 acres of surrounding forest and mountain, is now a National Historic Landmark. What a splendid setting in which to travel back in time, in luxury and comfort, to the days of the Old West.

The country and period of the weekend vary each year. Donald Westlake, author of more than forty mystery novels, has written the script the past six years. The Mohonk Mountain House has been transformed into a variety of settings, from a cruise ship, the S.S. Mohonkia, queen of the Black Star Line, to the luxurious London home of Sycophant Teasdale, a murder victim. In 1988, it will become the 1940s set of *The Maltese Herring*. I wonder if Humphrey Bogart will be there?

Social Climate

People from as far away as Texas and Florida converge on Mohonk for these weekends. They are all ages and from all walks of life. Some are there because they became hooked on the intrigue at a former year's mystery. Some are hooked on murder mysteries, games of intrigue, or the period of that year's setting. Some may have gotten the Thursday through Sunday weekend as a gift. Neiman-Marcus has even carried it in their Christmas catalogue as "the ultimate" Christmas present.

You'll find a number of the suspects have a hidden identity. They are murder mystery writers themselves, many of great renown. You'll have the opportunity to meet their other real-life characters as well. They'll tell you about books they are now writing as well as seldom heard stories about the creation of characters such as Rambo, with whom you're already likely familiar.

Even though you may come alone, you won't be alone for long. You're immediately assigned to a group of fifteen to twenty other guests. You eat together and meet together to discuss the latest clues you've uncovered and your current version of the murder. While there are always a few who really take things seriously, most people are there to have a good time, win or lose.

Remember to be kind when you question the suspects. About half of them will likely be judges on Sunday morning when each group presents its version of the murder. You wouldn't want them to be holding a grudge against you.

Activities

In addition to questioning suspects, there are more clues to be found when you actually visit the setting of the murder on Friday night. A Western fiddler and guitar player welcomed us to Turnip Gulch while we drank at Kitty Kat's saloon, visited the office of the *Gulch Gazette*, the livery stable, and a number of other spots around town. The suspects were all in town that night along with a number of other Turnip Gulch locals. They made us feel right at home.

There's always a big dance on Saturday night. We did a lot of square dancing and line dances, including the Virginia Reel.

You get your chance to be on stage, too, if you like. In addition to a prize for the most accurate solution, there is one for the most creative. Having no idea "who done it," my group went for creativity. Posses don't just announce their version of the murder, most act it out, complete with props. You're limited to five minutes per posse, but a few went over. What an exciting climax to a great weekend. I think some of our solutions were actually better than Donald Westlake's. They were certainly fun to put together and see performed.

Quite by chance, my posse fingered the unlikely Priscilla Buttons as the murderer. It turned out she had had an affair with Clint Hawk's brother Tom, and when she wouldn't marry him, Tom had threatened to tell the town. Knowing she'd lose her reputation and job, she killed him to keep him quiet. Then she killed his brother, Clint, who came to town, she thought, to look for Tom's murderer. She later had to kill Doc, too, to keep him from talking . . . and she looked so innocent.

There are nonmystery activities, too. You can walk the scenic trails on your own, or you can go on one of the guided hikes along the mountain trails or around Mohonk Lake. In the summer months there is horseback riding, golf, tennis, and swimming. You can tour the museums and greenhouse all year, and go cross-country skiing during the winter months.

The view from the over 200 balconies is breathtaking on one side over Mohonk Lake and Mohonk Mountain, and on the other side the Shawangunk Mountains and even the nearby Catskills. Your private balcony is a great place to sit and relax, if you can find the time. On the cooler days you may want to stay inside in front of your private fireplace. You automatically get a supply of wood, which the staff replenishes each day, along with kindling and paper to make fire-starting easy.

If you have a car, I'd also suggest driving the 6 miles back to New Paltz, a historic city in its own right. If you stop by *P & G's* on Main Street, you'll meet the locals. Wine and beer are only $1 during happy hour. A longtime resident of New Paltz told me he'd heard there really was a murder at Mohonk two years ago. Just goes to show how fantasy can become fact.

Preparing for Your Mystery Weekend

While the Murder Mystery Weekend at Mohonk Mountain House is not the only mystery weekend of this nature, it was the first and appears to be one of the most popular. The concept was developed by Dilys Winn, who had already founded Murder Ink, a New York City bookstore specializing in mysteries.

Not everyone is lucky enough to get a room. That's why the prize of a guaranteed reservation for the following year is so coveted. If you call the Mohonk Mountain House—(914) 255-1000 or (212) 233-2244—they will tell you on what day reservations will be taken. It's only one day a year, usually the first Thursday in December. Reservations are taken from 9:00 A.M. until they are fully booked, usually around noon. Payment is due in February. The same mystery is performed on two weekends each March, with a few changes in the script and the identity of the murderer.

Rates

For the three nights of the weekend a single room will cost from $330 to $588. A large double with a fireplace and balcony will be

$576 to $870. This includes all your meals. There is an additional $50 charge per person for the special mystery weekend events.

What to Take

To really get into the spirit of the event, you'll want to dress in period costumes from the time you arrive Thursday afternoon until your departure Sunday afternoon. Most people do. You'll want clothes for daytime wear as well as something more dressy for Saturday night. You may want to become your favorite character from the era and pick a costume that character would wear.

You should bring comfortable shoes and warm clothes for outdoor hiking. Even in March there are usually folks playing tennis, so bring your racket and warm-up suit. The lake will probably still be covered with ice and the horses in lower open pastures, but check with the management just before you leave home.

Getting There

Since Mohonk Mountain House is approximately a one-and-a-half-hour drive northwest of New York City, you should fly in to one of the area airports. Limousine service from the airports can be arranged through Mohonk ($130 each way), but I suggest picking up a rental car. The cost will be about the same as the limousine and you'll have the convenience of a car if you want to explore the countryside—time permitting, of course.

Along with your registration information, you'll receive detailed directions on how to get to Mohonk Mountain House.

Once you've visited the unspoiled setting of the Mohonk Mountain House for a mystery weekend, I expect you'll look for an excuse to return. The nineteenth-century character has been retained with all the conveniences of a twentieth-century resort center.

WHITE WATER RAFTING THROUGH THE GRAND CANYON

▶ ─────────────────────────────────────── ▶

GENERAL AMBIANCE	★ ★ ★
SOCIAL CLIMATE	★ ★
ACTIVITIES	★ ★

FOR TOUR ARRANGEMENTS CONTACT:
Outdoor Adventure River Specialists
P.O. Box 67
Angels Camp, CA 95222
(209) 736-4677

Or *contact your travel agent* and ask for OARS Grand Canyon trip

▶ ─────────────────────────────────────── ▶

I once thought I knew a lot about rivers, having sat on the shore and watched intently as they flowed by. I've always been drawn by the hypnotic lure of running water. I spent hours as a child along the edge of rivers dangling my feet or trying to catch the ever elusive newly hatched fish in the palm of my hand. However, once I slipped down the calm **V** into the white water of my first Colorado River rapid, I realized I had really known very little about rivers before that moment.

General Ambiance

I had been told that white water rafting was the thrill of a lifetime, but somehow I had expected it to be more like the many canoe trips I have taken. It was at the end of that first rapid that I realized how naive I had been. I was indeed in for the thrill of a lifetime and much more than just another river trip.

What's more, even with all the excitement of the river, the greatest

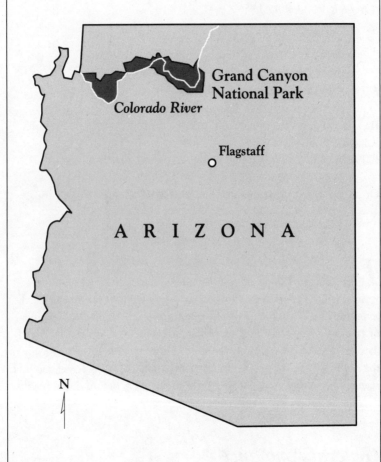

Grand Canyon
National Park

Colorado River

Flagstaff

A R I Z O N A

N

thrill comes from the towering magnificence of the Grand Canyon itself. Deservedly recognized as one of the seven wonders of the world, the Grand Canyon of the Colorado River is a huge natural museum where one can easily become lost in the enormity of creation.

One of the big advantages to taking an OARS (Outdoor Adventure River Specialists) trip through the canyon is that they don't destroy the magnitude of the silence with motors or with a large group of people. Each trip is limited to sixteen passengers, only four people per boat, and the only roar you'll hear is the roar of the canyon.

This trip can best be described as camping with room service. While you do need to pitch your own tent, if you use one, the tents provided by OARS are the easiest I've ever pitched. The river guides will do all the rowing and cooking, although you are certainly welcome to help. I soon learned that the cook table was a great place to relax with the guides and sample their special store of drinks. There was more than enough beer and wine to go around and the food was great. One of our guides was even proficient at cooking in a Dutch oven. He made a great cake and lasagna in addition to other "specialties."

Social Climate

It's the men and women you'll meet who make this adventure an especially appealing trip for a woman traveling alone. Most of your fellow adventurers will be in their twenties and thirties; many will be single. You'll also find more men than women, although the trip is popular with both.

My trip included a couple from Austria, their college-age son, and a good friend of his—both boys were kayaking. A woman flight attendant and a charming, energetic grade-school physical education teacher from Canada were also on the trip. In addition, we had a Manhattan attorney and a Boston salesman, neither of whom had ever been camping before. In fact, the only wool pants (included on the suggested clothing list) the salesman had to bring along were an old pair of suit pants.

You'll find a few days on the river will quickly unite even the most diverse individuals into a cohesive group. Here everyone is away from their usual rules and routines, stripped of their familiar symbols of role and status.

The river guides are a unique and very interesting breed of men and women. On my trip there were five seasoned river guides who had been running rapids for years, some over ten years. They were all men. Of the four trainees along, two were women. During the summer you might find these guides on Alaskan rivers, and during the winter months on the rivers of Africa, South America, or New Guinea. Others run rivers during the summer months and work on the ski slopes during the winter. For most, home was the waters. Their mail went to the home of relatives or a post office box.

One of our guides was a Colorado dentist with a wife and two kids "in my other life." One of the women trainees was a successful Alaskan fisheries consultant. Both were torn between the independent, rugged life on the white water rivers and life in civilized society. After only nine days on the river, in the canyon, I, too, felt the lure of life as an adventurer.

I expect these men and women are in many ways like the trappers and mountain men of yesterday. They've chosen life-styles that keep them close to nature and the wild. They move around a lot, and they stay clear of the big city most of the year. They're fit, intelligent, rugged philosophers who value their life-styles much as we usually value our own, and sometimes long for the romance of theirs.

Activities

While the primary focus of your trip on the Colorado River is the adventure of white water rafting, it's certainly not the only activity. The days you spend on the river will be a real escape from civilization to the solitude and fullness too often missing from our busy lives. You'll pass close to ring-tailed cats and bighorn sheep on seemingly inaccessible sheer rock ledges. You'll see beaver and peregrine falcons. You'll camp on sandbars or under rock ledges that the Anasazi Indians, the Ancient Ones, likely slept under 800 years ago. You'll also see the still intact remains of their granaries.

In addition, you'll experience the more modern history of man on the river. Your route is the same John Wesley Powell, the canyon's first and most famous explorer, took in 1869. You'll pass the *Ross Wheeler*, a metal boat left on the rocks beside the river in 1914 by the Russell-Quist party. On my trip we also passed the remains of a wooden boat that had lost its battle with the river. It lay broken, still held tight against a boulder at the end of Crystal Rapids. Later we learned the unfortunate incident had occurred only a few days earlier. While no one had been hurt, equipment had been lost to the river— a harsh reminder that a trip down the Colorado is still a daring and dangerous undertaking. Unlike the early explorers, on your OARS trip you'll have the advantage of a flexible rubber boat and the experience of boatmen who have made this trip up to fifty times before.

Not only will you experience the history of mankind at firsthand, but you'll experience the history of the earth at firsthand as well. Nearly a mile deep, 8 miles across, and 255 miles long from Glen Canyon Dam to Lake Mead, the Grand Canyon has an enrapturing story to tell. You'll go back an estimated 200 million to over 2 billion years. As you travel down the Colorado, you'll pass the various hues of rock, each of which represents a different millennium in the canyon's creation. You'll see the youthful bright gold and suntan-brown layers of sandstone, a mere 250 million years old. Then later you'll pass the 450-million-year-old redwall limestone stained a brilliant red by the iron oxide carried by the rain from the earth above it. In the inner gorge of the canyon you'll see the lines of age and experience worn deeply into the dark gray and black schist and granite. This is the oldest portion of the Grand Canyon.

By comparison, you'll find the story of the river a recent one. The sculpting of the canyon by the river has averaged an inch of down-cutting per century. It has been estimated that the river has done its work in a mere 40 million years. As you exit the canyon at the end of your trip, you'll go back up through the millions of years of the earth's formation. Millenniums will become mere moments.

Not only will you see the majestic canyon from the river, you'll also have the opportunity to hike up into the breathtaking side canyons, each more stunning than the last.

This is also *the* place to stargaze. I've never before nor since seen so many stars in the sky. One of the river guides on my trip was familiar with the constellations and was happy to point them out. I usually slept out under the stars, not bothering with the confinement of a tent. It was a special thrill to watch the stars literally move across the sky. New ones appeared in the sky above the south rim while others disappeared behind the walls of the north rim. At daybreak, I watched the stars slowly disappear. When I first awoke, all the millions of stars were usually still visible. Then the majority would fade, leaving the sky that I was familiar with seeing at home. I'd watch as the stars faded more, until only the major constellations were visible. Then day would come and sunlight would enter the Grand Canyon signaling the beginning of yet another day of adventure.

If you're really lucky you'll experience a thunderstorm in the Grand Canyon. I grew up in Seattle, which has lots of thunderstorms, but none came even close to the one I experienced in the canyon. That particular night I had camped halfway up a hill on a sandy plateau under a large rock overhang. Like most nights, I had not bothered with a tent. I awoke to a flash of silver before my eyes and then came the thunder. It roared down the canyon, filling it with greater and greater density as it came nearer. The roar totally filled the canyon. It was strong and carried the force of centuries and the magnitude of all the heavens. I was certain the whole canyon would crumble under its weight. Not the only one awake now, I soon heard the hoots and hollers of my fellow travelers on the sand bar below. A spontaneous tribute from our river guides to the spectacle of thunder and lightning from the heavens. Then came the rains. I was glad for my rock overhang. I wondered if the Anasazi had slept under this particular rock? What had they thought of the storms? Slowly, sleep came once again.

By morning the rains had stopped but the best was yet to come. Just across the river from our camp we saw the first of many of the massive cascading waterfalls we were to see as we traveled that morning. The sky, now clear and blue, made an incredible backdrop for the rushing white waterfalls now flowing through the well-worn paths in the redwall limestone. That night and morning alone made the trip an experience of a lifetime.

OARS Trip Itinerary and Options

You have your choice of three primary trips. You can go the whole 226 miles of the Colorado River with 150 rapids from Lees Ferry near

Flagstaff to Diamond Creek near Lake Mead (thirteen days). You can do just the easier rapids on the upper portion of the river from Lees Ferry to Phantom Ranch (six days), or you can meet the trip at Phantom Ranch and do the larger rapids of the lower portion of the Colorado (eight days).

I chose to do the eight-day trip partially because of time, partially because the awesome Crystal Rapids and Lava Falls are included in this portion of the trip, and partially because that allowed me to spend time at the south rim lodge area and walk down the Bright Angel Trail.

Preparing for Your OARS River Trip

This is one trip where you don't need a passport or visa and money won't do you any good. To experience and enjoy the canyon to its fullest you do, however, need to be able to do some hiking. There's something to challenge everyone on this trip. I did well on the 10- and 12-mile quick-paced hikes across Surprise Valley, a desert valley, and up steep canyons. But I'm not a mountain climber, so I skipped one trail, over a lunch stop, that required climbing an unsupported rope that led to a sheer rock cliff. Four people in our group did make the climb. All came back exhilarated, and two admitted that great fear was a part of the excitement and challenge.

Rates

The full thirteen-day trip from Lees Ferry to Diamond Creek, including all of your meals, all the wine and beer you can drink (unless you're a real lush), and the use of a tent and two watertight bags is $1653. The eight-day trip from Phantom Ranch to Diamond Creek will cost you $1269. The shorter six-day trip on the more gentle upper rapids will cost $895. You must also add 5 percent Arizona tax.

When to Go

When you decide to go is to a great extent a matter of personal preference. There are pros and cons to every season of the year. I went in early October. It was a good time because there were no motor boats on the river (they are not allowed to run after September 15). During our trip we saw only one other group of people. The rest of the time we had the canyon totally to ourselves. While the temperature got into the eighties, we did not have the scorching weather you'll find from late June through early September. Because it was late in the year, the hours of daylight were short, and it did get cold at night. We were, however, allowed to build a fire, which is not allowed during the hot summer months. When we got wet in the shade of the canyon, the 55-degree water felt every bit that cold. During the hot summer months, it's refreshing.

Were I to go again, I think I'd pick late May, early June, or mid to late September. In the spring, the days are the longest, the weather warm but not too hot, and the crowds haven't yet begun. I'd also pick mid to late September because it would be just a little warmer than the October trip I took.

Regardless of when you choose to go, experiencing the mighty rapids of the Colorado River is guaranteed to provide memories to last a lifetime. By the end of the week you'll find you've come to accept towering magnificence as a normal state of the world.

While thousands of people float down this grand river each year, thanks to their consideration of the environment and their consideration of those who will follow, they have left hardly a trace behind. I was especially pleased and surprised to find the animals are not afraid of people. Obviously they have not learned to see mankind as a predator. This speaks well of those who came before me. On the whole trip I found only two cigarette butts in the sand, which we picked up. Everything you take in must come out with you. The very important credo of the park department is "Take only pictures. Leave only footprints." If everyone adheres to this the grandeur of the canyon will remain for future generations to experience and enjoy.

What to Take

OARS will provide you with a complete equipment list. While they provide the food, tents, and waterproof bags for your equipment, you'll need to provide your own sleeping bag (they will rent you one for a small additional charge), dishes, and clothing. I thought the waterproof equipment bags were somewhat superfluous, and I wondered about the necessity of waterproof pants and jacket. To some extent, this depends on the time of year you take your trip. If you go on one of the first trips in the spring (before June) or on one of the last in the fall (late September or October), you'll definitely need waterproof clothing. While it can easily get up to 80 degrees in the sun, because of the high canyon walls, you'll be in the cool shade a lot, and the water is always a chilly 55 degrees. The rain gear will keep you drier and warmer.

I also found their suggested quick-drying clothing important. Blue jeans take forever to dry, as do cotton shorts. Nylon shorts dry quickly, as do the cotton shorts and pants made by Patagonia.

You'll want a pair of cloth tennis shoes. In addition, *Expeditions* (625 North Beaver Street) in Flagstaff sells a thonglike sandal with a nylon web ankle strap for about $20. I highly recommend picking up a pair for the trip. Thongs without the ankle strap are too easily lost to the wet sand and mud of the river. These stay on. Don't take any bottles. They are not allowed. I'd also recommend picking up a portable plastic "shower," available at your local mountaineering equipment store ($12–15). This ingenious black plastic device allows you to heat water with the help of the sun (black absorbs the sun's heat).

OARS will also send you *The Colorado River in Grand Canyon: A Guide* by Larry Stevens. Read it before your trip and bring it with you. It provides valuable information. I also suggest you take along *The Man Who Walked Through Time* by Colin Fletcher. This is a spectacular account of the walk he took along the rim the entire length of the Canyon.

Getting in Shape

If a regular exercise routine is not part of your life-style, you may want to begin a conditioning program well in advance of your trip (see p. 36 for pointers). It's not essential to be in good shape. You can make the trip without exerting yourself, but the reality is that you'll miss much of the beauty of the canyon and the exhilaration of the experience because you won't be up to the more strenuous activities.

Getting There

Because OARS will provide transportation only back to Flagstaff at the end of the trip, if you drive, I suggest leaving your car there. If you'll be flying, you can fly into and out of Flagstaff.

The best way to get to the South Rim Village from Flagstaff is to take the bus ($11.75). The one-and-a-half-hour bus ride will take you past stands of Ponderosa pine and the usually snowcapped San Francisco Peaks. The highest, Mount Humphrey, reaches 12,633 feet. The landscape here is a stark contrast to the equally beautiful yet very different desert canyon into which you'll soon descend.

You'll want to spend at least one night on the South Rim, then descend the Bright Angel Trail the next morning to Phantom Ranch on the Colorado River. This is where you'll meet the boats.

Checking Your Gear

One of your first stops at the rim should be the *Fred Harvey Livery Barn*, where you drop your gear to be taken down into the canyon by mule. In order to avoid a $10 late drop fee, your bag must be at the livery barn by 4:00 P.M. The mules leave at 3:00 A.M. sharp. Whatever you do, have your gear at the livery in time to go down on the mules. If you don't, you'll have to carry it yourself. You should keep back a small day pack with your overnight articles and the water and camera equipment you may want to carry with you as you descend into the canyon.

Tipping

Gratuities are, of course, never required. However, if you feel that your guides have provided you with services on your trip that go above and beyond the call of duty, it's appropriate to tip them accordingly. Most excursion operators suggest $5 to $8 per day per guest depending on the quality of service you feel you received.

In most cases, the group will collect the tip and present it to the head guide, often at the farewell dinner. He or she will share it equally with all other guides and trainees.

The South Rim Village

Where to Stay on the South Rim *

El Tovar Hotel ($85 to $105). Located right on the rim of the canyon, this is *the* place to stay, but you'll need to book early.

This majestic, historic hotel was built by the Fred Harvey Company in 1905 from native boulders and Oregon pine. Each room is uniquely furnished with period furniture. Even if you're not able to stay at El Tovar, be sure to have breakfast in their dining room. On either side of the massive stone fireplace in the dining room are equally large picture windows through which you can look out onto the sun-bathed hues of the canyon wall. The colors change from pink to gold as the day begins and as you dine on everything from the Mule Skinner's Special ($10.30) of filet mignon, eggs, hash browns, and toast to Smoked Salmon Benedict ($6.10). The smoked salmon is a wonderful treat with a light lemon hollandaise sauce. What an incredible way to begin a spectacular experience in the canyon. As you leave, for another $6.50, you can pick up a trail lunch from your waiter. Dinner here is first class, too, but since the sun has set there's no view.

Thunderbird Lodge ($79 to $85). Also located on the rim, this is a contemporary lodge with comfortable accommodations.

Maswik Lodge ($30 to $77). Located back from the rim, the deluxe rooms are comfortable and attractive with vaulted ceilings. Cabins (not heated) are available during the summer months.

The Bright Angel Trail

The Bright Angel Trail starts in front of the Bright Angel Lodge and descends 4,460 feet, nearly 8 miles, to Phantom Ranch on the Colorado River. The trail is well maintained and, although somewhat steep, an easy walk down. There are two rest houses with water at 1.5 and 3 miles below the rim. You'll pass the lush green Indian Gardens on your way down into the depths of the canyon. Depending on your physical condition and walking speed, the trip will take you three

---

* All the lodges listed here can be booked by calling Grand Canyon National Park Lodges (602) 638-2401.

to six hours. Be sure to allow enough time. If you get down early you can always spend time exploring Phantom Ranch, but you don't want to miss the boats.

Life on the River

Our first day on the river began much like those to follow. Sleeping outside, we awoke with the dawn, just as the sun was beginning to climb down the walls of the canyon towering above us. Our guides had already begun breakfast. We had a variety of hot and cold cereals, pancakes, sausages or bacon, and some mornings omelets.

Most of us had our tents down and much of our gear packed in our watertight bags before the sweet sound of "Breakfast; come and get it" rang out down the canyon. We were usually on the river by 9:00 A.M.

From a distance, Horn Creek Rapid, my first rapid on the Colorado River, looked deceptively calm. My only clues to the thrill and excitement to come were a dull roar in the canyon and an occasional massive thrust of water ahead on the otherwise quiet river. The roar sounded so much like an airplane that I checked the sky only to find it empty. I could feel the excitement mount as we approached "The Horn" and the boat in front of us dropped out of sight.

The full force of the rapid became apparent about the time our river guide skillfully edged our rubber boat into the center of the calm of the V. The exploding rapids were on both sides of us now. He kept us right on course down through the calm V to the tip, where we broke through on top of the crest of the biggest wave. The deep hole between the waves dropped us out of sight, much as it had the boat ahead of us, then tossed us back up on the crest of yet another wave. I gripped the side ropes as tightly as I could, trying often unsuccessfully to keep my eyes open to more fully experience the rapids for which I had come. As large waves broke over our heads, I understood the need for the waterproof equipment bags I had thought superfluous.

The ride wasn't over when we broke through the crest of the last big wave. A whirlpool at the end of the rapid caught one end of our boat and with great force whipped us around, nearly forcing us into an eddy that flowed back upstream along the bank. Only the strength and skill of our boatman kept us from being caught by the mighty river. As he pulled us through I became aware for the first time of the boils and whirlpools in the café-au-lait-colored river, and the stationary waves that appeared to be flowing upstream.

We had covered nearly 10 miles on the river and gone through four rapids before the lunch stop. Because our guides did all the cooking, lunch stops were a time for us to relax or explore the canyon. Each side canyon we stopped at was more beautiful than the last, and more difficult to leave when it was time to move on. Some lunch stops were on large sandbars.

The leisurely lunch break was often the time to use our portable showers, warmed by the sun on the morning's river ride.

We rode through eight more rapids and traveled another 8 miles before camping for the night. We had not seen another person all day, though we had passed a bighorn sheep grazing on a cliff near the river. He seemed unconcerned about our intrusion into his world.

Some group members gathered wood for our evening campfire, some helped the guides prepare dinner, others read, wrote in their diaries, or climbed the canyon hills. Dinner was a large salad, French bread, and lasagna, and while we ate we sat in a group on rocks in the sand and shared stories about other adventures, past trips, future trips, our hopes, dreams, and aspirations. Our newly made friends from Austria told us about kayaking on European rivers. Dusk had fallen.

Those of us who had left our flashlights with our gear were glad for the moonlight that lit the canyon as we walked back to our tents. I fell asleep to the music of the river with the stars over my head and dreams of more adventure in the morning.

MOROCCO: A CIRCULAR JOURNEY FROM CASABLANCA TO MARRAKECH AND BACK AGAIN

▶ ————————————————————————————————————▶

GENERAL AMBIANCE	★ ★ ★
SOCIAL CLIMATE	★
ACTIVITIES	★ ★

FOR TOUR ARRANGEMENTS CONTACT:
Moroccan National Tourist Office
20 East 46th Street
New York, NY 10017
(212)557-2520

Or *contact your travel agent*

▶ ————————————————————————————————————▶

*E*ver since I first saw Humphrey Bogart and Ingrid Bergman in the movie *Casablanca* I've wanted to visit Morocco and Rick's Cafe American. By the fifth time I'd seen the movie, I knew I had to go. When my dream at last became a reality and I was planning my trip, I actually became a little angry when I was told Rick's didn't really exist, it was only a Hollywood creation, and other parts of Morocco were more interesting than Casablanca. I later found that was both true and not true.

Fortunately, I visited Casablanca first. I then stopped in Rabat, Meknes, Fez, and Marrakech before returning to Casablanca for the flight home. I thoroughly enjoyed Casablanca, and even though I didn't find "Bogie," I did wander through the same Casbah. I found mystery and intrigue in Casablanca, where it's easy to step back a thousand years or more in time. Yet I found even more in Fez and Marrakech, both of which far surpassed my expectations. By the time I returned to Casablanca, it seemed civilized and modern in comparison.

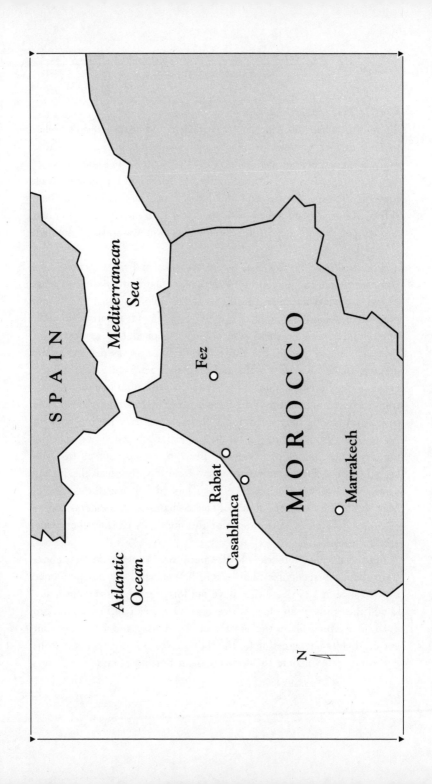

General Ambiance

To me, the charm of Morocco is in its sense of history and its ability to take the visitor back in time literally hundreds of years, because that's where much of the country has remained. Traditional water carriers dressed in bright red-patterned robes and hats still walk through the small towns and the larger cities alike. For .5 dirham (DH), about 5 cents, they will pour you a drink of water in their copper community cup from the full goatskin water sack strapped across their back.

The medinas, the casbahs, the restaurants, and most of the souks you'll visit were standing in much the same condition 200 to 300 years or more ago. While even the terms today hold a special charm and magic, you'll soon learn that the "medina" is the oldest part of the city, often walled. The "casbah" was originally a citadel or fortress. Not every city has a casbah, but those that do exist are as magical as the name implies, with large walls and ornately decorated gates, still the entrance to the city within. The "souks" are the rural markets where, from the beginning of time, the people from the mountains have come to buy the goods they need and sell the wares they have produced. As you walk from one to the other, and especially when you visit the tannery in the casbah of Fez, you'll need to remind yourself that you are still in the late twentieth century. I can vividly recall the feeling of awe and wonder I experienced as I looked out over the square in Marrakech filled with the flutes of snake charmers, fire-eaters, falconers, and storytellers performing for the hundreds of tribesmen gathered to watch.

Best of all, the Moroccans love Americans. We were the first country to officially recognize them when they gained their independence from France in 1956, and they have not forgotten. Morocco has maintained the spirit of an old Arab saying, "O traveler, if you come into my home, you will be the master of the house, and I will be your guest." The official greeting for the tourist, which I heard on numerous occasions, is "Welcome to Morocco, Your Second Home."

Social Climate

While the primary language is Arabic, almost everyone speaks French. English is the next most frequently spoken language followed by Spanish. If you're not proficient in a second language, you'll still have no problem in Morocco. The staffs at all of the large hotels are multilingual, as are the guides. Many speak ten to twelve languages fluently, which is why they hold their relatively well-paying jobs.

Even when I wandered off into small bedouin farming villages where the people spoke only Arabic, I found them warm and welcoming. They went out of their way to try to communicate with me. They greeted me by bringing their hands to their lips then touching my chest. Best of all, without speaking a word, I could understand; they made me feel welcome and comfortable as I wandered through their land.

While restricted and controlled, the women of Morocco are also protected and respected. The result, much to my surprise, was that I was not harassed by the men on the street. It was almost as if they wouldn't even consider such disrespectful and inappropriate behavior. In a country where about 30 percent of the women still wear veils and the others are covered from head to toe, it really should not have come as such a surprise.

While you will find a few discos in Casablanca, and the large resorts have cocktail lounges, the nightlife here is not the primary attraction. So, though you will meet other travelers, mostly from Europe and other African countries (very few Americans), this is not the place to go if your primary objective is meeting other single people.

Thanks to the French influence, the Moroccan upper class (there's really no middle class by our standards) are very charming and "continental." Most speak a little English as well as being fluent in French. The local men will be interested in speaking with you. On the streets I was hesitant to do so, being uncertain of their motives.

In the hotel lounges I felt more comfortable. The setting was safer. In Islamic Morocco the men still classify women as either virgins, wives, or whores. Women must still be virgins when they marry or no man will have them. There's no female sexual liberation here. On the other hand, men are expected to be sexually experienced. So where do they look for their experiences? To prostitutes or to Western women, whom they consider "loose" sexually. This is one of those countries in which it's particularly important to be careful that your friendly behavior is not interpreted as an invitation to sex. Don't invite a man to your hotel and don't go to his unless you want to be more intimate. If you're not interested in a man who seems interested in you, you can more easily exit by saying "I must go. My husband/ boyfriend/father is waiting for me." Then get up and leave.

Activities

You can enjoy sunbathing at the beach or pool one day, then ski down the slopes of the *Atlas Mountains* the next. You can relax in the luxury of a first-class resort after having walked through streets that have not changed in hundreds of years. Even the clothing worn by the people, and the donkeys used for transportation, have remained the same. You can drive through pine forests or ride a camel through the desert. All extremes are possible in this small country.

Safety

When I first told friends I was planning to include Morocco in this book, some (who had not been there) were shocked. "It's not safe! You're not going alone, are you?" was their first response. Much to my surprise, I found men and women alike were afraid to travel to this wonderful, hospitable country.

There are places in Morocco that are not safe, such as Tangiers, a border town much like Tijuana, where thievery is rampant. There are also things you just don't do anywhere in Morocco, such as leave your bags in the car unattended, especially overnight. When you park your car you'll also want to park where there is an official to watch it. He should have a round badge. For 1 DH (about 10 cents) he'll not only watch your car, but likely wash your windshield, too. The large hotels all have safe parking available. There are also areas you shouldn't go alone at night. Your hotel staff or guide can tell you which areas to stay away from.

Morocco is a poor country, so you may occasionally be approached by beggars. They mean you no harm. They only want you to give them money. With the exception of the very old, who usually sit quietly with their head bowed and hand open, I prefer not to encourage beggars by giving them money. Also, as a result of the general poverty, theft is a problem. If you must carry a purse, keep it close to your body, not over a shoulder, and do the same with your camera. If your hotel does not have a safe-deposit box, keep your traveler's checks and passports on you securely. This is a good county in which to wear a money belt. Varieties are available that can be pinned into a bra or you can devise your own from a handkerchief.

As in most big cities, if you use good common sense and take a few simple precautions, you will be less vulnerable. You'll also have a happier, less traumatic vacation.

Preparing for Your Trip to Morocco

Documents

You will need a valid passport to enter Morocco. American citizens do not need a visa. If you are planning to rent a car, you will also need a current International Driver's License.

When to Go

Whether you're looking for adventure, the unusual, or just an escape from a cold, dreary winter at home, December through April is the time to visit Morocco. Marrakech is an oasis town on the edge of the Sahara Desert, so even in late May or early June you can begin to feel the heat from the desert. The advantage of Morocco is that there is little rain at any time of the year. In my opinion early spring is the best time to visit, unless, of course, you want to ski.

Ramadan. For one month each year, Muslims abstain from eating and drinking during the daylight hours. This month, called Ramadan, commemorates the most holy month when God revealed the Koran to the Prophet Muhammad. As you might expect in a desert country, tempers can get somewhat short in the hot afternoons. In the late afternoons you will see Moslems crowding around *pâtisseries* to purchase their box of the wonderful Moroccan cookies, made from ground almond flour and honey. It is a testament to their strong belief in Allah that the box reaches home intact. I know I would have a difficult time resisting such delicacies. Prayer is especially important during this time, as is giving to the poor. It is considered good luck to give grain or money to the less fortunate during Ramadan.

I arrived in Casablanca in early June and hit the last three days of Ramadan. (It begins and ends with the new moon, so the dates will vary.) The end of Ramadan is a holiday. The short tempers are then replaced with celebration and, a short time later, the beginning of the Annual Folklore Festival in Marrakech. As a result, there are advantages and disadvantages to a visit at this time of year.

Annual Folklore Festival. The nomadic tribal life-style of the Berbers, the initial inhabitants of Morocco, has, of course, changed as Morocco has "developed." Many wandering tribes have settled into farming communities; others still move with their herds of goats. Today, the Berbers make up 60 percent of the population of Morocco.

This yearly gathering of the Berber tribes in Marrakech is one of the ways that their rich national heritage has been preserved. The full week of activities includes craft displays, street theater, and lots of music and dancing. The dancers wear full tribal regalia with colorful sequined robes, sashes, and jewelry unique to the area. Turbaned horsemen, firing muskets in the air, charge forward as if in battle. The women produce a shrill undulating chant like nothing I've heard before, and gyrate their bodies in movements much like the Tahitian hula.

These are not professional dancers brought in to entertain. These are the tribesmen and women from all around the area who have come to celebrate and honor their heritage. We're fortunate to be able to observe this sacred folkway. For more information, contact the Moroccan National Tourist Office, 20 East 46th Street, New York, NY 10017; (212) 557-2520.

Skiing. If you are a ski enthusiast as I am, you, too, will be surprised to learn there are two downhill ski areas in Morocco. While they claim to operate November to May, the locals inform me this is "of course" dependent upon weather. They are more likely to be operating late December through February. *Oukaimeden* near Marrakech is the best area. The lifts are primarily the old-style T-bars, and the housing facilities are not good. But it is close enough that you could stay in Marrakech and make the hour or so drive to the slopes in the morning. While I would not go to Morocco specifically to ski—there are bigger ski areas in the world—the slopes are better than anything Minnesota has to offer. And I plan on taking my next trip during January or February in order to get in a day or two of skiing. You can rent all of your equipment, so you need only bring suitable clothing.

What to Take

When you are packing for your trip to Morocco, keep in mind that Moroccan women are dressed in robes from head to foot. While the Berber women don't wear veils, the Arab women do. Modesty should be a real consideration in an attempt not to offend.

I would *not* take sleeveless or low-cut tops, or shorts. It's no fun having the local men talk to your breasts. I was appalled and embarrassed by two women at the front of a tour group as it walked through the streets of Marrakech. One was dressed in a white lace see-through top with short shorts. The fact that she was wearing a bra did little to help. The other was wearing a chamois fringe "dress" that barely covered her crotch. I listened closely as the group passed, and I must admit I was relieved to discover they were *not* speaking English. I wondered what the two veiled Arab women across the street thought as they passed by.

When you're packing, remember it can get very hot depending on the time of year you are traveling. Loose-fitting cotton clothing, either long pants or dresses, is the most practical and comfortable. And since few streets through the old towns are paved, and even those that are get dusty, you'll want clothes you can rinse out at night when necessary. I'd also suggest loose-fitting, long-sleeved shirts to protect you from the sun when you're out and about. Sunscreen is great around the pool, but it will end up collecting a layer of dust when you're out on the streets. Also bring comfortable walking shoes, sandals, and, of course, a bathing suit.

I'd suggest buying a kaftan in Morocco to wear to dinner in the evening instead of packing a dress. They're comfortable, inexpensive, and exotic—and they'll dazzle your friends. The less exotic ones are great for everyday wear or for entertaining back home. They also make great gifts.

It's a good idea to take a small number of items for gifts and/or to trade. T-shirts, candy, and especially the small credit card–size pocket calculators are especially good. When I brought out my pocket calculator in a shop in Morocco, the owner almost began to drool. In exchange for it, I had my pick of anything in the shop. I also traded a hair pick and a plastic card with a favorite saying for a couple of Fez hats in Fez. Gift giving is a tradition in Morocco. It should be something small so it can be reciprocated.

Money

The local currency is the dirham (DH), and you are not allowed to take them into or out of Morocco. You can buy dirhams at the airport exchange bureau when you arrive, at banks, or at the major hotels. The exchange bureau at Casablanca Mohammed V Airport is open continuously. The exchange rate used in this book is 9.6 DH equals US$1. In order to change dirhams back to U.S. dollars when you leave, you will need to show your original bank receipts. If you were in Morocco more than forty-eight hours, only 50 percent of the original amount will be exchanged. When you leave the country, the customs officer will ask you how many dirhams you have. While small amounts are not a problem, any amount could be confiscated.

Health Concerns

You will not need any particular immunizations in preparation for your trip to Morocco. You should, however, always check with your local health department for the latest recommendations. While the water is considered safe in the big cities, I only drank it when it was boiled for the more refreshing and memorable mint tea. I am usually not so cautious, but in Morocco I decided not to take the chance. Morocco is fortunate to have plentiful water in the north and in the Atlas Mountains to the east.

Getting There

The Casablanca Mohammed V Airport is new and modern. As you deplane and attempt to exit the airport, you'll have your first taste of Moroccan bureaucracy. Don't be surprised if the people on the customs lines don't move, except for the men who know someone and go around back to get their family's passports stamped. Be patient; eventually you'll get through customs. Watching the colorful dress of the women, especially those from the Sudan, will help pass the time.

Don't forget to change some money at the bureau office just outside of customs. This is also the area where you'll pick up your rental car.

Getting Around

I highly recommend a rental car. The roads are excellent, interesting, and the distances relatively short. There is no better way to see Morocco than by car. I'd stick with one of the big international companies, such as Hertz or Avis. Their rates are comparable with the small companies and their service is far superior. When I left the country there was no one to check my car in. I felt much better leaving knowing I was dealing with a reputable company that would not try to overcharge me. For a one-week rental with unlimited mileage, you can expect to pay approximately 2,000 DH.

While there is very inexpensive bus and train service, both can be full of people, as well as produce, going to and from the market. The buses are especially slow, stopping to let passengers off not only at every small town, but also at what appears to be the middle of nowhere.

The airfares between cities are surprisingly inexpensive (Rabat to Casablanca US$9; Marrakech to Casablanca US$17). But the airports are a long way from town, some more than 15 miles, so you'll need to take a cab or rent a car when you arrive anyway.

Guides

All guides should have an official badge. The going rate, always negotiable, is 80 DH for a full day and 50 DH for a half day of three to four hours. If you are interested, ask the people at the front desk of your hotel to arrange for a reputable guide to contact you. Don't hire one of the many small, or not so small, boys on the streets who will want to act as your guide. You will likely find that they don't know the language or the area, and they only want to take you to shops where they get a commission on everything you buy. Even an official guide gets a commission on your purchases—it's the way of life in Morocco. However, he will at least take you to reputable shops where you will not be overcharged. Guides must all pass a test and be fluent in a number of languages. If you do not have a rental car, your guide will arrange to hire one for the day, which will, of course, cost more.

If you're interested, you can also hire a guide to go with you to other towns. The advantage of this is that you'll have guide service along the way as well. Be sure it's agreed that he pays for his own food and room. The going rate for excursions is more, between 150 DH to 250 DH a day. You'll be expected to provide the car. When you hire him, be sure to specify what cities you want to see.

I highly recommend hiring a guide. The medinas and casbahs, with their narrow winding streets, are easy to get lost in. The maps available are inadequate. A guide will also keep the beggars away and make sure you don't miss any of the important sights.

Tipping

Tipping is an expected way of life in Morocco. You should tip often but in small amounts. You'll tip the person who watches your car 1 DH. Whenever you take a picture, you should tip the person 1 DH, or if someone guides you a short distance, a 1 DH tip will be gladly accepted. Tip cab drivers 10 percent, waiters 10 percent to 15 percent of the bill, depending on the elegance of the restaurant. If you negotiate the price for a guide in a city, you need not tip, unless he performs a special service, then tip him for that special service. A tip in U.S. dollars is especially desirable as Moroccans cannot obtain "hard" foreign currency at a bank.

Moroccan Cuisine

You'll experience some of the best cuisine in the world in Morocco. While likely the result of the French influence, the similarity ends at the quality. The primary meat is lamb, although Moroccans eat a lot of chicken. The mainstay of their diet is couscous. Its base is a steamed grain somewhat similar to rice. It is combined with vegetables and either chicken, mutton, or beef.

You'll also find brochette (shish kebab) made from a variety of meats, including lamb, beef, and veal. Another favorite dish is tajine, which is cooked and served in a special pottery dish with a large pointed lid. While it is usually made from roast lamb, sometimes camel meat is used. Favorite variations include onions and raisins, prunes, or olives and lemon. Poulet au citron (lemon chicken) is also a favorite—don't miss this Moroccan specialty.

My most memorable dish, which I highly recommend, is Pastilla aux pigeonneaux (pigeon pie). The best place to order it is Fez, although it is served throughout Morocco. It's a light pastry, somewhat like a meat pie, filled with a cinnamon and almond-flavored squab (pigeon) meat. Sometimes it will also contain chicken, which tastes very similar. It's excellent. This is an area specialty you won't want to miss.

Your meal will usually include a wonderful Moroccan salad of tomato and green pepper sautéed in garlic. It's served hot or cold. Dinner will be followed by mint tea and the wonderful almond and honey cookies.

Taking Pictures

Many Moroccans believe that you are taking a part of their soul when you take their picture, and that it may bring them bad luck. As a result, it is not okay to just take someone's picture, especially Arab women wearing veils. If you see someone turn their head away or cover their face, common sense should tell you it's not okay to take their picture, so please don't, for your own sake as well as theirs. A friend of mine had a man follow him, very upset, because he thought he had taken his picture.

Water carriers, performers, and small children have somehow managed to overcome this taboo and will allow you to take their picture, but only if you pay them. The usual rate is 1 DH, so be sure to carry a pocket full of 1 DH coins. They can get quite upset if they don't get paid. The performers in the square in Marrakech will try to get more. If you offer 1 DH, they'll want 2 DH. If you offer 5 DH, they'll want 10 DH. Don't be intimidated—once you've paid, be firm and continue on your way.

Treasures to Purchase

Morocco is one place you must bargain; you should never pay the first price asked. The more you buy, the better bargaining power you have. On large purchases, you can often pay as much as 50 percent less than the initial asking price. You should get at least 30 percent off on smaller purchases. You can also expect to get complimentary Coke or mint tea when you're shopping for such larger items as a rug, or if you're in a larger shop. This, too, is part of the custom.

In order to lighten your burden, I'd recommend shopping in one of the establishments that will ship your purchases home for you. While the items will likely be a little more expensive than those on the street, the quality will be more consistent and most accept major credit cards or a personal check.

In addition to the kaftans, you can buy beautiful lightweight Moroccan shirts and leather goods. Most of the leather is either goat or camel skin. You will also find shops with beautifully tooled silver, brass, copper, and nickel plates, bowls, candlesticks, cook pots, and so on.

Don't miss the shops selling spices, makeup, perfume, and toilet articles. They have everything from chunks of musk derived from the neck glands of the gazelle to chunks of henna and charcoal for under your eyes and to make the proper Berber tattoo on your forehead and chin. This is how the women designate which tribe they belong to. The henna is used as a hair conditioner and to draw intricate patterns on the palms and feet of young girls and women, which is done on special occasions for its beauty and to bring good luck. You'll also find a wide variety of spices and jars of colored powder to be mixed with water and used for eye shadow.

For a small tip, the shopkeeper may even apply the makeup for you, much as in the department stores back home. However, here you'll sit on the stool and watch Berbers and Arabs pass through the narrow streets of the medina on donkeys or carrying chickens to the market. There is very little resemblance to the beauty stores back home where the salesladies show you how to apply their wares.

CASABLANCA TO MARRAKECH

Casablanca

Morocco's major seaport and the most well known of her cities, Casablanca became the capital of the Berber kingdom in the eighth century. The actual date of the initial settlement of this now modern city of 2.5 million is uncertain. Casablanca translates to "white house," and indeed most of the buildings here, as well as throughout the rest of Morocco, are white.

Exploring Casablanca

As you drive into town you'll initially enter the center of the new modern city and *Mohammad V Square*. The broad avenue *Hassan II* is lined with modern buildings on one side and the *Park of the Arab League* with its palm-tree-lined walkways and gardens on the other. This is only the first of many indicators of how much the Moroccans love their royal family. Mohammad V is the father of the present King Hassan II, whose picture you'll see everywhere. Interestingly enough, the Moroccans have never seen his wife, and pictures of her are not available. Even the prominently displayed pictures of his daughter's recent wedding include only her and the king, never his wife.

You'll also want to see *United Nations Square* and *The Palace of Justice*. While you can go into the *Sacre Coeur Church* to see its spectacular walls of stained glass, you cannot enter the many spectacular mosques you'll see throughout the country. They are strictly places of worship reserved for Muslims only.

You should also take a walk along the boulevard overlooking the public beach on the northwest edge of town. On the drive from the center of town to the beach, you'll pass one of the many summer palaces of the royal family. Swimming pools that can be used for a fee (140 DH per day) are located here. The nightclubs are in this area as well.

Toward the end of the beach area are steps leading down to the *Crepuscule* restaurant, an ideal place to lunch or to simply sit overlooking the surf and sip mint tea.

One of the highlights of your trip to Casablanca is bound to be the market, where you can purchase everything from fresh meat and fish to shoes and flowers. The medina is the original Arab settlement, with narrow winding streets packed full of people on foot, donkey carts, turbaned men on horses, and women with large loads balanced on their heads. *The Casbah* is the part of town enclosed within the old fortress walls. Your guide will show you where Bogart wandered during the film that made this city famous. *The Mosque of King Mohammad V* built in 1936 is very near the entrance to the Casbah.

Be sure to ask your guide to take you to the *Pâtisserie Traiteur* in the Habous area. While the Moroccan almond and honey cookies are usually wonderful, these are by far the best in the country. They'll make you up a box of assorted varieties for just a few dirhams. This was my last stop in Casablanca before I caught my plane home, much to the delight of my friends.

You'll find Casablanca is many very different cities within one city. On a hill overlooking the medina and Casbah, you'll find a new modern section. Here are high walls with palm trees and guards at the gates of the villas of the prince and diplomats. In town you'll find a European-style shopping mall with Western-style clothes, very near to the dirt streets and ancient souks (small shops).

Where to Stay in Casablanca

Hotel Riad Salam, Boulevard de la Corniche (single 400 DH, double 500 DH). Located on the edge of the ocean not far below the Palace of the Prince, this is an excellent choice. Unfortunately, the rooms don't look out onto the ocean, but they do face a beautifully terraced pool with a gardened inner courtyard. The inlaid tile floors and walls in the lobby include a wall of water cascading toward the entry. The restaurant looks like a Moorish palace so typical of the nicer Moroccan restaurants.

Casablanca Hyatt Regency, Place Mohammad V (single 700 DH, double 800 DH). The striking beauty of this hotel begins with the black marble lobby floor with its colorful center tile pattern, bright red Arab rugs, and red Victorian furniture. Behind the main lobby is the Moorish palace–style *Golden Gates* restaurant, complete with a fountain. The *Maison Blanche* is an elegant European-style dining room. I, however, prefer the Moroccan *Dau Beida* restaurant with the low tables and thick cushion seats so typical of the country. From 9:00 P.M. to 3:00 A.M. *The Black House* nightclub and disco is open. It specializes in popular French music. They also have a *Casablanca Bar* that is loaded with Humphrey Bogart memorabilia, including posters from his movie that I coveted.

Hotel El Mansour, 27 Ave. De L'Armee Royale (single 350 DH, double 400 DH). In the center of town near Place Mohammad V, this hotel is comfortable, relaxing, and unpretentious. You'll find Moorish-style silver chandeliers hanging from the lobby ceiling. The rooms are bright, spacious, and nicely furnished. Their royal suite is indeed fit for a king with a colorful tentlike canopy over the bed.

Hotel Transatlantic, 79 Rue Colbert (single 130 DH, double 200 DH). An excellent value in the price category, this is where you'll run into travelers from the Sudan. The women in their brightly colored layers of fabric are stunning. The lobby has a pleasant Moorish-style lounge. The rooms are large and well maintained.

Where to Eat in Casablanca

Al Mounia, 95 Rue du Prince Moulay Abdellah. This is the finest restaurant in Casablanca. The typical Moorish palace–style interior is carried to the courtyard as well. Typical Moroccan dishes, including tajine and couscous (35 DH), are served. You can get a complete meal for around 80 DH.

Le Buffet, 88 Ave. Mohammad V. This European-style restaurant is pleasant, bright, and comfortable. The service is excellent and food good. A complete meal with wine will be under 100 DH.

Restaurant Riad Salam, Blvd. de la Corniche. A Moorish palace atmosphere with elaborate silver teapots and trays. Berber dancers entertain, beginning around 9:00 P.M. Dinners range from 60 DH to 300 DH. Your waiter will even sprinkle rose water over you from a special silver decanter at the end of your meal.

From Casablanca to Rabat

As you leave Casablanca with the Atlantic on your left, you'll first pass flat bedouin farmland with small villages between. Each has its own mosque with its tall square tower rising above the village. You'll pass herds of sheep and goats, often with small children dutifully tending them.

About 80 kilometers from Casablanca, in the middle of the farmlands, the speed limit will decrease to 40 kph. If you watch closely, you'll see a sign with a picture of a crown indicating that the red brick wall with the green tile top on your left is the summer palace of King Hassan II.

You'll pass a stretch of deserted sandy beach before turning left toward Rabat. After that you'll pass a number of summer ocean villas belonging to the wealthy, including the king's two sons. They're always surrounded by high walls and guarded by soldiers. They're just outside of Rabat.

Rabat

The high ancient walls of the casbah will be visible as you enter Rabat, the capital of Morocco and the primary home of King Hassan II. I recommend checking into the Hotel de la Tour Hassan and, of course, unloading your car before exploring the town. This is *the* place to stay in Rabat.

Exploring Rabat

Founded by the Romans in the first century, the remains of *Chellah*, a fourteenth-century Roman city, are now being restored. You'll be both amazed and charmed by the large, awkward straw nests of storks perched on top of the ruins of Chellah. You can walk through the remains of the old Roman baths on the sites in front of the entry gates.

Nearby you can walk through the 48-acre grounds of Hassan II's elaborate palace. While you cannot enter the actual palace, you can stroll the gardens with their beautiful fountains. The mosque where the king prays every Friday he's in Rabat is on the grounds, as is a special building where he greets diplomats. King since 1961, he is exceptionally popular with the people. This is not a country where it's a good idea for a visitor to speak negatively about the monarchy. He has improved the educational system, medical care, and the irrigation system for the farmlands.

The glory of Rabat is the *Hassan Tower*, built in the Twelfth century. The *Tomb of Mohammed V* is on the same square above Rabat. This elaborate tomb is guarded by turbaned soldiers in white robes on horseback. In addition, prayers are said continuously over the tomb as they have been since Mohammed V's death in 1961. When you go there you can hear the Arabic chanting of the prayers. On the hill behind the Hassan Tower are the various embassies. You'll enjoy wandering through the medina, the old section of town, and the casbah. Many of the newer buildings as well as the old ones have green tile roofs for good luck.

Where to Stay in Rabat

Hotel de la Tour Hassan, 26 Ave. Abderrahmare Annegai (single 400 DH, double 500 DH). While not as large as King Hassan II's palace, this hotel of the same style is almost as elegant, and you'll certainly be treated like a queen here. The Moorish style throughout includes arched ceilings of inlaid tile with tiled walls and gray marble floors accented with bright red Arab carpets. The canopied lounge on the upper level has sheltered more than one prince. Soft piano music can be heard on the garden terrace. This is indeed a grand palatial hotel.

Hilton International Rabat, Aviation Souissi (single 250 DH, double 300 DH). A luxury, European-style hotel with tennis courts, pool, putting green, and elegant dining rooms.

Where to Eat in Rabat

Cafe Restaurant Saadi, 84 Ave. Alal Ben Andell. For 17 DH to 45 DH you can eat a typical Moroccan meal in this simple cafe in the new section of Rabat near Blvd. Mohammad V.

Koutoubia, 10 Zankat Pierre Parent. Near the casbah, this traditional-style restaurant features tajine and couscous. A complete meal will run 60 DH to 75 DH. An excellent restaurant that's reasonably priced.

Jour et Nuit, 4 Rue Ahfir. Open day and night, this large restaurant is a local favorite and can be crowded with long waits. While you can get Moroccan food here, they offer hamburgers, spaghetti, and omelets as well. They have a pleasant courtyard area.

Rabat to Meknes

If you rise relatively early, you can spend much of the day exploring Meknes then go on to Fez to spend the night. By the time you reach Meknes, you are too close to the Palais Jamai in Fez to spend the night in any other hotel.

As you leave Rabat driving east toward Meknes, you'll pass through the miles and miles of cork forest. Occasionally you'll see rows and rows of cork, the bark of the trees stacked like logs. The bottom portion of the tree will appear black where the bark has been stripped away. You'll also pass eucalyptus forests and olive trees as well as vineyards and fields of mint, lavender, and sunflowers, their heads all bowed in the direction of the sun.

As you get closer to such Berber villages as Tiflet, the road becomes crowded with donkey carts, motor scooters, and bicycles. The donkey is still the primary means of transportation in the villages and even on the boulevards in the major cities. The smell of mint is strong as you approach Meknes.

Meknes

You enter the imperial city of Meknes through the spectacular heavily decorated gate Bab El Mansour in the seventeenth-century walls that still surround much of the city. There's an immense and beautiful stable that once housed 12,000 horses and a granary as big as a cathedral in which their feed was stored. There is an ancient pool covering nearly 10 acres nearby; it was once used to irrigate the gardens. The mosque here, which houses the body of Moulay Ismail, one of the monarchs of Meknes, is the only mosque in Morocco open to non-Muslims.

I'd suggest buying a handful of fresh mint leaves prior to your walk through the medina of Meknes. This was the only area in Morocco where I saw and smelled decaying garbage.

When King Hassan II is in town he stays at another of his palaces located here, *Par el Makhzen*. Nearby you'll find the *Bab Er-Rih* (Gate of the Wind) and the *Garden of the Sultans*.

Volubilis

If you can see Meknes in half a day, you'll also have time to see the ancient Roman ruins of Volubilis. It's on a dramatic windswept plain not far from Meknes. Excavation was begun in the early 1900s and covers over 100 acres. Guides are available to show you through the ruins.

Fez

Less than an hour's drive farther will bring you to one of the most incredible cities in the world, Fez—an ancient city, an aristocratic city, a city filled with mystery. Initially founded in the eighth century, Fez has one of the oldest mosques in North Africa, the ninth-century *Qarawiyin Mosque*. Part of the mystical quality of Fez is evoked by the call to prayers you'll hear from the mosques at dusk, again two hours later, and then at sunrise. From your balcony in the Palais Jamai you can look out over the medina in awe as you listen to the chants from the hundreds of mosques, each of which independently chants in Arabic, a language very foreign to American ears. The rates of the chants vary, as does the pitch; some are shrill, others very low. Some are close and others are far away, barely audible. The effect is enchanting and hypnotic. You will know you've entered into a world that is in many ways still as it was hundreds of years ago.

Exploring Fez

The mystery of Fez is found in the ancient part of town, the medina. I entered with a small crowd of people through the ancient gates *Bab Boujeloud* that date from the fourteenth century. One man, riding his donkey, had live sheep in saddlebags on either side of the donkey and another in front of him, all bound for market. A small boy was carrying two live pigeons by the feet. Another donkey had six large crates of Coca-Cola balanced on top of his back. A short distance inside I passed a man sitting in a doorway with two live roosters tied by their feet beside him as he plucked another, freshly killed. Many of the women, in veils and robes, were balancing jugs and large baskets on their heads. Still another donkey had so much hay on his back that his size was doubled, and just the tip of his nose protruded as he passed.

The stalls on the maze of streets are endless and wonderful, filled with brass, copper, silver, candies, incense, candles, nuts, dried fruits, pottery, fabrics, clothing, and pointed shoes of leather and fabric worn by men and women alike. Different areas offer different goods. You'll also pass ancient mosques, palaces, and *medersas* (former schools) now abandoned except for the occasional visitor. You will want a guide to help you find your way back to the twentieth century.

Make sure you go to the *Tanner's Quarters*. While the stench here is not as bad as that in the Meknes medina, take a handful of mint leaves with you anyway. As you enter a short narrow passage, you'll no doubt pass a large pile of skins with horns still attached lying in the corner. In the tannery you'll see well-worn cement dye vats. Men wearing only shorts, their bare legs and feet the red color of the dye, walk between and through the vats dyeing the hides. In another area, men similarly dressed are working with sticks in vats of lye bleaching the hides. For a small tip one of the workers will lead you up a narrow stairway for a better view of the thirty to forty vats in the open area below. While more of each step was worn away than remaining, I hesitated touching the wall to keep my footing for fear of forever smelling like this godforsaken place.

You'll want to see *Nejjarine Square* with its mosaic fountain with the *Fondouk*, an eighteenth-century stable that housed camels and donkeys downstairs and the merchants and visitors who rode them to town upstairs. This medina is worth hours or days of wandering and exploring.

Fez Carpets

If you're interested in buying a carpet in Fez, I'd recommend going to the *Palais Salam* (9 Kettanine) in the medina. Originally built as a House of Music in the fourteenth century, the building alone is worth a visit. The walls and floors are made of intricately inlaid tile and marble. (The marble was obtained by trading the Italians 1 kilo of sugar for 1 kilo of marble.) The enclosed center courtyard is three stories high with exquisite brown Berber rugs, red Arab rugs, and blue Fez rugs draped everywhere. Since 1956, this building has housed the cooperative of 1,500 area women. They make the rugs by hand in their homes and bring them to the shop to be displayed and sold.

The Berber rugs can be identified by their earth tones. These rugs are the loosest weave, with 60,000 knots per square meter. The tighter Arab rugs have 90,000 knots per square meter; and Fez rugs 160,000 knots per square meter. The Berbers have no written language. Their rugs have been their literature. Tribes or individuals would make rugs with their distinct pattern to present as gifts. Before being sold, the rugs are evaluated for their quality and a government label is affixed to the back.

They almost make buying too easy at the Palais Salam. They accept credit cards or even a personal check and they will, of course, ship your chosen treasure home. To ensure you get the rug you wanted, you'll be asked to sign the back of the rug before you leave the store.

Where to Stay in Fez

Palais Jamai, (single 420 DH, double 580 DH with medina view— well worth the 40 DH to 80 DH extra to look from your balcony onto the ancient city).

Located within the ancient walls of old Fez, the pre-Moorish architecture was designed to bring pleasure and peace to the soul. It was originally built by the Jamai family in 1296 as a place to escape from the city to the restful pleasure of trickling fountains. The tiled courtyard garden has fragrant orange and apricot trees as well as medicinal herbs. It was purchased for a hotel in 1930, and was completely restored to its former splendor. An oasis of peace, charm, and luxury, it now has a pool in the garden, two excellent restaurants, a nightclub, and shops.

When you exit the lobby door and turn left you enter the magic of the medina. The location and setting combined make this hotel one of the best in the world and *the* place to stay in Fez.

Hotel Merinides, in Bordj Nord (single 400 DH, double 500 DH). This modern luxury hotel is located 4 kilometers out of town on a small hill above Fez. The bluff-side pool is attractive and inviting, as is the Parisian-style cafe, bar, and nightclub.

Where to Eat in Fez

Restaurant Tijani, in the medina. Entered through a narrow passage with tiled walls, this restaurant is a real find. Couscous, tajine, and other Moroccan specialties are served from 10:00 A.M. to 7:00 P.M. (40 DH). The interior is that of a very small old Moroccan palatial home with low pillow seats, small round tables, and mosaic tile walls. The rooms are alive with wonderful colors and odors.

Al Firdaous, in the medina. Just beside the Palais Jamai as you turn to enter the streets of the medina, this restaurant will be on your right. The drums and Berber dancers don't begin until 9:30 P.M., so you'll want to eat late. For 40 DH to 70 DH they offer all the Moroccan specialties, including excellent local wine. The pastilla (pigeon pie) is better here than anywhere else I tried it. The tajines are also exceptionally well prepared. The inner courtyard is covered by a canopy two stories above. Beautiful old rugs hang on the mosaic tile walls built over 200 years ago.

Palais des Merinides, 99 Zkat et Rouah. Also located in the medina, this is another excellent choice for authentic Moroccan cuisine and ambiance, and they offer an excellent pastilla. Dinners range from 60 DH to 80 DH.

Fez to Marrakech

I found it especially hard to leave Fez. On my next visit I'd like to stay longer, but the drive to Marrakech was pleasant and Marrakech was even more spectacular. It's a full day's drive, 520 kilometers, along the Atlas Mountains. Midway, at Beni Mellal, a number of tourist resort hotels with pools and nice restaurants have sprung up, a nice place to stop if you'd like to break up your drive. However, there's not much else here. Unless you simply want to relax around a pool, I would suggest continuing on to Marrakech.

Ifrane

You'll drive through the picturesque town of Ifrane with its stone buildings and green tile roofs. It's spotlessly clean. You can see one of the king's many castles on the hill above town. This is the smaller of the two ski areas in Morocco, and you can rent ski equipment if you'd like. The slope is just 18 kilometers out of town. They even have a *Chamonix Restaurant*.

As you continue on your way to Marrakech, you'll pass the villages of *Azrou* and *Khenifra*. Look for the large stork nests in the valley with four to five large birds in a single nest. You'll also pass tents that are the temporary homes of bedouin herders. They move frequently during the summer as they follow their herds. At harvest time you'll pass whole families cutting the wheat by hand and tying it into small bundles.

As you get closer to Marrakech, the buildings become a deeper and deeper pink until they look like adobe.

Marrakech

Nothing I had ever experienced in the past evoked the degree of wonder and amazement the *Djemaa El Fna Square*, the center of life in Marrakech, did. This is where the Berbers and Arabs come to perform, sell their wares, and watch others perform. This is where you'll see dancers, acrobats, soothsayers, palm readers, and jugglers. This is where you'll hear the flutes of the snake charmers and musicians playing instruments you've never seen before.

Marrakech is an oasis. It sits on the edge of the Sahara in the midst of 30,000 acres of over 120,000 palm trees planted in the eleventh century. Winston Churchill, a frequent visitor, spent hours painting these palms during the darkest periods of World War II. He came here to find peace, health, and his former vitality.

Marrakech, from its very beginnings, has drawn tribesmen and women from the mountains to its souks to buy and sell. Since the selling of wares and the buying of provisions is so important to the tribal, nomadic life-style, the souks have always been under the protection of the religious and political powers, as a place where even enemies could meet without risk. Much like the villages you've seen as you approach, the buildings of Marrakech are a deep rose pink. Once the center of the Islamic world, it is still the jewel.

Exploring Marrakech

Even in the new, quite modern quarters of Marrakech, the large, busy boulevards will have nearly as many horse-drawn carts as cars. I recommend parking and walking through the souks. You will see an occasional car, and my guide often thought I was crazy for wanting to walk "when we have a perfectly good car," but somehow a car seemed so out of place on these narrow ancient streets. They belonged to the horse and donkey, not to a car. Besides, you'll see so much more on foot. I found getting from one sight to another just as interesting if not more interesting than the places I had come to see. The streets hold the life of Marrakech.

You can still see many of the old gates leading into Marrakech: *Bad Doukkala*, *Bad Ailen*, *Bad Debbagh*, *Bad El Khemis*, and *Bad Taghzout*. You'll also find the most famous mosque in Africa, *Koutoubia Mosque*. This twelfth-century, light-green mosque rises 226 feet to tower over Marrakech. After visiting Djemaa El Fna Square, you'll want to wander through the souks nearby.

The fourteenth-century *Monument Ibn Yussef*, once used as a university, and the *Bahia Palace and Moorish Gardens* are a must. In former days, the king's harem lived at this palace, each woman with a separate elegantly decorated room off the main courtyard. The jasmine trees in the garden add to the magic of the history made here. The *Saadian*

Tombs, with the remains of the Saadian monarchs, are near the *Mellah*, the Jewish quarter of town. The Saadis traded 1 kilo of salt for 1 kilo of gold for the tombs.

The *Dar Si Said Museum* is especially interesting. Here you'll not only see jewelry more than two centuries old from the various Berber tribes, their elaborate robes and copper and nickel utensils, but you'll also see the first Ferris wheel for children, which is more than a hundred years old. The palace is of the typically ornate Moorish inlaid tile with an inner courtyard with fountain. The ceilings are carved and painted cedar wood. Many of the walls are covered by Berber kilims, rugs made by the tribes as gifts for great feasts.

Most of all, however, take time to wander through the souks, the streets, and the beautiful gardens of Marrakech.

Where to Stay in Marrakech

Mamounia Hotel, Ave. Bad Idid (single 750 DH, double 960 DH). Completely remodeled in 1986, this hotel remains the most elegant in Marrakech. It was from the top floor of this hotel that Winston Churchill painted the picture later shown in London depicting the orange and olive tree gardens with the snow-covered peaks of the Atlas Mountains off in the distance. It offers refined Moroccan luxury, excellent service, and relaxing gardens.

Hotel Es Saadi, Ave. Qiadossa (single 320 DH, double 380 DH). The famous casino of Marrakech, which opens daily at 9:00 P.M., is located on the grounds. The hotel offers European-style luxury. Its walled gardens include a pool with a refreshing breeze from the waterfall near the lobby.

Hotel Safir (single 325 DH, double 375 DH). The lobby is dark but pleasant. This luxury hotel blends the feeling of East and West. The large pool in the palm-treed courtyard is pleasant and inviting.

Hotel Palais El Badis, Ave. de la Menara (single 250 DH, double 300 DH). A pleasant Moroccan-style lobby, with a large garden and pool. All rooms overlook the pool. The staff here is helpful and pleasant.

Where to Eat in Marrakech

Restaurant Fantasia Chez Ali, outskirts of Marrakech. For 209 DH a person, you can experience the same spectacular "Fantasia" and feast that marks the birthday of King Hassan II. This event is a noteworthy example of traditional Moroccan folklore and pageantry. You'll dine on couscous, tajine, Moroccan salad with mint tea, and almond-honey pastries under large canopied tents with large cushions, low tables, and Arab rugs on the ground. The food is served from a large platter and it's customary to eat with your hands or scoop up the food with pieces of bread. If this doesn't appeal to you, you can always use the silverware provided. It's easy to feel like a member of a wealthy bedouin family. Berber dancers perform while men chant and play unusual instruments and drums. The highlight is the festival of gunpowder, with the frenzied dash of turbaned men on horseback firing muskets into the air amid the riders' piercing cries.

Restaurant El Bahia, Rue Raid Zitroun Jdid. You have a choice of three complete menus (150 DH to 180 DH), each of which includes tajine and pastilla. You'll wish you could eat all three. Five separate groups will perform while you dine. The two shows begin at 8:30 P.M. and 10:00 P.M. You'll see Berber dancers, jugglers, belly dancers, drummers, and acrobats. The restaurant is traditional Moorish style, which by now you should have grown accustomed to and feel comfortable in.

Restaurant Dar Es Salam, Rue Raid Zitroun El Kedim. Complete meals of tajine, brochette, and poulet au citron are 110 DH to 150 DH, a bargain at any price. This seventeenth-century building has carved cedar ceilings and inlaid tile walls. It's worth going just for the setting, although the food is just as exotic and appealing.

Bahja, Mamounia Hotel. Even if you're not staying at the Mamounia, don't miss this elegant Moroccan-style restaurant that specializes in Moroccan cuisine.

Around Marrakech

If you have time, I'd suggest a drive to *Oukaimeden*, the largest ski area in Morocco. Even if you don't ski or it's not the season, the Berber villages built on the sides of the mountains are fascinating.

If you have more time, you may also want to drive south to *Agadir*, *Taroudant*, and to experience the Sahara.

Marrakech to Casablanca

Eventually you must leave the ancient, mythical city of Marrakech. And once you leave that oasis, the 258 kilometers back to Casablanca is over land that is bleak and barren. Both the landscape and the heat rising from it are a constant reminder of the desert's nearness. There are few villages in the first 100 kilometers, although you'll likely pass a donkey cart or a camel caravan seemingly in the middle of nowhere. I wondered where they were coming from and going to. How long would their trek take them?

When you arrive again in Casablanca it will look so civilized in comparison to the wonders you've experienced since you were last here. Be sure to leave time to stop by the *pâtisserie* to pick up a box of almond-honey cookies. You'll be taking a small piece of Morocco home for you and your friends along with once-in-a-lifetime experiences and memories.

AMAZON RIVER CRUISE

▶ ─── ▶

GENERAL AMBIANCE   ★ ★
SOCIAL CLIMATE   ★ ★
ACTIVITIES   ★ ★

FOR TOUR ARRANGEMENTS CONTACT:
Society Expeditions
3131 Elliott Avenue, Suite 700
Seattle, WA 98121
(800) 426-7794

Or *contact your travel agent* and ask for the Society Expedition
    Project Amazon Trip

▶ ─── ▶

*T*he mighty Amazon River flowing through north central Brazil has always carried a certain mystique and sense of adventure. When I think of the Amazon, I think of thick jungle filled with brightly colored exotic birds, monkeys crossing the top of the forest canopy, and jaguars stalking the ground below. I think of witchcraft, voodoo, alligators, and piranhas. Myth and fantasy? Not so. While life in Brazil today is in a state of rapid change, as in many previously remote parts of the world, the mystique and adventure of discovery still remains.

General Ambiance

Brazil, which covers more than half of the South American continent, is one of the most diverse countries in the world in terms of its plants and wildlife. No one even knows how many species of plants exist in the Amazon region. While over 30,000 species have already been classified, scientists estimate as many more exist that have not been identified. Coming from a country where individual plants and animals are often followed and studied, it's hard to fathom being unknowledge-

EQUATOR

Manaus

Amazon R.

Belem

Fernando
de Noronha

B R A Z I L

Recife

Salvador
de Bahia

Brasilia

S O U T H   A M E R I C A

Rio de Janeiro

Atlantic Ocean

N

able about the species present. It's a little easier to grasp the magnitude of the task once you realize that while an acre of woods in the United States may contain a dozen or so different kinds of trees, a botanist from Manaus recently identified 290 different species on one acre of forest outside that very city.

A big advantage to exploring the Amazon with Society Expeditions, your host on this adventure, is that you will also be exploring the area with scientists collecting specimens, many of which will likely prove to be species never before identified. On my trip, Dr. Iain Prance, curator of Amazonian botany at the New York Botanic Garden, collected his 30,300th specimen for their herbarium (a museum of dried specimens). According to Brazilian law, half of the specimens he and other scientists collect must remain in Brazil. Most are kept in the Rio or Belém Botanic Garden collections. Being in the jungle with an expert such as Iain provides a unique sense of exploration and discovery.

On this adventure, you will travel the 1,000 miles of the Amazon from Manaus to Belém. The largest and most beautiful tributary, the Rio Negro joins the Solimoes River to officially become the Amazon at Manaus. This spectacular blending of the café-au-lait-colored Solimoes and the deep black Negro is called the Marriage of the Waters. Because of the difference in their viscosity, they run side by side for some time with a distinctly visible line of demarcation before their waters merge.

You'll experience the best of both the wild and civilized worlds traveling down the Amazon aboard the *Society Explorer*. After time ashore in dense jungle, you'll return to the ship's air-conditioned comfort with its unlimited supply of hot water running through your private shower. You'll have plenty of time to relax before your usual gourmet evening meal.

Social Climate

As on other Society Expeditions trips, you'll find your fellow adventurers to be a well-educated and well-traveled group. You'll share a special sense of awe at the beauty of the diversity of nature and the uniqueness of travel on the Amazon.

While you'll likely get to know most of the hundred people (maxi-mum allowed) on the ship, you'll get to know those with whom you share a particular interest even better. With tables seating four to seven and frequent celebrations, you'll never eat alone. While the ship is large enough for you to always find an area for solo contemplation, the group spirit will tend to draw you into the many activities.

Activities

Excursions

The activities usually begin early; there's so much to fit into each day. You can sleep in if you choose, but the first Zodiac (rubber raft) excursions usually leave just after 7:00 A.M. and return around 9:00 A.M. If you're an early riser, you can enjoy coffee and freshly baked pastries in the Penguin Lounge prior to your morning excursion. The usual buffet of fruits, cheese, pastries, hot cereal, eggs, and omelets cooked to order will be ready when you return. The early morning excursions divide the larger group into smaller groups of eight to twelve plus a scientist. Some will go birdwatching, others fishing, still others on general exploration or to collect examples of unusual plants and flowers.

You may go up a small tributary to fish for piranha, sting ray, pira-rucu, or any variety of fish I'm certain you've never even heard of before. I'm not usually too excited about fishing, but here the fish were so plentiful and of such unique varieties that it was a great ad-venture. Our guide, Mo, born and raised near Manaus, was proud of his fishing skill. I enjoyed fishing for piranha, which are attracted to raw red meat. They're feisty little things, some not so little. I must admit their sharp teeth gripped the meat and hook so firmly that I often accepted Mo's offer to rescue my hook so I could catch another fish. Our cook filleted the fish for dinner. They were quite tasty.

There's always at least one or two Zodiacs with birders and an ornithologist aboard. I'm not a birder and have never gone birding prior to my experience with Society Expeditions. I was surprised to find out how exciting bird watching can be, especially on the Amazon River. One morning I watched hundreds of parakeets in flight not far from the bow of our Zodiac as the sun was rising pink in the sky. A native family in a dugout canoe with a not-quite-triangular sail at its bow greeted us as we went farther up the small tributary, the "road" to their home.

Dawn is a busy time for the birds and animals. The jungle is filled with activity. The tree ducks perched on the large branches of trees beside the tributary looked as awkward as the snowy egrets look graceful as they patiently fished for breakfast along the water's edge.

If you'd prefer, you can also do general exploration. You'll likely stop and visit a Caboclo family and see firsthand how they live. The Caboclos, Amazonian river people of mixed native Indian and Portuguese blood, live in houses built on stilts over the river. Their homes have palm-thatched roofs and either wood or woven palm leaf walls. Their lives are completely oriented around the river. They eat the fish from it, drink it, swim in it, wash themselves and their clothes in it, throw their refuse into it, and travel on it. There are no roads here. Instead of cars, bikes, or scooters, kids, even very young kids, paddle around in dugout canoes. While there are some villages where a number of families have built homes together, you are more likely to pass individual homes where a man and woman live with their eight to twelve children, much like our early farm families.

The Amazonian Caboclos live in harmony with the river on their doorstep and the jungle behind them. The jungle provides an abundance of fresh fruit, including bananas, limes, pineapples, and mangos. The giant old Brazil nut trees are another source of sustenance. In addition, the Caboclos will often clear a small area near their home to plant sugar cane, manioc, and even coffee. Unfortunately, the forest jungle vegetation is based on a very fragile ecosystem. Cultivated land will produce crops for only about five years before the nutrients are depleted. Their homes last only about two years before they need to be replaced. Since land is free to the squatter, the families usually move on to another area instead of rebuilding in the same place.

Other excursions will include visits to Indian villages where you'll watch them cook manioc, weave baskets, make paddles and canoes, and harvest their small fields. You'll visit the schools, sawmills, and general store. Through your Portuguese-speaking translators, you can ask the schoolteachers, children, and storekeeper about their lives and answer their questions about yours.

Lecture Series

Once or twice a day we were fortunate to hear from our resident scientists. They spoke about the crucial problem of deforestation in Brazil, about mammals of the Amazon, and about orchids and their unique method of pollination. We learned the truth about the Amazon myths and legends, as well as about the current political situation. Mo gave us a lecture on "Sex, the Hungry Piranha, and Other Fish Stories." We also learned about the life of a Caboclo family from an anthropologist who had been studying a village for many years. His wife had grown up in the area he is now studying.

Best of all, these scientists and local experts were available to answer our questions and to show us the area when we went ashore. Since they were traveling with us they were also available later to answer individual questions as well as share fascinating stories about their experiences in Brazil and along the Amazon.

Preparing for Your Trip Down the Amazon River

Rates

The rates vary according to your cabin selection. The owner's suite goes for US$10,600 on this eighteen-day cruise; the least expensive cabin with a small porthole just above water level will cost US$4,290. This cabin is just as large and has the same facilities as the next three more expensive cabins (private bathroom with shower, desk, closet, hair dryer, and small chest of drawers). The difference is the size of the window (larger is more expensive) and the location (the rear of the boat; the higher up, the more expensive). My suggestion would be to go with a midrange Yacht Deck cabin (US$4,890). Here you'll be above the waterline with a good size porthole. The more expensive Boat Deck cabins have a walkway between their large windows and the ocean. This does not allow for much privacy if you want to leave your drapes open so you can look out your window.

The price of your trip from Manaus to Rio de Janeiro will include everything you'll need or want on this trip. Unlike many other ship tours, with Society Expeditions there is absolutely no hidden charge.

From the moment you arrive at your destination city, every meal, tour, hotel room, and transportation charge will be taken care of by the Society Expeditions representative. You need only relax and enjoy the luxury of the Amazon.

If you have the time, inclination, and extra money, for an additional US$4,000 you can begin your trip thirteen days earlier in Iquitos, Peru. Some people feel this is the most interesting portion of the river because of the opportunity to visit remote Indian tribes.

Documents

U.S. citizens need a valid passport and a visa to enter Brazil. To get a visa, your passport must be valid for at least six months after you plan to leave Brazil. You'll also need a round-trip airline ticket and three passport-style photographs. While you do not need to send in your ticket, you will need the ticket number so the Brazilian consulate can confirm your reservations. Applying for a Brazilian visa can involve a lot of red tape. The most inconvenient problem is that they will not mail your visa to you. It must be picked up by you or your representative. I recommend using a visa service (see p. 29). Your visa will be valid for ninety days and may be renewed once.

When to Go

September, October, and November are probably the best months to travel on the Amazon. You're less likely to experience high humidity, because the rainy season hasn't begun yet (December through February in the north; June through September in the south). Because Brazil is located so close to the equator, the temperature varies little. You can expect warm tropical temperatures in the high seventies and low eighties. It will be warmer, in the nineties, during the summer months (December through February).

What to Take

Loose-fitting, wrinkle resistant cotton clothing is ideal. There are usually two shipboard occasions, the Captain's Welcome and Farewell dinners, for which you will want to wear more dressy attire. Otherwise, informal resort wear is the rule. Shorts are discouraged in the dining room at dinner, but slacks and a cotton shirt or dress will do nicely. Lightweight slacks and a loose-fitting shirt with long sleeves will keep you cool and comfortable yet provide some protection from the direct rays of the sun, the jungle vegetation, and the occasional insects. While sandals are fine for the beach, tennis shoes are essential for your walks through the forest and up the short but sometimes steep and muddy hills to visit Indian villages. They're also ideal for wet Zodiac landings.

You might also want to bring along a light sweater or jacket for cool evenings. Don't forget your bathing suit, sunglasses, a floppy hat for protection from the sun, and lots of sunscreen.

While I seldom found it necessary, there can be a couple of occasions when insect repellent was essential. I prefer the spray because I can put it on my clothes.

It's also a good idea to take a small travel alarm. Since not everyone gets up early, the early morning wake-ups are not announced over the intercom, and there are no clocks in the cabins. You won't need a hair dryer—there's one in each cabin—unless you plan to stay over after your cruise. The current is 110 (U.S.), so you don't need a converter for other items.

Take a few extra disposable pens and pads of writing paper. The schools you'll visit have very limited supplies and the Society Expeditions staff will usually collect any extra writing materials to leave as a gift in exchange for their hospitality. Remember, they don't speak English, so our schoolbooks will be of little value to them.

Don't forget your camera and plenty of film. While film is available on the ship, it will be more expensive. It's a good idea to carry extra batteries for your camera; these are less likely to be available.

Even if you are not a "birder," a pair of binoculars will help you spot the abundant wildlife.

Language

The official language of Brazil is Portuguese, but many residents also speak English.

Money

In attempt to control rampant inflation, the cruzeiro was replaced by the greatly devalued cruzado in February 1986. The cruzeiros still in circulation are now worth one-thousandth their original value (drop "000"). Your rate of exchange will vary greatly. The official rate of exchange, which you'll get in Brazilian banks and whenever you use your major credit cards, is CZ$14.2 for one U.S. dollar. The change houses in Brazil will, however, give you CZ$24 to CZ$28 for your dollar. The change office at the Miami airport offers one of the better exchange rates, CZ$23 to CZ$25 per dollar. You'll have to carry U.S. currency to get the best exchange rates in Brazil. The change houses will not usually cash traveler's checks. When they do, they are cashed only at a much lower rate, about CZ$14 to CZ$20. Traveler's checks must be cashed at banks and hotels for the official rate.

Health Concerns

Food and Water. Since you'll be living aboard the *Society Explorer*, you will not need to worry about exposure to contaminated food or water. You will, however, have the opportunity to eat ashore. Each time you reach port, a list of suggested local restaurants will be made available. These are the recommendations of the contact for that city (a local) or a staff member from a prior visit. The food is generally the best available and the setting pleasant. Even the most expensive Brazilian restaurants are inexpensive by our standards with the exception of Rio, of course.

Malaria. The strain of malaria in Brazil is chloroquine-resistant. So if you decide to take a medication prophylactically, you should keep that in mind. Mosquito repellent is likely the best protection for the nights you are out after dusk.

Getting There

When you check in at the Miami airport, you will need to pay a US$15 departure tax prior to boarding your plane for the five-hour flight to Manaus. You actually have a treat in store for you on your flight to and from Brazil if you fly on Varig Brazilian Airlines. Until I flew Varig, I thought there was no airline that could challenge the high standards in service and scheduling that I had enjoyed whenever I flew Lufthansa. Varig Brazilian Airlines has. They maintain the published schedule and their routes are direct to and from Brazil. You won't have long layovers in a Bolivian airport—a problem with other carriers.

The seating is not crowded and you'll have plenty of leg room. The food is great, and the rich Brazilian coffee is served in a large china cup with a smile.

Be sure to check which carrier Society Expeditions has scheduled for the group flight. If the carrier is not Varig, I strongly recommend you ask to be booked on a Varig flight to Manaus and especially from Rio. The flight home is a long one even when you fly direct. Why spoil a wonderful adventure with an unnecessarily long flight home?

Tipping

While on the trip no tipping will be necessary on Society-sponsored activities, including meals ashore. When you're on your own, you should tip 10 percent to 15 percent of the price of the meal or cab.

At the end of the trip, while you're paying for your shipboard purchases, a box for gratuities will be available at the pursar's office. A tip of US$6 per day is suggested. It will be divided among the crew to ensure that everyone who has made your stay a pleasant one will be equally rewarded.

Treasures to Purchase

Brazil is one of those parts of the world where it's especially important to consider the impact of your purchases. You'll have the opportunity to purchase potions made from parts of dolphins, whales, and turtles as well as numerous other plants and animals. You can purchase skins of snakes and spotted cats. You'll find many items decorated with the colorful feathers of endemic birds and jewelry made from whalebone.

While some of the items may be attractive and certainly unusual souvenirs, their purchase will encourage the slaughter of more animals, some threatened, some endangered, and some already greatly declining in number. Think before you buy in Brazil.

There are many treasures to purchase that are not made from endangered species. Leather sandals and shoes are a good example. For as little as US$3 you can buy a well-made, comfortable pair of leather shoes. Woven hammocks go for between US$7 and US$15 depending on the size and material. They have inexpensive men's shirts that, while not of the highest quality, are a good buy for US$5 to US$10. For a more unique gift, you might try a machete, about US$12. You can purchase perfume made from sweet grass (US$1 to US$5 per bottle) or coat hangers with a sweet grass sachet (US$1 to US$2). Bowls made from coconut shells are a unique item for 25 cents. You can also get Brazilian coffee for as little as US$2 per pound.

Rio is the place to buy clothing. You'll find all the latest fashions—the quality varies as does the price. Salvador de Bahia is the place to purchase leather items. You'll find everything including shoes and sandals (US$2 to US$15) made from a good grade of leather. Collapsible leather suitcases are a great buy for US$20. You'll also find white cotton dresses with brightly colored sashes for US$20 and even elaborate lace dresses for up to US$300.

Thumbs Up

This is one of the many parts of the world where you will *not*, I repeat, *not* want to use the American hand signal that everything is okay (first finger touching thumb in a circle). In Brazil, this is an obscene gesture suggesting sexual intercourse. Instead, you should use the thumbs-up sign. You'll see the Brazilians using this often to indicate thanks, you're okay, it's okay, or I understand.

YOUR EXPEDITION CRUISE

Manaus

It's a good idea to leave two or three days early and plan to spend this extra time in Manaus, a vibrant cosmopolitan city on the edge of the Rio Negro. The Negro is the largest tributary of the Amazon and the most beautiful. The dark color of the water results in stunning mirrorlike reflections of the jungle along its banks and the billowy clouds above. While the Rio Negro carries only 40 percent of the total volume of the Amazon River it meets, that represents four times as much water as the Mississippi pours into the Gulf of Mexico.

Exploring Manaus

A boomtown in the late 1800s, much of the grandeur remains. The most famous building is the opera house (*Theatro Amazonas*), which was built in 1896. From the black-and-white-patterned floorboards to the 14-karat-gold ceilings, this building is exquisite. You'll find Italian marble Corinthian columns with carved jokers (from Greece) surrounding red velvet mahogany chairs for the audience. The Amazon is famous for its many varieties of wood, and you can see an incredible selection in this building alone. Don't miss the ballroom on the balcony level with its imported, made to order paintings and exquisite star-patterned floor and marble columns.

Great musicians and singers from around the world have performed here ever since the opera house opened. Don't miss a chance to see a performance in this historic building. Its grandeur is in stark contrast to the simplicity of life you'll soon see along the banks of the Amazon.

You also shouldn't miss the *Palace of Justice* nearby. Built in 1880, it, too, has the alternating black-and-white wooden floor with decorative ceilings and pastel-colored walls. You'll likely be greeted by an informal guide. Ask to see the president's office in one wing and the courtroom at the opposite end. From the second-floor balcony you can look out over the round-tiled dome of the opera house across the main street.

Another highlight of my trip was a visit to the *public school*. If you continue a few blocks down the main street (Ave. Eduardo Ribeiro) separating the opera house from the Palace of Justice and walk up the steps, you'll be in school. You'll need to find someone to give you a tour, possibly an English-speaking teacher. The lower grades are on the main floor, the upper grades on the top floor. The school may be a stark contrast to the one back home. Except for the wooden desks and chairs, a blackboard and a few books, the rooms are bare. The students, however, seem happy and enthusiastic. If you have a Polaroid camera, be sure to bring it with you. You'll be a big hit with the kids. The teachers, who also work in private schools, donate their time in this free public school.

Also near the opera house is *The Cathedral*. Not a church, this is *the* night spot. Appropriately, Sunday is the big night out in Manaus.

If you want to find authentic artifacts and unusual souvenirs, don't miss the *House of the Humming Bird* (Casa Do Beija Flor) on Rua Quinto Bocaiuva, 224. For US$50 you can get an authentic blowgun. It'll cost you another US$30 for a palm bark bag of darts (without the poison, of course). You'll find jewelry, musical instruments, baskets, wood carvings, and much, much more. Each item will come with a map indicating its area and tribe of origin. This is one shop you should not miss while in Brazil.

Where to Stay in Manaus

The best hotel in Manaus is the *Tropical Hotel Manaus*, telephone 92-238-5757 (single or double CZ$2,500). You'll need to be sure to make your reservations early and be aware that they often overbook. While a luxurious resort with elegant shops and restaurants, it is about twenty minutes from the heart of town. They will, however, provide free bus transportation.

If the Tropical is booked, try the *Plaza Hotel*, Ave. Getulio Vargas, 215; telephone 92-233-8900 (single CZ$1,300, double CZ$1,380), in the heart of town. While not a resort, the rooms are clean and pleasant and it's an easy walk from all the sights. If you ask at the front desk, they'll provide you with a map and directions.

Where to Eat in Manaus

One of the better restaurants offering international regional cuisine is the *Taruma* at the Tropical Hotel. Be sure to try one of the many Amazon River fish selections from around US$5 to US$10. I'd also highly recommend the rustic *Panorama* (Rua Recife, 900) with its excellent selection of local specialties for under US$5. *La Barca* (Rue Recife, 684) is another favorite with the locals.

My favorite restaurant was *Palhoca* (Estrada da Ponta Negra) on the outskirts of Manaus. You'll want to begin your evening with a local rum drink, Caipirinha, made from local rum, Cachaca, lemon, and sugar. Their pirarucu (a large Amazon River fish) is a special treat. Other local fish specialties include baked tambaqui, stewed tucunare, and the popular fried jaraqui. You'll usually get a side order of thick manioc flour flavored with coriander and tucupi (a fermented manioc extract).

Manaus to Belém

As you leave Manaus on your 1,000-mile voyage to Belém, you'll pass the *Marriage of the Waters*. From then on you'll be sailing on the muddy white waters of the Amazon River.

Caiman Hunt

The excitement begins that first night when you go out after dark to hunt caiman (a South American crocodile similar to the alligator). As your Zodiac cruises upstream on the Lago del Rei, you'll see the red of their eyes along the banks, lit by the flashlight's beam. Each group is anxious to catch the first and the largest caiman. Like rabbits, they are transfixed by the light, allowing you to slowly and carefully approach them, then even more carefully grab them behind their large heads, avoiding the sharp rows of teeth. We chose to let the big ones, over 6 feet, go along their way. We brought a 4-foot caiman back to the ship for comparison and observation before returning it to its habitat. The sound of the croaking frogs and the vision of thousands of fireflies dancing beneath the jungle canopy resulted in a unique and memorable experience.

Boca de Valeria Indian Village and Rubber Plantation

We were welcomed by the entire village at Boca de Valeria. We followed them from the water's edge up the dirt path to their village of palm-thatched buildings. The villagers showed us how they weave and the kids posed for pictures. We stopped at a rubber plantation on our way back to the ship and saw how the rubber is harvested.

Altar Do Chao

The "Altar of the Earth" has been a hill of religious significance for hundreds of years. Just a short distance from a long sandy beach, the majority of passengers relaxed in the sand while seven of us scaled the front of the hill. Using a machete, Mo, our guide, hacked his way through the thick jungle growth from the beach where we had landed to the foot of the hill.

It was a steep climb toward the top, making our successful ascent of the summit more exciting. The view when we reached the summit was spectacular. We watched the beginning of the sunset before returning to the beach to join the others for a barbecue.

We finished eating just as a spectacular tropical storm hit. We reembarked amid a torrential downpour. I was surprised by the high waves produced by the river. That day I really felt like a true adventurer.

Jurupai

In Jurupai we visited the home of a Caboclo family. Their daughters took us up on the hill and through an area they had cleared for cattle and planting. As we walked back into the forest with our guides from the New York Botanical Gardens, we saw orchids in bloom on the trees. The woman who greeted us showed us the "headache tree" (Jatropha Curcas). After being baked, a single seed from this tree is said to cure even the most severe headache.

Olaria

Before our Zodiacs were even in the water, small children from this sawmill town were jumping from their dugout canoes into our boats hoping for a ride. We were constantly surrounded by friendly smiling children. The town had grown up across the river from the sawmill where the men work. The mill is owned by a company from South Carolina. They transport the wood, primarily virola, back to the United States, where it is used to make furniture.

Only the largest virola trees are taken. The abundant natural re-seeding of this fast-growing tree makes the harvesting of this particular species of wood less dangerous to the fragile ecosystem of the forest. Deforestation is a crucial problem in Brazil.

Belém

Pronounced "Be-ling," this city of over a million inhabitants sits at the mouth of the Amazon River. Shortly after our early morning arrival, we visited the market, which includes a section referred to as the voodoo market, where we found a wide selection of potions and herbs, things to treat ills and make spells. Like the rest of Belém, it's a fascinating place to visit.

In the afternoon we visited the *Botanical Gardens* where one of our scientists works. We also had the opportunity to visit the experimental station of the *Goeldi Museum* on the edge of town. We had plenty of time for sightseeing and to wander around town and along the water-front before our departure.

For lunch I suggest you try pato no tucupi (duck cooked in jambu leaves making a thick sauce) or farofa de pirarucu (manioc and dried pirarucu fish with coconut sauce). A full dinner at *L'aem Casa* restaurant will cost about CZ$85 (under US$5). Other suggestions for lunch include *Rest Avenida*, which specializes in seafood, and *Na Brasa* for barbecued meats.

Belém to Rio de Janeiro

We had three days at sea before our first stop on the way to Rio. The time passed quickly with lectures, sumptuous meals, and relaxing and reading on deck. With the elections approaching, our lectures focused on the economic and political situation of Brazil. Our lecturers, well versed on the Brazilian political scene, provided us with insights on the current political-economic status of Brazil.

We also learned more about the exploitation of the Amazon forests and water basin. We learned how continued deforestation poses a threat not only to Brazil but to the rest of the world as well. The video *The Decade of Destruction* that we saw on board showed the protest of the native Brazilian Indians against the destruction of their land. We also learned of ways small farmers had found to make an adequate living, to feed their families, and yet not destroy the land.

Fernando de Noronha

A real highlight of the trip was our swim off Fernando de Noronha Island in the Bay of Dolphins. From Greek myths to present-day accounts, dolphins are known for their fascination with people. They have been credited with saving the life of more than one tired swimmer.

No one knows why the dolphins prefer this particular bay. We passed a number of similar bays as we approached the Bay of Dolphins. They were all deserted, and we wondered if we would be disappointed. But our anticipation erupted into excitement as we saw the first spinner dolphins leap from the water and literally spin four or five times in the air. They really were here! Our Zodiacs were soon surrounded by thirty to forty friendly dolphins jumping in front of us in groups of three or four, some leaping far into the air and spinning. It was now apparent that this small bay was teeming with dolphins, likely well over 150 magnificent creatures.

We quickly anchored our Zodiacs and took to the water with our welcoming friends. I had thought it was exciting seeing their aerial acrobatics around the boat, but the real excitement came when I was actually swimming with them. I was often surrounded by twenty to thirty inquisitive creatures at a time. They would swim within a few inches of my body or my outstretched hand, always just beyond my reach. As they passed they would look at me with their ever-present smile. I could even hear their high pitched vocalizations. They were talking to me. They were all talking at once. What an incredible, once-in-a-lifetime experience. They swam past, then leapt into the air, coming back to look at me as if wondering why I didn't do likewise.

We swam with the dolphins for over two hours. No one wanted to leave these magnificent creatures. We finally climbed back into our Zodiacs, exhausted and invigorated by the experience. As we left the bay, they swam beside our boats. We would never forget the Bay of Dolphins off this small desertlike island in the Atlantic Ocean.

Recife/Olinda

Of these sister cities, Olinda, founded in 1537, is by far the more beautiful. Our tour took us to a cathedral situated on a hill in Olinda that overlooked the sea and the palm trees sprinkled throughout the city. Recife is often considered the Venice of Brazil because of its many canals and bridges.

One of the most interesting "urban renewal plans" we saw in Brazil was the Recife jail, now a fascinating market. Each tiny "cell" is today a shop filled to the brim with handmade clothes, leather items, local crafts, jewelry, and much, much more.

Dinner with a small group of fellow travelers at one of the many seaside restaurants completed another day of adventure in Brazil.

Salvador de Bahia

Pronounced Salvador de "By-ear," this is the center of voodoo in Brazil, and my favorite city. What a fascinating place to spend a day. It is here that you will see the adolescent boys on the streets playing the *berimba* (a bowlike instrument with a coconut at one end) and performing the *capoeira* (a form of "fight-dance" vaguely similar to break dancing). This is a very controlled, ritualized dance. The women and young girls wear full white cotton dresses with bright sashes, a striking contrast to their dark black skin.

You won't want to miss the elaborate gold altars of the Church of San Francisco or the Lacerda elevator that connects the town at sea level to the town above on the hill. While the *mercardo* (market) here is not as spectacular as the restored jail in Recife, few are. The leather items for sale offered the most unique selection and the best value in Brazil. The quality was good and the prices low.

For lunch I'd suggest the *Casa de Gamboa* on the hill overlooking the port. Their maqueca de ouro (seafoods cooked in saffron served with manioc) was wonderful. The food was a little more expensive here. Lunch with hors d'oeuvres and a couple of drinks came to nearly US$20 per person. While expensive by Brazilian standards, it was a superb meal. The old house in which this restaurant is located exudes charm and warmth.

Rio de Janeiro

We arrived in Rio as the sun was rising and the moon was dipping from sight behind Sugarloaf Mountain. Our visit here was short. A number of people chose to stay on a few days in order to have more time to walk down the Copacabana and Ipanema beaches or explore the many cosmopolitan shops, the museums, and sample the first-rate restaurants available. Rio has a Botanical Garden with over 7,000 varieties of local plants including towering palms and the rare Victorian water lily.

If you haven't visited an H. Stern jewelry store yet, you should do so in Rio, if not to buy then at least to look at the emerald jewelry and the exotic birds fashioned from beautiful blue, purple, and gold stones.

Where to Eat in Rio

If you're interested in regional food, I'd suggest *Aractaca* or *Moenda*. For more formal dining you might want to eat at *Le Saint Honae* with its breathtaking view of the beach from the thirty-seventh floor. The cuisine is French. The old-fashioned *Ouro Verde* also offers fine French cuisine in an elegant setting.

You should try one of the famous barbecue houses for at least one meal. They are scattered throughout Rio. For a fixed price (about US$8) you get as much as you can possibly eat. In addition to a well-supplied salad and dessert bar, you'll be offered a variety of barbecued meats. Men will bring long swordlike skewers to your table and start cutting off slabs of roast beef, pork, chicken, spare ribs, and spicy sausage until you tell them to stop. You'll also be served fried plantains (a type of banana) and manioc.

Where to Stay in Rio

There are a number of first-class hotels along the waterfront, such as *Caesar's Park*, *Othon Palace*, *Rio Palace*, *Copacabana Hotel*, *Hotel Leme Palace*, and the *Hotel Ouro Verde*. All would make excellent choices. They are, however, not on the beach; they are separated from the crowded public beach by a busy four-lane street.

In Rio I would recommend staying at the *Rio Sheraton Hotel*, Ave. Niemayer 121 (single US$76, double US$95), located at the end of Leblon Beach—actually on the water's edge. It even has its own private sandy beach. You won't need to fight the crowds here, and you'll have a spectacular view of the city at night. Ask for a room facing the city. There is a pleasant barbecue restaurant next to the pool at the water's edge. Just on the edge of all the excitement, this hotel offers a peaceful and elegant retreat.

Safety in Rio

While I had only pleasant experiences, Rio has a reputation for crime. It's a place where you should be cautious. Don't walk alone at night in areas that aren't frequented by tourists. Ask at your hotel. You'll want to keep your purse and camera around your neck and shoulder and be sure your valuables are secured at all times (see p. 66).

If you don't have to hurry home, spend at least one additional day in Rio. It's an exciting, vibrant metropolis. Knowing you have another day or two of excitement will make it easier to say good-bye to the friends you made on the Society Expeditions cruise ship.

As I sat having dinner with a couple of newly made friends from the cruise in the waterside restaurant of the Sheraton, we watched the *Society Explorer* sail out of the Rio harbor. She was filled with a new set of adventurers just beginning their voyage of discovery. We toasted the staff on board, the wonderful times we had had, and our return to the *Society Explorer* for our next cruise.

CHAPTER 8
▶ ▶ ▶

Rest and Relaxation in the Summertime

PARIS TO LONDON ABOARD THE VENICE-SIMPLON ORIENT EXPRESS

▶──────────────────────────────▶

GENERAL AMBIANCE	★ ★ ★
SOCIAL CLIMATE	★ ★
ACTIVITIES	★ ★ ★

FOR TRAVEL ARRANGEMENTS CONTACT:
Venice-Simplon Orient Express
One World Trade Center, Suite 1235
New York, NY 10048
(800) 524-2420

Or *contact your travel agent* and ask for the Venice-Simplon Orient
   Express Trip

▶──────────────────────────────▶

*T*here was a time between the two great wars when the grace and
luxury of the rich and famous was extended to travel. To them it was

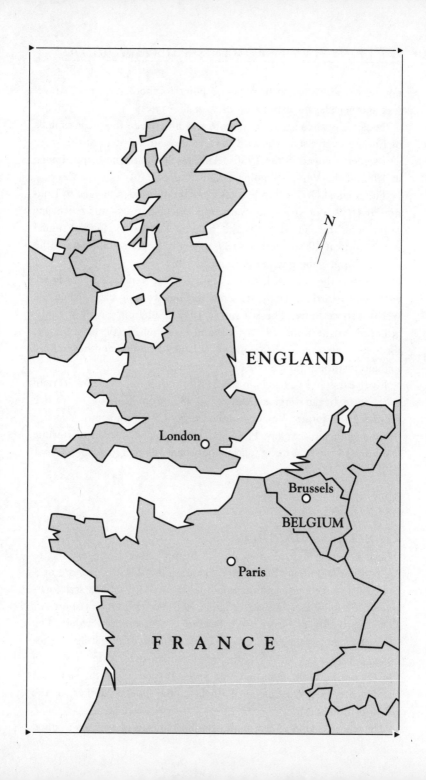

not simply a way to rush from one point to another. Instead, travel was another elegant expression of their life-styles.

Today it is once again possible to travel between the great capitals of Europe in the style the lords and ladies and the stars of the stage and screen enjoyed in the 1930s. And it's all due to the reappearance in 1982 of the Venice-Simplon Orient Express.

The original Orient Express left Paris on its maiden voyage to London in 1889. For years afterward, the Orient Express was *the* means of travel for the chic. In 1906, the Simplon Tunnel (the longest tunnel in the world at 20 kilometers—12½ miles) was opened, shortening the time to Venice and giving the train its name.

In 1962, the former luxury Pullmans were replaced by ordinary cars, which carried mainly students and the working class, while the wealthy chose to fly. The last run in 1977 resulted in a rush of media attention to the train, which indicated there might still be a market for luxury rail travel. That same year, James B. Sherwood began buying and restoring the famous old carriages.

Five years (and £11 million) later, the world's most celebrated train once again began service (May 25, 1982) from London to Venice following the former Venice-Simplon Orient Express route. You can now, once again, explore Paris and London, and instead of rushing from one to the other, the journey between will be a highlight of your trip.

General Ambiance

The cars, each with its own unique history, have been restored to their former grandeur. Built in the twenties and thirties, they are decorated with mahogany and burwood panels with Edwardian-style marquetry of landscapes, flower garlands, and baskets. Others sport Art Deco marquetry or Grecian urn designs in a green holly wood. The dining cars and private cabins have thick, comfortable built-in couches covered in velvet, with pink-fringed Victorian-style lamps and fresh flowers on the table. You may find yourself traveling in the same car that once carried the Queen of England, the Queen Mother, or the Duke of Edinburgh.

The elegant lounge car, with continual music played on a grand piano, provides an excellent opportunity to meet the other passengers all dressed for the occasion. You'll find the men in jackets and many of the women in hats—and the more adventuresome in period clothes from the twenties and thirties. It is indeed like stepping through a time tunnel into the elegant era of the thirties.

While the journey between Paris and London will certainly be the highlight of this and possibly many other trips, when considering the general ambiance, you cannot forget the two magnificent metropolitan centers you are traveling between. Paris has always maintained a special elegance and grace. While I have heard many stories of the French being rude to the foreign traveler, on my many visits I have never had such an experience. While living in Europe I visited Paris often and I am still entranced by the charm of this city.

London is an especially comfortable city for Americans to visit because there is no language problem. The signs and directions are easy to read, and when one asks a question, the answer is easy to understand. You'll quickly feel at home in London even though it's a big city.

Social Climate

In France, your ability to speak the language, even a little, will greatly enhance your social contacts. You'd be amazed, however, at what an interested Frenchman will do to communicate even if you don't speak French. The men of France really do live up to their reputation of loving women and letting you know they appreciate you for just being a woman. The best is that they do so without being pushy, aggressive, or expecting anything in return.

In London, the ease of conversing is a great advantage. The British do not live up to their reputation of being stuffy. In fact, I found them endearing and helpful to the visitor. It's acceptable for a woman to wander into the ubiquitous neighborhood pubs in the evenings, and it can be a lot of fun. Unfortunately, they roll up the sidewalks between 10:00 and 11:00 P.M., but until then you'll have a great time.

While you're on the Orient Express, you'll find the majority of people will speak English. Most will be middle- to upper-middle-class European tourists. I did, however, meet a number of travelers from the U.S. The lounge car, with the music and a full selection of drinks, facilitates interaction with your fellow travelers. An interesting hat is a great conversation piece.

Activities

One of the advantages of this itinerary is that you can explore two exciting yet very different cities to your heart's content, then sit back and be pampered in the style and luxury usually only available to the very wealthy. With even a week in each city, you'll only scratch the surfaces of things to do, places to go, and people to meet.

You could spend days in Paris just sitting at sidewalk cafes watching the people. You can visit the famous Louvre, Nôtre-Dame, the Eiffel Tower, and Arc de Triomphe. You can look out over the city of Paris from the steps of the Sacré-Coeur. At night you can enjoy the excitement of the Folies Bergères, the Moulin Rouge, or Club 79 Disco. Best of all, the French food, even in the small, out of the way restaurants, deserves its first-class reputation. This is the place to eat well.

When you arrive in London you'll have no doubt you've arrived in a new country. What a great opportunity to go to the theater and the pubs. You'll want to be sure to see Westminster and Buckingham Palace. London and Paris are both great cities in which to shop for treasures. They are two of the greatest cities in the world.

Preparing for Your Trip

Rates on the Venice-Simplon Orient Express

The Venice-Simplon Orient Express makes two trips each week from London to Venice, where the train connects with a special boat to Istanbul. The London-Paris portion of the trip includes the Channel crossing for US$265 per person without a cabin, US$365 with a cabin. You really won't need a cabin on this trip, though it's an added luxury to have one, if you feel like splurging a little.

The entire thirty-two-hour trip, one way from London to Venice, is US$820 plus US$160 for a private cabin. Since stops are made along the way, you may chose to go only as far as Zurich (US$640), Innsbruck (US$640), or you may decide to stop over in a city and catch the next train. In addition, they have recently added a seven-day boat trip to Istanbul. For another US$922, you get on a luxury cruise ship in Venice. Your first stop is Piraeus prior to stopping at the spectacular city of Istanbul. From Kusadasi, the next stop, you can visit Ephesus, one of the most spectacular ruins in the world. Then it's on to Patmos, Katakolon, and back to Venice.

You should book your Orient Express trip early.

Documents

You will need a valid passport to enter France and England. You will also need a visa to enter France. Health certificates are not necessary when entering from the United States.

When to Go

While Europe is beautiful year-round, London can be cold in the fall and winter. The average temperature in both Paris and London is only slightly above 70 degrees during July and August—it is in the low seventies in London and mid-seventies in Paris. Since most Parisians go on vacation during August, it is, in my opinion, an excellent time to visit. While a few restaurants will be closed, most are open. The Parisians you meet are likely to be less hurried. May and June are also good choices, though you are more likely to run into spring showers and crowds. September is my favorite month for visiting Europe. The schools have started, there are fewer tourists, and the weather is generally good, even if a little cool.

What to Take

While it is not essential, I strongly recommend taking a hat to wear on the Venice-Simplon Orient Express ride. If you are more creative you might try to recapture the style of dress of the twenties and thirties. I guarantee you'll have a more sensational trip if you do. You cannot overdress on the Orient Express.

Both Paris and London are also great cities in which to dress your best. The French like style, even when it is informal. If you decide to splurge and go to one of the better French restaurants, you'll find the better dressed you are, the better your reception will be. I'd wear the hat you brought for the Orient Express ride.

Paris is a city for walking, so take comfortable shoes. Even during the warmest months, London can get cold in the evenings, so you'll want a sweater or light jacket. Unfortunately, it rains year-round. A small fold-up umbrella will come in handy. If you decide not to bring one and it rains, they are for sale on most street corners for a few dollars. Most of the summer rains pass quickly, however. If you stop for a drink or duck into a store, you'll likely walk out into blue sky and sunshine.

Money

The rate of exchange varies greatly, so check just before you leave town. The exchange rate used in this book is US$1 equals 1.5 British pounds, and US$1 equals 6 French francs. In both countries, you will get your best rate of exchange at a bank. When the banks are closed you can still change money at Victoria Station in London and the Gare du Nord, Gare de L'Est, and Gare de Lyon in Paris. There is a change office open on the Sealink to Great Britain as well. While the exchange rate is usually relatively poor, most large hotels will change money for their guests as well.

Treasures to Purchase

Paris has been setting the pace in fashion for years. You'll find the *Champs-Elyseés* lined with shops packed full of high fashion, and most are open from 9:00 A.M. to 7:00 P.M. While you will find the best here, you can expect to pay a high price. The leather is also of excellent quality in the shoes, handbags, and gloves. The only real bargain I found was perfume. The selection is excellent and the price much less than back home. You'll find a much better selection in town than at the Duty Free Shop.

You'll want to at least wander into the *Galaries Lafayette* (40 Boulevard Haussmann). They carry a little bit of everything, including the famous French perfumes (on the ground floor) and a wide selection of dresses. Most of the styles are two years ahead of what is popular in the States, so you'll be able to wear your new Paris dress much longer than its American counterpart and still be chic.

If you're a little more conservative, you might find the styles in London more in line with your taste. I especially like shopping for clothes in London. While still very stylish, they seem to fit my office needs better.

London is also an excellent place to buy crystal and china. Wedgwood and Waterford are sold in most shops with less well known but just as attractive brands. You'll also find the great names in fashion here as well as in Paris: Ralph Lauren, Louis Vuitton, Dior, Gucci, and many others.

For a special souvenir of your trip, stop by 76 Oxford Street. Here you'll find the Venice–Simplon Orient Express Collection. They carry exact replicas of the crystal, china, and silver used on the train and in the twenties. You can also buy Orient Express car replicas, scarves, key chains, ashtrays, books, and shirts on the train. These make an excellent reminder of a wonderful adventure in luxurious travel.

While in London, don't miss the latest "hit" with London shoppers, the massive *Virgin Megastore* on Oxford Street. It's a razzle-dazzle record store with everything from a mini coffee shop to life-size wax figures of rock stars, including John Lennon and David Bowie. It also has more than 500,000 albums and videos. They even have an extensive music catalog. If there's a hard to find album you've always been looking for, this is the place to find it.

PARIS

▶ ─── ◀

Paris has drawn Americans and Europeans alike for generations and for good reason. Paris is, as Hemingway called her, "a moveable feast." When you think of gourmet food and high fashion, you likely think first of Paris. In my opinion, everyone should visit Paris at least once in their life. Indeed, when I was surveying women in an attempt to decide what to include in this book, Paris was the one city most often mentioned as the place for a dream vacation.

Paris has also, however, received considerable bad press as a city that is rude to tourists. For the most part, this is undeserved. While you certainly do not need to speak French to travel in Paris, it is the one city where you will get a better reception in the shops, small restaurants, and small hotels if you at least try to speak their language. A French for travelers tape will provide you with enough language skills that if you try what you have learned from the tape, you'll find the French will answer you in perfect English.

The French are really much more receptive to a non-French-speaking visitor than we would be to a non-English-speaking one. How would you react to someone who came into your office or place of employment and started speaking French to you? This is exactly what many Americans do in France. In the large hotels, the staffs are multilingual and will politely respond in perfect English. In the shops, restaurants, and hotels where the staffs or owners do not know English well, they may be more uncomfortable with the language and thus more uncomfortable with you. They may even, understandably, resent your expecting them to fumble with your language when you are unwilling to try theirs.

So don't stay away from Paris because you can't speak French or because you've heard stories from other Americans about a bad reception. Instead, accept that the French are proud of their country and language just as we are, and don't be afraid to sound a little silly because you speak their language poorly.

Getting There

There are special buses to town from both of the Paris airports. They leave every fifteen minutes. The fare is 35 F and it takes about forty-five minutes to reach the city, longer during rush hour.

You can also catch a free shuttle bus that will take you to the Boissy Rail, which then takes you to the Gare du Nord. From there you can take the Metro or a cab to your hotel. The Metro is under 4 F for a single one-way ride. A taxi from the airport to the center of town will be 150 F to 180 F, much less than you'd pay in New York City.

Getting Around

The Paris Metro is convenient and inexpensive. You can buy individual tickets or you can buy ten first-class tickets for 42 F or second-class tickets for 26.50 F. You should watch your valuables; there have recently been theft problems in the Metro. When going short distances, you'll probably want to walk. Paris is so beautiful and there is so much to see that it's often a shame to go underground. Your Metro tickets can also be used on the bus. While better for sightseeing, the bus is a much less efficient system and the taxis are more expensive than in London.

Exploring Paris

You haven't seen Paris until you've seen the *Arc de Triomphe*, *Nôtre-Dame*, the *Louvre*, the *Eiffel Tower*, and strolled along the boulevards and through the gardens. The free map available at all tourist information offices will have these sights—and more—well-marked along the Metro stations. The *Champs-Elyseés* is the world's most famous boulevard for shopping or just for sitting at a sidewalk cafe and watching people. The Arc de Triomphe at one end adds grandeur to its splendor. You won't find your bargains on the Champs-Elyseés. To look for bargains, you'll have to go to the left bank of the Seine. There are many wonderful little shops on the streets near the *Sorbonne University*.

The best view of the Eiffel Tower is from the Jardin du Trocadéro. If you're lucky, you'll catch the skate boarders running obstacle courses made of soda pop cans with unsurpassed skill beside the spectacular fountains. Parisians and tourists alike watch in great numbers, amazed at their competence.

Napoleon's tomb, at the *Hôtel des Invalides* (really a palace and church) and the *Musée de l'Armée* should also be high on your list. *La*

Sainte Chapelle, near Nôtre-Dame and less well known, is in some ways even more spectacular with its extensive stained glass.

A new and very unique museum, the *Musée D'Orsay,* with its nineteenth-century art, is a rich addition to the already rich cultural heritage of Paris. It's located on the left bank in a renovated train station. Don't miss it.

On Sunday, especially, I always enjoy sitting on the steps of the *Sacré-Coeur* with its beautiful white dome. It's a great place to look out over most of Paris as well as to people watch. Then I stroll through the artist quarter of *Montmartre.* You can still buy paintings in the square beside the church and walk the crooked little streets where Renoir, Van Gogh, and Toulouse-Lautrec once wandered.

Paris has many wonderful gardens. The *Jardin du Luxembourg* is my favorite. I especially enjoy watching the small boys sail their boats in the pond. The *Jardin des Tuileries* along the right bank of the Seine was originally a park for the French royalty. Thanks to the revolution, it's now for the pleasure of all.

Paris at Night

Paris has a number of spectacular, world-renowned nightclubs. The most famous include *The Lido* (595 F), *The Folies Bergères* (475 F), and *Moulin Rouge* (575 F)—these prices include transportation (approximately 100 F). You can go to the Lido, for instance, on your own without dinner for 330 F. Don't miss these spectacular shows. They are of the same scale as the Las Vegas extravaganzas, only better. You'll be seated with other people, many of them tourists. While their first language may not be English, they will likely speak English better than you'll speak French.

One of the most famous discos in the world, *Club 79 Disco,* is located at 79 Champs-Elysées. It opens at 10:00 P.M. Drinks (even a Coke) start at 80 F. Champagne will cost 380 F. The wine bars, now common in Paris, are an excellent place to stop and meet people. The food here is good, too.

Where to Stay in Paris

As in most of Europe, you can always book a room by going to the Tourist Information area at the major train stations. In Paris, these are the Gare de Lyon, Gare de L'Est, and the Gare du Nord. There is also a downtown office (127 Av. des Champs Elysées, telephone 47-23-61-72). It is open from 9:00 A.M. to 8:00 P.M., Monday through Saturday. Rooms in Paris are rated: ★ (160 F to 250 F); ★★ (260 F to 380 F); ★★★ (450 F to 600 F); ★★★★ (650 F to 800 F); and L ★★★★ (900 F to 1,800 F and up). I'd suggest at least a three-star room. These are clean, have a private bath, and usually include breakfast.

Hotel des Deux-Isle, 59 Rue Saint-Louise-en-l'Ile; telephone 43-26-13-35 (single 385 F, double 485 F; breakfast 28 F). You'll need to book one to two months in advance to get into this seventeenth-century mansion that has been turned into a small (seventeen-room) hotel. Located on an island just a few blocks from Nôtre-Dame, this attractively decorated hotel with bright overstuffed lounge chairs in the lobby is an excellent choice. The surrounding area is one of the most interesting parts of Paris.

Hotel Lancaster, 7 Rue de Berri; telephone 43-59-90-43 (single 1,100 F to 1,300 F, double 1,500 F to 1,750 F). Located just off the Champs-Elysées, this elegant hotel was originally built in 1889 as a private residence. In 1928, Mr. Wolfe turned it into a hotel that has housed reigning monarchs and leaders in government, the arts, and business. Much of the current furnishings and artwork was purchased with the estate. The restaurant opens onto the original interior court-yard garden, and the lobby was once the area where carriages pulled up to the front door with guests. The lounge areas and the rooms have retained the charm of a private estate. I highly recommend this hotel.

Hotel Raphel, 12 Ave. Kleber; telephone 45-02-16-00 (single 720 F to 1,100 F, double 990 F to 1,400 F, breakfast 60 F). Located just two blocks from the Arc de Triomphe, this is one of the truly grand large hotels in Paris. The elegant and stately beauty of the dark wood and carved antiques throughout the public areas are enhanced by the friendly, helpful attitude of the staff as well as by the soft music that greets you. The quiet bar is a nice place to chat with other interesting guests. A remarkable value for the price, this is another excellent choice.

George V, 31 Ave. George V; telephone 47-23-54-00 (single 1,500 F, double 1,990 F). *The* hotel in Paris when J. Paul Getty stayed here, the George V went through a period where only the reputation of its grand days remained. It was badly in need of the remodeling that is currently under way. The new kitchen is already in place. With a newly acquired award-winning chef, a major expansion of the restaurant is now in progress. The rooms and lobby areas have all been completely redone. This extensive remodeling promises to return the George V to its former elegance. Hopefully, it will once again become *the* place to stay in Paris.

Prince de Galles–Marriott, 33 Ave. George V; telephone 47-23-55-11 (single 1,300 F to 1,650 F, double 1,500 F to 2,100 F). The next-door neighbor of the George V, this hotel has currently taken over as one of *the* large hotels of elegance and luxury. Its high lobby ceiling holds an elaborate crystal chandelier and the surrounding public spaces feature antique furniture and impressive bouquets of flowers. The Regency Bar is comfortable and is a good place to meet other visitors to this incredible city. Even if you don't stay here, you might want to try dinner in their restaurant near the attractive inlaid tile inner courtyard (entrées from 95 F to 140 F, 195 F for the menu of the day). Most rooms overlook this courtyard.

Hotel Royal Victor Hugo, 6 Ave. Victor-Hugo; telephone 45-00-05-57 (single or double 500 F). This new hotel, not to be confused with the much older Victor Hugo, is close to the Champs-Elysées. It will likely jump in price soon. The small, attractive lobby is decorated almost entirely with white marble, brass, and mirrors. Palm trees give it a soft, fresh feeling. An excellent value. You will need to take extra traveler's checks along if you stay here; they do not accept credit cards.

Where to Eat in Paris

Paris has some of the most celebrated restaurants in the world. Among these are *Maxim's* (3 Rue Royal), *Tour d'Argent* (15 Quai de la Tournelle), *Le Grand Vefour* (17 Rue de Beaujolais), and *Lasserre* (17 Ave.

Franklin D. Roosevelt). At all of these, the presentation of food is as impeccable as the quality. The chefs are the finest in the world. You will need reservations, and I suggest you dress your best to ensure good service. With wine, you can expect to pay US$75 and up for your meal.

While you may want to splurge one night, the rest of the time you will find there are a number of smaller and much less expensive restaurants, bistros, and cafés scattered all over Paris. In these you can pay as little as 45 F for an excellent lunch, 60 F for a superb dinner. A 12 percent to 15 percent charge will usually be added to your bill.

Paris even boasts having the oldest restaurant in the world, *Café Procope*. I highly recommend it. Founded in 1686, it was at one time *the* cafe for anyone with a name, or hoping to make a name, in the arts. La Fontaine, Voltaire, Rousseau, and Balzac were once regulars. In addition, Robespierre, Danton, and Marat met here during the revolution. The food is of the best French quality. A full, three-course dinner will run 75 F to 100 F.

Around Paris

If you have time, I recommend taking a tour of the *Palace of Versailles*. About fifteen minutes from town, this is one of the most incredible palaces in the world (only King Ludwig II outdid the French royalty in the splendor and elegance of his palaces). The gardens are as spectacular as the palace and the apartment of Mme. de Pompadour, which you can visit while here.

PARIS TO LONDON ON THE VENICE-SIMPLON ORIENT EXPRESS

▶ ── ▶

You'll know this train is unique and you'll feel special from the moment you step onto the blue carpet in front of the special check-in counter.

You'll find it on the platform in front of the train at the Gare de L'Est in Paris. The friendly, English-speaking staff in tailored suits will give you your cabin or seat assignment and take your luggage to be stowed in the luggage compartment. It's best to keep only one small bag in your compartment, since the trip from Paris to London takes just one day.

Shortly after leaving the station in Paris at 9:00 A.M., brunch is served in the dining car. Those traveling alone are usually asked to join others at a table. Be sure to make your preference known to the steward who will greet you in the dining car. The white linen, sparkling crystal, and cutlery glitter next to the black-lacquered walls with inlaid mother-of-pearl deer running through woods and swans swimming on lakes. The fresh flowers and silver buckets with champagne on each table add to the festive excitement of travel and dining on this great train. Brunch begins with scrambled eggs and salmon brought by waiters in starched white jackets with gold buttons and shoulder braid. It is followed by lobster in a butter sauce, served from a silver tray, then fruit arranged in a pastry shell with a light raspberry sauce. *Gourmet* magazine would be proud to feature this meal as a centerfold.

There is plenty of time after brunch to walk through the train, compare the cars, and read about their history, or relax in the lounge car and listen to piano music while sipping an "Orient Express" (orange juice and rum) or your own favorite drink. By now everyone will be caught up in a camaraderie of the travel experience, feeling pampered and as elegant as your surroundings.

When you look past the beauty of the cars, you'll enjoy the French countryside with its red-tiled farm villages, grazing cattle, and rolls of hay in the fields. When you reach the coast of Bologne four hours later, the porter will collect your cabin luggage, which will be transported for you onto the boat for the channel crossing. You'll be escorted to a comfortable VIP lounge on the boat reserved for Orient Express passengers. Here the continual beverage service will make the two-hour crossing seem short.

When you arrive in Folkstone, England, you'll need to claim your luggage and transport it less than 50 feet through customs before returning it to the Orient Express crew for transport to London on the final leg of your journey. This transfer has been exceptionally well orchestrated and occurs smoothly and seemingly effortlessly.

The train that will meet you in Folkstone is a collection of restored dining cars, each one more elegant and luxurious than the last. You will be shown to your car, affectionately called by names such as Minerva, Audrey, Phoenix, and Perseus. There you'll once again step into the elegance of a past era in a place where time has stood still.

As the train pulls out of the station, afternoon tea will be served. If it's low tide, you'll pass by rows of small wooden fishing boats sitting on the sand awaiting the next tide to rescue them from their awkward stance. The English countryside seems to have changed little from the days when other ladies sat where you now sit sipping tea and eating scones with clotted cream and homemade strawberry jam. You'll pass through the fields and watch the planting or, at another time of year, the harvest.

If the scones aren't tempting you, try the fruitcakes; they're especially good with the Ceylon tea poured into your china cup from a silver teapot. You'll likely peer past pink carnations and daydream of days long ago and lifetimes now mostly forgotten. Your history lessons of this once faraway country will seem much more important now than they did when you were in school.

London's Victoria Station comes into view much too quickly. I found it difficult to come back to today as I walked the length of the train into bustling, hurrying London.

LONDON

▶─────────────────────────────────────▶

Much of the history I learned as a child was in some way related to the past ties of America with Europe, and especially with Great Britain. Indeed, much of that history still remains, for London is an old city.

Getting Around

The underground system is fast, safe, and inexpensive; for £.50 to £.60, you can go most places in the city. For £1.70 you can buy a pass good from 9:30 A.M. until the last train at night. Whenever you ride the underground, hold onto your ticket. You'll have to turn in a one-ride ticket or show your pass as you exit. The famous double-decker buses are slower during rush hour, but just as safe and inexpensive. Cabs, which look and feel more like small limousines, are also cheap and ubiquitous in London.

Exploring London

Not only will you find the remains of history in the *British Museum* (Great Russell Street), but you can visit some of the homes of the people who made the history, people such as Dickens (48 Doughty Street), and Keats (Wentworth Place, Keats Grove), or you can see their likenesses at *Madame Tussaud's* (Marylebone Road) if you prefer.

Of course, you won't want to miss *Buckingham Palace*. If you visit at 11:30 A.M. any day when the queen is in residence (signified by a flag flying from the roof), you can see the spectacular changing of the guard, which lasts nearly an hour. The *Tower of London*, where the crown jewels are on display, is perhaps the most spectacular sight. It's well worth the frequently long wait. If you arrive before 10:00 A.M., you'll miss the tour buses. The *Houses of Parliament*, where the House of Commons sits at 2:30, Monday through Thursday, and 9:30 on Friday, is also worth a visit. *St. Paul's Cathedral*, more famous today as the site of the marriage of Prince Charles and Lady Diana, and *Westminster Cathedral* are nearby. If you'd like, for as little as £2.5, you can make your own brass rubbing in Westminster Abbey. *Trafalgar Square*, a tribute to Lord Admiral Nelson, Great Britain's most famous naval officer, is spectacular with its bronze lions around Nelson's column. The *National Gallery* is just across the mall. The *London Zoo* with its giant panda bear, is just across *Regent's Park*. It's beautiful to walk through when the roses are in bloom. *Hyde Park*, with *Speaker's Corner* (near *Marble Arch*), active early Sunday afternoon, extends over 340 acres.

London is still a great place to shop for crystal, china, and clothes. If the clothes in Paris are a little too extravagant for your taste and pocketbook, you'll likely find the styles in London more in line with both. *Harrods* is worth a visit just to see the food department with its decorative inlaid tile walls, ceiling, and floors as well as the decoratively displayed fish with water streaming over it. You'll find everything else you could want here as well, from furs to china. It's a large modern department store in an elegant old red-brick building. After shopping at Harrods, I suggest lunch across Basil Street at *Wolf's*, where you can watch the chauffeurs pull up in their Rolls-Royces.

If you're feeling a little extravagant, shop at *Knights*. You'll find a number of "By Appointment to the Queen" shops at this new arcade between Brompton Road and Knightsbridge. They sell quality gifts, including fisherman knit sweaters at British *Knitwear*, and luscious chocolates at *Charbonnel et Walker*. For fancy soaps and scents try *Penhaligons*.

After shopping I'd suggest tea at the *Ritz Palm Court*. It's become popular so book early. The first sitting is at 3:15 P.M., the next at 4:30 P.M. There's also a Sunday Tea Dance in their restaurant from 4:30 to 6:30 P.M.

London at Night

London Theaters

London has a large and very active theater district. If you stop by the fourth floor of Harrods you can pick up a free up-to-date theater guide with the latest information on musicals, comedies, ballet, thriller, and repertory theater in London. You can also book the play of your choice with the available seating chart. Theaters in London are quite inexpensive by New York City standards.

The Mouse Trap, currently in its thirty-fourth year at *St. Martin's* theater, is the longest-running play in the world. I recommend seeing it and having dinner before the play at *Wheeler's Ivy* restaurant across the street. Established in 1911, Wheeler's was a place frequented by Winston Churchill, Noel Coward, Edgar Wallace, and Lillian Braithwaite. It's open from 6:15 to 10:00 P.M. Entrées range from £8.50 to £9.50. They feature seafood.

I'd also suggest you see what's playing at the *Theatre Royal*, on

Drury Lane. It's one of the oldest still functioning theaters. It opened in 1663. Its rotunda has entrances labeled "The King's Side" and "The Prince's Side" to prevent a repeat of the evening King George III ran into his worthless and scandalous son the Prince Regent at an opening. A five-minute walk from the Theatre Royal is *The Lamb and Flag*. Opened in 1627, it is the oldest pub in historic *Covent Garden*. It's a good place to stop before the theater.

London's Pubs and Wine Bars

London has a wealth of neighborhood wine bars and pubs that welcome visitors. In addition to ale, wine, and beer, you'll find interesting deli-style snacks including meat pies. You'll meet more area locals than tourists at these old and well-worn places.

Where to Stay in London

While it's always a good idea to book ahead, if you did not do so there is a hotel reservation booth in Victoria Station. They can always find you a place to stay. A bed and breakfast will be clean though not luxurious, and begins at £25.

Hyde Park Hotel, 66 Knightsbridge W1; telephone 235-2000 (single £125, double £135, breakfast £6 to £8). If you're looking for an elegant old established hotel, this is *the* place to stay. Located right on Hyde Park near the center of the shopping area, the location is excellent. You enter by walking up marble steps banked with gold-topped red marble columns under a sparkling crystal chandelier. The entire lobby, including the walls, is variously colored and patterned marble.

Dorchester, Park Lane, W1; telephone 629-8888 (single £145, double £175, breakfast £6 to £9 extra). Another old established hotel in the grand style on the edge of Hyde Park, but a little less conveniently located for the shops and the Underground. While just as elegant, the difference is the result of more recent remodeling. A more up-to-date appeal.

The Ritz, Piccadilly, W1; telephone 493-8181 (single £120, double £140). This landmark hotel still retains its elegant old style with marble floors and walls with gold detail. The lobby bar, with its skylight ceiling and gold statue and doorman with top hat and tails, offers all you expect to find in this grand city. Convenient to the Underground.

Basil Street Hotel, Basil Street, SW3; telephone 581-3311 (single £36 without private bath, £65 with; double £57 without bath, £ 86 with). If you like small hotels, I highly recommend this one. Located near Harrods, the Underground, and Hyde Park, the location is the best in town and the ambiance is even better. The lobby floors are parquet with red oriental rugs and antique furniture. The carved wood stairway off the lobby leads to the rooms, restaurant, and lounge above, where you may choose to have afternoon tea.

Vanderbilt, 67 Cromwell Road; telephone 584-0491 (single £50, double £70). While this hotel is farther from the center of town, it's just off an Underground stop. The large white columns out front lead to an attractively remodeled lobby area with a marble fireplace and crystal chandelier.

Rubens Hotel, Buckingham Palace Road; telephone 834-6600 (single £57, double £67). Located across from the palace stables, this small, older hotel is comfortable and well located, and a good value for the price.

Royal Westminster, Buckingham Palace Road; telephone 834-1302 (single £85 to £105, double £105 to £135). While the exterior makes it obvious that this large hotel is new, the interior has been nicely furnished in red and white marble with beautiful antique furniture. Also near the palace stables and Underground, the location is convenient.

The Cadogan Hotel, 75 Sloane Street; telephone 235-7141 (single £85 to £105, double £105 to £125). Once the home of Lillie Langtry, this elegant old small hotel has retained its charm and appeal through its renovation. An excellent location near town and the antique shops. Though not close to the Underground, it is an excellent value for the price and I highly recommend it.

Where to Eat in London

Like everything else in London, including the pubs and wine bars, the restaurants close early. The last seating is usually between 9:00 and 9:30 P.M. Unfortunately, unlike Paris, London is not known for its food. While the food is usually good, it is simple fare. If you're going to diet, do it in London.

One of the smaller, less-known places you should not miss is *Sherlock Holmes* (10 Northumberland Street). If you get to this small informal restaurant early enough, you can get a table that looks into a facsimile of Sherlock Holmes's study filled with memorabilia such as his hat and pipe. The restaurant upstairs and pub below are also filled with old pictures and clippings of the many greats such as Clive Brooks, who have made this super detective famous. Just off Trafalgar Square, it's a good lunch stop (noon to 2:00 P.M.) and dinner stop (6:00 to 9:30, Monday through Saturday). Entrées range from £5.45 to £9.85.

Hatfield House (Hatfield; telephone 62823). The old palace hall of Hatfield House where Queen Elizabeth I spent much of her childhood and held her first Council of State in 1558 is now an Elizabethan-style restaurant. You'll need reservations here, so call ahead or book a tour. For £16 (£27 with a tour, which includes round-trip transportation) you can dine in traditional Elizabethan style with Henry VIII, Elizabeth I, and Charles II. Jugglers and fire-eaters will entertain throughout the evening. It's a great place to go if you're alone and want to join "the group" as everyone is seated at long tables. It's a difficult place not to get to know your neighbors. Wine, beer, and mead (a sweet honey-flavored drink) are unlimited.

Cockney Tavern Music Hall (18 Charing Cross Road). Another similar type of entertainment worth taking in over dinner is Cockney Night at the Cockney Tavern Music Hall. Here you'll be served a four-course meal and listen to colorful old English Cockney entertainment. The wine and beer are unlimited. Tours are available through a number of agencies that include transportation for £26 to £29.

Talk of London Cabaret (Drury Lane). If you'd like a more formal evening watching an old-style cabaret, then listening to a show band after your four-course dinner, you might try this London cabaret. Tours with transportation from your hotel are available for £26 to £29.

Around London

If you have the time, I strongly suggest seeing the areas outside of London, either on the many half-day or full-day tours available or by renting a car and exploring on your own. Some of the places you won't want to miss are the towering stone columns known as *Stonehenge;* *Bath* with Roman baths built 2,000 years ago; *Stratford-Upon-Avon*, the birthplace of William Shakespeare; *Warwick Castle*, a fourteenth-century castle with a collection of Rubens and Van Dyck paintings; *Canterbury*, with its famous cathedral; *Cambridge* and *Oxford*, where you can wander through the narrow streets of the villages and the halls of these world-renowned universities; *Leeds Castle*, one of the most beautiful castles in the world built on an island; and, if you'd like, you can also spend a day at the races.

Your Departure (or Arrival)

If you depart (or arrive) from London, you'll find London's Heathrow and Gatwick airports easily accessible from downtown. Stanstead and Manchester airports are much farther away (Manchester is 188 miles from London). Be sure to check which airport the flight departs from before booking.

To get to Heathrow Airport (15 miles west of London) take the Piccadilly underground line west to the end of the line; you'll be at the airport (£1.20). Most airlines depart from the very last Underground stop, which services three of the four terminals. If you prefer, a cab from town will be under £20. The Underground link goes to Gatwick Airport (27 miles south of London). It will cost about £4 and take 35 minutes.

No matter how long I've stayed, and I've been to London for up to two weeks at a time, it's not long enough. There is so much to do in and around this incredible city.

BERMUDA: THE FRIENDLY ISLANDS

▶────────────────────────────────▶

GENERAL AMBIANCE   ★ ★

SOCIAL CLIMATE   ★ ★ ★

ACTIVITIES   ★ ★ ★

───────────────

FOR TOUR ARRANGEMENTS CONTACT:
Bermuda Department of Tourism
310 Madison Avenue
New York, NY 10017
(212) 818-9800

Or *contact your travel agent*

▶────────────────────────────────▶

*I*f you're at all hesitant about traveling alone, make your first solo trip to Bermuda. Not only for its beauty—the plethora of fragrant blooming tropical plants and trees and the expanse of long white sandy beaches at the edge of crystal clear azure waters—but most of all because the people of Bermuda are so incredibly welcoming to strangers. The Bermudian charm and hospitality immediately make you feel like a longtime family friend. They even speak English in this foreign country. I never felt alone here, and I never felt uncomfortable about my safety. I was able to totally relax along a deserted beach, day or night, alone.

If you're interested in relaxing in a lush tropical paradise then Bermuda is the place for you. But don't look too far south on your map.

Not only do most people look for Bermuda down around the Bahamas, they also refer to *the* island of Bermuda. Bermuda is actually an archipelago of more than 150 islands located far out to sea (about 600 miles) at nearly the same latitude as Charleston, South Carolina. The seven primary Bermuda islands are connected by a series of bridges, including the smallest drawbridge in the world. As you travel between these small islands you will be struck by the rainbow of green,

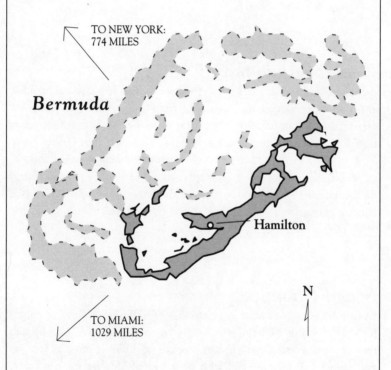

TO NEW YORK:
774 MILES

Bermuda

Hamilton

N

TO MIAMI:
1029 MILES

yellow, orange, pink, and purple vegetation growing down to the edge of white sandy beaches, and meeting cool blue waters. You'll also find yourself intoxicated by the fragrance of jasmine, oleander, and honeysuckle, which fills the air throughout Bermuda.

While the first known visitor to Bermuda was a Spaniard believed to have landed in 1515, it was the 1609 shipwreck of the British flagship *Sea Venture*, captained by Admiral Sir George Somers, that led to the colonization of Bermuda. Bermuda is today the oldest self-governing British colony.

General Ambiance

Add the charm, grace, and tradition of the British to a tropical paradise and you'll experience the appeal of Bermuda, which has somehow managed to incorporate only the best of its British heritage. It offers tradition and formality without stuffiness. Elegant manor houses stand amid tropical gardens, and while the men often wear a jacket and tie, as required by many establishments, they are worn with shorts and knee-high socks more often than with long pants. The result is a curious combination of the formal and the tropical, so typical of the spirit of Bermuda.

Social Climate

Even a short stop to look at a map inevitably brings at least one local resident offering to help you find your way. If you're unfortunate enough to run out of gas on your moped—as I did—almost as soon as you stop you'll be besieged with help and quickly be on your way. The local Bermudians, both the men and the women, are open, warm, and welcoming, offering friendly conversation and assistance before it's requested and without your feeling hassled or in any way intruded upon. Any woman knows the sometimes not so subtle difference between friendly conversation and a "hi" that commands an answer. Unlike many places I've traveled throughout the world, the latter was not the case in Bermuda.

I also felt comfortable wherever I went in Bermuda, day or night, from crowded bars and nightclubs to deserted beaches and back roads. I was able to travel alone in Bermuda without even a hint of discomfort. I heard the same from every other traveler and local I met. Being isolated on only 22 square miles of land in the middle of an ocean seems to have created a feeling of community similar to that found in a small town.

Activities

Blending a tropical life-style with the traditional British way of life, Bermuda offers a wide variety of activities. The beaches are some of the most beautiful in the world and it is still possible to find out-of-the-way deserted areas with fine soft white sand and crystal clear vivid blue waters. In addition to windsurfing, sailing, water skiing, and body surfing, because of the British influence, every Sunday during the summer you can also watch the traditional dinghy races. (The locations vary. Check with any yacht club.)

Horseback Riding

Spiceland Riding Center on Middle Road in Warwick offers the most spectacular trail ride I've ever seen. Much of the time you are actually on the beach with your horse sidestepping a little as the waves come in, much as you and I do. The horses are well trained and well mannered. Some will challenge the expert rider and others will accept even a first-timer. It's a trail ride that should not be missed. For US$30 you get an hour-and-a-half trail ride with a hearty breakfast after the ride. Private lessons (US$35 an hour), trail rides (US$15 an hour), and group lessons (US$15 an hour) are available. They also offer a sunset trail ride (US$15).

Cricket

While the Bermudians are a delight any time of year, I'm told the time to really experience them is the end of July or the first of August at the annual two-day Cricket Match between the east and west ends of the islands. If you miss this special holiday time of continual gaiety and carnival-like festivities, you can still find a cricket match in progress somewhere any Thursday or Sunday afternoon during the season.

Helmet Dives

Surrounded by reefs, Bermuda boasts some of the best scuba diving and snorkeling in the world. For a unique view of the sea life you can take a helmet dive. Using a helmet that covers your entire head (and not getting your hair wet or smudging your makeup, if that's a concern) you descend some 20 to 30 feet to the clear, sandy ocean floor, where you can see the ubiquitous ocean parrot and angelfish, purple sea fans, clusters of sea sponges, mollusks, and sea urchins in the Sea Garden.

Sailing and Windsurfing

You can rent sailboats (and motorboats) in Salt Kettle, as well as at a number of other locations. You can get to Salt Kettle from Hamilton by taking a ferry from the Front Street Terminal or you can ride along the peninsula on the south side of the Hamilton Harbour. Windsurfing lessons are available at the Glencoe Hotel in Salt Kettle, and they have large sailboats for charter as well. If you can sail, be sure to explore this delightful harbor and its many small islands.

Sea Gardens

For the less adventurous, the Sea Gardens can be comfortably viewed from specially built glass-bottom boats. The *Looking Glass* offers a dinner cruise five days a week that was a highlight of my last trip to Bermuda. After cruising through the Sea Gardens and some fifty small islands, the *Looking Glass* stops near the western tip of the islands at the *Village Inn Restaurant*. Here you'll enjoy a spectacular barbecue dinner of Bermuda fish chowder, pork (supposedly the pigs are descendants of those left by the first Spanish visitor in 1515), conch fritters, chicken, and baked Alaska—all served on the restaurant's patio at the water's edge. The entertainment while you dine is great fun and includes a sing-along before boarding the *Looking Glass* for the cruise back toward the lights of Hamilton. The open bar on the boat is included in the price, making the package a real bargain at US$42. If you're lucky, your captain may even take you by his "dream home." While we all have ours, few include two islands connected by a private bridge, five private docks, and a home nestled in a secluded bay worth around $4 million.

Relaxing on the Beach

The most beautiful, but unfortunately also the most crowded and commercial, beach is located at Horseshoe Bay. While you won't want to miss seeing this beautiful white sandy bay, I don't recommend this beach for a relaxing afternoon. I'd avoid it, as the locals do, and move to Long Bay. About a half mile farther down the south shore, it's here or at Elbow Beach where you'll meet the locals.

If you really want to find peace and solitude, ride your moped around the island (be sure to wear your bathing suit). Then feel free to stop and relax, swim, or sun wherever you come to one of the many small, isolated, and usually deserted sandy coves.

Preparing for Your Trip to Bermuda

Documents

U.S. and Canadian citizens do not need a visa to visit Bermuda. You do, however, need a return or onward ticket and either a passport (valid or expired), a birth certificate, a signed U.S. voter registration card, a U.S. reentry permit, a U.S. naturalization certificate, or a U.S. alien registration card. If you plan to stay for longer than three weeks, you must obtain permission from the Bermudian immigration officials upon arrival at the airport.

When to Go

Located at about the same latitude as Charleston, South Carolina, Bermuda has a similar climate, and it gets too cold to swim at the beach during the winter months. The most popular tourist months are

May to November, when daytime temperatures will be in the mid-eighties, evening temperatures in the seventies. During the winter months, the daytime highs will be in the sixties and seventies.

What to Take

The average temperature in Bermuda is 70 degrees and it seldom gets below 50 degrees. In the off-season winter months, it can get cold, especially at night, so you'll need a sweater and warm jacket. You'll also want a raincoat for the winter showers. During the summer, the showers are usually brief and easily ignored.

While you'll primarily need only resort wear, because of the British influence, some of the better restaurants expect more formal attire at night; nice slacks or a dress will do. Short shorts, bathing suits, and halter tops are not appropriate on the shopping streets, when viewing Parliament, in the restaurants, lounges, or hotel lobbies.

Money

I was quite surprised when I went to the bank to change money on my first day in Bermuda. They gave me American dollars for my traveler's checks. For better or worse, the Bermudian dollar is now tied to the American dollar instead of the British pound. This means there is always a one-to-one exchange rate. Their money rises and falls with ours.

You'll usually get American dollars back as change when you make a purchase. You may, however, get a combination of Bermudian and American dollars and coins, depending on what the shopkeeper has on hand.

Getting There

Bermuda does not currently have a national airline carrier. Pan American World Airways does, however, offer excellent service to and from Bermuda. Their schedules are convenient and they fly to the major gateway cities. The best news is that their fares are surprisingly low. While most airline food is poor to passable, I must say that the food on my Pan Am flights to and from Bermuda was excellent. That seems appropriate since the food in Bermuda was so consistently good as well.

Airport Transportation

For US$7 you can take a bus from the airport to most hotels—your travel agent should prearrange this—but a cab is more convenient. If you share one with another incoming passenger, it will be the same price, or less. Much like all other Bermudians, the local cab drivers are full of information and exceptionally friendly.

Departure

U.S. citizens can take out US$400 in merchandise and one liter of alcohol per forty-eight hours in the country. A US$10 departure tax will be collected at the Bermuda airport upon departure.

Customs

Both coming and going I was through customs before I realized what was happening. Quite unusual, you clear U.S. Customs when leaving Bermuda rather than upon reentering the U.S.

Getting Around

You are not allowed to drive a car in Bermuda unless you live on the island. But there are a number of other options.

Cycle

For around US$18 a day, less for multiple days, you can rent a moped. If there is not a rental office at your hotel, there will be one nearby that will deliver. Anyone who can ride a bike can ride a moped. You'll see businesspeople in suits and ladies in dresses riding around on mopeds, as they are the primary form of transportation in Bermuda. You do need to remember to stay on the *left*-hand side of the road and use your right hand to signal a right-hand turn, not your left as Americans typically do. I enjoyed my moped so much I found it hard to part with it at the end of my visit.

Helmets are required and are provided with your moped, as are locks for the bike. While the speed limit is 20 mph, most cycles only go that fast downhill, so you need not be concerned by the lack of a speedometer on most mopeds. You'll also likely not have a gas gauge. Be sure you're shown how to engage the reserve gas tank (and pedals, if you have a pedal bike). I ran out of gas not knowing I had a reserve tank. Fortunately, a local who did know stopped to help even before my bike had come to a complete halt.

Bus

Bermuda has an excellent bus system. For 75 cents to US$2, depending on the distance, you can reach almost any location. Exact change is required. You can save even more by buying tokens at the Washington Street terminal in Hamilton. Bus stops are marked by green-and-white-striped poles.

Taxi

There are a number of taxis around Bermuda. They hold one to four passengers and do not charge extra for additional people. You'll of course save money by sharing a cab, a common practice on the island. A cab ride from one end of Bermuda to the other will be about US$30.

Taxi Tours

If you are interested in a taxi tour of the area, the drivers of cabs with the blue flags are licensed tour guides. For US$16 an hour, they will provide you with a comprehensive tour of Bermuda. I suggest doing so over two days. In about three hours you can see the west end one day and in another three hours you can see the east end another day. Once again, you'll recognize a substantial savings, and have more fun, if you find two or three others to share the cab.

Ferries

For US$2 per person plus US$2 for your bike, you can take a ferry from Hamilton to Somerset Island. They leave almost hourly. You can obtain a schedule at the Ferry Terminal on Front Street in Hamilton. This is a relaxing way to spend an hour and get a feel for the number and size of the many small islands of Bermuda.

For US$1 you can also take a ferry (passengers only, no bikes allowed) from Hamilton to Paget, Warwick, or Sandys.

Horse-Drawn Carriage

The best place to catch a carriage is near the Ferry Terminal on Front Street. For US$7.50 per half hour, you can enjoy the sights from your carriage.

Treasures to Purchase

Fine British china and crystal is available in Bermuda for approximately 30 percent less than in the United States, although I certainly recommend checking your local discount houses first if you plan to make a purchase. Don't forget you will need to pay duty if you exceed your allowed limit of US$400 for all purchases. If you send your treasures home there is postage and insurance to be added as well.

While I had a difficult time even thinking about the cold weather back home while in the warm Bermuda sun, there is an excellent selection of Icelandic wool sweaters, jackets, scarves, and hats as well as fine woolens and tweeds to buy.

There are many Irish linen stores, but I was disappointed by the quality of most. I also thought the well-advertised pottery factory was not much more than a tourist trap. The *Lili Perfume Factory* on the other hand was interesting. The fragrances produced and for sale on the premises—such as jasmine, lily, sweet pea, passion flower, and oleander—are unique and difficult to choose between. You will find the perfume prices at the factory are the same as at the airport.

Once you taste the traditional Bermudian fish chowder spiced up with sherry pepper sauce and black rum, you'll want to pick up both condiments to take home. You'll find the sherry pepper sauce in souvenir shops and the black rum in the liquor store. If you buy 2 or 4 liters of rum, you can avoid paying the local tax and the store will deliver directly to the airport for you to pick up as you clear customs. (You will, however, have to pay duty on the amount over the one liter limit.)

Where to Stay in Bermuda

Before you decide where to stay, you'll need to consider the type of vacation you want and the type of atmosphere you prefer. In Bermuda, you can choose among large luxury resorts that you really don't need to leave, small hotels, and guest houses. You can also be on or off the beach, in town, or quite isolated.

Hamilton, the capital of Bermuda and the only large city, is located nearly in the center of the islands, in Pembroke Parish (district). It has the most sophisticated clubs, excellent restaurants, the best shopping, and beautiful beaches. It is also a convenient spot from which to explore both ends of the islands, on alternate days. As a very charming local single told me, "Accessibility should be your first consideration when deciding where to stay. . . . Besides, when I meet a lovely lady, it's more convenient for me to pick her up and take her home if she's not isolated on the tip of the islands." If you're getting a ride, taking a cab, or riding your moped home, you may want to consider the distance. For those reasons, I recommend staying in the Hamilton area.

Another consideration should be meal plans available. Some hotels offer room only, others require that you pay for meals whether you dine there or not. Personally, I prefer the Bermudian plan, which includes the room and breakfast only. All other meals can then be eaten out or in, as you prefer. (The prices quoted are for the room only unless otherwise stated.)

Hamilton Area

The Hamilton Princess, Hamilton (single US$130 to US$185, double US$130 to US$191). Located on the west shore of Hamilton, this hotel offers luxury and convenience. The *Gazebo Lounge* features top nightclub entertainment on the premises and the three top clubs are only a few blocks away along Front Street. The Princess also has a pool and a patio on the water's edge.

The Bermudian Hotel, Hamilton (single US$120 to US$185, double US$120 to US$200). This modern resort sits on a small hill on the west end of Front Street overlooking Hamilton Harbour. Restaurants, lounges, and pool at the hotel; beach club access available (true of nearly all hotels).

Stonington Beach Hotel, Paget Parish (single US$104 to US$150, double US$158 to US$206). This small luxury hotel is located ten minutes out of Hamilton on one of the most attractive beaches on the island. All of the rooms have balconies with ocean views (I especially like being able to hear the surf at night). Situated next to a school of culinary arts, the *Overlook Restaurant* at the hotel serves the students' superb meals. While the beach is only a few feet away from most rooms, there is also a pool off the main lobby. There are two tennis courts and a tennis pro available for lessons.

Elbow Beach Hotel, Paget Parish (single US$140 to US$230, double US$145 to US$335). This large resort is located on Elbow Beach next to the Stonington Beach Hotel. There are a cocktail lounge, pub, gourmet restaurant, grill, and coffee shop on the premises. Five tennis courts (lit at night), access to golf course, and a private health club as well as a pool are available to guests.

Outside the Hamilton Area

There are a few resorts outside the Hamilton area that are spectacular enough that you may want to consider them if you prefer large hotels with all the amenities. These include:

Marriott's Castle Harbour Resort, Tuckers Town (single and double US$180 to US$220). Thirty minutes east of Hamilton, surrounded by one of the most spectacular ocean-front golf courses on the island and next to the famous Mid-Ocean golf club (private, but open to Marriott guests), this is the newest of Bermuda's luxury resorts. A formal lounge off the main restaurant features nightly entertainment and overlooks the patio and garden below, which are on the edge of the sea. The knotty Bermudian pine entry is spectacular, as is the high-beamed lobby with red and white marble floors.

The tasteful artwork and flowers everywhere exude the feeling of class and luxury.

Sonesta Beach Hotel, Southampton Parish (available with breakfast and dinner only: single US$178 to US$278, double US$198 to US$298). This luxury resort is located on a private beach with twenty-five landscaped acres of grounds. A solar-dome pool, complete European health spa, shops, nightly shows, bar, and restaurants make this a resort you may not want to leave. Specials are available that include tennis, scuba diving, or spa facilities.

Southampton Princess, Southampton Parish (available with breakfast and dinner only: single US$180 to US$270, double US$220 to US$320). While the main resort is located on a hill, a private beach is available a short distance away. Tennis courts, a sun deck and pool, a number of excellent restaurants, shops, and bar and nightclub make this a self-contained resort. Specials are available that include tennis and golf.

Salt Kettle House, Salt Kettle Road, Paget Parish (single US$31 with breakfast, double US$50 to US$60 with breakfast). The best-kept secret in Bermuda, this small house, located on the water, is across the harbor from the city of Hamilton, a two-minute walk from the Salt Kettle Ferry dock. Though there is no beach or pool, there is a private dock. This is an excellent choice for the money.

This is in no way an exhaustive list of accommodations. For a complete listing, write the Bermuda Department of Tourism, Suite 201, 310 Madison Avenue, New York, NY 10017.

Where to Eat in Bermuda

I found the restaurants and food in Bermuda to be consistently good. Bermudian delicacies you should be sure to sample include mussel pie, conch stew, steak and kidney pie, conch fritters, and Bermudian fish and lobster (when in season, September through March). Especially interesting is the fish chowder. While it tastes good as served, it is transformed into a culinary delight when a touch of sherry peppers and Bermudian black rum are added.

While there are many excellent restaurants located throughout the islands, there are a few you should not miss. These include:

Mikado's, Marriott Castle Harbor Resort; telephone 3-2040. Even if you don't stay at the Marriott, don't miss Bermuda's only Japanese restaurant. This is a favorite of locals, and you'll likely meet more Bermudians here than tourists. Seating is at a community table for eight with your meals cooked at the table. The management makes a point of seating single women with other singles, rather than couples, whenever possible and it usually is. Located at the most luxurious island resort, the people you will meet here are usually the type you'll want to meet. The food is superb and the atmosphere and other guests interesting (US$35 to US$50 for a complete meal with drinks).

Fourway's Inn, Middle Road, Paget Parish; telephone 6-6517. This old Bermudian home built in 1727 is consistently recommended by locals as *the* gourmet restaurant. Formal yet not stuffy, this restaurant offers a variety of seafood (lobster, US$31), steak (from US$18), and special Fourway fettuccine (US$16.50). They even offer Beluga caviar at US$50 an ounce for an appetizer. While there are no joiner tables, the management and staff are friendly and will keep your meal interesting.

There is also piano music nightly. The bar is in the old slave quarters of the estate.

Tom Moore's Tavern, Bailey's Bay. This restored seventeenth-century home on the bay, the oldest building in Bermuda, is another restaurant that should not be missed. Tom Moore, an Irish poet, wrote his best-known works while a guest here. It has been a restaurant for more than eighty-five years.

There are four small dining rooms, but the most spectacular is the Admiralty Room with its dark cedar fireplace. Lunch includes sandwiches and salads (US$4.75 to US$7.25). Dinner features a variety of entrées of fish, meat, or quail (US$19.75 to US$23.75) with assorted fish cakes, hash cakes, or conch fritters (US$7.50) as starters.

Fort William, Government Hill, St. George's; telephone 7-0904. This informal restaurant and pub is located in one of Bermuda's oldest forts. Originally built in the early 1600s, it was rebuilt into a gunpowder house in 1887. You enter through the old tunnel dug into the side of a mountain, which now feels like a time tunnel carrying you back hundreds of years. On Friday nights (if there are enough reservations) they produce a banquet fit for King William himself (US$25 per person). Book your place a week ahead. The usual dinner menu (served between 6:30 P.M. and 10:30 P.M.) includes a crusty meat pie of the day (US$9.50) and a variety of steaks and fish dishes (US$10.75 to US$14).

St. George

Pub on the Square, King's Square; telephone 7-1522. One of the few places open early for breakfast, this old English-style pub has a small balcony with seating overlooking the historic town square. Lunch (10:00 A.M. to 1:00 P.M.) includes sandwiches, salads, and kidney pie (US$3.50 to US$9). Dinner (6:30 P.M. to 10:00 P.M.) includes ribs, steaks, and a variety of seafood (US$7.50 to US$15).

White Horse Restaurant, King's Square. On the water's edge with outside seating next to the crystal clear blue water, this restaurant is an excellent place for lunch on a hot day. Lunch (noon to 6:00 P.M.) includes sandwiches, salads, and an excellent fish chowder (US$3 to US$12.50). Dinner (6:00 P.M. to 10:00 P.M.) includes everything from sandwiches (US$3.50) to surf 'n turf (US$18.50). This old English-style brick and tile restaurant with tables made from polished logs is a friendly place to eat and relax at the bar (open until midnight).

Carriage House Restaurant, Water Street; telephone 7-1270. This restaurant is located a short walk up Water Street from King's Square on the shore. In addition to an elaborate brunch—with music provided by a guitarist—they offer a daily special (US$8 for soup, entrée, dessert, and coffee), hot and cold sandwiches, a number of house specialties including seafood, fettuccine, and steak, as well as a salad bar (US$6.50 to US$12.75).

Fisherman's Wharf, Water Street; telephone 7-1515. Located farther down Water Street, this is also on the water. Lunch includes everything from sandwiches (US$3.50) to lobster pie (US$16.50). The nautical atmosphere with fishnets and floats hanging from the ceiling is appropriate for the view out over the moored boats in the harbor. Tuesday and Saturday are barbecue nights—for US$16.95 you get a complete dinner including wahoo (mackerel), steak, and ribs.

Summerset

Village Inn, Waterford Bridge; telephone 4-1398. On the water's edge overlooking the bay and Hamilton beyond, this makes a great stop for lunch (noon to 3:30 P.M.). Salads run US$3.50 to US$5, fish entrées US$9.50 to US$10.50, hamburgers US$4 to US$5. The best time to eat here is with the *Looking Glass* dinner cruise. Leaving the Hamilton Ferry Dock at 6:00 P.M., cruising through the Sea Gardens on a glass-bottom boat (with a complimentary bar), you arrive at the Village Inn at approximately 7:30. The excellent barbecue dinner includes pork, chicken, conch fritters, Bermuda game fish, papaw, and baked Alaska with your coffee for dessert. Calypso music and a sing-along make a superb evening even more special. No one is seated alone in this festive, party atmosphere (US$21.50 dinner only; US$42 with Sea Garden excursion and tour of bay). The dinner cruise is well worth the time and expense and was a highlight of my trip.

Plantation Club, Harrington Sand Road; telephone 3-1188. Not a private club, this warm island restaurant is inviting with its pink colors, rattan chairs, and ubiquitous plants. On cool evenings, dinner is served out on the patio under the canopy. This is a good lunch stop after visiting the spectacular Leamington Caves. The staff here is especially helpful and informative. Lunch (noon to 2:30 P.M.) includes salads, hamburgers, sandwiches, and sea food (US$2 to US$9.25). Dinner, more formal and expensive, includes an excellent selection of seafood and specialties (US$10.25 to US$17). Beluga caviar is served as an hors d'oeuvre for US$30 per ounce. Other hors d'oeuvres range from US$4 to US$8.

Glencoe, Salt Kettle; telephone 6-0407. Situated on the point of the bay, this restaurant is near the Salt Kettle Ferry, about a ten-minute moped drive from the city of Hamilton. Outdoor seating is available. The main dining room faces the water on two sides. It is a wonderful place from which to watch the boats in the bay and the lights of the houses beyond. The tables are close enough to encourage conversation between them, a frequent occurrence in the islands. At lunch (noon to 2:30 P.M.) and dinner (7:30 P.M. to 9:30 P.M.) you can get Glencoe's famous fish with banana, an excellent selection. Their meats are tasty and tender and somewhat unusual. I recommend the filet of beef in a goat cheese sauce. Dinner entrées range from US$15.75 to US$17.75.

Southampton

Henry VIII, South Shore Road; telephone 8-1977. On a hill over-looking the Sonesta Hotel at the turn-off at Gibb's Lighthouse, this friendly, lively Tudor-style pub is an island favorite. You can get all the Bermudian favorites here, such as mussel pie, and fish chowder, and the English favorites, steak and kidney pie and roast beef and Yorkshire pudding. Lunch includes salads and more traditional meats and seafood (US$7.50 to US$12). Dinner is more formal (US$14 to US$19.25).

Hamilton

Mr. Onions, Par-la-Ville; telephone 2-5012. Attractive and casual with a large bar and eating area decorated in dark green and brass, this restaurant is open for lunch (noon to 3:00 P.M.) and dinner (5:30 P.M. to 11:00 P.M.). The bar is open until 1:00 A.M. A favorite spot for locals to stop for a deli sandwich (US$3.75) or steak dinner (US$14.75), there is a wide selection of seafood and barbecue as well.

Lobster Pot, Bermudian Street; telephone 2-6898. Another favorite of the locals for informal dining. Featuring primarily seafood from US$7.95 to US$33.25 for a 2-pound lobster. The nautical effect is carried to the lobster pots hanging from the ceiling.

Exploring the Islands

St. George's

Located on the east end of Bermuda, near the airport, St. George's is the second oldest English town in the New World. Here you will find yourself surrounded by three centuries of history. It was on the shores of St. George's that Sir George Somers and the 150 men, women, and children sailing with him to Virginia, the oldest English settlement, were shipwrecked in 1609. They later built two vessels to carry them on the remainder of their voyage. For US$1.50 you can tour a replica of the larger of the two ships, *The Deliverance*, on Or-dinance Island, just off King's Square. To get a feel for the conditions of travel in 1610, you need only step below deck. You are immediately struck by the low ceilings and cramped quarters that held men, women, and children; provisions; livestock; and everything else that could be brought aboard. Everything they needed to begin their new lives was stowed on this small boat. The stories these colonists eventually brought back to England are said to be the basis of William Shakespeare's *The Tempest*. Their tales of the richness of the islands in hogs (left by an earlier Spanish explorer), fish, tobacco, and whales in the neighboring harbor sped its colonization by the Virginia Company in 1612.

This island was known as Dunking Stool Island until 1795. As the sign on the dunking stool in front of the *Deliverance* states, it was used primarily to humiliate women when they disobeyed their husbands and broke social norms—an unfortunate reminder of the need for men to keep "their women" submissive.

This sheltered harbor still provides moorage for the simple and the grand sailing vessels. The boats tied up along the docks are in many ways as interesting as the historic buildings in the square behind them. You'll see the freshly painted brass-trimmed yachts of the wealthy with corporate executives and their wives being greeted by a brass band and the town crier as they enter the harbor. You'll also see old wooden sailing vessels badly in need of paint with a man and woman living aboard. This is a life-style I for one have always fantasized about "one day" experiencing. Some of these people are temporary sojourners on a much-too-brief vacation; others left their professional or corporate positions years ago to enter this new dimension of existence.

There is also a short, well-rounded statue of Sir George on the island. He appears to be laughing lustily at the curious combination of old and new, wealthy and possession-free "explorers" now finding refuge in the harbor.

King's Square is the center of St. George's. It's a great place to park your bike and begin your tour on foot. The old *Town Hall* is located here (next to the visitor's center). It contains old furnishings made of the unique Bermudian cedar and also photographs of past mayors and the stories of political intrigue.

Just a short distance up King Street is *Bridge House*, built in the early 1700s. Once the governor's home, it is now an art gallery and craft shop owned by the National Trust. The oldest building in Bermuda, *State House*, built in 1620, is farther up King Street. The House Assembly met here when St. George's was the capital of Bermuda. If you're in town in April, don't miss the annual peppercorn ceremony, when the Masonic Lodge, which now maintains the building, pays its annual rent of one peppercorn.

In the other direction from King's Square up Water Street, you'll find an antique *Carriage Museum* with a collection of carriages, the only form of transportation in Bermuda until 1946 (US$1 admission). Nearby is *Tucker House*. Here, for US$1.50, you can view an excellent collection of Bermudian cedar furniture, silver, and portraits of former residents. At the end of Water Street is the straw factory.

If you go up one block to the main street, you'll pass a number of modern-day shops with clothing and jewelry before you reach *St. Peter's Church*. While I do not always visit churches—they seem so plentiful as to become repetitious—this one is unique. The roof is typical of the buildings throughout Bermuda: open cedar beams supporting a limestone roof. On either side of the doors there are statues of the king and queen brought from Westminster Palace, where the English parliament meets in London. They were placed here to commemorate the first meeting of the Bermudian Parliament, held in the church in 1620. If you exit by the side door, you'll pass the ancient weather-beaten stones of the church cemetery among the tropical plants. The inscriptions on most are no longer legible. The ones that you can read commemorate the very famous as well as the slaves (who are located in a separate area on the west side of the main churchyard).

If you leave through the back gate and turn right, you'll pass *Featherbed Alley* with its print shop (a working replica of the Gutenberg printing press is housed here) and Historic Society Museum. Before leaving town, you may want to visit the *Old Rectory* on Broad Alley north of St. Peter's, and the *Somers Gardens*, with its indigenous trees, flowers, and shrubs, on Duke of York Street.

Outside St. George's

If you return to the main road and continue through town, you'll pass *Gates Fort*. This small restored fort, named after Sir Gates, one of the survivors of the *Sea Venture* shipwreck, guards the eastern entrance to St. George's Harbour.

Continuing around the point you'll pass a number of white sandy beaches, some deserted, some quite busy. If you were smart enough to have brought or worn your bathing suit, I highly recommend a refreshing dip in the ocean at the beach that appeals most to you.

Don't miss *Fort St. Catherine* (US$1 admission). The cool, narrow passages of the stone structure feel much as they must have when this was an active nineteenth-century fort. There is an interesting collection of muskets, cannons, reproductions of the British Crown Jewels, as well as the fort's cookhouse and duty room complete with soldiers in uniform.

As you continue over the hill back to St. George's, you'll pass *Fort William*, now a restaurant and pub. This is a great place to stop for lunch or a cool drink.

Continuing toward Tuckertown you'll go over the swing bridge with its reminder to carriage drivers to "Walk Your Horse Please," then across the bridge causeway over the especially stunning blue waters of Castle Harbour. Just across the bridge is the *Blue Grotto Dolphin Show*. These hourly shows feature two well-trained dolphins performing to voice commands in the stunning setting of the naturally formed Blue Grotto. It's a lot of entertainment for US$3.

If you're interested in learning how perfume is made, continue on the main road past the Bermuda Pottery store and the *Swizzle Inn* (actually, you may want to stop here for a rum swizzle, an island specialty). The *Lili Perfume Factory* is located just past the main intersection of North Shore Road, Wilkinson Avenue, and Blue Hole Hill. It's on your left. It was established by Madeline Scott in a 200-year-old building. After the free tour you'll have a chance to sample and, of course, purchase fragrances made from the jasmine, oleander, lily, and passion flowers grown on the islands. They also produce a man's cologne made from local cedar wood. This is a wonderful way to take home the fragrances you've been enjoying as you rode along the picturesque, flower-lined lanes.

If you take Wilkinson Avenue west, you'll pass the *Crystal Caves* (US$2.50 admission) with stalactites hanging from the ceiling and stalagmites rising from the ground to meet them. The story is that these magnificent caves were discovered in 1907 by two small boys who climbed 120 feet down a hole after their cricket ball. A pontoon bridge now replaces the former, more intriguing, boat ride back into the water-filled cave. Further down the same road you'll pass the smaller but less commercial *Leamington Caves* (US$2). The enthusiasm and information presented by the guides through these caves make the visit one not to miss.

The *National Arches,* although difficult to find, are also an important stop. Continue toward Tuckerstown past the Castle Harbour Resort and turn left onto the South Road through the Mid-Ocean golf course. As you near the end of the South Road, the road will branch. Keep right and go through the pink stucco gate to the Mid-Ocean Club. Take the first left at the road to the beach then keep right to the parking area at the National Arches with its pink beach. Be sure to wear your bathing suit here. The changing rooms are private and you won't want to miss this public beach. (You'll get the best picture of the arches from the path to the left above them.) As a result of the breakup of the red coral reef offshore, the sand here has a pink hue. The brilliant blue waves are great for body surfing or just playing in the water.

Devil's Hole, farther west on Harrington Sound Road, has been an attraction with visitors since 1830 and a natural aquarium since 1847. Giant turtles, parrot fish, large groupers, an immense green moray eel, and an array of other reef fish swim in this collapsed cave still fed by the ocean (US$2.50 admission). The modern *Bermuda Aquarium Museum and Zoo* is not far away (north on Harrington Sand Road in Flatts). Opened in 1928, the aquarium houses an array of colorful area fish with self-guided (free) microphones providing comprehensive information on life in the coral reefs. Among other things, the museum documents Dr. William's famous 1934 one-mile record dive with a replica of the original bathysphere he used. The small but attractive zoo was added in 1967.

If you're in Flatts at 10:00 A.M. or 2:00 P.M., you can catch the boat for a helmet dive (bring you own towel and bathing suit). With this large helmet you can walk on the ocean floor and feed the fish without even getting your hair wet. (Call 2-4434 for reservations.)

If you go back south to South Road, you'll pass *Spittal Pond*. This wildlife sanctuary is just north of *Spanish Rock*. If you walk through the sanctuary and up the hill (look closely for a sign here and there; the path is obscured in many places) you'll find Spanish Rock on a high cliff overlooking the ocean. The bronze plaque dated 1543 is in the place where carvings were found in the rock. Originally believed to be Spanish in origin, experts now speculate that the initials were carved by Portuguese sailors who were shipwrecked here.

Almost back to the town of Hamilton on South Road you'll pass *Verdmont* on Collector's Hill (US$2 admission). This is another stop you shouldn't miss. This fine, late-seventeenth-century home contains an interesting collection of Bermudian cedar furniture and portraits of former inhabitants painted by a local artist. Even more interesting is the tale told by an elderly Bermudian lady of the history of the home and its residents. Not only does she know the history, she's a part of it herself. You'll feel like a guest in her home, privy to the local town gossip.

West of Hamilton

If you pick up the free *Guide to Bermuda Beaches* published by the Looking Glass Boat Tours, you'll find most of the spectacular soft white sandy beaches of Bermuda are west of Hamilton along South Road. Stop and walk along the surf, especially at *Stonehole Bay* and *Horseshoe Bay*. (If you take the *Spiceland Stable* breakfast trail ride, this is where you'll come.) They are truly spectacular. If you turn right onto Lighthouse Road (at the Henry VIII Restaurant), you'll reach *Gibb's Lighthouse*. The view from the top, 362 feet above sea level, encompasses the entire area and helps give you a feel for the number of small islands that make up Bermuda (US$1 admission).

As you continue to the northwest tip of Bermuda, you'll pass over the world's smallest drawbridge. At 22 inches wide when open, it's just enough for the mast of a sailboat to pass through. This scenic drive ends at the *Bermuda Maritime Museum*. This former dockyard for the British Royal navy now has a number of exhibit halls. The artifacts housed here tell the story of life in Bermuda for the past 300 years. Queen Elizabeth acknowledged the importance of this museum by attending its opening in 1975. The *Bermuda Arts Center* is just next door. Both close at 5:00 P.M., so don't arrive too late. You'll want to be able to spend some time wandering through the buildings and around the pond, a collapsed cave made into a safe harbor for unloading munitions. If you'd like, you can catch the ferry back to Hamilton for US$2 plus US$2 for your bike. The forty-five-minute ride is both a relaxing and scenic way to end your day.

The City of Hamilton

The current capital of Bermuda and the hub of activity, Hamilton is the primary port for ocean-going cruise ships. *Front Street* is *the* place to shop, with its stores well stocked with crystal and fine china from England, linen from Ireland, and woolens from Iceland. The *Department of Tourism* is located here on Church Street in Global House. It's behind the *Sessions House*, where the Supreme Court and House of Assembly can be viewed (no shorts, jeans, or halter tops, please). The chief justice, speaker of the house, and barristers wear the traditional black robes and white wigs. Seated on large elaborately carved dark wooden benches, they present a very grand, formal image.

The *Cabinet Building* on Front Street is another area landmark. The grounds around the building occupy an entire block and are as spectacular as the building. The *Bermuda Library* and the *Post Office* next door are on Queen Street in front of the *Par-La-Ville Gardens*. You'll want to visit all three. The *Historic Society Museum* on the first floor of the library has a number of pictures of early Bermuda and a spade used by Winston Churchill to plant a cedar tree at Government House in 1942. If you wander through the park you'll see old ladies feeding the birds and cats (together) and businesspeople eating their lunch.

Nightlife

Many of the popular informal bars are located on Front Street. Among these are *Rum Runners*, *Cock 'n Feathers*, and *Longtail*. They're lively, comfortable, and the clientele are friendly without being imposing. You won't be alone long in any of these, but neither will you feel obligated to stay or leave with whomever you've spent time talking.

Hamilton also has a couple of very sophisticated discos. *The Club* just off Front Street on Bermuda Street (US$7 cover) and the newly opened and currently very hot *Cocacabana* (US$8 cover), whose owner, Donna, has really put together a classy disco. This, too, is a great place to meet locals as well as visitors. If a cruise ship is in town, it will be especially busy. The *Disco 40* and *40 Thieves*, also on Front Street, are popular with the younger crowd.

While you're out and about in Hamilton, don't miss the Night Club Show at the Hamilton Princess Hotel. The manager prides himself on "knowing people" after seventeen years in the business. Single women are never seated alone in this lounge with its comfortable elegant setting. He's quite proud of his matchmaking skills—no obligation here either, of course. For US$20 you'll not only get two drinks, but you'll enjoy a spectacular show and who knows what else. If you're looking for a more subdued evening, they have a piano in the lobby, off the bar. The crowd here is consistently friendly and tasteful.

I have no doubts that you will agree that the people of Bermuda are more consistently charming, friendly, and helpful than any you'll meet anywhere. I only hope we can each take a little of their hospitality to our hometowns and make our visitors feel as comfortable.

AN EXPEDITION VOYAGE THROUGH THE PANAMA CANAL

▶─────────────────────────────────────▶

GENERAL AMBIANCE   ★ ★
SOCIAL CLIMATE   ★ ★
ACTIVITIES   ★ ★ ★

─────────────────────────

FOR TOUR ARRANGEMENTS CONTACT:
Society Expeditions
3131 Elliott Avenue, Suite 700
Seattle, WA 98121
(800) 426-7794

Or *contact your travel agent* and ask for the Society Expedition
  Project Lands of Cortez

▶─────────────────────────────────────▶

I have always longed for an escape from my usual routine, and one
of my dreams has always been to sail on the open seas. On a number
of occasions I have met people with the same dream who have actually
left their profession and friends and exchanged their home on land for
a sailboat on the sea. Some have now been sailing for years. Others
did it for only a few months before returning to the security and crea-
ture comforts of a life on shore.

The majority of dreamers—certainly myself and perhaps you, too—
are not willing to totally divorce themselves from their lives and friends
on land indefinitely; they long for the adventure of the high seas, but
on a more limited basis. Those of us who fit into this category are
fortunate today, because there is a ship, the *Society Explorer*, that was
built and is operated specifically with you, me, and our dreams in
mind.

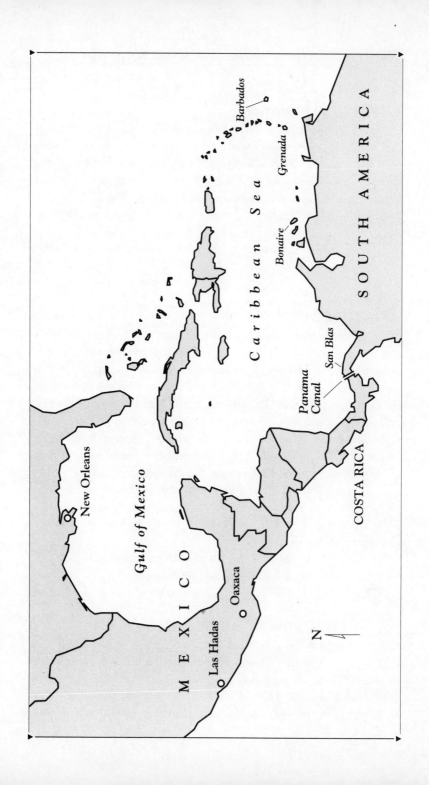

General Ambiance

Operated by Society Expeditions, headquartered in Seattle, Washington, the *Society Explorer* is indeed as close as I've ever come to a cruise that feels like being on a family ship. By the time I left the ship eighteen days after boarding, I honestly felt as though I were leaving home. I made many friends whom I still cherish. The ports of call, often remote, were thrilling and the service on the boat was first class, but it was the passengers, the Society Expeditions staff, and the scientists on board who really made the adventure spectacular.

Social Climate

You'll immediately become a member of the family when you board the *Society Explorer*. With ten Society Expeditions staff and sixty-five crew members on board, everyone is well attended to. Everyone from the captain of the ship to the waiters and waitresses in the Marco Polo Restaurant experiences the world together. Name tags worn the first few days facilitate remembering everyone's name.

Tables seating groups of seven in the dining room encourage mixing with new groups of people. The stories told over meals were often so fascinating that I found I didn't want the distraction of eating until the tale was complete. You'll find you are sailing with real adventurers: people who have sailed the Drake Passage in gale force winds on a 36-foot sailboat, or who have uncovered pre-Columbian gold on digs in Panama.

No matter how much of the world you've already seen, you feel both humbled and excited by the adventure stories told by staff and passengers alike. I came away with a whole list of new places I knew I had to see.

As on most ships, the crew are often geographical bachelors if not real bachelors. While they are seldom too aggressive and readily accept a "no," they will undoubtedly make you feel appreciated and desirable. These are sophisticated sailors who are used to interacting with women of class. They are very sensitive to your limits and very respectful of them. They are also very charming and a pleasure to sail with.

Activities

Specifically built for expedition travel, the *Society Explorer* is unique because its shallow draft allows it to sail into ports most cruise ships could not manage. In addition, the ship carries small inflatable Zodiacs (rubber rafts developed by Jacques Cousteau) to shuttle passengers into even more remote landing sites. This unique capacity, coupled with the knowledge and extensive preplanning by the Society Expeditions staff and scientists, results in a rare combination of ports of call.

You may well find yourself landing on an island where no human being is known to have previously set foot. Best of all, you will do so with ornithologists, marine biologists, and anthropologists who are the leading experts in the particular part of the world you're visiting. As a result, not only do you have the opportunity to experience the beauty of the setting, the bird and animal life, and the original inhabitants through your own eyes, but even more enticing, you will experience each area through the seductive lure of a scientist's point of view. On more than one occasion I myself was excited by the sight of a rare bird or animal because of the unbridled thrill of the naturalist who had never seen this rare species before himself. I also found I saw so much more when I walked through a tropical rain forest with people who knew what to look for. For example, I walked right past a three-toed sloth that was quickly pointed out by the naturalist close behind.

The *Society Explorer* has a maximum capacity of only a hundred passengers. And while interests vary, each individual's needs are well managed by the very professional staff. Small vans or cars that can easily be dispatched in different directions are used for transportation much of the time. If you'd like to see the Gold Museum in Cartagena, Colombia, for instance, and that was not included in the original tour, the staff will quickly find you a guide and rent you a cab, all at their expense. Their objective is to make sure you see what you want to see, and thus have the best vacation possible. They are not interested in fitting you into their mold, as many companies will insist is necessary. They want to meet your specific needs, and they manage to do so.

The ship carries up-to-date snorkeling and scuba diving equipment (including a compressor) and an experienced dive master who is also a marine biologist. I especially enjoyed the option to explore the world from under water. No group is too small. On more than one occasion I dove alone with the dive master while other passengers wandered through the shops and back streets of island villages, visited wildlife sanctuaries, or explored historic points of interest.

You'll always have the option of staying on board the ship as well. This is a real vacation/expedition ship, and you decide how much or how little you want to do each day. If you want to rise early and do aerobics on the top deck or have coffee and fresh-baked Danish you can do so. Or you can sleep late.

When at sea, the scientists, mostly published researchers, will present succinct, easily understood synopses of their work relative to the area you'll visit next. Even if you haven't had time to review the list of suggested readings before coming on board, you'll feel well prepared by the time you reach a new area. In an hour lecture complete with slides, you'll hear a comprehensive review of the formation of the earth and the shifting of the continents; the effects of El Niño on marine life; the species of birds, fish, and marine mammals in the area; the history of the local inhabitants and their folk crafts, and much, much more.

Preparing for Your Trip through the Panama Canal

Rates

The cost of your voyage will, of course, depend on the type of accommodations you select. The least expensive Explorer-level cabin will cost US$5,450, the highest priced Boat Deck–level cabin US$7,050, and the owner's suite US$9,450. The price includes all your meals, excursions, side tours, and transfers plus your cabin for eighteen days. Unlike most other cruises, there are no additional, hidden costs. The cabins are virtually the same size offering the same amenities (private bathroom with shower, desk, closet, hair dryer, and a small chest of drawers). The suites are, of course, larger. The primary difference in price is the size of the window and location. The least expensive cabins have a small porthole just above the waterline at the less stable front end of the ship. The Boat Deck cabins are on the upper level and have a large rectangular window. My advice would be to go with a midpriced Yacht Deck cabin (US$6,250). You'll be above the waterline and have a good-sized porthole. The more expensive Boat Deck cabins actually afford less privacy because their windows look out onto a walkway.

If you choose to begin the trip a week earlier in San Diego, the additional cost begins at US$3,150 for the Explorer Deck. A Yacht Deck cabin will cost US$3,625, Boat Deck US$4,070, and the owner's suite US$5,430.

Documents

You will need a valid passport. You will also need visas for Panama, Colombia, and Costa Rica. You can obtain these directly from the individual consulates, but I recommend using an express visa service (see page 29).

What to Take

You'll find there is very little temperature change so close to the equator. The daytime temperature will usually be around 80 degrees Fahrenheit, 70 degrees at night. You'll want to wear loose-fitting cotton slacks, shorts, or dresses most of the time. Shorts are discouraged in the dining room at dinner. While you'll only really dress up two or three nights, I suggest a nice summer dress or skirt and blouse for dinner most other evenings.

Because you'll be going to isolated beaches on remote islands, you'll experience a number of wet Zodiac landings. Wet may mean ankle-deep water or small waves that make shorts or a bathing suit ideal. You should have sandals that can get wet and sandy, and a pair of tennis shoes for walking through wet and sometimes muddy tropical rain forests are a must.

While the small ship's store does carry a few toilet articles and extra film, you should take an adequate supply of everything you need. They also sell T-shirts, which make a great extra change of clothing. Take lots of sunscreen and a floppy hat to protect you from the sun's burning rays around the equator.

There is a laundry on board with reasonable rates. While I would not trust them with fine silks, they do well with cottons and blends. Expect a two-to-three-day turnaround time.

Don't take expensive jewelry. You won't need it. Costume jewelry can dress up a daytime outfit nicely for the evening.

Each cabin has a built-in hair dryer, so you can leave yours at home. The electricity for your curling iron, if you decide to bring one, is conveniently 110 just like at home. It's a good idea to bring along a small alarm clock. While the staff will wake you on the mornings that early activities are planned, you may want an alarm to assure you'll be up from an afternoon nap for a lecture. The lectures are much too good to sleep through.

Money

Your American dollar will be readily accepted in every country except Mexico, where you'll need pesos. The *Society Explorer* purser has a limited amount of pesos (US$25 per passenger). Once in town, the hotel will be able to exchange more. Many shops are also willing to take American currency. However, they will not make change in American currency, so small bills are essential. The ship's purser is also able to exchange a limited amount of large bills for smaller ones, but it's best to bring smaller bills along.

Getting There

As you exit the passenger terminal you'll find your Society Expeditions representative awaiting your arrival. If you've arrived in Manzanillo, Mexico, you'll find him or her after you collect your luggage and clear customs. From that moment on it's all carefree travel for you. They will introduce you to any fellow travelers who arrived on your flight and load you and your luggage into a cab for the drive to your hotel.

Tipping

From the moment you are met at the airport by your Society Expeditions representative, you need no longer worry about tips or money. Everything is included. Your first night at the hotel prior to boarding the ship you will be on your own. The bill, however, is on Society Expeditions, except for alcoholic beverages. You should simply add 10 percent for service and sign your name and room number. Your Society Expeditions representative will settle the bill before your departure.

Your last day on board the ship, when your shipboard accounts are settled, a tipping box will be provided. Society suggests that you leave US$6 per person per day in an envelope and put it in the box. While you can, of course, give individual tips to those who provided a special service, this is discouraged. All tips collected in the gratuities box will be divided evenly among the crew.

Treasures to Purchase

A real advantage to travel by boat is that you don't need to lug your treasures around with you. You can store them on the boat until it's time to fly home. Even then the staff will transport your bags from your cabin to the airport for you.

Don't forget to bargain when you're shopping. If you buy with a friend and purchase two or three items between the two of you, you'll of course get a better price. You'll have more fun, too.

On this trip you'll have an opportunity to purchase items to which few people have access. Don't leave home without at least one extra bag.

Mexico

You won't need to bring a large wardrobe with you when you visit Oaxaca in south-central Mexico. For US$3 to US$10 you can purchase beautiful hand-embroidered cotton blouses, skirts, and dresses. For US$25 to US$200 you can even purchase copies of the folk dresses you'll see the local dancers wearing and that you'll see in the local museums. Each area has its own unique style. You'll also find beautiful woven shawls (US$5 to US$15) and colorful belts (US$1 to US$3) as well as attractive costume jewelry (US$1 to US$20). There are woven rugs and wall hangings (US$3 to US$30), tablecloths (US$3 to US$15), and yarn dolls (two for US$3). When you visit the Mayan archeological sites you'll be able to purchase carved masks and statues made from the local jadeite stone (US$3 to US$30). I'd suggest offering them about half their original asking price. Don't be afraid to hold firm and walk away. You'll be surprised how often they'll follow and eventually accept your price or at least one closer to it.

Panama

To me, one of the most exciting shopping opportunities was being able to buy *molas* from the Kuna Indians on the small isolated San Blas Islands of Panama. Molas, which are made only by the women, are today considered one of the most highly developed forms of contemporary folk art in the world.

Molas are elaborately designed, patterned reverse appliqué panels of color. The more elaborate the design, the higher the price. You can buy the individual panels (US$5 to US$20), or you can buy them made into blouses or dresses (US$25 and up). Molas that portray a timely sport or political message will be the most valuable collector's items in the years to come. Other mola motifs include myths and a variety of local plants and animals. The quality of a woman's molas determines her status and prestige within the group. The mola is today the only export for the Kuna Indians. It is thus the basis of their economic system in this matriarchal society where wealth is passed from mother to daughter.

Colombia

You'll want to take your credit card and checkbook ashore in Cartagena, Colombia. This is the place to buy emeralds. While they aren't cheap, they are exquisite. The gold used in the settings is all 18k instead of the 14k used in the United States. You can buy any size and quality of set or unset stone. I strongly recommend visiting a jeweler you trust before leaving home. Ask him to show you what to look for in a stone. Because the stores must pay a commission when you use your credit card, you can usually bargain for a better discount if you're using traveler's checks, cash, or a personal check. Even with a major credit card, you should expect a discount of at least 10 percent, 20 percent to 30 percent with another source of payment. If the salesclerk you're dealing with says the discount is not possible, ask to speak with the manager. The more expensive the item you're purchasing, the higher your discount should be.

If you're really not interested in getting quite so elaborate a piece of jewelry, you can also buy copies of pre-Columbian jewelry, the typical black and white Panama straw hats, baskets, and high-quality leather bags.

Grenada

The spice islands of Grenada grow cinnamon, nutmeg, cloves, mace, and ginger as well as cocoa. You'll find these available in decorative souvenir baskets for US$1. You can also purchase larger quantities of individual spices. They make especially nice gifts for friends back home.

THE EXPEDITION

▶ ───────────────────────────────── ▶

Depending on your time constraints, you can board the *Society Explorer* bound for the Sea of Cortez in San Diego, or you can board in Manzanillo one week later for the last eighteen days of the expedition.

Baja Peninsula

Your first stop after departing San Diego is the Isle de Guadalupe followed by Islas San Benito. Here you can walk right up to the California sea lions and elephant seals who breed on the island and look them in the eye. Previously on the brink of extinction, their numbers are once again growing. This is just one of the many highlights of the trip.

Before reaching Isla Isabela you'll pass Lands End, a long stretch of sandy beach where the Pacific Ocean meets the Sea of Cortez. They actually meet in the center of a large land arch which extends to the very tip of the Baja Peninsula. Lunch will be at the elegant Hotel Cabo San Lucas, whose patio extends out over the sea. You'll visit wildlife sanctuaries as well as have time for shopping, wandering through the village, and swimming at the beach.

You'll be able to get so close to the blue-footed boobies nesting on Isla Isabela that they'll fill the screen of your lens without a zoom. You'll also travel by Zodiac up the mangrove-choked waters to *La Tovana Springs* for a picnic and swim in the crystal clear waters.

Manzanillo

The final group of passengers will board the ship at the Las Hada Resort in Manzanillo, where they have spent the previous night. This $34 million resort was the setting for the movie *10*, starring Bo Derek. The architect is said to have had no budgetary limits when he built this Moorish-style luxury resort. It is a fitting spot for new passengers to begin a Society Expeditions cruise. The resort manager, a friendly chap, makes a point of personally greeting each passenger.

Oaxaca

After a day at sea, you'll arrive at Puerto Escondido and be transferred by air to Oaxaca. You'll arrive just in time to celebrate Mexican Independence Day (September 16) in this isolated mountain village surrounded by emerald green hills. You'll spend two nights at the Hotel El Presidente. This tastefully restored monastery was built in 1576. A hotel since 1976, it has been declared a national treasure. From here you visit the archeological ruins of Monte Alban and Mitla. These Zapotec Indian cities date back to 600 B.C. While extensive ruins have been uncovered, they retain much of their mystery. With all of our expertise, we can only speculate on the meaning and use of many of the buildings. You next fly to Puerto Madero, still in Mexico, where you meet the ship and sail, that afternoon, to Costa Rica.

Costa Rica

You'll make two stops in Costa Rica, the first on the Peninsula de Nicoya, where you'll see a variety of seabirds, two- and three-toed sloths, and spider monkeys. There'll be time for a swim and barbecue on the isolated white sandy beach. If the water is calm, you can snorkel and scuba dive. Should you want even more isolation, a short walk will bring you to a number of smaller beaches where your solitude will only be disrupted by an occasional troop of monkeys swinging from the treetops or the call of the large macaws and seabirds.

The next day you have your choice of a strenuous trek more than 10 miles round-trip or a shorter one-mile hike in Corcovado National Park, the only virgin rain forest remaining in Central America. Here you'll likely see endangered species of mammals as well as exotic rare birds and lush tropical foliage. Local naturalists who have been doing research in the area for years will join you. Your visit will triple the average number of thirty to forty visitors who come here by sea each year. Don't be surprised if you interrupt agoutis; you'll be using their jungle pathway. This large rodent escaped extinction as a food source for the Costa Rican people because its urine is red. The Costa Ricans assumed it was a female menstruating and would not eat it.

If you watch the high forest canopy, you'll likely spot coati-mundi. They remind me of a small fox with a long nose. We interrupted a large troop of twenty to twenty-five who, one after the other, dropped great distances to the forest floor. They then scurried off like clandestine raiders of the forest. While these scavengers were introduced on many tropical islands to decrease the rat population, they unfortunately also devastated the seabird population.

You'll likely spot a variety of parrots, toucans, brilliant blue morpho butterflies as large as your outstretched hand, and a variety of hummingbirds, such as the purple crowned fairy, which are as mystical as their names. The forest is so still you'll hear the hum of their wings before you actually see them.

My favorite discovery was the leaf cutting ants. They actually clear a "highway" through the forest floor by removing fallen leaves and other debris. They then use this highway to carry a piece of leaf more than twenty times their size to their nest. You'll see hundreds of these ants scurrying home in single file down one side of their highway, then up the other side to collect another piece of leaf. They don't eat the leaves. They store them underground until the fungus they do eat grows on them.

As we started back to the ship from a tall cascading waterfall 5 miles away, a torrential downpour hit. The rain was warm and actually lifted our spirits rather than dampened them. During the three hours it took us to walk out of the forest, over 2 inches of rain fell. Our pathway soon became a river; small streams we had crossed on the way out became thigh-deep rivers. At one point our small party of eight had to form a human chain to cross the swift current of a river that was nonexistent when we walked into the forest. When we left, there was no doubt that we were adventurers not tourists, participants not onlookers. Appropriately, as we left this mystical wonderland, spotted porpoise escorted our Zodiac back to the ship.

Panama and the Canal Transit

Late afternoon of the next day you'll stop in Los Santos, Panama. You'll drive through the countryside and at night have dinner at a local restaurant where you'll be entertained by local dancers. Then it's on to the real highlight of the trip, the Panama Canal transit.

Panama Canal Transit. It takes eight to nine hours to cross the 50 miles through the Panama Canal. Entering on the Pacific Ocean side, you are first raised 85 feet through a series of three locks to the level of Gatun Lake. Sailing, much to my surprise, in a northwesterly direction, you are then lowered 85 feet through another series of three locks to the level of the Atlantic Ocean. I was also surprised to learn that four small trains attached to the ship pull her through the canal locks. The ship does not use her own power. A special pilot and crew to handle the steel lines attached to the trains come aboard for the transit.

As you cross the Continental Divide, you'll see a monument to the men who gave their lives building the canal. The monument sits on the side of the cliffs that loom above you.

Gatun Lake, which you cross, was the largest artificial body of water in the world from the time of the opening of the Panama Canal in 1914 until Lake Mead was formed by the construction of Hoover Dam.

Every boat using the canal must pay a toll. While the toll is based on tonnage, there is a minimum fee of US$125. It costs the *Society Explorer* approximately US$8,500 to transit this path between the two oceans. The *Queen Elizabeth II* pays the highest toll of US$99,065.

I was unprepared for the real thrill and sense of history the crossing evoked. We celebrated our crossing first with champagne and hors d'oeuvres on the top deck as we anchored amid giant cargo ships in Gatun Lake, and then later with lunch on the pool deck. A couple of my fellow passengers had made the crossing before, one more than thirty-five years earlier. For them it was an especially nostalgic trip. Little had changed in all that time. I wonder what it will be like in another thirty-five years. The United States has agreed to transfer control of the canal to Panama on December 31, 1999. The Panama Canal Commission, a U.S. government agency, will continue to operate the canal until then.

Another of the many highlights of this trip will be your next stop— a remote series of 375 San Blas Islands, 12 miles off the coast of Panama. Approximately thirty-five of the larger islands are inhabited by the Kuna Indians. They have lived here since the 1850s. In the early 1900s, Panama tried to force their assimilation by banning their traditional dress and ritual. The Kuna rebelled in 1925 and won autonomy as a group.

When I awoke early on the first day of our visit here, I looked out my porthole to see the *Society Explorer* surrounded by men and women wearing their colorful traditional dress sitting in small boats I later learned were called *ulus*. Beyond the boats I could see a couple of islands with primitive huts made from palm fronds. The *ulu*, a boat carved from a single log, is still the only form of transportation here. Some had large sails, some oars, and others small motors. Smiling and waving to us, the people were waiting impatiently to sell us molas. They watched from their boats as eight of us did our aerobics on the top deck. I still wonder what they thought of our display.

After breakfast we launched our Zodiacs and went ashore to one of the larger islands. This was our chance to purchase their attractive folk art. The women were dressed in brightly colored red, yellow, and purple woven cloth dresses with molas on the front and back. Each wore a gold ring through her nose and gold rings on her fingers. This finery is purchased with the money earned selling the molas. The women drove a hard bargain, understandably resistant to accepting a lower price even though bargaining is part of the fun of the sale. The sale of molas, the only export of the islands, has been the salvation of the economy. Since only women make molas it has brought them considerable prestige and power.

We saw an occasional albino, a problem resulting from the inbreeding that occurs on these small, isolated islands. To prevent further inbreeding, albino boys are raised as girls. Their ears are pierced and they are taught to make molas.

Colombia

In contrast to the isolation of the Kuna Indians of Panama, is the time you'll spend the next day in Cartagena, a city of nearly a million people. It's a good idea to leave all your jewelry on board the *Society Explorer* and to be cautious of your valuables in this walled city of treasures established in 1533.

As we left the dock area we passed truckload after truckload of Colombian coffee awaiting shipment. The coffee is available on the streets for as little as US$1 per pound. Coffee is the official primary crop of Colombia.

Most of the city is built on a series of islands connected by bridges. An imposing monastery built in 1608 sits on the only large hill overlooking the town. From the monastery's patio you can see the entire area, the 6 miles of wall surrounding the old city, the fortress left by the Spanish, the port, and the new modern section of town.

The cuisine on the *Society Explorer* is of such a high quality that the meals off the boat can seldom compete. That was not the case in Cartagena. Lunch at the *Club de Pesca Restaurant* was superb. We sat under the trees on the waterfront patio within the walls of the old city. Various seafoods, including shrimp in a coconut sauce, and a whole selection of desserts, including flan, left a memorable impression.

After lunch, those who wished wandered through the *Gold Museum* and Inquisition building in the old city, others shopped in the more modern section of town with shop after shop filled with emeralds, and still others visited the *Botanical Gardens* twenty minutes out of town.

Like most other stops, it would have been nice to have had another day or two in this emerald city of many faces on the edge of the Caribbean Sea.

Bonaire

After another day at sea with lectures by the scientific staff, you'll arrive at one of the top scuba diving spots in the world. I have made some incredible dives in some of the best places, but Bonaire deserves its reputation. The coral reefs surrounding the island contain more than 1,000 species of marine life. The fish are often found in large schools and will swim up and look you in the face. The colors and varieties are truly spectacular. If you are an avid diver, I recommend foregoing the morning trip to the flamingo colony, even though the birds are spectacular in their own right. Once you make your first dive on Bonaire, you'll want to make another before lying back on the soft white sand of the *Bonaire Beach Club Resort* and reliving the beauty and excitement you experienced under the sea. As the sun sets over the smaller island of Little Bonaire you'll return to your ship and set sail for Grenada.

Your Last Day at Sea

As you sail for Grenada, you'll spend your last day at sea. Somehow everyone seems to realize that the trip is nearing an end. A now-cohesive group is about to be disbanded. New friends, some very close, will soon go their separate ways. Addresses are exchanged and plans made to get together again.

Another highlight of the cruise is the crew show, which is held this night. Our crew, who come from the Philippines, Germany, Switzerland, and other parts of the world, sang and danced to their hearts' delight and most of all for our enjoyment. The festive tone set by the show turned into the best party on board, lasting until the wee hours of the morning.

Grenada

While few spots in the world can equal Bonaire for scuba diving and snorkeling, the diving around Grenada is excellent by most standards. Unlike the flat, desertlike climate of Bonaire, Grenada is a tropical paradise with lush green hillsides and sparkling white beaches. If you choose not to join the main group you can arrange your own taxi tour for about US$10 an hour. Choose this option and you'll have plenty of time to both scuba dive and see the island.

The ship anchors in *St. George's Harbor*, picturesque with houses of various colors perched on the emerald hillside. It was here and at the site of the new airport that most of the fighting took place when American troops were sent to Grenada in 1983. You'll find 90 percent of the population still grateful. As one man told me, "America was our liberator, not our conqueror. We are now free of the Cuban and Soviet troops that were here in such great numbers." I saw a number of T-shirts that said, "Thank you America for Liberating Grenada."

If you'd like, you can take a boat taxi to the sandy beaches nearby for US$7 each way. When your boat taxi leaves, you need only arrange a pick-up time for your return.

The conch, fresh fish, and lobster served here are excellent. The rum punch drinks, made with locally produced rum, are large and strong but wonderfully refreshing. As a result of the lush tropical landscape there is little poverty in Grenada. Even with very little land, which is still available to squatters, a family can plant enough food to live a subsistence life-style from the land and sea much as the islanders have done for centuries.

Even if Grenada were not the last port before Barbados and home, it would be hard to leave the friendly inhabitants of this picturesque island. One couple I spoke with had been vacationing there for three months and were still not ready to go.

The parting is made somewhat easier by the anticipation of the captain's farewell dinner that night. As our German captain made a point of saying, "In Germany they do not say goodbye, they say auf Wiedersehen, which means until we meet again."

Barbados

Unfortunately, Barbados is only scheduled as a transfer point to catch a plane and fly to Miami and homeward. If you have the time, I strongly recommend having the Society Expeditions staff arrange for you to spend a couple of nights at a local hotel before your flight home.

While I was not able to do so, a small contingent did stay. I really would have liked to join them.

*   *   *

As you depart the ship and say goodbye to the crew, staff, and your fellow travelers, you will at once be aware of both the loss in parting and the rich experiences and friendships that you take with you. For a short period of time you became a family on a very unique expedition ship with an even more unique group of travelers. You sailed the open seas together. You shared your past memories of adventure and forged new memories with one another. While you now go your separate ways, part of your spirits will always remain together. You have become Society Expeditions explorers. Seventy percent of you will return for another voyage to adventure.

BADEN-BADEN SPA AND THE GERMAN COUNTRYSIDE

GENERAL AMBIANCE	★ ★ ★
SOCIAL CLIMATE	★ ★
ACTIVITIES	★ ★ ★

TO BOOK A BEAUTY WEEK CONTACT:
Lancaster Beauty Farm
Brenner's Park Hotel
An der Lichtentaler Allee
7570 Baden-Baden, West Germany
Telephone: 07221/31457

A good friend of mine was recently awarded a Ph.D. after nearly eight years of continual work. The birth of twins midway through the program had made it a very stressful eight years, and there was a real need to totally remove the last bits of stress. After much thought and discussion, a decision was made—spend a week at a spa. It worked.

In my opinion, the best way to experience a spa is to visit one of the traditional European spas and see a part of Europe as well. This section takes you to the spa at Brenner's Park Hotel in Baden-Baden, Germany, a favorite of the rich and famous. Your itinerary will include a Lufthansa flight to Munich, then by rental car to Garmisch-Partenkirchen, Oberammergau, the castles of King Ludwig II, and Konstanz on your way to Baden-Baden. Before flying out of Frankfurt, you'll stop at Düsseldorf, the German fashion capital, Koblenz, and take a Rhine River cruise to Wiesbaden.

The German Tourist Bureau (747 Third Avenue, New York, NY 10017), Lufthansa Airlines, or your travel agent are all excellent resources to help you plan your route. The places you can see are only

limited by the amount of time available. I would suggest taking one or two weeks in addition to your week at the spa in Baden-Baden.

The spa as a water cure traces its history back 2,000 years to the ancient Greeks and Romans. Strong believers in the medicinal effects of the hot healing springs, they constructed luxurious bath facilities around the spring for recreation and relaxation as well as for the curative effects.

Spa waters are usually clear hot springs containing abundant minerals and gases. In Europe, where their curative properties are better accepted than in America, specialists analyze the mineral content of the various spa waters and recommend certain spring waters for certain ailments. While most people soak in the waters, some choose to drink them. Even if you don't suffer from any injuries or sore muscles, you, too, will likely leave praising the spa's rejuvenating powers as have Julius Caesar, George Washington, Mark Twain, and Franklin D. Roosevelt. Good health is our most important attribute, one worth care and attention. Today, a European spa is a place to go to improve your general sense of well-being, health, and beauty. A place for the release of tension and the removal of stress. Attention is dutifully paid to all of these needs when you spend a week at the Brenner's Spa in Baden-Baden.

For generations, Baden-Baden has been considered to have the best spas in the world. European royalty, the famous, and the not-so-famous all come to this charming old-world German town to be refreshed and revitalized.

There are two public spas in Baden-Baden, the old *Friedrichsbad* and the new *Caracella Baths*, where you can enjoy the refreshing natural mineral waters. There are also private spa programs, which include a combination of exercise, diet, and massage, as well as general health evaluation and care. The most famous, the most complete, and the most luxurious of these spa programs is located at the Brenner's Park Hotel, *the* place to stay in Baden-Baden whatever your reason for coming.

General Ambiance

A European spa is a place to go to relax, to be taken care of, and to be rejuvenated. In Baden-Baden, at the Brenner's Park Hotel and Spa, you will find yourself being pampered in luxury. The pace is slow moving and uncompetitive. The decisions about what you will eat and what programs you will participate in and when, are left up to you. They are not dictated and regimented as is often the case at the American counterparts.

The staff here is accustomed to catering to some of the most wealthy people in the world. The service is skilled and impeccable. Every guest is treated with care, discretion, and the utmost courtesy. This is one of the few hotels I've been in where everyone on the staff, from the director to the chambermaid, went out of his or her way to greet you at every opportunity. On my first visit I felt like a guest who had been returning for years, as some do. This is not your average hotel, nor does it feel like a hotel. It's individual and personal, just like your week's program will be.

Social Climate

What better place to meet interesting people than at one of the most famous spas in the world. While most Europeans do speak English fluently, your ability to speak German will, of course, increase your options. You'll spend a week with up to twenty other "Lancaster Ladies," as you'll become known. Most will be European, in their mid-thirties to late forties, and upper middle class. Some of the wealthiest women in the world make this a yearly beauty retreat. Typically, 20 to 30 percent of the participants are from the United States.

The very charming and personable director of guest relations, who will greet you upon your arrival, makes sure to provide opportunities for you to get to know the other guests. She will also make sure you participate in group activities only as you see fit. You will not feel obligated to be with a group. While the exercise programs are for everyone to join, most beauty treatments are individual. Being part of a group, you need never eat alone, unless of course, you prefer to.

There are lots of people outside the group of Lancaster Ladies whom you may choose to meet. The hotel lobby and cocktail lounge are both convenient and comfortable places to meet the other very charming guests, many of them European businessmen.

If you're in Baden-Baden during the big spring and August race, you'll find the city is full of the rich and famous. This is both an advantage and a disadvantage. If you don't have a lot of self-confidence, not to mention a smashing wardrobe, or if you really want to relax, you might prefer a different week. On the other hand, if you like rubbing shoulders with the elite, Brenner's Hotel is the place to be and Grand Race Week is the time to be there. Dress to the hilt. This is one time you will want to bring along your best suits, dresses, and jewelry—and don't forget your hats, heels, and gloves. You'll even see a few shoulder furs.

Activities

In addition to the truly elegant facilities at this top-notch spa, one of the big advantages of staying at the Brenner's Park Hotel is its association with the Lancaster Beauty Farm and Schwarzwald Clinic. I'd suggest a weekly program that takes advantage of the Lancaster Beauty Farm facilities as well as the spa program. Most people combine the two. Some people have their plastic surgery done at the Schwarzwald Clinic then recoup in a resort setting instead of a hospital. Their friends at home are then only aware of how much better and younger they look.

Sports

Baden-Baden also has an abundance of options for the sports enthusiast. Very near the hotel you'll find well-tended clay tennis courts, horseback riding, golf, and wonderful areas for hiking and jogging just outside the hotel doors. The hotel staff will even find you a partner for tennis if you need one. In winter there is cross-country skiing and a couple of small downhill ski runs nearby.

The Arts

In addition to numerous private art galleries in the area, the Brenner's Park Hotel periodically holds its own art shows. There are also in-house concerts with cocktail parties during which to meet the other guests. Every day at 4:00 P.M. there is an excellent free classical music recital in the garden in front of the casino. These concerts are a tradition at the spas. They are intended to lift the spirit as the body is revitalized, and they do.

Casino

Baden-Baden is the home of one of the most spectacular casinos in the world. Located just a short walk from the Brenner's Park Hotel, the casino was established in 1827. It is a magnificent palace, worth visiting just for its sheer beauty.

Horse Racing

Both flat races and steeplechase are held at the track 7 miles northwest of Baden-Baden. Established in 1858, it is one of the oldest and most famous racetracks in the world. The spring meeting and Baden-Baden's Grand Race Week (at the beginning of August) are a highlight of health resort life. The latter is the most important horse-racing event in Germany.

Around Baden-Baden

Baden-Baden is located in the "Schwarzwald" or Black Forest region of Germany. Driving just out of town you can see this beautiful forest with its quaint, sleepy villages. A number of them—such as Eisental, Affental, Bühl, and Neuweier—are wine-growing centers, so be sure to sample the regional wine. It will be even more special after you've driven through the vineyards where it was grown.

A Brenner's Spa–Lancaster Lady Week

On the day of your arrival (usually Sunday), the director of guest relations, Margarette, will invite all the newly arrived "Lancaster Ladies" for a drink or tea, as you prefer. This will give you a chance to meet the other guests and learn more about the area and the week ahead. I thoroughly enjoyed Margarette. She is charming, casual, and a wealth of information. She will be your colleague and ally at the spa.

The next day, Monika, the manager of the Lancaster Beauty Farm, will greet you and provide you with more details about that aspect of your stay. You then receive an individual cosmetic and skin analysis. Your individual treatment program will be put together by the specialist with whom you will work throughout the week.

Each day you'll receive a full body rub and pack to remove the dead skin cells, stimulate circulation, and remoisturize your body. You'll also receive a complete facial daily, including the most soothing, relaxing facial massage imaginable. You'll emerge feeling pampered, luxurious, and youthful.

An extensive makeup course, a manicure, and pedicure are also included. Mineral and gas baths are available and can be scheduled into your program if you'd like.

Recognizing that rejuvenation must come from the inside as well as the outside, the spa makes available a number of exercise classes. These include yoga, gymnastics, swimming, and water gymnastics. Participation in other area sports is also encouraged. The classes are scheduled daily and extra individual instruction is available. You are never pushed to attend. You and only you determine your daily schedule.

If you'd like, the hotel restaurant also offers a tasty 1,000-calorie-a-day diet. It is essentially the same gourmet food served to the other guests without the rich sauces, starches, or dessert.

Like so many Lancaster Ladies, you may decide to make a week at Brenner's Spa a part of your yearly routine.

Preparing for Your Trip to the Spa

Rates

A usual program lasts one week. For a full seven days, including a single room with shower at the elegant Brenner's Park Hotel, three gourmet meals each day (gourmet reduction diet upon request), spa, and beauty program, you pay only 2,124 DM to 2,600 DM from January 6 to March 31 and 2,303 DM to 2,719 DM from April 1 to January 5.

For a week's stay including all the above plus a complete physical exam and routine lab work at the Schwarzwald Clinic, the cost is 4,181 DM for a single, 3,924 DM per person in a double room.

Documents

You need a valid passport to enter Germany; however, you do not need a visa.

When to Go

September always has been my favorite month to visit Europe. By then the hordes of kids, many from the U.S., have returned to school. The Europeans have returned to work, too, so all the restaurants are operational again. The weather is beautiful, usually in the seventies with lots of sunshine. The weather begins to warm for summer in mid-April and usually stays comfortable until mid-October. Unbearably hot weather is unusual anytime during the summer months. The winters can get cold and you may encounter snow.

You'll need to make your reservations at the Brenner's Park Hotel early if you want to go during Baden-Baden's Grand Race Week (at the beginning of August). If you do attend this event, it will be a highlight of your trip. Horse racing starts in the spring.

If you arrive between the last week in September and the first week in October, you'll be there in time for the Munich Oktoberfest, worth the trip itself. Make your Munich reservations early; it gets crowded. Many small towns and villages will have their own wine fests during the month of September. These celebrations are often more fun than the Munich festival. While these wine and beer festivals are indeed a time when everyone drinks too much, it's still more of a family affair than a drunken brawl. The Germans are happy drunks. Instead of fighting with each other, they sing and dance. They are also very welcoming of a woman alone. They usually go out in groups of ten to twelve men and women. You'll soon be asked to join more than one group, and it won't even matter how much German you can speak. *"Prosit,"* their favorite toast, will be sufficient.

What to Take

While informal resort wear will be fine most of the time, you will want to dress up a little for dinners at Baden-Baden and *really* dress for the casino. This is one of those places where the better dressed you are, the better you are treated—and the better you feel about yourself.

Don't wear jeans, short shorts, or skimpy tops in the hotels (especially not Brenner's Park Hotel) or around Baden-Baden. Resort-type shorts are, however, fine for daytime wear during the hot summer months. You will also need a swimsuit and a nice cover-up to wear as you go from your room through the hotel to the pool. Lancaster began as a producer of sunscreens, so you may want to try their products instead of your usual sunscreen.

The electrical current in Germany is 220 volts, so take along a converter or only bring those appliances that work on the European voltage.

Money

The German mark (DM) is the currency used. The value of the DM in relation to the American dollar has varied greatly in the past few years from less than 2 DM per dollar to over 3 DM per dollar. This fluctuation will, of course, greatly affect the cost of your trip. You will get your best exchange rate in the local banks.

Health Concerns

You do not need any immunizations to travel in Germany. You can drink the tap water anywhere except while traveling on the trains.

Getting There

One of the advantages of going to a European spa is that you have the opportunity to enjoy another culture and country while "taking the cure." For no extra charge, Lufthansa Airlines will allow you to fly into one German city and out of another. I recommend doing just that. I suggest flying into Munich and out of Frankfurt in order to see the best of Germany. You can pick up a rental car at the airport and drop it off before your departure. While the Brenner's Spa will pick you up at the airport, even one-way pick-up is expensive (Frankfurt 530 DM, Stuttgart or Strasbourg, France 220 DM). You can rent a car from Hertz for less than US$100 per week with unlimited mileage if you reserve it ahead of time using their toll-free number.

Lufthansa has always been one of my favorite carriers to Europe. It's especially good to start hearing German the moment you board the plane. All of a sudden you feel as if you've reached the edge of that other country. By the time you get to your destination, the sounds of the German language have become familiar and more comfortable. For those concerned about flight safety, you'll be glad to know that Lufthansa has the best maintenance program of any airline and the newest fleet of planes. In fact, I'm told their planes are the only ones Boeing will take back in trade, as they continually upgrade their fleet. This typical German efficiency results in fewer breakdowns, delays, or plane exchanges than is the case with many of their competitors. As one woman told me, "Their planes are so consistently on schedule that I can set my watch by their afternoon flight to Frankfurt." They also have an excellent flight schedule. I have gone from Munich to Frankfurt in the morning, gotten a few hours of sleep on board, left Frankfurt at 1:00 P.M. and arrived in New York City in the early afternoon, which allowed me plenty of time to get a connecting flight home by early evening. With a good night's sleep, I suffered little from jet lag.

Getting Around

While the trains through Europe are wonderful (they run frequently, are always on time, and are safe), I'd suggest renting a car for this trip. The German countryside has more charm and sense of history than you can possibly imagine. Also, while not essential, you'll find it convenient to have a car in Baden-Baden. Besides, driving on the German autobahn (expressway) is an experience no one should miss.

You should reserve your car prior to your departure to ensure the lowest rate. Arrange to pick it up at the Munich airport. As you exit the baggage claim area you'll see the car rental booths directly in front of you.

Driving in Germany

I strongly recommend that you ask for a pamphlet explaining the European road signs when you get your International Driver's License or write the German National Tourist Bureau, 747 Third Avenue, New York, NY 10017. You will need the license to rent a car, and you'll need to know the signs to get around. While most are pretty obvious, not all are and it's best to be prepared.

Most of the time I would suggest keeping to the small back streets that wind through the countryside between small, very attractive villages. Except on the autobahns, there is a posted speed limit. It is usually 60 kph in the small towns and 100 kph between them.

You must travel on the autobahn, where there is no speed limit, at least once. It is a totally unique driving experience. There are, however, a few things you should keep in mind when you do. First, be sure to always keep to the right, except when passing. Cars in the left-hand passing lane are usually traveling in excess of 220 kph (140 mph), so be sure there is plenty of room before pulling out in front of one.

When in the passing lane, you should pay an equal amount of attention to the cars behind you and to those in front of you. If you see a car approaching and flashing its headlights, you should speed up and move right immediately. According to German law, if you are in the passing lane and someone hits you from the rear, you are at fault for blocking traffic. But don't worry, this is rare. The German drivers don't want to get into an accident any more than you do.

In addition, when making a left-hand turn you are required to check to see that no one is passing on the left. If you should turn in front of them and be hit, you are considered at fault for not having cleared to the rear.

Check your car insurance before you leave home. While most policies cover liability in the States, few do so in Europe. If yours does not, I strongly suggest the optional coverage.

Overall, I find European drivers careful, and courteous. There is no reason to be nervous about driving here. You need only be aware of the expectations and drive accordingly.

Tipping

You should tip in Germany as you would in any major U.S. city (except New York City), about 15 percent. You should, of course, use the DM equivalent rounded off to the nearest DM; however, U.S. dollars will always be accepted.

I strongly recommend that you tip well upon arrival at the Brenner's Park Hotel, and that you introduce yourself to the maître d' and tip him at your first meal (see p. 60).

Treasures to Purchase

German beer steins are available in silver and crystal as well as porcelain and ceramic. Some are very simple, practical, and inexpensive, while others are works of art. In addition, you'll find that beautiful down comforters, lace window curtains, and wooden incense burners, wooden Christmas ornaments, and cuckoo clocks are available in most towns and villages. Baden-Baden, being a resort town of the wealthy, also has many designer shops you will likely want to at least browse through.

Where to Eat in Baden-Baden

Unfortunately for you if you have decided to cut down on calories while in Baden-Baden, there are a number of excellent restaurants. When gambling was outlawed in France, the wealthy of Paris flocked to the casino at Baden-Baden. In addition to the beautiful villas you will see along the famed Lichtentaler Allee and lovely antique furniture, they also brought their cuisine. Like the villas and the French antiques, the superb cuisine has remained.

Restaurant Schloss Neuweier is an elegant restaurant, in a castle built in 1549, that should not be missed whatever your diet restrictions. It is the castle of the popular Neuweier vineyard, which surrounds it. Located a short drive from town in the midst of wine country, they offer complete meals from three courses (38.50 DM) to eight courses (133 DM). You'll enjoy the cuisine in much the same style as the knights and their ladies did in the sixteenth century.

Schloss Eberstein, ten kilometers from town, is actually located in the old buildings on the edge of the castle perched on the side of a high hill. While the food is good and the view excellent, I found the service rather slow. Entrées range from 12.80 DM to 23 DM.

Just a short walk toward the center of town from the Brenner's Park Hotel is the *Restaurant Stahlbad*, where the food is too good to miss, even on a diet. Worst of all, it's the chocolate mousse that is the most spectacular. Considering myself a connoisseur of chocolate, that is always one of my indulgences. The presentation was so attractive, with a light raspberry sauce poured over the top, that I initially hated to eat it, but was I ever glad I did. Their entrées—lamb, seafood, and poultry—were of equal quality (42 DM to 95 DM). In addition to an interesting interior dining room, they have an especially comfortable covered garden seating on the park. The help was friendly, gracious, and competent.

While there are a number of other local restaurants, I personally didn't find any that could equal the Brenner's Park Hotel dining room in quality and ambiance.

EXPLORING THE GERMAN COUNTRYSIDE: MUNICH TO BADEN-BADEN

▶────────────────────────────▶

I highly recommend that you take some additional time while you're in Germany to explore the countryside. One week prior to your week at Baden-Baden and one week after the spa is a good way to break it up. I usually fly into Munich, an attractive cosmopolitan city worth at least a couple of days. Garmisch-Partenkirchen and Oberammergau are nearby and require a stop. You'll miss the best part of Germany if you miss these Bavarian towns. Konstanz, on the lake called the Bodensee, is a convenient place to stop between Bavaria and Baden-Baden, but I'd suggest spending any extra time you might have in Bavaria.

After your week at the spa, if you are planning to fly out of Frankfurt, drive to northern Germany and the towns of Heidelberg, Trier, Düsseldorf, Wiesbaden, and Koblenz. You should also take a Rhine River cruise.

Unless you're visiting Munich during the Oktoberfest, you don't need to make reservations ahead of time in most German cities. In fact, I'd recommend not doing it. Instead, retain your spontaneity by booking a room as you go. Every German town, even most small villages, will have a Tourist Information Center. It's usually marked with a large "I" on a blue and white sign. They're often at the train station. The Tourist Information people will find a room for you within a few minutes for a small fee (usually 3 DM). Specify your price range and whether you want a private shower, bath, toilet, or parking included. They will also give you directions to your hotel, in English.

Munich

Exploring Munich

Munich has a lot to see and do, day and night. Don't miss *Marienplatz* with the famous musical clock in the central tower of the Rathaus (town hall—I've always thought this was an appropriate name for a town hall). If you follow the signs to the *Cafe Glockenspiel* (you enter up an elevator at the rear of the building to the fifth floor), you'll find an elegant little cafe with the best view of the clock tower in town. They serve wonderful little German cakes as well.

You should also visit the famous *Hofbrauhaus* just around the corner from the square. Inside you'll find a lusty, large room with wooden tables and chairs with high carved backs and the music of a live German "umpah" band. While tourists are attracted to this large hall in droves, so are the Germans, many of whom will be in traditional Bavarian dress. They only sell beer by the liter (6 DM). It's quite a sight to see the waiters and waitresses carrying 6 liter mugs in each hand. It's also quite a sight to see the tables covered with empty liter mugs. If you come alone—and even if you come with a friend—you'll soon find yourself part of a large fun-loving group who may or may not speak English.

Be sure to take a stroll along the large shopping malls that lead to and from Marienplatz. At one end of Kaufinger Str., you'll run into *Karlsplatz* with its large attractive fountain. The old arched gates leading into the old city of Munich have been preserved here. As you walk these streets you'll pass historic churches and homes as well as high-fashion shops.

You'll also want to be sure to see the restored *Residenz Complex,* which will give you an idea of the opulence of the life of the rulers in Old Munich. While you will see beautiful antiques and paintings in the Residenz, there are more in Munich's museums. These include the *Alte Pinatothek* (Barerstr. 27); *Bayerisches Nationalmuseum* (Prinzregentenstr. 3); *Glyptothek* and *Antikensammlungen* (Konigsplatz) and the *Deutsches Museum,* a massive museum on its own island in the Isar River near *Maximilian Park.*

I attended the 1972 Olympics at the Munich Stadium. Even if you weren't there during the excitement of the games, you may want to visit the park that remains. If you visit *Theresienwiese Park* you'll be at the site of the yearly Oktoberfest. This, too, is an event you'll not want to miss if you're around the area the last week in September and the first week in October.

Where to Eat in Munich

You'll find a number of excellent small restaurants and cafes in Munich, many of which have outdoor seating. The people walking by provide excellent entertainment. One of the cafes you won't want to miss is the *Cafe Glockenspiel* (Marienplatz).

I also enjoyed the *Augustiner* (Neuhauser Str. 16) with its outdoor seating on the mall. They have a number of Bavarian specialties for 5 DM to 28 DM. These include Wurstsalat (sliced meats with a vinaigrette dressing) and Munchner Leberknodelsuppe (chopped liver dumplings in a broth). They're good—don't be afraid to try them. The *Weinstadl* (Burgstr. 5), near the Alder Hof, is another excellent choice with entrées for 9 DM to 19 DM. For more formal dining you won't beat the *Konigshof Restaurant* at the Hotel der Konigshof.

Where to Stay in Munich

Just after you exit the baggage claim area at the Munich airport, you'll see the black and gold Munich Tourist Information sign to your right. This should be your first stop if you don't have a place to stay. For a room in a small hotel with a private shower, toilet, parking, and breakfast, you can expect to pay 135 DM. Nice rooms without a private bath are considerably less. The large hotels are considerably more. The tourist highlights of Munich are clearly marked on this map. I'd suggest taking advantage of this service and spending your first night or two in Munich. It's a beautiful city and you'll likely find yourself tired earlier in the evening than you anticipate as your body adjusts to the time change.

Most of the moderately priced small hotels in Munich are excellent. If you want a large elegant hotel, try the *Hotel der Konigshof* (Karlplatz 25) or the *Hotel Bayerischer Hof* (Promenadeplatz 6). Both are centrally located luxury hotels.

From Munich to Baden-Baden

From the first time I visited the small, quiet town of Oberammergau, it has been my favorite German village. While most people will suggest Garmisch as your first stop out of Munich, and I certainly enjoyed Garmisch, too, my preference is to only stop in Garmisch for lunch and to wander around town, but then to go on to Oberammergau to spend a night or two.

The roads are well marked out of Munich to Garmisch-Partenkirchen (95S), about 50 miles away. You'll soon be on the autobahn south (blue signs with a picture of a double highway) driving through pine forests heading toward a massive mountain range, the Alps—even in summer their glaciers are covered with snow. Continue past small Bavarian farming villages, each with its own church with the round, onion-top steeple and boxes of colorful blooming flowers in every window of the homes.

Garmisch-Partenkirchen

Exploring Garmisch-Partenkirchen

Nestled in a small alpine valley beneath the majestic Alps, Garmisch-Partenkirchen is a favorite of ski enthusiasts during the winter months. This picturesque Bavarian village is indeed a jewel.

St. Martinkirche on Marienplatz is an excellent example of the Bavarian rococo-style church. It looms over Garmisch in exquisite grandeur. The streets and shops in town are a wonderful place to while away the hours. I recommend wandering through the equally charming and picturesque residential areas. (After spending a few days in Bavaria, I always want to come home and plant flowers everywhere.)

Whatever the time of year, take a ride to the top of the *Zugspitz*, 9,787 feet high. The view is breathtaking. The base is located between Garmisch and Partenkirchen, two towns that have united politically into one.

In addition, try to see the ski stadium and ski jumps from the 1936 Olympics, which were held here. There is also an Olympic ice stadium and an indoor swimming pool complex.

Where to Stay in Garmisch

Clausings Post Hotel, Marienplatz 12, Garmisch; telephone 08821 (single with bath 110 DM, double 130 DM to 180 DM). If you have the time to spend a night here, *the* place to stay is this member of the consistently high-quality Romantic Hotel chain. This charming Bavarian hotel, with its golden hunting horn hanging out front, is one of the best examples of Bavarian hospitality. Located near the post office on the main square, its restaurant with outdoor seating is a favorite of locals and visitors alike. It has two other restaurants and a bar on the ground floor that feel more like being in a castle wine cellar than a hotel.

Oberammergau

Just 10 miles from Garmisch and you're in the incredible town of Oberammergau, where the Passion Play is performed only once every ten years. Most of the population participates in this play, which depicts the life of Jesus, including the Last Supper, Betrayal, Crucifixion, and Resurrection. The play was first performed in 1634 by the villagers in thanks for being spared from the Black Plague. The next performance will be in 1990. While I've had people tell me they bought tickets at the door, most purchase theirs years in advance.

If you've ever wanted to retire to a quaint mountain hideaway, this is the place to do so. While it can certainly be exciting to see the Passion Play here, I prefer Oberammergau the nine out of ten years when it's less crowded. When not performing, the inhabitants' primary occupation is wood carving. The carvings are of high quality, but the prices match. Bargains are few and far between. The pieces carved by the residents of the village carry a special emblem to identify them. Ask any shop owner to show you.

Exploring Oberammergau

The open and friendly residents of Oberammergau welcome visitors, especially when the play is not on. This is a village in which to slow your pace and begin the rejuvenating process on your way to the spa—time moves slowly here. It is also a good place to watch the young and old in traditional Bavarian dress. Don't miss the life-size wood carving in town of the wood-carver carrying his backpack full of wares, or the cows in the barns right in town, on the main streets.

If you follow the walking path along the rock-lined creek (it runs in front of the Hotel Alois Lang) you'll come to the public indoor/outdoor swimming complex, open from 9:00 A.M. to 5:30 P.M. You can use it all day for 8 DM or three hours for 6 DM. There is also a sauna available for another 9 DM. Farther up the path is the base of the gondola that takes you to the restaurant at the top of the mountain for 12 DM (round-trip). During the summer you'll likely see hang gliders launching from the top of the steep cliffs, then gliding out over the mountains and the village far, far below.

Where to Eat in Oberammergau

While German food is usually good, in my opinion, Oberammergau has some of the best Bavarian restaurants. My favorite is the *Theatre Cafe*. The entrées, which may range from 8 DM to 22 DM, include an incredible mafia steak (16.50 DM). You can enjoy this pork steak with a light curry sauce on the patio under a fruit-laden apple tree. Another favorite is the *Hotel Turmwirt Restaurant*. The entrées here include a number of Bavarian specialties from 10.80 DM to 24.50 DM. Their pepper steak (29.50 DM) is excellent, but little can beat their selection of wild game (18 DM to 37.50 DM). A pottery jug signed by the cast of the 1984 Passion Play commemorating the 350-year anniversary sits on a windowsill. The knotty pine walls and ceilings are typical of the Bavarian charm. You an also get wild schweinbraten (roast pig, 13.50 DM) at the *Gasthof von Stern* not far away. Other entrées range from 7 DM to 23 DM. In addition, they offer a house specialty, a complete meal for around 15 DM. The *Hotel Walf* offers Bavarian specialties in an attractive setting from 9.50 DM to 29.50 DM.

Where to Stay in Oberammergau

For as little as 25 DM a person, you can get a bed and breakfast room in a home. You'll see signs on the homes saying "Zimmer Frei" (Rooms Free). Just stop in. If you'd like, the Tourist Information Office near the river on the main road can also book you a room.

Hotel Alois Lang, St. Lukes Strasse 15 (single 85 DM to 100 DM, double 140 DM to 160 DM). One of the most attractive small hotels in town, the Alois Lang is located beside a small river away from the traffic. Out front, the lawn has the hotel's name spelled out in flowers.

Hotel Alte Post, Dorfstrasse 19 (35 DM to 55 DM per person). A charming Bavarian hotel in every way, this, too, is an excellent choice. Its location in the center of town is convenient.

Around Oberammergau

Between Garmisch and Oberammergau you'll see a sign pointing the way to King Ludwig II's castle, *Schloss Linderhof*. Parking is 1.50 DM and a tour of his only completely finished and furnished castle is another 6 DM. There is often a wait. You may want to go early in the day to avoid the tour buses from Garmisch. This is Ludwig's most spectacular castle, with a gold fountain pool out front and a thirty-step waterway leading to the pool in the rear of the estate.

A short drive from the Linderhof is *Schloss Neuschwanstein*. And the easiest way to get here is to take the back road into Austria before returning to Germany near the town of Füssen. This castle was made famous when Walt Disney used it as the model for his Disneyland castle. Once again demonstrating the opulence of the mid-1800s, this castle should not be missed. Tours for 6 DM are a real bargain and worth the long wait.

Located on the hill opposite the Neuschwanstein, *Schloss Hohen-schwangau* was destroyed by Napoleon and restored by Maximilian, Ludwig II's father. Ludwig II spent much of his youth here. While not as elaborate as the one he later built, it is nonetheless spectacular and full of history. It was the residence of the royal family until 1912. It has been a museum ever since.

Konstanz

Constance is the English name for this sea resort on Lake Constance, which borders Germany, Switzerland, and Austria. The Germans call it Konstanz and the lake Bodensee. The most direct route from Füssen to Konstanz will take you in and out of corners of both Austria and Switzerland.

Konstanz is more a town of history than one of beauty. The flowers and rural charm of Bavaria are conspicuously missing here. It has an interesting old section that is well worth exploring and is a convenient stopover between Oberammergau, Bavaria, and Baden-Baden in the Black Forest.

Where to Stay in Konstanz

Steigenberger Insel Hotel (single 120 DM, double 195 DM). This is *the* place to stay in Konstanz. Located on a small island at the point were the Rhine River flows from Lake Constance, this thirteenth-century Dominican monastery has been carefully restored into an elegant luxury hotel by the Steigenberger hotel management group. Many of the original paintings and furnishings are still on display on the walls around the ancient inner courtyard. Ferdinand Graf Von Zeppelin was born here in 1838, and the hotel bar is named in his honor. There are two fine restaurants on the premises.

Hotel Barbarossa, Obermarkt 8 (single 59 DM, double 104 DM). Centrally located in the old part of town, you'll likely hear local musicians in the square in front of the hotel. This fifteenth-century building is well maintained. Much lower in price, the quality of the surroundings are a big step down as well.

Hotel Deutsches Haus, Marktstrasse 15 (single 60 DM, double 115 DM to 130 DM). Also well located and similar in quality to the Barbarossa, its lobby is attractive and the rooms spacious.

Exploring Konstanz

The Insel Hotel is at one end of the attractive, flower-lined city gardens, which dominate the waterfront. At the other end you'll find the old Council Building (*Konzilgebaude*) in which the 1417 papal election took place. There is now an attractive restaurant, the *Konzil-Gastatte*, in the lower portion of this building with seating looking out over the park gardens, the ferry docks, and the sea (entrées range from 4 DM to 24 DM). If you take the passage just past here under the main street, you'll enter the old historic streets of Konstanz. Walking tour maps of this part of town are widely available and very helpful. Ask at your hotel.

Be sure to see the *Rosgartenmuseum* in a well-maintained Gothic Guildhouse of the butchers. The *Rathaus* (town hall) is where Mesmer, the originator of the theory of animal magnetism and hypnosis, lived from 1812 to 1814. You'll also want to see the *Rhein Bridge Gate*, the *Hus Haus*, and the *Insel Mainau*, a 110-acre botanical garden with a baroque palace and church.

EXPLORING THE COUNTRYSIDE: BADEN-BADEN TO FRANKFURT

▶──▶

I recommend going the long way to Frankfurt, by way of Düsseldorf, Koblenz, the Rhine River, and Wiesbaden. At the very least, if your time is short, stop in *Heidelberg* to see the magnificent *Heidelberg Castle* and have lunch at the *Hotel Ritter* (Hauptstrasse 178) or at the *Heidelberg Castle Restaurant.*

On my last visit to Germany, my then five-year-old German godson Johannes asked me about my castle in Mound. We were driving from his hometown, which has a castle that was built before Columbus reached the New World, to Heidelberg to visit the Heidelberg castle. He was disbelieving when I first told him neither Mound nor Minneapolis has a castle. He had grown up in an area where most towns had a great old castle looming on the hill above. It was a fact he took for granted.

If you do have the time, I'd suggest taking the small roads through the German countryside, possibly through Trier to Düsseldorf.

Trier

The oldest German city, Trier, has been the northern headquarters of a number of Roman emperors beginning with Augustus. Now a wine distribution center, it celebrated its 2,000th anniversary in 1984. It is situated in the Mosel Valley and the entire city is a museum of history. Don't miss the *Porta Nigra*, of which the town is very proud. It is much more than an old gate to the city. You'll also want to see the *Liebfrauenkirche*, a thirteenth-century Gothic cathedral.

Düsseldorf

Most visitors migrate to Düsseldorf's more famous neighbor, Cologne, and in so doing miss this exciting and vibrant city. The site of many international trade fairs and congresses, Düsseldorf, a city of half a million, is also the fashion capital of Germany.

Where to Stay in Düsseldorf

There are two excellent hotels from which to choose.

Steinberger Park Hotel, Corneliusplatz 1 (single 325 DM to 420 DM, double 375 DM to 520 DM). Centrally located between the park and the old part of town, this luxury hotel is an excellent selection. The staff is especially friendly and helpful. In the traditional Steinberger Hotel tradition, considerable attention to detail has been paid in the restoration process. The rooms are spacious with all the modern conveniences.

The *Hotel Breidenbacher Hof,* Heinrich-Heine-Alle 36 (single 260 DM to 350 DM, double 370 DM to 450 DM). The newly decorated, elegant lobby, lounge, restaurant, and bar are often the center of activity in this very active town. The antiques set off the marble decor nicely.

Exploring Düsseldorf

The old part of Düsseldorf bordering the Rhine River is the place to be day or night. These walking malls are packed full of shops and restaurants with people eating and drinking, inside and out, just simply enjoying life to its fullest. You'll find shops with designer fashions as well as souvenirs. *Konigsalle* is *the* shopping street. It's easy to spend money in the boutiques and jewelry shops here. The restaurants, pubs, and cafes are first class as well.

You'll also want to see the *Kunstmuseum* (Ehrenhof 5), in the *Hofgarten,* which is also worth a visit. This magnificent park has swans swimming on its lake, flowers and shrubs throughout, and local citizens strolling or sitting and just relaxing.

Düsseldorf to Wiesbaden

I suggest leaving your rental car in Düsseldorf and experiencing the rest of Germany on the famous train system and aboard a Rhine River boat. You haven't really experienced Germany until you've ridden the trains and cruised the Rhine River.

If you rise early you can catch the 9:00 train to Koblenz, leaving time to explore the city, have lunch there, and still catch the Rhine River boat to Wiesbaden.

The Train to Koblenz

If you have the chance, I recommend taking the all-first-class *Rhinegold Express*. This is the modern-day version of the even more luxurious trains of yesterday, among them the Orient Express. Since it is an express, it won't stop in every station. If Koblenz is not listed, it won't stop and you'll need to take a less famous train.

It is highly unusual for a German train to be even one minute late. They arrive at their designated track on time (check the arrival schedule labeled *Anfahrt*) and leave on time (check the departure schedule labeled *Abfahrt*). The time in the station will be short. If you have a first-class ticket, stand where the board says the first-class cars will be located. The cars will have a large "1" for first class and "2" for second class next to the door. There will also be designated smoking and nonsmoking cars with the usual international signs.

Most important, not every car on a train continues the full route. Be sure to check the sign on the outside of the car you board, next to the entrance, to see that it has Koblenz listed as a stop.

The trains in Germany are efficient, well run, and an excellent way to get from one location to another quickly. They usually include a restaurant car for long trips, which adds to the feeling of having stepped back in time. If you haven't purchased your ticket in the station, don't worry, you can buy one for the same price from the conductor on the train. He'll also make sure you're in the correct car to get to your desired destination, Koblenz, one hour and ten minutes away.

Koblenz

Koblenz, founded as a fort by the Romans in A.D. 14, lies at the juncture of the Moselle and the Rhine rivers. The elegant old homes and churches stand today in tribute to its history. The *Deutsches Eck*, located at the point where the rivers meet, was initially unveiled in 1897. Since 1953, it has been seen as symbolic of Germany's unity.

If you caught the 9:00 A.M. train, you'll have about four hours to walk around town and have lunch before the boat leaves. I'd suggest checking your bags in one of the train station lockers for 2 DM. (The boat won't arrive until boarding time and there is no storage on the piers.)

Directly across the street from the train station is a round building that houses the Tourist Information Center. They'll provide you with a map and show you where to find the old town, shopping streets, the Deutsches Eck, and the *Ehrenbreitstein Fortress*, a royal residence in the seventeenth and eighteenth centuries.

Rhine River Cruise

Koblenz is a favorite starting point for boat trips up the Rhine River. You can buy your ticket for the river cruise at the dock. Koblenz to Wiesbaden (57.60 DM) is the most interesting portion of the Rhine. You'll pass one historic castle after another perched on the side of the hill. You'll also pass the famous *Lorelei Cliffs*, which descend almost vertically to the river. These cliffs have been the focus of legend, song, and poetry.

The all-first-class Köln-Düsseldorfer (KD Rhine Line) boat offers an excellent selection of Rhine wine for you to enjoy as you pass through the most famous wine-growing region of Germany. On lazy summer days, the lounge chairs on the open decks are usually crowded with sun worshippers. The six and a half hours will go quickly as you travel through ancient history. This river was the primary form of transportation for the lords and ladies who lived in the castles you pass.

Nothing moves too quickly here, including the ferries you will see transporting vehicles across the river from one picturesque village to another. It will be evening when you reach Wiesbaden, your destination. Pick up your luggage, which had been stored for you, as you disembark. One of the waiting cabs will gladly take you to your hotel in town for 12 DM to 15 DM.

Wiesbaden

Exploring Wiesbaden

Beginning with the *Bahnhof* (train station), Wiesbaden is a jewel of a city. An appropriate place to end your journey, it was also a delight of the ancient Romans who so enjoyed the spa. The rulers and the wealthy have enjoyed these waters and been renewed by their healing powers for centuries.

You can easily see this city on foot. In a very few blocks you'll go from the elegant old *Casino* and *Kurhaus* (Kurpark), dedicated by Emperor Wilhelm II in 1907, to just as elegant shops with the latest designer favorites. You'll want to be sure to see *Marktplatz*, an old town square where you'll find the Renaissance-style *Rathaus* and red-brick *Martkirche*. Local festivals are still held here.

There is also a beautiful theater (Kurpark). Seats range from 17 DM to 20 DM. Even if your German isn't good, you'll likely enjoy an evening in this attractive setting.

Where to Stay in Wiesbaden

The *Central Hotel*, Bahnhofstr. 65 (single without bath 58 DM to 95 DM; double with full bath 140 DM), is well named with its convenient location one block from the Bahnhof, from which you will eventually depart to go to the Frankfurt airport and home. Have breakfast in their pleasant sun-filled lobby, overlooking the park. The front rooms are spacious with high ceilings, antique beds, and private patios.

The *Hotel Schwartzer Bock*, Kransplatz 12 (single 115 DM, double 190 DM), is not only one of the world's oldest hotels (opened in 1486) but one with the most old-world charm. You're greeted by red marble columns and rich warm marble and antiques throughout the hotel. In town, near the casino, the location has remained central. No two rooms here are alike, ranging from Empire to contemporary in style. In keeping with the theme of this trip, there is even an in-house spa with a thermal swimming pool. It is a great value.

The *Hotel Nassauer Hof*, Kaiser Friedrich-Platz 3 (single 315 DM, double 395 DM). Newly remodeled, and with high prices to match, this is indeed a grand old hotel on the outside, new inside. Across from the casino, the location is excellent, but in my opinion the setting does not justify the price.

When you're ready to leave town—or when you must go, as you'll likely never be ready to leave—you can catch a train to the Frankfurt airport from the Wiesbaden Bahnhof. This bahnhof probably has the nicest restaurant I've ever seen at a bahnhof. If you have time for a last farewell glass of Rhine wine or rich German beer, it's a good place to stop.

PORTLAND AND COASTAL MAINE: A NEW ENGLAND HIDEAWAY

▶ ─── ▶

GENERAL AMBIANCE	★ ★
SOCIAL CLIMATE	★
ACTIVITIES	★ ★

FOR TOUR ARRANGEMENTS CONTACT:
Prince of Funde Cruises, Ltd.
P.O. Box 4216, Station A
Portland, ME 04101
(800) 341-7540

Or *contact your travel agent* and ask for the USAir Fly-Drive-Cruise
Tour

▶ ─── ▶

*W*e all have times when we want to "really get away." We don't want
excitement or romance, we don't have the energy for adventure. We
need to go to a place where we can sit comfortably and just be. If
that's the situation in which you currently find yourself, Portland and
the coast of Maine is just the escape.

I always find solitude and a soothing peacefulness in the sound of
the waves lapping on the shore and the sight of sea gulls soaring
above. Sitting back on the deck of a ship and watching the nearly 300
islands of Casco Bay pass by is a special form of relaxation. If driving
through rush hour when you're late for work is a real drag, then the
drive along the stunning coast of Maine from one small fishing village
to the next is a drive of ecstasy.

For this R&R New England hideaway, you'll start in Portland,
Maine, on Casco Bay. Portland was described by a London newspaper
as "the San Francisco of the East," and I would agree. After a couple
of days in this charming New England city you'll begin your drive
north on scenic U.S. Route 1.

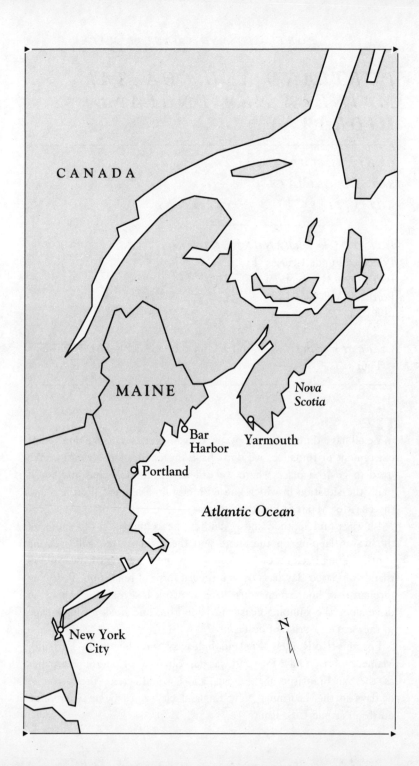

Your first stop will be Freeport, Maine, the home of L. L. Bean and many other factory outlet stores. You'll go on to Thomaston to spend the night. If you have the time, I'd suggest another night's stop at Camden. If time does not permit, continue on to idyllic Bar Harbor on Mount Desert Island for your next overnight. Here you'll visit Acadia National Park before taking the Bluenose Ferry to Yarmouth, Nova Scotia. Your cruise on *The Prince of Funde* from Yarmouth back to Portland will complete your holiday away from home.

General Ambiance

Whenever Maine is mentioned, I picture waves breaking over large rounded boulders with a brilliant blue sky above and billowing white clouds slowly floating by. It also brings to mind fishing boats tightly packed into a safe harbor and off in the distance a lighthouse keeping its ever-vigilant watch over the rockbound coast. This is a spectacular part of Portland and the coast of Maine; however, it is only a part.

Social Climate

Portland is a big city, though on a small scale. While the people are friendly, most are not there on vacation. You might pass a few minutes in conversation with them, but as in any big city, they will soon need to be on their way home or back to work.

Things change once you begin your drive up the coast. The pace slows considerably. While there's lots to see and do, the people you'll meet won't be rushing off to jobs or families. They, too, will be here for fun and relaxation. But even the shop owners and the others you'll meet who live and work along the coast seem to work at a slower pace. You are their real "industry," and they want to make sure you find all you're looking for so you'll return.

A real advantage of the bed and breakfast lodgings in which you'll stay is the casual opportunity they afford to meet the locals as well as other visitors like yourself. In many ways, staying at a B&B is like visiting a little-known aunt. The proprietor will have time to chat with you and she'll be sure to introduce you to her other guests, if you've not already met. You can visit while you have wine on the veranda in the evening and over breakfast in the morning. You'll find some of her guests visit every year, insisting on the same room, of course. After a while she does almost become family, only you won't find her sitting up by the window at night waiting for you.

Activities

This isn't meant to be one of those action-packed vacations, though you'll find there's plenty to do. You'll wander through small fishing villages and perhaps sit by the water's edge for hours watching the sea gulls, the waves, and the boats offshore. You'll probably want to take a ferry ride while in Portland prior to your cruise on the M/S *Scotia Prince*. You can do as much or as little as you please.

Preparing for Your Trip to Maine

What to Take

For the most part, you'll want casual resort-type clothing—cotton dresses, shorts, and tops. Although casual will be fine everywhere you visit, you may want something just a little dressier for dinner in Portland. Don't forget your comfortable walking shoes; you'll certainly need them. In the spring and fall you should take a sweater or light jacket for the evening. Even during the summer months the ocean breeze can be cool, especially when you're on the water, so I'd suggest a sweater or shawl.

Though the water is cool, usually 55 degrees, you'll want your swimsuit for the beach. No one says you have to go in the water. Be sure to take your camera and plenty of film. And don't forget your sunglasses to filter the harsh glare of the sun bouncing off the water.

When to Go

Things close down here during the winter months then open again in the spring. By late May the weather has warmed and the lilacs are in bloom. The days are warm and the evenings cool throughout the summer months. Then, by mid-October, it's fall and winter will soon be approaching. I suggest going before school lets out in June or after they've reopened in September. That way you'll miss the families visiting Acadia National Park.

Getting There

The Prince of Funde Cruise line, which operates M/S *Scotia Prince*, has gotten together with USAir to offer special Fly-Drive-Cruise packages. By purchasing their package you can get your flight from any U.S. city served by USAir, your cruise to Yarmouth, and rental car all at the reduced rate. To get their rate from your city, call their toll-free number (800) 341-7540. They offer a variety of packages ranging from three to eight days, and you can always extend your stay.

Getting Around

A car is not absolutely necessary in order to see the city of Portland, as most attractions are within walking distance. However, to enjoy the beauty of the surrounding area, a car is essential; there is no public transportation to the outlying areas.

Once in Bar Harbor, you can turn in your rental car for a bicycle ($11 a day) or a moped ($23 for the first two hours, $5 an hour after that).

Treasures to Purchase

You'll find a number of galleries, antique shops, and fine crafts stores featuring everything from blown glass, lithographs, silk screens, Art Deco, and Art Nouveau to period jewelry and pottery. On *Fare Street*, which parallels Portland's waterfront commercial street, you'll find shops specializing in wood crafts, baskets, imported clothing, and brass. Don't miss tiny *Wharf Street* behind Fare Street. It's here you'll find art galleries, gift shops, and canvas shops as well as a cafe. An especially interesting shop nestled among the many others is *Ecology House* (7 Exchange Street). It features sculptures, books, stained glass, "endangered species" T-shirts, gold and silver jewelry, and tapes for relaxation.

For a unique gift, get a lobster "packed for travel." The *Great Maine Lobster Company* (2 Portland Fish Pier, Portland; telephone 772-0106) and the *Harbor Fish Market* (9 Custom House Wharf, Portland; telephone 775-0251) will pack them for you.

In Bar Harbor you'll find similar items as well as shells in every size and shape, and hand-knit sweaters. They also have a number of outlet stores, although not nearly as many as you'll find in Freeport. Shopping doesn't end at dark here, but continues bathed in the soft glow of the colonial lamps lining its wide brick-paved sidewalks.

EXPLORING COASTAL MAINE

Portland

Portland was settled in 1628 as Casco. Then, as now, it relied heavily on its port with lumber, fishing, and shipping as its major industries. Henry Wadsworth Longfellow, born and raised in Portland, wouldn't recognize the city today. While the old coexists with the new, more has changed than remains the same.

Portland is a bustling city in which you will immediately feel at home. Hours can be spent wandering the neighborhoods, viewing the architectural styles that range from Italianate and Carpenter Gothic to Colonial Revival and Greek Revival. One of my favorites was a Victorian brownstone remodeled after an Italian villa.

While Portland is the largest city in Maine, it is tiny compared to New York or Chicago, or even Boston for that matter. Portland has the feel and warmth of a small town with the advantages of a large city.

There is something for everyone in Portland. Fine museums, good theater, endless shops jammed with old lithographs, antiques, crafts, clothing of every kind, including a shop specializing in vintage recycled clothing and antiques, and old and rare out-of-print books. In addition, Portland has a strong arts community, and nearly every pub and bar features evening entertainment.

One of your first stops before beginning your tour of Portland should be Greater Portland's Visitor's Center at 142 Free Street. Here you can pick up brochures, maps, and additional information about the city. You can also obtain information ahead of time by writing the Chamber of Commerce of the Greater Portland Region, Portland, ME 04101, or by calling (207) 772-2811.

The downtown area of Portland is patrolled by mounted police—a charming way to provide extra safety.

Exploring Portland

I found the best way to start getting a feel for the city was to wander around the *Old Port District,* which is bounded by Congress Street, the Franklin Street Arterial, Commercial Street, and Temple Street. This area has been transformed from old shipping warehouses and boat buildings into a delightful collection of restaurants, unique boutiques, gift shops, and impressive galleries. This quaint village-within-a-city with its cobblestone streets, turn-of-the-century lampposts, and small parks is ideally suited to shopping or just wandering down the narrow streets window shopping and people watching.

Every Wednesday and Saturday, from 6:30 A.M. to 1:30 P.M., on Federal Street right off Market Street, there is a *Farmer's Market.* It's a wonderful place to talk to the local people and hear about the area. They sell everything from fresh fruits and vegetables to homemade jams and jellies to fresh flowers and bedding plants.

I found myself being drawn back to the Old Port area time and time again, and on every visit I would find a new treasure to explore and enjoy. The entire ambiance of the area transports you back to the turn of the century. Most of the buildings have been expertly restored, keeping intact the flavor of a bygone era.

Victoria Mansion, 109 Danforth Street, Portland, between State and High streets; telephone (207) 722-4841. Open June 1 through August 31, Tuesday through Saturday from 10:00 A.M to 4:00 P.M. In September, open from 10:00 A.M. to 1:00 P.M. Admission: $3. Tours continually.

Victoria Mansion has been beautifully restored to its original splendor. It was built in 1858 and many feel it is one of the finest examples of nineteenth-century architecture to survive in the United States. As was true of all the restored homes I visited in Portland, there are no restraining ropes placed in the rooms, so you have free access and the opportunity to experience the rooms as they once were. While touring the home, I had the eerie feeling that the family just stepped out and would return at any moment. I highly recommend seeing this mansion, a ten-minute walk from the Old Port area.

Wadsworth-Longfellow House, 485 Congress Street, Portland; telephone (207) 772-1807. Open June through September, Tuesday through Saturday from 10:00 A.M. to 4:00 P.M. Garden open year-round from 9:00 A.M. to 5:00 P.M. Admission: $2.50. Tours continually.

Located in the heart of downtown Portland, this house, the boyhood home of Longfellow, is an absolute must. Built in 1785, it today contains furnishing belonging to and reflecting the life-style of Longfellow. I found the kitchen particularly interesting, containing many cooking utensils used during Longfellow's time.

Tate House, 1270 Westbrook Street, on the corner of Congress Street; telephone (207) 774-9781. Open June 15 through September 15, Tuesday through Saturday from 11:00 A.M. to 5:00 P.M., Sunday from 1:30 P.M. to 5:00 P.M. By appointment May 15 to June 14 and September 16 to October 15. Admission: $2.50. Continuous tours.

Built in 1755 by Captain George Tate, Tate House has been restored to its original condition. A unique feature of this home is a central chimney with eight fireplaces. The Tate House is a fifteen-minute drive from the heart of Portland.

The Portland Observatory, 138 Congress Street, Portland; telephone (207) 774-5561. Open when the flags are flying, Memorial Day to Labor Day. Admission: $1. The Observatory is about a thirty-minute walk from downtown Portland past the main shopping district of downtown, beautiful old homes that have been restored and old homes that have not been restored, intriguing secondhand furniture stores, an old cemetery, beautiful churches, and little neighborhood shops of every description. Built in 1807, the observatory was originally a signal tower for the merchants and shipowners, so they would know of approaching ships hours before they docked. It was closed at the turn of the century when progress in communications made signal flags unnecessary. It was reopened in 1939 as a historic point of interest. There are 102 steps to the top—well worth the climb as you, too, will agree when you step out on the open deck and look south over the ocean and magnificent Cape Elizabeth. Walking around to the west you'll see Portland, with all its unique architecture, spread out at your feet. I especially enjoyed the eastern view overlooking beautiful Casco Bay and the more than 300 islands reaching as far as the eye can see.

Casco Bay Cruises

At least one cruise out into the bay is an absolute must. There are several cruise lines, each with a variety of cruises, so there is one to fit every schedule and interest. For example, the *Bailey Island Cruise* is a four-hour cruise that departs every Sunday through Wednesday at 10:00 A.M. and 2:00 P.M. from Portland. If you choose the 10:00 A.M. crossing, you can stay on at Bailey Island and dine at one of the six fine island restaurants before leaving at 4:00 P.M.

The *Portland Head Light* cruise is an hour-and-fifty-minute cruise that departs Portland every Thursday through Saturday at 10:15 A.M., 12:30 P.M., and 4:00 P.M. This lectured cruise takes you through Casco Bay's most scenic highlights, including Whitehead Passage, Diamond Island Cove, and Pumpkin Knob. Cost: $6.

The *Calendar Island by Sunset* cruise departs at 5:30 P.M. This two-and-a-half hour cruise is the one the locals use to go between islands and back and forth to Portland. It is a beautiful time of the day to be on the bay and it is wonderful to meet the local islanders. On my trip there was an interesting and diverse group of passengers, including young lovers wanting to watch the sunset, entire families with mounds of luggage, including their pets, and an excited little boy with his day's fishing catch proudly clutched in his hands. Cost: $6.

Portland Museum of Art, 7 Congress Square, Portland; telephone (207) 775-6148. Open October through Memorial Day, Wednesday through Saturday from 10:00 A.M. to 4:00 P.M., Thursday until 9:00 P.M., Sunday from noon to 4:00 P.M. Summer: Tuesday through Saturday from 10:00 A.M. to 5:00 P.M., Thursday until 9:00 P.M., Sunday from noon to 5:00 P.M.

Built in 1983, this museum houses an extensive collection of paintings, sculptures, ceramics, and early American and Federal period decorative arts and furniture. I found the collection of Winslow Homer paintings especially impressive. In a new city it is sometimes hard to find the time to visit an art museum; however, this one is well worth "finding" a few hours.

Portland Head Light, Fort Williams Park, Cape Elizabeth. Another must while visiting Portland, this lighthouse was commissioned in 1771 by George Washington. It is the world's most photographed and oldest lighthouse in continuous use in the country. Unlike the majority of the nation's lighthouses, which have been automated, Portland Head Light is still manned by the U.S. Coast Guard. Its 200,000 candlepower light is a welcome sight for boats of all sizes in stormy or foggy weather. The ocean front running on either side of the lighthouse is magnificent. There is a path down onto the rocks on the left side of the lighthouse and for the brave it affords a breathtaking view of the ocean and the head light. The lighthouse is located in the town-owned park and is open from dawn to dusk year-round. Accessible from South Portland by following Route 77 to Broadway (about a mile from the Portland–South Portland Bridge), left on Broadway, and right on Cottage Road, which becomes Shore Road.

A coastal town between Scarborough and South Portland, *Cape Elizabeth* is surrounded on three sides by water and boasts some of the most magnificent homes in the area. It is surrounded by the town-owned *Fort Williams Park and Beach* and is open to the public. Two state parks are located in Cape Elizabeth: *Crescent Beach*, a beautiful expansive sandy beach, and *Two Lights*, on the rocky coastline. Town residents are proud of the historical *Spurwink Church*, open to visitors during the summer months, and often the setting for summertime weddings.

Where to Eat in Portland

The Red Snapper Restaurant, 396 Fore Street, Portland; telephone 773-4363. This large and very popular restaurant offers something for every occasion. The bottom floor is small and opens onto a small patio and outside eating area that has a view of the harbor and is an excellent place to relax, sip a cool drink, and watch the people stroll by.

The large airy upstairs area opens onto Fore Street, one of the busy

Old Port arteries. The menu consists almost entirely of seafood, with five to eight seafood specials each night ranging in price from $9.50 to $15.95. The fish dishes are rated for flavor from delicate to pronounced. Food is top quality, the service excellent, and the atmosphere pleasant and reasonably casual.

Horsefeathers, 193 Middle Street, Portland; telephone 773-3501. This is a popular meeting place for Portlanders. A large and varied menu had many excellent seafood dishes, which I found was the rule rather than the exception all over Portland. The food is excellent, but at Horsefeathers that is only the beginning. Every evening from 5:00 P.M. to 8:00 P.M. they offer hors d'oeuvres, along with the ever-present popcorn; then, from 9:15 P.M. to midnight, there is live entertainment—a variety of bands, folk singers, etc. On Sunday you are in for a treat if you happen along between 4:00 P.M. and 8:00 P.M., when they have live jazz. Horsefeathers is open every day from 11:30 A.M. to midnight. No reservations are needed; it's a relatively casual place.

Rib Room (Senesta Hotel). Gourmet dining amid the most elegant surroundings. Food and service excellent: broiled and stuffed lobster, $18.50; shrimp scampi, $14.50; breast of chicken, $11.95. The couple at the next table had the chateaubriand and bouguetier for two, which looked marvelous ($34.95). Even though restaurants like this are sometimes intimidating to "loners," this one is not. I felt completely comfortable. The restaurant is open from 5:30 P.M. to 10:00 P.M.; reservations are recommended.

Greenhouse Restaurant (Senesta Hotel) provides casual dining, in a very light and airy-feeling room filled with large plants. Of course, they feature fresh seafood. The restaurant is open from 7:00 A.M to 2:00 P.M. Standard lunch and breakfast menus. Breakfast ranges from $2.50 to $8.25; lunch from $2.95 to $9.95.

Top of the East Lounge (Senesta Hotel). Open from 4:00 P.M. to 1:00 A.M., you get an absolutely spectacular view of Portland from here. Free hors d'oeuvres during the cocktail hour, live entertainment every evening. A perfect way to make the transition from a busy day to evening. Also a good place to end the day, sipping a cool drink while looking out over the lights of Portland. Sunday brunch is served from noon to 2:30 P.M. ($11.95), and is an unusually large selection—a must if you are in Portland on Sunday.

Deli One, 106 Exchange Street, Portland; telephone 772-7115. A wood-paneled bar and restaurant with a comfortable and warm feeling. If you go all the way through you'll come out into a secluded, tree-lined outdoor patio. It's a wonderful place to have a meal. Moderately priced with all the usual deli items, American cuisine, homemade soups, salads, sandwiches, daily specials, and an especially large dessert menu. They have live music in the evenings and are packed every Saturday night. It's a good place to go for an informal Saturday evening with the local Portlanders. The restaurant is open from 7:00 A.M. to 10:00 P.M., Monday through Friday; 9:00 A.M. to midnight, Saturday; 9:00 A.M. to 9:00 P.M., Sunday.

Wine Seller, 34 Exchange, Portland; telephone 775-1100. The *New York Times* called this "Portland's Most Elegant Restaurant" and it very well could be. If you want a refined, quiet, excellent dinner, this is the place. I found it moderately priced for its quality: filet of beef Wellington, $15.95; pecan chicken, $11.75; steamed salmon, $14.75. There is a lounge in the basement that is quiet and dark if you are looking for a place to relax away from people for a time. The restaurant is open from 5:30 P.M. to 9:30 P.M.

Blue Moon, Fore Street between Union and Exchange. This is an upbeat, fun place to have a meal. It was the busiest place I saw on Saturday evening. People were lined up at the door. They do not take reservations, and it is semiformal and friendly with helpful waiters. Moderately priced at $12.50 for seafood kabob or $12.95 for beef tenderloin. Again, they offer many seafood selections. Dinners range from $7.50 to $13.95. Open for lunch and dinner, Monday through Saturday, closed on Sundays.

Two Lights Lobster Shack, 225 Two Lights Road, Cape Elizabeth; telephone 799-1677. After your trip to Portland Head Light, you might want to treat yourself and stop by the Lobster Shack, located in a small building right on the ocean. The restaurant was mentioned to me by almost everyone I talked to in the Portland area. The food is served cafeteria-style and you can either sit in a glass-enclosed front room or take your food out on the front lawn and sit at the picnic tables. Or, my recommendation would be to climb down on the large area of rocks closer to the ocean to enjoy your wonderful meal. I highly recommend the lobster roll or the crab roll. They also serve shrimp, fried clams, hamburgers, and hot dogs. The food is moderately priced and you could not ask for a more beautiful setting in which to eat it. The restaurant is open seven days a week, from 11:00 A.M. to 8:00 P.M., April through October. After you've finished eating, you can spend time just sitting and watching the ocean break against the long expanse of rocks or you can wander along the rocks.

Where to Stay in Portland

Senesta Hotel, 157 High Street, Portland, ME 04101; telephone (207) 755-5411 (April to October: single $80 to $85, double $90 to $95; November through December: single or double $65). The Senesta Hotel is conveniently located in downtown Portland within easy walking distance of the Old Port District. It is a charming, elegant hotel decorated with an old-world warmth and style. There is a lobby bar that is a wonderful place to relax and people watch after a busy day or to sit and have a cup of coffee while you plan your day. The lobby lounge is open from 11:30 A.M. to 11:00 P.M. They have three restaurants: *The Rib Room*, *Greenhouse Restaurant*, and *The Top of the East*.

Ramada Inn, 1230 Congress Street, Portland, ME 04102; telephone (207) 774-5611 (January to June: single $56 to $66, double $66 to $76; July to October: single $62 to $82, double $72 to $92; November to December $58 to $68, double $68 to $78). The Ramada Inn is a new hotel with the warmth and charm of an older hotel. It has a beautiful pool area complete with sauna and Jacuzzi. Besides a restaurant, it has a lounge that has a Happy Hour Monday through Friday complete with hors d'oeuvres. This hotel is about a five-minute drive from downtown Portland. A car is necessary if you stay here.

Holiday Inn—Downtown, 88 Spring Street, Portland, ME 04101; telephone (207) 775-2311 (single $55 to $80, double $65 to $90). A bright, clean, newly decorated hotel located within four blocks of the Old Port area. Restaurant, lounge, live entertainment, and indoor pool.

Freeport

Freeport is located twenty minutes north of Portland on Route 1. It is the home of *L. L. Bean* and over seventy other retail stores and factory outlets. If you are a shopper, this is the place for you. The factory outlets include specialty shops, food and wine shops, linen, footwear, housewares, sporting goods, crafts, jewelry, and even ribbons. Some of them offer savings of up to 80 percent. Plan to wander around not only the stores on Main Street but also the nooks and crannies on the side streets and farther out from the village. If you like to shop, leave Portland rather early.

Thomaston

Instead of spending the night in Freeport I suggest you continue on to Thomaston. It's approximately 75 miles from Portland on Route 1. The drive from Portland to Thomaston is very pretty, but you won't see much "water."

Thomaston is a very small, quiet town with only one restaurant, *Harbor View Tavern* (1 Water Street, Thomaston, ME 04861; telephone [207] 354-8173), but it's a very warm and charming place. It looks out over the water and has an outside patio. Dinners range from $8.95 to $12.95 and the food is very good. There's also a small bar. It's open Monday through Saturday from 11:30 A.M. to 9:00 P.M. No place in town is open after 9:00 P.M. I had quiche, easily the best I have ever had.

You'll want to stay at the *Belvedere*, a bed and breakfast lodging at 163 Main Street; telephone (207) 354-8759 (open May 1 through October 31: single with shared bath, $27; double with shared bath, $37). The Belvedere is a gracious Victorian home that originally belonged to a sea captain. When you walk through the front door you truly feel as if you have walked through a time machine and landed in the early 1900s. It is a perfectly relaxing place to spend the evening. You'll find antiques, mementos, and knick-knacks from around the world in every room. Every nook and cranny has a beautiful piece of antique furniture that appears to have been made especially for it. The pillows and bedspreads are hand-crocheted. They even have a cat and a dog. Breakfast is served in the dining room with the other, usually very interesting, guests. While I was there I met two couples, a husband and a wife who were bicycling down the coast, and an artist and his wife.

To really get the feel of the seashore, continue down the peninsula to *Tenants Harbor*, a wonderful little seaport town. If you forgot to bring a good book for the quiet evenings, you'll find *Roseledge Books* has a great selection. Colleen Coughlin, the owner, will help you find just what you're looking for. You can sit on the steps of her porch and watch the boats in the harbor or have lunch at the *Eastwind Inn* nearby. You'll find many large and small yachts anchored in the bay while the owners enjoy this quaint little village.

Bar Harbor

At Bar Harbor, within minutes of each other, you'll find rugged, granite-faced mountains; posh dining facilities offering gourmet cuisine; wilderness forest sheltering quiet, clear lakes; a shopping district steeped in old-world charm; and the ever-present sea with its constantly changing moods and colors.

Bar Harbor is located on Mount Desert Island approximately 160 miles from Portland. From the 1840s to the 1920s, Bar Harbor slowly changed from a barely accessible, little-known island fishing village to one of the most famous "watering places" of America's elite. The first Bar Harbor hotel was opened in 1855, and by 1888, the town boasted eighteen hotels. During this period, longtime summer visitors began to buy land and construct their own cottages. The 1890s saw some 175 summer homes built in Bar Harbor, most of which were huge fanciful structures designed by top architects of the day.

By 1900, the days of primitive "rusticating" were gone forever. Bar Harbor had become a summer haven for the very wealthy, and they brought with them all the glitter, glamour, and sometimes outrageous antics that made up the fabric of their social lives.

The Depression and World War II profoundly altered the fortunes of most of Bar Harbor's summer inhabitants. While the Great Fire of 1947 destroyed a full third of Bar Harbor's 222 cottages, the fire itself was not responsible for the decline of Bar Harbor's Golden Era. By the time of the fire, many of the cottages were already empty or for sale.

Luckily, Bar Harbor has been able to gracefully survive the transition from its days of opulence to its present fame as the home of one of America's most beautiful national parks. Today, Bar Harbor offers summer visitors the natural grandeur that attracted its original visitors while retaining much of the charm of its Golden Era.

Mount Desert Island

Mount Desert Island is bordered by rugged cliffs and sand beaches, scented by tall pines, topped by lofty mountains, and colored by bustling waterfronts and cozy villages. Much of the island is a quiet, unspoiled national park. *Somes Sound*, the only true fjord on the Atlantic coast, nearly cuts the island in half as its 7-mile length slices between sheer cliffs.

Acadia National Park

On February 26, 1919, Acadia became the first national park east of the Mississippi. Acadia is a 38,523-acre preserve of luminous natural beauty situated on Mount Desert Island. While most of the sights and sounds we associate with the park come from the sea, the people who come here are not immune to the appeal of the forest, just as the people who think only of climbing Cadillac Mountain (1,530 feet, the highest point on the Atlantic coast) find themselves wondering about the strange marine world far below. Acadia has a special charm and magnetism all its own. It truly is a land that inspires poetry in the most prosaic of souls. There is room to revel in the opulence of nature at her most free and best, whatever mood may set the scene from day to day. Blue skies dip low to define islands, peninsulas, and a sea that stretches to a far horizon. Hours can be spent relaxing near the sea watching harbor porpoises, one of several kinds of whales found in Acadian waters, crest the waves in a graceful ballet, or, a little farther down the coast, harbor seals may be bobbing in the swells; with their short muzzles and gentle eyes they are puppylike in their appeal.

A very special part of Acadia National Park are the carriage roads. In 1917, John D. Rockefeller conceived the idea of constructing carriage roads as an alternative to the main road system and free from the uproar of the "infernal" combustion engine. Today, in the spirit of that tradition, park users can peacefully hike, bicycle, and ride horseback along the 46 miles of roads that wander aimlessly and delightfully through the park. One of the arms of the road breaches the talus slopes on the west bank of *Jordan Pond*, another climbs high on the shoulder of *Sargent Mountain*, then drops down to hug the shore of *Upper Hadlock Pond*, still another encircles *Eagle Lake*. Wherever the roads may lead, they gently beguile you with a sense of solitude and an appreciation of the harmony present in nature. There are sixteen stone bridges along the carriage-road system. One of the most magnificent is *Duck Brook Bridge*, a three-arch tour de force completed in 1929. Like the other bridges, it was constructed of hand-hewn granite in a long, laborious process. Rockefeller allegedly remarked that the bridges might as well have been built of diamonds for all they cost him. As you stroll across the beautiful bridges enjoying the almost palpable silence, broken only by the occasional chattering of a red squirrel or the singing of the many birds, you will agree that the results were well worth the effort and cost.

Begin your trip at the Park Visitor Center and be sure to pick up a park map and watch the fifteen-minute introductory film, *Search for Acadia*. I found the film informative and interesting. The park's most popular drive is the 27-mile Loop Road. It was constructed with the scenic views in mind and directs you to some of the most dazzling scenery: Sand beach, the cliffs past *Thunder Hole* (where the ocean waves roar into a rock crevice and shoot 40 feet into the air), *Otter Cliffs*, and *Cadillac Mountain*, which has the most spectacular view of the island. Plan a leisurely stroll along the Shore Path or the Jordan Pond self-guiding nature trail.

There is no end to the activities available in the park: boat cruises, evening slide programs, photography seminars, star gazing, nature walks covering a wide variety of topics, *Wildwood Stables* offering horseback rides, deep sea fishing excursions, trips with lobstermen, a sail through island-studded offshore waters, whale-watching trips, and, last but not least, if you're ready to cool off on a hot summer day, a quick splash at *Sand Beach*. (Beware, however, ocean temperatures rarely rise about 55 degrees.) If you prefer warmer water, try *Echo Lake*, which you can reach via State Route 102. You may obtain all the information you need regarding park activities at the Visitor Center; it's open year-round, seven days a week, from 8:00 A.M. to 8:00 P.M.

If you enjoy visiting museums, there are several that highlight Acadia's story. In the park located at Sieur de Monts Spring are the *Nature*

Center, which contains exhibits on the natural and cultural heritage of Acadia; the *Abbe Museum*, which houses an extensive collection of Maine Indian artifacts; and *Acadia Wild Gardens*, which is a spectacular formal garden of wildflowers and other plants native to the park.

If time permits take a trip to the west side—or as locals call it, the "backside"— of the island, which will take you to traditional down-east towns such as Bass Harbor and Bernard. The docks in these towns are covered with lobster traps and the harbors filled with fishing boats.

Where to Stay in Bar Harbor

Cleftstone Manor, Route 3, Eden Street, Bar Harbor, ME 04609; telephone (207) 288-4951 ($35, with shared bath to $125; 10 percent to 15 percent less for single). Cleftstone Manor is truly an oasis reflecting restful yesterdays. It is a magnificent thirty-three-room Victorian "cottage" set on a hill about a mile from downtown Bar Harbor. It's open from mid-May through mid-October. The interior of the restored mansion includes an impressive collection of fine art, antiques, imported lace curtains and wall coverings, goose-down comforters, and hand-crocheted bedspreads. After a long day you can enjoy a cozy fireside chat, a well-stacked library, chess, games, puzzles, and a countrylike stillness that soothes away daily frustrations. Tea is served every afternoon from 4:00 P.M. to 5:00 P.M.; between 8:00 P.M. and 10:00 P.M. there is complimentary wine and cheese to be enjoyed in the elegant living room by the fireplace or surrounded by luscious plants in the wicker-filled sunroom. This is a wonderful time to meet the other guests and hear about their daily activities—and possibly learn about some hidden place you have not yet explored. A stay at the Cleftstone includes a lavish breakfast of fresh fruit, juices, inn-baked breads, muffins, coffee cakes, imported English and herb teas, and hot coffee. The perfect place to enjoy your breakfast is the sunroom overlooking the beautiful grounds—and with the room itself filled with plants you feel as if you're breakfasting in a garden.

Manor House Inn, West Street, Bar Harbor, ME 04609; telephone (207) 288-3759 ($69 to $120, two-night minimum stay). A spacious, comfortable, twenty-two-room Victorian mansion situated on a tree-lined acre of land in a residential, historic district of Bar Harbor. Open mid-April through mid-November, the inn combines the convenience of an in-town location with an out-of-town atmosphere. There is an absolutely wonderful veranda running along the front and one side of the mansion. After an activity-filled day it is the perfect place to sip a cup of tea and watch the world pass by. The inn is so beautifully restored to authentic turn-of-the-century decor that you can easily become lost in the surroundings and have a moment's jolt when you see a "modern" car drive by. Each morning you will be treated to a superb continental breakfast featuring fresh native blueberry muffins, home-baked breads, fruits in season, coffee, and tea. (This is where I plan to stay when I go back.)

The Ledgelawn Inn, 66 Mount Desert Street, Bar Harbor, ME 04609; telephone (207) 288-4596 (All rates are double occupancy: $65 to $125, the Grand Suite is $145 a night; off season rates: $45 to $95). When you enter the beautiful foyer with its elegant sweeping staircase, grand fireplace, and numerous antiques, you feel as if you took a step back in time. Ledgelawn was built in 1904 and most of the furnishings are originals. Many of the rooms have working fireplaces, verandas, private entrances, and sitting areas. There is even a swimming pool and Jacuzzi, a modern-day update. The inn is conveniently located just a few blocks from the heart of Bar Harbor.

The Ledgelawn Inn Bar is open daily from 4:00 P.M. to midnight. It is located at one end of the living room and extends to the back veranda overlooking the tree-shaded backyard and carriage house. Complimentary continental breakfast is served daily from 8:00 A.M. to 10:00 A.M. in the living room and on the back veranda, and includes fresh fruit, orange juice, blueberry cake, other baked goods, hot chocolate, coffee, and tea.

Where to Eat in Bar Harbor

Parkside, corner of Main and Mount Desert streets; telephone (207) 288-3700. Open 11:00 A.M. to 9:00 P.M., the Parkside is a house turned into a restaurant. It is on the corner at the end of busy Main Street right across from a park. The outdoor seating area overlooks the park and is shaded by large oak trees and edged by low pine bushes. There is seating on the veranda running along two sides of the house. The inside is cool yet at the same time warm and charming with highly polished floors and many small eating areas.

A variety of seafood dishes are served ranging in price from $7.95 to $10.95 with several lobster specials and a nice selection of steak and chicken. The food is great and the rolls homemade.

Everything seemed a little slower paced sitting at Parkside. It is a very quiet area, yet there are people walking by to watch and children playing in the park. They are far enough away that they are seen but not heard.

Quarterdeck Restaurant, One Main Street, Bar Harbor, ME 04609; telephone (207) 288-5292. The Quarterdeck opens at 4:30 P.M. It is common in Bar Harbor not to have a set closing time; they close when there is no more business. The Quarterdeck overlooks Frenchman's Bay so you can enjoy the coming and going of a variety of boats from the Town Pier or the backdrop of the islands in the bay while you enjoy some of the finest seafood in Bar Harbor, including baked stuffed lobster, sole marguery hollandaise au supreme, scallops Kirkpatrick, or Maine lobster. Prices range from $9.95 to $12.95. There is also a good selection of steak and chicken from $7.95 to $13.95.

Galyn's Gallery, 17 Main Street, Bar Harbor, ME 04609; telephone (207) 288-9706. The restaurant opens at 11:00 A.M. This informal restaurant has a small deck from which you can look out on the bay. Located on a busy shopping street, it's a great place for people watching. The upstairs, with its small bar, is the place to be. You'll be surrounded by people and hanging plants. They have a standard menu with a lot of seafood, steaks, and chicken ($7.95 to $12) and a large lunch sandwich menu ($2.95 to $7.95). This informal restaurant seems to be a meeting place for locals, especially around 5:30 P.M. in the bar.

Things to Do in Bar Harbor

Lobster Fishing and Seal Watching Trips on the Katherine, Frenchman's Bay Boating Company, West Street, Bar Harbor; telephone (207) 288-3322. The one-and-a-half-hour trips depart Monday through Saturday, at 10:00 A.M., 12:15 P.M., 3:45 P.M., and 5:30 P.M. (Off season, call for times.) Cost: $9. The 36-foot *Katherine* carries sixteen passengers. You will learn about the lobster industry while watching the crew haul traps from the ocean floor. This cruise affords you the wonderful opportunity of seeing sea urchins, starfish, and sea cucumbers. After all the traps have been serviced, you will head for a small island to look for harbor seals who may be basking on ledges or swimming in the nearby water.

Windjammer Cruises, 1 West Street, Bar Harbor; telephone (207) 288-3322. This two-hour trip departs from Frenchman's Bay Boating Company on West Street at 9:00 A.M., 11:15 A.M., 1:30 P.M., 4:00 P.M., and 6:15 P.M. Cost: $13.50. On this very special cruise you will sail through the sparkling waters of Frenchman's Bay standing on the foredeck of *Bay Lady II* with the breeze blowing through your hair and the sound of the wind in the rigging. You'll pass the granite shores of the Porcupine Islands and the majesty of Cadillac Mountain rising from the sea. Beer, wine, and soda are sold on board.

Other cruises available include a naturalist cruise (two hours), sightseeing (one or two hours), VIP sightseeing (two and a half hours), sunset cruise (one hour), and a half-day deep-sea fishing cruise (four and a half hours). There is something to fit everyone's taste and schedule. I suggest you stop by Frenchman's Bay Boating Company on West Street next to the Municipal Pier or call for all the brochures explaining the various cruises. Prices range from $5 to $7.75 and $15 for the half-day fishing cruise.

Coastal Kayaking Tours, P.O. Box 45, 48 Cottage Street, Bar Harbor; telephone (207) 288-5483. There is nothing quite like exploring the surf-laced beaches and the glacier-carved shorelines of the coastal islands firsthand. The waters of Mount Desert Island are ideally suited for travel and exploration by sea kayak. With miles and miles of protected coastline and many offshore islands, the paddling opportunities are endless. There is no need to be concerned if you have never set foot, or seat, in a kayak. Before you depart, you'll receive expert instruction on kayak navigation. The large, stable, one- and two-person kayaks, which are equipped with rudders, make paddling easy and fun to learn.

You'll find being a participant rather than a passenger will make this the highlight of your trip to Bar Harbor. As you glide across the clear waters you'll see an inspiring view of Maine's rugged coastline that few people ever experience; a close-up view of porpoises, seals, shore birds, and, if you're lucky, even a whale. You'll also see the magnificent oceanfront mansions that are not visible from the roadside. On one of our island stops we spent some time beachcombing for shells.

You can take a half-day tour, an early-morning sunrise tour, or special naturalist tours. The tours generally run $24 a person per day with a double kayak. If you would like to explore on your own, you can rent a kayak for $20 for a single and $25 for a double per day. The staff at Coastal Tours will be glad to help you select a place to paddle; however, they restrict rental kayaks to freshwater areas. It is important to make reservations at least one day in advance.

Bluenose Ferry to Yarmouth

Book your ferry trip through your travel agent or the Canadian National Railways office. The trip will cost $31 during the high season. Low season rates, which begin mid-September, are $23.25 per person. This six-hour crossing to Yarmouth begins with an all-you-can-eat buffet breakfast after which you are free to see a movie, have a drink at the bar, try your luck at the casino, stroll the decks, or visit the outdoor lounge to soak up some sun before you dig into the buffet luncheon.

Yarmouth

You'll have the evening and night free to explore Yarmouth. As the gateway to Nova Scotia, Yarmouth is a refreshing resort town with scenic drives in every direction. The *Golf Club*, established in 1904, is noted for its turf on fairways and greens. They welcome visitors.

The first English settled here in 1761, although there had been French explorers at this picturesque site prior to that time. The stone fences surrounding the area farms seem to have existed for centuries and will likely remain for centuries to come. In addition to herds of cattle, you'll find fields of strawberries that supply nearby cities.

Don't miss the museum on Collins Street run by the Yarmouth Historical Society. The display includes a carved, inscribed Runic stone suggesting that the Norse explorer Leif Eriksson visited these shores centuries before Columbus.

June to September you'll see the fleet of fifty or more herring seiners leave the public wharf at Yarmouth and file out to sea. You need not rise early; they don't depart until 7:00 P.M.

Where to Stay at Yarmouth

The Prince of Funde Cruise Company, P.O. Box 4216, Station A, Portland, ME 04101; telephone (800) 341-7540, will include your hotel in their package. Ask them for details.

Grand Hotel, 417 Main Street, Yarmouth, Nova Scotia; telephone (902) 724-2446 (single US$68 to US$83, double US$77 to US$92). On Main Street, only five minutes from the ferry terminal, the location of this hotel is ideal. I'd suggest paying a little more and getting their upgraded "Echelon" room. They have one of the better restaurants in town as well as a coffee shop and a lounge with live entertainment Monday through Saturday. Ask for a room with a harbor view.

Rodd's Colony Harbor Inn, 6 Forest Street, Yarmouth, Nova Scotia; telephone (902) 742-9194 (single US$62, double US$73). The inn is located just up from the ferry terminal. The lounge (*Hawthorns*) with recorded music and restaurant with a large selection of seafoods are popular with the locals.

Prince of Funde Cruise from Yarmouth to Portland

The trip back is a real bargain. Depending on the time of year, it will cost between $34 (economy cabin, May through June 19) to $65 (cabin with private bath, June 20 through September 24). Prince of Funde Cruises, Inc., offers fourteen tour options ranging from this twelve-hour cruise to a full week of sailing. Check with them when planning your trip. You may decide you'd like to spend more time aboard ship.

Leaving late morning, on your return daytime sail from Yarmouth, you can sit on deck and enjoy the sea breeze, relax in the lounge, or enjoy the entertainment, which includes a casino, on this luxury ship, the M/S *Scotia Prince*. You can even watch a feature movie. Enjoy a late breakfast or an early afternoon buffet. You'll arrive in Portland in the early evening.

Your New England vacation is over. You have seen the beauty of the Maine coast and you have rested in the former home of a sea captain. You have spent time removed from the stress and strain of your everyday routine. Refreshed and restored, you are once again in control, ready to conquer the world.

CHAPTER 9

Special Interest Trips

A FLAMENCO DANCE TOUR OF SPAIN

▶─────────────────────────────────▶

GENERAL AMBIANCE	★ ★ ★
SOCIAL CLIMATE	★ ★
ACTIVITIES	★ ★

FOR TOUR ARRANGEMENTS CONTACT:
National Tour Office of Spain
Water Tower Place, Suite 915
East 845 N. Michigan Avenue
Chicago, IL 60611
(312) 944-0215

Or *contact your travel agent*

▶─────────────────────────────────▶

*F*lamenco is not just a type of Spanish dancing, as many people believe. It is an outward expression of a philosophy and a way of life. So the best way to understand the Spanish is to understand flamenco. In addition to reading about flamenco, the best way to understand it is to spend time in Spain and, of course, to learn to dance flamenco yourself.

While some instructors can be found in the States, the best are still found in Madrid and Sevilla. This trip begins in Madrid with lessons at one of the oldest schools of flamenco. On the way to Sevilla for more lessons, stops to enjoy the culture and the wonders of Spain in Toledo, Jaén, Granada, Torremolinos, Marbella, Ronda, and Arcos de la Frontera are suggested. Returning to Madrid, stops in Zafra, Trujillo, Salamanca, and Ávila will round out your understanding of the country and the people of Spain.

The Beginning of Flamenco

Flamenco as an art form, as well as a way of life, appears to have come about in response to the Spanish Inquisition in the sixteenth century. As persecuted peoples, the Jews, Muslims, and Gypsies were expelled from Spain by the Christians. Those Gypsies who remained were forbidden to speak their language, to practice their religion, or to live nomadic, "unproductive" life-styles. Many fled to the hills of Andalusia, the southern region encompassing Sevilla. It was here that "flamenco" developed—and flourishes today.

At the time of the Inquisition, Arabic was a common language in Andalusia. The Arabic term *felagmengu*, meaning "fugitive peasant," was applied to the people hiding in the hills. Music and dance was the way they expressed their suffering. In Spain today, though you will see non-Gypsies performing, only a real Gypsy who has grown up within the life-style is accepted as having real *gracia*, real passion of expression.

Flamenco, much as the bullfight, serves as a means for commoners to break free of their daily burdens and routine; it is also a reminder of the past and of the Gypsies' acceptance of their life-style. The vibrant and explosive flamenco music and dance, much like the Gypsy life-style, excites the imagination with its fluidity, grace, and lack of attachment. The Gypsies of today have retained an admirable lack of respect for material possessions. They perform for the essentials. In good times, a Gypsy family may perform for a week and earn enough to live and play for a month. To a Gypsy it seems as if non-Gypsies work all of their lives for things they don't need or really want.

General Ambiance

Spain is a country with considerable charm and beauty, which any tourist can see. However, through your contact with the Gypsies in your dance lessons you will have the unique opportunity to gain a feel for the country at a deeper and more enriching level.

The beautiful Spanish cities such as Sevilla are enrapturing all in themselves. When you add the spell of schoolgirls spontaneously dancing Sevillanas (a flamenco folk dance) to Gypsy guitar music, you are transported, drawn into the spirit of the country and nearer to the heart of the people.

Activities

This section focuses on flamenco. While dance lessons are, of course, recommended as the best way to learn Gypsy culture, you could certainly choose to just travel the route and watch the dancers instead of becoming an active participant. Arcos de la Frontera is an excellent place to exchange your dancing shoes for riding boots for a while, if you are so inclined.

You will find your days and weeks filled with the enchantment of Spain, from the cosmopolitan capital of Madrid with all the excitement of a major world metropolis, to the carefree holiday atmosphere of the Costa del Sol, the "coast of the sun," where you can bask in the sun as the long stretches of golden beaches beckon you with the sound of the surf and the warmth of the sand beneath your bare feet.

You'll find the hillside villages replete with the history of the ages. Time is itself breached as you enter castles and monasteries of the past, now parador hotels. You'll walk the streets Velázquez, Cervantes, and El Greco once trod. In Jaén you may even sleep in the same bed in which de Gaulle once slept.

Bullfights

If you've never seen a bullfight, I'd recommend you see one here. It is much more than a sport or a contest of equals. The bullfight is a central part of the cultural and artistic expression of the Spanish. It is a tragedy of death, and while there is danger for the matador, sometimes even death, it is the bull who is sacrificed.

Bullfights take place from early spring until mid-October. You can see them in the ancient bullring in Ronda or the beautiful Plaza de los Toros in Madrid. Sevilla has one of the most famous bullrings. The tickets are sold according to areas: *sol* (sun), *sombra* (shade), or *sol y sombra* (part sun, part shade). The seats in the shade are, of course, the most expensive, but on a hot day it's worth the extra expense.

The fight begins with a spectacular parade. All the participants are present, the picadors on horseback, the banderilleros on foot, and the matadors with their elaborate costumes. An afternoon usually includes six bulls, killed by three matadors.

Social Climate

Spanish men, unfortunately, still find it necessary to reinforce their macho, their sense of their own manhood, by not letting a woman walk by unscrutinized. I find the usual catcalls and whistles of American construction workers difficult enough to endure, but nothing equals the hissing of the Spanish. It takes quite a while to get used to their behavior. For the most part, the men behave in a manner they have come to believe is expected. Getting angry or upset is only a waste of energy; so as long as they didn't pinch (at least I was not pinched in Spain), I could ignore them and continue on my way.

Acceptable within the Spanish culture as a way to call a waiter or to get someone's attention, *pssst*, while at first rather offensive, becomes commonplace. Though I personally could not bring myself to use it to catch a waiter's attention, after having been in Spain a few weeks there were times I at least considered it. I had to keep reminding myself that this hissing was not disrespectful. Put into the proper cultural perspective, it was mainly a way to get someone's attention.

Spain is one of those countries in which it is helpful to speak a little of the native language. While you can certainly "get by" without speaking Spanish, your trip will be greatly enriched if you're able to communicate with the locals, even if only with a very basic vocabulary. I recommend taking a course in conversational Spanish from a local community college prior to your trip as well as listening to language tapes on your way to and from work.

The Spanish are not as sensitive as the French to a foreigner who does not try to speak their language. It is not crucial to them that you try their language before they will speak yours. However, fewer Spaniards than French know English. It's always best to try the few foreign language words you know, no matter how limited your ability may be. It will make the natives more comfortable trying their few words of English. With a lot of sign language mixed in, you'll probably do just fine.

The men, women, and children of Spain are warm and friendly. They are a charming and welcoming people as a group, greatly adding to the enjoyment of a visit.

When to Go

April, May, and October, though high season and, therefore, more expensive, are the best months to travel in Spain. June, July, August, and even early September, though the rates are the lowest, can be unbearably hot. March and late September are good times to take advantage of moderate rates and still avoid the hottest weather. Late September and October is the best time to catch the master flamenco dancers in Madrid teaching classes, having returned from dance tours.

Preparing for Your Trip to Spain

Documents

You need a valid passport in order to enter Spain, but a visa is not necessary for an American citizen. There is no tax to either enter or depart Spain.

What to Take

Although you'll only need the bottom half of your two-piece bathing suit on the Costa del Sol, throughout the rest of Spain you'll find the people dress very conservatively. A short-sleeved, loose-fitting dress or slacks (not shorts, except at the coastal resorts) and a blouse will do well day or night. More risqúe attire may be misinterpreted by Spanish men as reflecting your character. You'll also want shoes in which you can literally walk miles.

For your dance lessons you'll need a short-sleeved leotard top, short cotton socks, a long full cotton skirt (if it's polka dot with a ruffle or two at the bottom, you'll look just like a native), and flamenco shoes (you can buy these in Madrid).

I also highly recommend taking along two books: *Iberia* by James Michener and *The Art of Flamenco* by D. E. Pohren.

Money

Your best rate of exchange will always be obtained at a bank. Hotels, while convenient, usually give a slightly lower rate and airports often give the poorest. There is a fee charged for changing money at most places. It may vary from US$1 to US$3 for each US$100 changed. You will, of course, also get less when you change your pesetas back to dollars as you leave the country. Since you will need pesetas for your cab from the airport, you may want to buy some before leaving home. The conversion rate used in this section is 140 pesetas (Pts) per dollar.

Getting There

The primary air carrier to Spain is Iberia, though Aviaco has a number of charter flights. I suggest a direct flight to Madrid, avoiding flights that stop in Malaga for customs before continuing on to Madrid. Don't be surprised if your Iberia flight attendant appears to be Don Quixote reincarnated instead of your usually smiling stewardess—mine had to have been.

Getting Around

Once in Spain the best way to get around the country, especially to the castle paradors, is by rental car. You'll need your U.S. driver's license and a major credit card in order to rent a car, even if you intend to pay for it with cash. It's also a good idea to have an International Driver's License. The smaller car rental companies sometimes require one. The major companies—such as Hertz, Avis, and Budget—have a number of offices in Madrid. You should, however, make a reservation for a car before leaving home in order to take advantage of the lower rates. For just over US$100 per week plus 33 percent tax and insurance, you can get a car with unlimited mileage. Gas will cost another US$2, or thereabouts, per liter. You'll find the Spanish drive much as they wait in lines—everyone pushing in from every direction. Yet somehow they seem to avoid accidents. Don't expect other drivers to let you into traffic. Unless you're lucky and get another tourist, you could wait all day. When in Spain, drive like the Spanish.

You don't need a car in Madrid. The Metro and bus system is excellent and inexpensive (Metro 40 Pts and bus 35 Pts).

A taxi from the airport to a downtown hotel in Madrid should cost about 1,000 Pts (about US$7). The tip is included; like the cab fee, it is regulated by the government. Insist that the driver leave you at the door of your hotel. A favorite trick is to drop you at the corner out of sight of the hotel doorman and then try to charge you much more than the going rate.

Treasures to Purchase

Leave your expensive jewelry at home. Flashy costume jewelry or pink coral and gold jewelry sold throughout Spain is what the Gypsies wear. Although this jewelry can be expensive (20,000 Pts to 65,000 Pts), it does make a wonderful souvenir.

Spanish pottery, unique to each region of the country, also makes an excellent purchase. The *Galerias Preciados* in Madrid has a wide selection from the various areas, as well as Lladro porcelain statues and leather goods. To get to Galerias Preciados take the Metro to Puerta del Sol, go up the Calle de Preciados (a walking mall), past El

Corte Ingles (a large department store with everything from castanets and shawls to toilet articles). The cool air blowing out the front door of El Corte Ingles can be very inviting, drawing you inward. The front door of the Galerias will be farther up the mall on your right on the corner of Calle Romanos.

If you continue down Calle Romanos to number 14 (about two blocks) you will be at *Menkes*. Menkes sells flamenco shoes for around 9,000 Pts. They are either black or dyed to match your dress, with a round toe, 2-inch heels, and an elastic strap over your foot. Menkes will also make your flamenco skirt from a selection of fabric available.

You'll often find Gypsies playing flamenco folk songs on the guitar and serenading you while you wander around this mall. A rest stop on one of the many mall benches will quickly put you in the flamenco mood. A couple of 5 Pts coins will keep them singing.

To have a flamenco dress made to order, contact Keiko Watanabe, Calle Ayala 156, Madrid 9, Spain. She'll charge around US$300. You can also wait and purchase a flamenco dress when you get to Sevilla at Creaciones Maricruz, on the corner of Calle Cuna and Calle Orpesa just off the Plaza de Salvador. They will cost 35,000 Pts to 40,000 Pts. While you'll prefer a skirt for your classes, these dresses are a wonderful luxury.

Where to Stay in Spain

While I suggest accommodations, the Spanish Tourist Bureau publishes an extensive official *Spanish Hotel Guide* that you can buy for 475 Pts. It is a very useful aid, and can be obtained by writing the National Tourist Office of Spain, Water Tower Place, Suite 915, 845 North Michigan Avenue, Chicago, IL 60611.

Whenever possible, I suggest staying at a parador, which is a hotel run by the Spanish government. Most are historic sites located in the older, more interesting parts of town. Many are often restored castles or monasteries. They are moderately priced (7,000 Pts to 8,000 Pts), the food is consistently excellent and so are the facilities. I found them especially comfortable when traveling alone. They were a safe, often luxurious refuge at the end of the day where I could relax and have everything necessary easily accessible. Your parador reservations can be made by writing the National Tourist Office of Spain, Water Tower Place, Suite 915, 845 North Michigan Avenue, Chicago, IL 60611. Some fill up far in advance, so write as early as possible.

A proper tip for having your luggage taken to your room is 100 Pts.

A Change of Schedule

I've never had such an easy time adjusting to the daily schedule as I did in Spain. I actually found jet lag to be an advantage. While the shops open early and the hotels serve breakfast from about 7:30 A.M. until 10:30 A.M., anyone who can will probably sleep late. The stores close and the restaurants open for the large afternoon meal from 2:00 P.M. until 5:00 P.M. (the hottest part of the day). The shops then open again and stay open until around 9:00 P.M.

About the time we Americans are ready for dinner (5:00 to 6:00 P.M.), the restaurants are just finishing serving the afternoon meal. Except for *tapas* (hors d'oeuvres) served with drinks, there's no food available until late at night. Eight to 10:00 in the evening is the time for drinks and *tapas* before dinner, which is usually eaten after 10:00 P.M. The time to go to the disco is after midnight. They stay open and active until 3:00 or 4:00 A.M. Most flamenco *tablados* have an early show at 9:00 P.M. (for the tourists) and a later show at 11:00 P.M. for the Spanish.

Spanish Cuisine

There are a number of specialties you won't want to miss while you're in Spain. A typical Spanish breakfast will include coffee, hot chocolate, and *churros*, much like long doughnuts.

For lunch I'd suggest you try the *entremés*, an assortment of hors d'oeuvres. They will be different everywhere you go. Some will be hot, others cold. They are often very small portions of salads, a fish or egg dish, vegetables, or meats.

If you get hungry before the restaurant opens for dinner, the *tapas*, hors d'oeuvres, served in bars with a drink will tide you over. Each bar will have its own specialty. It's perfectly acceptable for women to stop in Spanish bars alone. You'll meet many Spanish women there alone, too. If you stick to the community bars in Madrid, avoiding the more popular tourist stops, you'll find you can get a great glass of Spanish wine (the red is the best) or beer, *cerveza*, and some *tapas* for 21 cents. Try a side order of *calamar* (squid). It's excellent. Sherry (*vino de Jerez*) is also a popular before-dinner drink.

Save room for dinner because the Spanish cuisine is great. The *paella*, a saffron rice dish filled with seafood, is a specialty of Andalusia. Try it while you're in Sevilla. *Rape* (angler fish) is a sweet ocean fish that's popular in much of Spain. *Langosta* (lobster) is also available prepared more creatively than in most American restaurants. Trout Navarre is also a popular dish, prepared by stuffing the trout with bacon or ham.

You'll find the pastries are not nearly as sweet as in France or even Germany, except for *flan*, an egg-custard with burnt caramel sauce that is always a great way to end a meal.

EXPLORING SPAIN

▶ ──────────────────────────────────── ▶

Madrid

Madrid became the capital of Spain in 1606. Today, Madrid, with a population of 4 million, is still the center of Spain. All of the main roads radiate out from kilometer "0" in Madrid's Puerta del Sol. While Sevilla remains the heart of flamenco, many excellent dancers and teachers are today located in Madrid, making it a great city from which to begin a flamenco tour of Spain.

Where to Stay in Madrid

Palace Hotel, Plaza de las Cortes, 7.28014 (single 12,500 Pts, double 16,500 Pts). Conveniently located across from the Prado, this five-star hotel is, in my opinion, *the* place to stay in Madrid. While luxurious, it is not stuffy. Its breathtaking stained-glass dome lounge and select shops, boutiques, and restaurants are charming. It also houses an Iberia Airlines office, making flight confirmations or changes convenient.

Hotel Ritz, Plaza de la Lealtad, 5.28014 (single 22,000 Pts to 28,000 Pts, double 28,000 Pts to 40,000 Pts). If you don't mind paying the price, this is considered one of the top hotels in Europe. It is elegantly appointed with carved marble staircases and a lovely garden for afternoon tea (US$5). As one might expect, the clientele is primarily a part of the old establishment.

Hotel Emperatriz, Calle Lopez de Hoyos, 4.18014 (single 7,500 Pts, double 8,525 Pts). This four-star hotel, though not as elegant as the above, is comfortable and attractive. It is conveniently located on a main bus route and is still a short cab ride or a long walk to the Prado.

Flamenco in Madrid

Flamenco tablados. There are a number of flamenco *tablados* in Madrid. The best is probably the *Corral de Moreria*, at Calle de Moreria 17, where Blanca del Rey dances. For 1,700 Pts you get a drink of your choice and an incredible show. Dinner is also available if you want to come early and eat. Most entrées are from 1,000 Pts to 2,000 Pts plus another 1,600 Pts for the show. I'd suggest dinner elsewhere and a drink at the cafe outside on the cliff overlooking the palace, the red-tile roofs of the suburbs of Madrid, and the tree-covered hills beyond (Calle de Bailen). Other excellent flamenco *tablados* include *Las Brujas*, *Arcado Cuchilleros*, and *Los Canasteros*.

Flamenco Dance Lessons in Madrid

Taking classes in Madrid is a wonderful way to get to know the people. Not only will you meet Gypsies and Spaniards, but you'll also meet Canadians, Japanese, and other Americans who have come to learn from the masters. Some came years ago and decided to stay, others will have but a few days or weeks. If you're lucky, you'll be invited to a *juerga*, a flamenco party, where you can really experience the spirit of flamenco.

To get to the flamenco school in Madrid where many of the masters began and others now teach, take the Metro to *Anton-Martin* in the old part of the city. Walk down Calle del Amor de Dios about half a block to number 4 (on your left). You'll find large brown doors with brass handles and wooden planks well worn by generations of flamenco dancers, some of whom have gone on to great fame. It was in this school that Carmen was first spotted by Antonio Cades.

Once inside, go through the black doors on your right. The small office, may be empty, but you'll hear the sounds of castanets, flamenco music, and the heels of flamenco shoes snapping just beyond. A bulletin board lists the classes and instructors. Classes typically cost 3,000 Pts a week—one hour a day—with a master such as El Ciro or La Tati. It will cost 2,000 Pts a week for a less well known instructor. You can also arrange for private lessons—one hour will cost around 2,000 Pts. Check the going rate with the Spanish students in your class; some instructors like to charge foreigners more.

I would suggest you take a combination of private and group classes from various instructors. Start with a couple of private lessons before joining the group classes. In the group lessons, the steps are not always broken down into their parts. If you've had no previous experience, you may soon find yourself lost. While some instructors will speak a little English, not all do. You should take your level of Spanish into consideration before choosing an instructor. This is one of the reasons it's best to learn some Spanish before leaving home.

New students are expected to stand at the back of the class. Most classes have mixed levels, so the better students will be up front. You may find a rare class geared toward beginners. In Madrid, Merche Esmeralda, Maria Magdalena, and Ciro seem the best for beginners. Paco Romano is an excellent instructor, but he tends to be easily frustrated by slow learners and loses his temper. If this should happen, remember it is *his* problem, and don't take it personally. It's part of their accepted cultural style.

After Class

Madrid has much to offer both after hours and between classes. Get a good map and explore the wonders of this incredible city. Don't miss the *Rastro* (flea market) on Sunday morning near the Puerta Toledo along part of the old wall of Madrid. It goes on forever. If you are selective you can find some handcrafts for a good price. To get there take the Metro to the Molina stop. A walk through the *Parque del Retiro* (Retiro Park) with its gardens, lakes, and sidewalk artists is also a wonderful way to spend a morning or afternoon. The *Prado Museum* can best be seen in a number of short visits so as not to become overwhelmed. Don't miss Picasso's *Guernica*, housed in a separate building next to the Retiro Park in back of the main Prado building.

While Madrid has many beautiful boulevards and plazas well worth a visit, one of my favorites for sitting and relaxing is the *Plaza de Mayor* with the Gypsy women dressed in black who sell flowers, read palms, and predict good fortune. While you're there, don't miss the caves near the plaza. Once hideouts of the *bandoleros*, they now house restaurants and bars such as *Luis Candelas*. You may even see a modern-day *bandolero*, complete with musket, wandering about. These are excellent places for drinks and *tapas* between 8:00 P.M. and 10:00 P.M.

The *Bar Moka* near the school is a favorite place for the dancers to stop for a drink after the exhaustion of classes. There are also a plethora of small neighborhood bars where you can get a glass of *tinto* (red wine) and *tapas*, the house hors d'oeuvre, for 30 Pts (that's about 20 cents). This wine is good and you get "the feel" of the neighborhood as well.

Madrid to Sevilla

If you leave Madrid early you can stop and see both Toledo and Consuegra, then overnight to Jaén. Toledo, one of the most beautiful cities in Spain, is only about an hour from Madrid on Highway N401.

Toledo

Toledo was the capital for a millennium, and few cities in Europe can match its beauty or historic significance. The cathedral, with its paintings by El Greco, Goya, Rubens, and Van Dyck among others, is well worth the visit alone, as is the *Alcazar* fortress, with its unmatched sense of history and survival. There's much more to see in Toledo, and if you can, you may want to spend a day or two.

Consuegra

If you continue from Toledo on Highway C400, you will pass the windmills on the hill near Consuegra in the region of La Mancha. Stately and forlorn, they stand alone on a hill near the ruins of a castle. While you see windmills in other parts of the region, those of Consuegra offer a special magic and mystery. These are the long-armed giants Don Quixote once challenged.

Jaén

Spending the night at the castle parador in Jaén (pronounced Hine) is well worth the 335-kilometer drive from Madrid. In the spring, the highway is lined with bright red poppies and the brilliant green of the wine vineyards and olive groves. The deep red earth of the region makes an incredible backdrop for the whitewashed haciendas with their red-tile roofs. The road cuts through sheer red rock cliffs as it winds up from the fields into the mountains on the way to Jaén.

Plan your trip in order to arrive in time for dinner at the castle parador perched on top of the hill with its commanding view of the valley below. For 2,200 Pts you can sample a number of dishes. The combination of castle ambiance with tapestries dating from 1285 and Andalusian cuisine make it a meal you should not miss. The parador itself is part of recent history as well as ancient history. It was a favorite holiday stop for de Gaulle. If you're lucky you may even get the room in which he stayed.

After a walk through the castle, the fragrant pine trees, and a buffet breakfast at the parador, you can continue on to Seville by way of Granada.

Granada

While the *Alhambra* of Granada, its gardens and royal residence, are well worth a visit, the town below is congested. I suggest following the signs through town to *Parador San Francisco* located within the Alhambra. Don't park partway up in the park, though the Gypsies will try to get you to do so. Continue following the signs to the parador. You can park there without being hassled by Gypsies—and without having to walk the rest of the way up the hill. If you can't get into the parador here and still want to spend the night, try the *Hotel American* just next door, also within the old walls. It is a quaint hotel and not really American at all. You'll need to make reservations a couple of weeks in advance.

Granada to the Costa del Sol. From the hills of Granada you descend to the Mediterranean Sea and the sandy beaches of the Costa del Sol. Málaga is easily accessible with an international airport just out of town, but even in the off season it will likely be very congested. I suggest you skip it in favor of either Torremolinos or Marbella.

Torremolinos

While Torremolinos is more like the coast of Florida than the sleepy fishing village of days past, it has inviting sandy beaches. The *Parador de Golf* in Torremolinos is surrounded by its own golf course, which provides more privacy. Its beach is usually deserted except for a few fishermen with 10- to 12-foot poles propped in the sand, the lines far out in the surf. It's a short 10- to 15-minute walk into town along the beach, although once in the midst of the crowds, I found myself anxious to return to the quiet of the beach in front of the parador.

Torremolinos also has quite good flamenco *tablados*. *Taberna Flamenca Pepe Lopez* on the Plaza de la Gamba Alegre in the center of town has interesting folk dances in addition to flamenco and is worth the visit.

Marbella

Marbella, just a short drive farther down the coast, is truly the playground of the jet set. The *Puerto Banus* with its designer shops and cafe-lined harbor is an interesting place to spend an afternoon people watching and looking out over the yachts and masts of sailboats in the harbor.

This is also a great place to splurge and spend a few nights in one of the five-star luxury resorts, such as the *Marbella Club*, *Los Monteros*, or the *Don Carlos*. For around 15,000 Pts to 30,000 Pts (US$100 to US$200) a night, you can bathe topless in the hot Mediterranean sun, swim in the pool overlooking the sea or the sea itself, and play golf or tennis with the rich and famous. The Don Carlos is the European headquarters of the Women's Tennis Association. Such tennis greats as Billie Jean King, Catherine Tanvier, and Andrea Temesuar and Spanish pros play in tournaments here and often offer clinics.

Ronda

While you'll probably not want to leave the luxury of the Costa del Sol, a stop in Ronda will make your departure more palatable. This ancient city up in the barren mountains has somehow retained its character and avoided the inevitable urban sprawl now outside of Toledo. If you get there early you'll miss the tour buses arriving from Sevilla, and you can wander through the well-worn streets of the town with the schoolchildren. It's a great place for a late breakfast on your way to the castle parador of Arcos de la Frontera to spend the night.

Arcos de la Frontera

The well-maintained castle parador, with its magnificent view of the old town walls and cathedral, is the highlight of Arcos, unless you like horseback riding. If so, you may decide to spend a few days and take individual or group lessons at the riding school *El Tesorillo* just out of town. Evelyn Gross, who speaks English, is the person to contact (telephone 959–70–1359).

Sevilla

Sevilla is the heart of flamenco and by far the most beautiful city in Spain, if not all of Europe. The boulevards and the crescent-shaped Plaza de España, erected in 1929 for the international exposition, far surpassed the grandeur I had anticipated. The numerous parks and formal gardens with fountains and small waterways are a wonderful refuge from the heat of the afternoon. By far the most intriguing and most unique area is the Barrio Santa Cruz, the former Jewish quarter with its narrow, cobblestoned streets between whitewashed stucco buildings and flowers everywhere.

Where to Stay in Sevilla

Hotel Alfonso XIII, San Fernando 2 (single 12,000 Pts, double 18,000 Pts). If you are looking for elegance and grandeur, this five-star hotel is the place to stay in Sevilla. More like a Moorish palace than a hotel, the inner courtyard is filled with tropical plants and surrounded by the marble floors and mosaic-tile walls of the lobby. The high carved wooden-beam ceilings continue through the lobby and into the elegant formal dining room and library areas. Its fair-sized pool is next to the hotel's own formal rose gardens with numerous orange trees for shade.

Doña Maria, Calle Don Remondo 19 (single 4,000 Pts to 7,000 Pts, double 7,000 Pts to 11,000 Pts). If you want a more intimate though still luxurious setting, the four-star Doña Maria near the cathedral is a remarkable find. For a relatively modest price you can spend the hot afternoons enjoying a view of the cathedral and Giralda tower from the small but refreshing rooftop pool.

Hotel Murillo, Lope de Rueda 7, Rueda (single 2,000 Pts to 3,000 Pts, double 3,200 Pts to 5,400 Pts). There are a number of small hotels in the Barrio Santa Cruz such as the quaint Hotel Murillo. This comfortable two-star hotel is located just a few doors from the pension where Ramone Barroll lives and teaches flamenco dance. Since the streets are much too narrow for a car, your luggage will have to be carried or brought in on a pushcart.

Flamenco in Sevilla

Flamenco tablados. Sevilla has no problem in attracting the very best flamenco dancers. *Los Gallos* at 11 Plaza Santa Cruz in the Barrio de Santa Cruz is one of the best shows in town (1,600 Pts for entrance and one drink). Shows are at 9:00 P.M. and 11:00 P.M. and both are crowded. This is also an excellent place to watch the dancers and then request private lessons from your favorite. (Most dancers teach for the extra income.) Both Ramone Barroll and Manola Marin often dance here.

Another excellent *tablado* is *El Arenal*, located near the bullring at 7 Calle Rodo (1,600 Pts for entrance and one drink). If you arrive early, stop at El Mason on the corner for *tapas* (hors d'oeuvres) and *tinto* (red wine). You'll look out onto the walls of the bullring and be surrounded by pictures of famous bullfighters from the past. You'll also see a good show at *El Patio Sevillano*, 11–A Paseo Cristobal Colon, for 1,700 Pts.

Flamenco Dance Lessons

Ramone Barroll will give you a private lesson for 2,000 Pts an hour in the courtyard of his pension. His landlady will clap, applaud, and yell *olé* when you do especially well (Lope de Rueda 12, telephone 217695).

If you'd prefer a group lesson, Manola Marin has an especially attractive dance studio located across the river in Triana, where many Gypsies now live. Here you can join an hour and a half lesson for 500 Pts or take a whole week of lessons for 2,000 Pts. The dance studios, with their white stucco and mirrored walls and unfinished wood floors, look out onto a small private courtyard—an especially pleasant setting when you add the live flamenco guitar to which you will be dancing. Manolo's Academia de Baile is located at Rodrigo de Triana 30. To get there go across the Bridge de Triana. Park your car by the river as the street you will want to go up is one way in the wrong direction. Continue up the Calle Jacinto and take the second left onto Rodrigo de Triana. It's one long block down on your right (telephone 340519).

After Class

In addition to trying the *tapas* and *tinto* or watching flamenco, you should see the sights of Sevilla. The *Alcazar*, with its Islamic palace built in the fifteenth century and incredible formal gardens and pools, is a pleasant spot to spend the hottest part of the day. The fragrance of roses and orange trees is often enhanced by the sound of flamenco guitar being played for local schoolgirls, who may well dance a Servillanas for you in the ancient garden under the 400-year-old magnolia tree.

With its history and intrigue, the *Barrio de Santa Cruz* was my favorite area in which to wander. It is scattered with shops and restaurants where you can stop for a refreshing drink. The *Museo de Bellas Artes* is an important stop, especially Salle VI with its red, white, and gray marble floors and elaborately decorated dome ceilings and paint-ings by Velázquez and Bartolome Esteban.

In addition to the *Plaza de España*, the *Plaza de América*, and the *Park Maria Luisa*, don't miss the *Cathedral* and *La Giralda Tower*, the *Tower of Gold* along the river, the *bullring* (one of the most beautiful in Spain), and, of course, the previous Tobacco Factory, now the *University of Sevilla*, where, in Bizet's opera, Carmen worked.

For an especially relaxing afternoon, take the boat from the *Tower of Gold* up the Guadalquivir River past the *Sevilla Yacht Club* and the shipyards. Sevilla was once Spain's major port. Cádiz has now taken over the honor, but large vessels still make their way up to Sevilla. For 600 Pts, the hour ride on the cool river is a refreshing bargain.

There is no shortage of restaurants in Sevilla. My favorites were the small establishments sprinkled throughout and around the Barrio de Santa Cruz. *El Diamante* (Calle Meson del Moro 10) has an in-credible buffet from 2:00 P.M. to 9:00 P.M. for 450 Pts that includes a variety of fish and salads, as well as fruit. Nearby is the *Meson El Tenorio* (Calle Meson del Moro 16) and the *Meson Don Raimundo*. Both offer a lunch menu that ranges in price from 400 Pts to 1,000 Pts. My favorite, however, was Antonia Miranda's *Restaurant Giralda* (Calle Justino de Neve 9), very near to the wall of the Alcazar. Antonia, a real treat herself, makes a good paella (400 Pts), and one of the best flans I've eaten (only 50 Pts).

Just down the wall is another favorite stop for a drink or a meal, the *Alfaro Restaurant* (Calle Lopez de Rueda 4). With outdoor seating beside the gardens, this was an especially good place for people watch-ing.

The *Rio Grande* restaurant (Calle Betis 70) is across the Guadalqui-vir River in Triana, the Gypsy area. It has an outdoor bar on the side of the hill overlooking the river. It's a wonderful place for a drink and *tapas* in the afternoon, although a complete dinner for 1,500 Pts is a much better buy.

Sevilla to Madrid

Zafra

Approximately two hours (135 kilometers) north of Sevilla on High-way N630 in the province of Extremadura is the town of Zafra. The *Parador Hernan Cortez* located here is a peaceful, quiet place to spend the night (3,500 Pts to 4,036 Pts, breakfast is another 600 Pts). It is situated in an old castle with a plant-filled courtyard and small pool. The old castle walls form one side of the pool. The small town square near the parador, the sidewalk cafes, and the *Plaza de Toros* of Zafra just beyond make it a pleasant place to wander in the afternoon.

Mérida

Continue north on N630 another 62 kilometers and you'll enter Mérida, the best preserved Roman ruins in Spain. The *Roman amphi-theater and bridge* that arches about half a mile over the Guadalquivir are worth a stop alone. You may even run into an old man from the area who spends much of his time hanging around the ruins pointing out a picture on a postcard that shows him fishing under the bridge. (The picture was taken in 1974.)

Trujillo

If you've ever wondered what life in a convent is really like, spend a night at the parador in Trujillo. This former convent is now a four-star hotel (6,500 Pts to 7,500 Pts). While you don't exactly live the way the nuns did, you can wander by the same ancient walls they once passed. There are still two active convents in the area.

The town nearby is also fascinating, with its *Plaza Mayor* built on several levels and dominated by an imposing statue of Francisco Pizarro, a local hero; an old *Moorish castle*; and many smaller palaces. Storks have built their large nests on nearly every tower and wall. I suggest spending two nights here and taking a side trip to Guadalupe.

Guadalupe

The 80 kilometers from Trujillo to Guadalupe will take a good two hours to drive because of the sharp switchback roads. You may prefer to take the bus so you can relax and enjoy the lush green mountain scenery. The Virgin of Guadalupe has made this city one of the most famous sites of Christian pilgrimage. The statue was found by Gil Cordero in 1325 after being buried over 600 years while the Muslims were in control of the area.

She is housed in a magnificent monastery. (Somehow a convent would seem a more appropriate resting place for her.) The shrine is one of the richest in the world. Gifts of jewelry, robes, and crosses are sent here from all over the world. The monastery museum contains a unique collection of richly embroidered antique vestments and fifteenth-century carved chairs.

Salamanca

If you take Highway N521 back to Cáceres then continue north on N630 another 219 kilometers, you'll reach Salamanca. While a little out of your way, this beautiful city with its hidden treasures from the past is well worth a visit. The four-star parador located here has a commanding view of the city below. Unlike the one in Trujillo, this parador is new and spacious. Its restaurant serves high-quality regional specialties with the traditional excellent service seen throughout the paradors of Spain. It also has a swimming pool.

Salamanca is an ancient city ruled at one time by Carthaginians, Romans, and, much later, by the Moors. It was the center of much wealth, which accounts for the splendid architecture and art that has remained. The *University of Salamanca*, founded by King Alfonso IX, is today recognized throughout Europe.

You can still walk over the stone bridge built by Hannibal across the Tórmes River. The enclosed *Plaza Mayor* is just as spectacular as the one found in Madrid. There are also a number of magnificent cathedrals representative of the various cultures that inhabited the city throughout history. The major thoroughfare passes the unique *Casa de las Conchas*, a fifteenth-century palace with a facade of beautifully carved shells.

Avila

Returning to Madrid on N501 you'll pass Avila (99 kilometers). This small remnant of the Middle Ages has retained much of its original mystique with its remarkable eleventh-century encircling walls. It was here that the Carmelite nun, later to become Saint Teresa, was born. The *convent of San José*, which she founded in 1563, is still active today. It contains a number of her mementos. While she lived and studied in more than one convent, the *Monasterio de Encarnación* in Avila, now a museum, is one of the most interesting. Leave Avila on highway N501 and connect with N6 to be back in Madrid in just over an hour (109 kilometers).

By the time you return to Madrid, you will not only have seen much of Spain, but you will have learned flamenco and, through it, gained an understanding of the Spanish people which few tourists have.

THE RING IN SEATTLE

▶━━▶

GENERAL AMBIANCE   ★ ★
SOCIAL CLIMATE   ★ ★
ACTIVITIES   ★ ★

FOR TOUR INFORMATION CONTACT:
Seattle–King County Convention and Visitors Bureau
1815 Seventh Avenue
Seattle, WA 98101
(206) 447-4240

▶━━▶

You need not be an opera enthusiast or even a Wagner enthusiast to enjoy a visit to Seattle and Wagner's theatrical spectacular, *Der Ring des Nibelungen* (The Ring of the Nibelung), a series of four operas. Seattle is the only city in the Western Hemisphere where you can see the complete *Ring* performed. It has been performed here each August since 1975.*

The Ring is Richard Wagner's chief work, completed in his late years. First performed in 1876 in Bayreuth, Bavaria, *The Ring* unites poetry, drama, great music, and song.

Der Ring des Nibelungen

The Ring cycle consists of four plays intended to be performed on four successive evenings. The prologue to the other three, *The Rhine Gold* (*Das Rheingold*), is followed by *The Valkyrie* (*Die Walküre*), *Siegfried* (*Siegfried*), and *Night Falls on the Gods* (*Die Götterdämmerung*).

Beginning in 1986, "supra titles" have been projected over the stage

---

* Recent scheduling and budgeting changes may affect the presentation of *The Ring* some years. Before making your plans, call the Visitor's Bureau to see if other operas are being substituted.

N

Seattle

WASHINGTON

providing the English translation of the libretto. While I love to hear the sounds of a foreign language, and I have a special fondness for German, I found this a wonderful innovation. No matter how much you've already read about the opera or how many lectures you have attended, there is nothing like also being able to understand the action word for word as it unfolds on the stage. I wish more opera companies would follow this practice—it might encourage more people to buy tickets.

The Ring cycle is the story of a ring forged from Rhine gold. It initially brings power to the person who possesses it, but later it brings death and ruin. The four plays begin with a world inhabited by mystical dwarfs, fairies, giants, and gods. But the world is waiting for man to rise up and redeem it from their ineffective government.

The initial poem was written in response to the political revolution of the mid-1800s, when the Socialists were attempting to replace a capitalistic order. It is also, however, a drama of today, with issues involving conflicts between love, power, greed, integrity, and self-respect.

It's a story alive with vitality and struggles still real today. The music is alive as well, bringing forth the image of fire, water, the trilling of birds, the hush of a forest, the thunder of a dragon, and the horn of a young woodsman. This is an opera for the ordinary person to see and enjoy.

General Ambiance

Not only will you have the opportunity to attend the principal international artistic attraction of the Pacific Northwest, *The Ring*, but you will do so in one of the most beautiful cities in the United States, Seattle.

Even though I grew up in Seattle, it was not until I moved to Minneapolis that I really came to appreciate its snowcapped mountains reflecting into lakes filled with fishing boats, ferries, and multitudes of sailing vessels of every size and shape. No longer a regular witness to the beauty of Puget Sound on a daily basis, I am struck by its greatness even before my plane lands. Mount Rainier greets each visitor to Sea-Tac Airport and bids you farewell.

I'm also struck by the casual dress and life-style of the people who live in Seattle. During the winter most of the men resemble rugged lumberjacks, with their beards and heavy wool shirts. You seldom need more than a jacket in the mild Seattle winters.

Social Climate

In general, Seattle is a relaxed, friendly town where people usually say "hello" as you pass them on the street. Add to that the activities of the Wagner Festival and you have an excellent social climate for meeting other people.

One of the big advantages of participating in a festival of this nature is that it provides contact, over an entire week's time, with people who have a similar interest. You'll be attending special lectures and tours with people you'll also see that night at the opera. Since many people will be in town specifically for the festival, you'll find it very natural to have dinner or a light snack between the lecture and opera with someone you've met. With all the new, exciting information, you won't be at a loss for dinner conversation. You may also decide to explore Seattle with one of your newfound friends.

Activities

The Wagner Festival of *The Ring* in Seattle offers a full week of things to do. While the four operas are the center of activity, you'll find much more available.

Wagner Festival Activities

Opening Night Reception. The festival begins with an opening night reception following the curtain of *Das Rheingold*. You'll need to purchase your ticket to this gala event in advance ($25). The buffet and wine reception offers you a chance to meet the cast and creators of *The Ring*. It is an excellent way to begin your week of magic in Seattle.

Lecture Series. Each year an eminent critic is brought to town for a lecture series on *The Ring*. The lecture on each opera precedes the performance. You can attend all four for $40; individual tickets are $12 each. Prior registration is recommended. Each opera is discussed in detail, using musical examples and emphasizing the points of special interest and significance.

Backstage Tour. One day each year, usually just before the last performance, you have the opportunity to take a backstage tour. This tour will greatly enhance your understanding of the technical magic of stagecraft. During your one- to one-and-a-half-hour tour, you'll become privy to many of the details essential to the production. You'll learn that it took 50,000 man-hours and 5,000 gallons of paint to build the new set (construction began in 1984 and was completed in 1986). It takes the equivalent of fifteen 40-foot semitrailers to store the sets. You'll also learn the secret of how the trick sword works and how the fires are started, the chemicals used, and something I've always wondered, how the set is so efficiently and quietly changed in the dark.

Your tour will include the makeup room, where you'll learn all the women wear synthetic wigs rather than human hair because of the humidity, and that it takes them an average of two hours to do their makeup, costume, and wig, in that order. You'll see the spectacular horses, worth $15,000 each, close-up and learn that the women riding them have no control at all. They are each moved by two men on cue.

You'll go into the orchestra pit for a unique view of the stage and audience, and into the musicians' lounge. Before leaving, the musical assistant will talk with you about the music and answer your questions. You'll feel informed and knowledgeable about both the opera and the production when you leave.

Tours begin every thirty minutes. The first is at 10:00 A.M. Group sizes are limited, so be sure to register early to get your assigned starting time ($10).

Special Events. In addition, the festival will include special recitals and plays. These will be listed on the schedule available in February.

Evergreen Classic Horse Show. Held at the same time as *The Ring*, this horse show has in the past designated a "Ring Day." A special bus for equestrian enthusiasts will leave the Opera House in the morning and return midday. Tickets ($25) include your transportation, admission to the horse show, and lunch. You'll see the vivid pageantry of the horse and rider performing and be back in plenty of time to attend the next *Ring* Festival event.

Seafair in Seattle

The Wagner Festival is traditionally held in conjunction with Seafair week in Seattle. In addition to the *Torchlight Parade* in downtown Seattle at twilight, don't miss the *Hydroplane Races*. This is an event I grew up looking forward to each year. Either from a boat or from the shore, the spray from the "tails" of these boats is a fascination and a thrill to watch. The local newspaper, *The Seattle Times*, will have a listing of these and other events.

Preparing for Your Trip to Seattle

Preparing for the Opera

You will certainly get sufficient information to understand and enjoy the opera from the program, the English "supra titles," and the lectures prior to each performance. But like anything else, the more you know the more you will broaden and expand your enjoyment. With this in mind, I suggest you pick up one of the books about *The Ring*, or even the libretto.

A book I found easy to understand and complete without being overwhelming was *The Perfect Wagnerite: A Commentary on the Niblung's Ring* by George Bernard Shaw.

Obtaining Your Opera Tickets

The cycle of four operas is performed over a one-week period. Typically, two cycles are performed each year. The schedule is usually available in February, at which time you can order tickets by writing to the Seattle Opera, P.O. Box 9248, Seattle, WA 98109, or by calling (800) 426-1619. Seats for the series range from $72 to $236. Individual performance prices vary. While you may be able to buy tickets at the door prior to the performance, the more popular productions are sold out months in advance. I suggest ordering your tickets as soon as possible for a better seat selection as well.

Any of the 3,117 seats in the Seattle Opera House will be superb just because you have the opportunity to be there. However, according to the assistant conductor, the best seats for viewing the opera are the first three rows of the ground floor ($59 per seat, $236 per cycle) and the best seats for listening to the music are the second balcony, center ($55 per seat, $222 per cycle).

What to Take

Seattle enjoys a moderate climate, and August is usually the warmest month, with temperatures ranging from the seventies to mid-eighties, cooler in the evening. Though August is usually a dry month, rain is what keeps Seattle so green, so take a lightweight raincoat or umbrella. The air can get chilly when you're out on the water, so you'll need a light jacket or sweater for the boat rides or for strolling along the waterfront.

For the most part, the people of Seattle dress very casually day and night. You'll find the dress at the opera will vary from slacks to the very formal. Casual wear, summer dresses a little on the dressy side, will be the most predominant. I suggest you dress comfortably.

If you don't have your own opera glasses you can rent them at the theater for $2. Be sure to bring a driver's license to leave for collateral.

Take your hiking boots or tennis shoes if you plan to go climbing in the mountains. You'll find a number of books in the local bookstores with "101 Hikes" in the Cascade or Olympic Mountains, which are nearby. When I can find the time to get up into the mountains, it's inevitably a highlight of my trip. The alpine meadows and deserted mountain lakes formed by melting snow are found in few other parts of the country.

Getting There

The Seattle-Tacoma Airport (Sea-Tac) is located approximately thirty minutes from downtown. A cab will cost $18 to $23. Bus service is available to town from the airport for $5.

Treasures to Purchase

If you're a skier, you might want to stop at the *K2 Ski Company* factory outlet store on Vashon Island (telephone [206] 463-3631). You can purchase new skis with the paint smudged for half the usual price. REI (Recreational Equipment, Inc.) also has a large outlet store in Seattle (1525 Eleventh Avenue). Here you'll find clothing and equipment for camping, climbing, and skiing. Many of the items are truly unique. The September 1986 issue of *Cosmopolitan* also mentions REI as a great place to meet men in Seattle. There are certainly a lot of them there.

Since Seattle is on the water, you'll find a number of shops that sell carved wooden sea gulls perched on logs. Watercolors and prints of nautical scenes are ubiquitous. Many are very tempting, as is much of the American Indian jewelry and artifacts. I also have a small wooden ferryboat I purchased to hang on my Christmas tree. These are for sale at a number of shops in the *Market*. You'll find a large selection of handcrafted items in this area.

If you want the ultimate souvenir of your trip to *The Ring* in Seattle, *Fox's*, on the corner of Fifth and Union, sells "The Ring Ring." For $60 you can purchase a unique, gold-plated sterling silver ring. Fourteen karat gold is also available for much more.

Exploring Seattle

A big city, Seattle has a wealth of attractions for the visitor. You'll find you can spend days wandering along the waterfront, in and out of the shops housed in old piers. You can smell the salt water and watch the ferries go off to the various islands in the sound. The Olympic Mountain range makes a spectacular backdrop, with its snowcapped peaks. Be sure to wander through the *Pike Place Market*, an open-air market overlooking Elliott Bay. The small restaurants nestled between shops make an excellent place for lunch or morning coffee. You can rest your feet while you daydream about the mountains or the boats sailing by.

While you're on the waterfront, stop at the *Seattle Aquarium*. Unique, it sits on the edge of one of the most diverse aquatic habitats in the world. The award-winning exhibits include a saltwater marsh and a beaver dam you can peer into. It is especially interesting to view the sea otters and harbor seals in their natural habitat. You'll pass a working salmon ladder leading to a hatchery from which thousands of fish are released each year.

North of the piers is a unique park area, *Gas Works Park*. Here the giant pipe remains of a gas plant have been painted for children to climb. They sit on the top of the hills that roll gently down to the lakefront. This is also the beginning of a bike and walking path that goes through Seattle, past the University of Washington, all the way to the Ste. Michelle Winery at the other end of Lake Washington. Best of all, it's flat most of the way and a wonderful ride, although it's quite a distance (26 miles each way).

Freeway Park, with its waterfalls and plateaued lawn areas, is actually located on top of Interstate Highway 5. Not far from here you'll find the third largest *Chinatown* in the country, with a number of excellent restaurants. The *Hongkong* (607 Maynard Avenue South) is a favorite of the locals. This is also a great area in which to purchase pork buns for a snack to be enjoyed in any one of Seattle's many parks.

Pioneer Square is a large, beautifully restored historic district. This is where Seattle had its beginning as a port and logging community. Don't miss *Waterfall Garden* in the center of the Pioneer Square district. Located on the corner of South Main Street and Second Avenue South, this garden oasis has a 22-foot-high waterfall. There are tables where you can sit and relax.

While you're near the waterfront, I suggest taking a *Harbor Tour*. For $4.50 you can go out onto Elliott Bay and see the large ships in the active shipyard up close. If you're lucky, you may even catch a banana boat unloading. The Seattle skyline from the harbor is spectacular as well.

The *Space Needle*, originally built for the 1962 Seattle World's Fair, remains a unique landmark towering over the downtown area. There is a revolving restaurant and an observation deck at the top of this 605-foot structure. The view of the city, the Sound, and the mountains is breathtaking day or night. The *Seattle Center* at the base of the Space Needle contains the *Plaza of the States*, *Coliseum*, a number of exhibition halls, and the *Pacific Science Center*. The *Opera House* and *Bagley Wright Theater* are also in this area. (Check in *The Seattle Times* to see what events are being held at the theater while you're in town.)

Take time to sit and enjoy the *International Fountain* in the Seattle Center. This is Seattle's only computer choreographed walk-in fountain (the water is synchronized with the music). You can take the *Monorail* from this area back to downtown.

The *Ballard Locks*, with their salmon ladder, are another popular attraction. Vessels, large and small, are lowered up to 26 feet from Lake Union to Puget Sound, from fresh water to salt water. The grounds, with their *Carl English Gardens*, make your visit especially nice.

Woodland Park Zoo, one of the nation's top ten zoos, is known for its natural habitats. The 5-acre African savanna houses a variety of wildlife. You can also visit the swamp and the Nocturnal House ($2.50 admission).

The *Boeing Company*, one of the largest manufacturers of aircraft in the world, is headquartered in the Seattle area. The 747, the world's largest jetliner, is manufactured at their Everett plant (30 miles north of Seattle). For tour information call (206) 342-4801. The *Museum of Flight* is located in the original 1916 Boeing factory, the *Red Barn*, located in Seattle near Boeing Field ($2.50 admission).

The *Rainier Brewery* is in the same general area. It, too, is open for tours (1:00 P.M. to 6:00 P.M.) with free samples of beer at the end of the tour.

Even if you're not a true sports enthusiast, you may want to see the Seattle Mariners, a major league baseball team, in the *Kingdome*. Call (206) 628-3555 for schedule and ticket information.

Another must is the *Seattle Underground Tour*. For $3 you can spend one and a half hours in the city that lies beneath Seattle's Historic Pioneer Square district. Wear comfortable shoes and bring a jacket if the weather is cool.

If you get a chance, drive across the Freemont Bridge at the north end of Lake Union. You'll see a unique group, always appropriately dressed for the weather, waiting for the bus. These bronze statues of travelers are a real delight.

Ferries

Another good way to see the city is to take a short ferry ride. The main terminal is at the end of Columbia Street at Colman Dock next to *Ye Olde Curiosity Shop*. For just a few dollars you can ride on the ferry with the sea gulls following across Puget Sound to the navy yard in *Bremerton*, to *Vashon Island* or to *Orcas Island*.

Where to Stay in Seattle

Stouffer Madison Hotel, 515 Madison Street; telephone (800) 468-3571 (single $65, double $95). This luxury hotel has maintained the traditional Stouffer quality with attention to detail, and they have done so for a very reasonable rate. For $85 you can be guaranteed a Puget Sound view; for $95 you'll have your own corner suite. Weekend rates at 50 percent off are available for selected rooms. In addition to well-appointed, spacious rooms, they have gone out of their way to ensure quality, down to the incredibly fluffy feather pillows. They have even made rising a little more pleasant by providing a complimentary newspaper and coffee or tea with your morning wake-up call. A health club, pool (massage available), restaurants, and lounge are also on the premises.

Alexis, 1007 First Avenue at Madison; telephone (800) 426-7033 (single $115, double $135). This 1901 building was totally renovated in 1982 to an elegant, soft pink, mauve, and gray contemporary style. Located in the heart of downtown Seattle near the waterfront and Pike Place Market, it has the feel of a country inn and is listed on the National Registry of Historic Places. Down comforters and wood-burning fireplace suites are available upon request ($260). There's a small, intimate bar on the ground floor. The formal restaurant serves fresh local seafood specialties. Best of all you don't need to worry about tipping if you stay here. The rates include all tips for doormen, bellmen, valet, parkers, and maid service. Only the restaurant, bar, and room service are not included.

Seattle Sheraton Hotel and Towers, 1400 Sixth Avenue; telephone (206) 621-9000 (single $109 to $139, double $139 to $159; Towers: single $150 to $170, double $170 to $190). Five blocks up from Pike Street in downtown Seattle, this hotel is a "hotel in a hotel." Separate express check-in is available on the thirty-second floor for the top three floors, considered "The Towers." Complimentary continental breakfast, high tea (2:00 P.M. to 4:00 P.M.), and cold hors d'oeuvres (5:00 P.M. to 7:30 P.M.) are provided free of charge for the Towers guests. If you want to feel pampered, it's worth the additional cost. Hotel bus service is available for the forty-minute ride to the airport ($5).

The Westin, 1900 Fifth Avenue; telephone (206) 728-1000 (single $95 to $160, double $120 to $185). The twin-tower Westin remains one of Seattle's fine hotels. There are four restaurants on the premises, including *Trader Vic's*, a well-established local favorite. There is also an attractive *Market Cafe*. An indoor swimming pool, fitness center, and four lounges should meet your needs. On weekends, their most expensive rooms at the top with a waterfront view are available at 50 percent off the usual rate.

The Four Seasons Olympic Hotel, 411 University Street; telephone (206) 621-1700 (single $130, double $150). A hotel with historic elegance. This ornate Italian Renaissance–style hotel has been a landmark and *the* place to stay in Seattle since its opening in 1924. In 1979, it was placed on the National Registry of Historic Places. The recent restoration has enhanced its original old-world charm and achieved the restoration goal of making it a world-class, luxury hotel. The solarium spa complete with indoor pool, sauna, and fitness center is uniquely attractive. The touch of class continues with brass elevator doors engraved with sailing ships. The *Georgian* dining room offers fine French cuisine, the *Shuckers* the finest local seafood, and the *Garden Court* a variety of seafoods and omelets in an informal garden setting. Highly recommended.

Where to Eat in Seattle

Benihana of Tokyo, Fifth Avenue and University Street. This is a great place to go not only for the food but to meet other visitors and locals. They fill up their tables and cook in front of you, so everyone ends up eating with a small group. Complete meals range from $10.25 to $17.50. Happy hour with a selection of hors d'oeuvres is from 4:30 P.M. to 6:30 P.M.

Georgian Room, Olympic Hotel. Even if you're not staying at this elegant historic hotel, you should stop in for dinner. You'll find everything, including local trout ($16.95), cooked to perfection and delivered with impeccable service. The old-world elegance of the dining room is consistent with the charm of the building and staff.

At the Lakeside, 2501 North Northlake Way. This informal restaurant on Lake Union specializes in seafood. You can arrive by car or boat. Daily specials include all the crab you can eat ($15). Lunch entrées range from $4.75 to $6.25, dinner for $10.75 to $22.95.

Triples, 1200 Westlake Avenue North. Also located on the edge of Lake Union, this informal restaurant offers everything from seafood ($8.95) to steak ($18.95). As you dine, you look out over the masts of sailboats moored on the pier in front of the restaurant. An added treat: you'll likely be able to watch seaplanes land and take off; there's a training school next door.

Ivar's Captain's Table, 333 Elliott West. This is the top of the line of Ivar's restaurants in Seattle. Ivar is a local institution, a local boy who made it big. The seafood offered is good, plentiful, and reasonably priced. The decor is completely nautical.

Pier 70, Pier 70. My favorite seat in this restaurant is on the end next to the floor-to-ceiling windows overlooking the water. Not far from the main ferry terminal—originally a working pier—you can count on seeing large ferries and sleek sailing ships pass between you and the snowcapped Olympic Mountains on the other side of the sound. This is a beautiful setting for an informal lunch.

The Old Spaghetti Factory, 2801 Elliott Avenue. Across from Pier 70, you can get just about any kind of spaghetti sauce you want here, including an unusual clam sauce. Very informal with interesting and unique antiques throughout the restaurant.

Cutter's Bayhouse, 2001 Western Avenue. Located at the north end of the Market, this informal restaurant has modern copper ceiling lights, cane-backed chairs, and oilcloth on the tabletops. It looks out over the spectacular Puget Sound and Olympic Mountains. The continental cuisine ranges from pasta ($7.95) to seafood ($12.95). While they use a lot of garlic in their food, the flavor is satisfying.

Side Trips Around Seattle

Tillicum Village Salmon Bake and Tour

This four-hour tour to Blake Island leaves from Pier 56. This is your opportunity to visit the birthplace of Chief Seattle and eat salmon baked over an alder fire in a cedar log house. As you feast on the salmon, the air filled with the mixed aroma of cedar and alder, you'll be whisked back centuries to a rare display, the song and dance of the native Northwest Coast Indians. Take time to walk the nature trails on the island and examine the crafts and artifacts on display before the forty-five-minute return boat trip. Call (206) 624-5813 for information and reservations ($27.50).

Victoria

Steam to Victoria, British Columbia, on the *Princess Marguerite* cruise ship. Daily round-trip service is available. I recommend spending the night at the *Empress Hotel* in Victoria, however, so you have more time to explore that very British seaport. You can sail in luxury with a private cabin and enjoy lunch on board in the dining room.

Port Townsend

If you have a rental car, I highly recommend taking the ferry to Winslow, then driving across the Hood Canal Bridge to the sleepy fishing town of Port Townsend. This National Historic District is the best example of a Victorian seacoast town north of San Francisco.

Mount Rainier National Park

The 14,410-foot Mount Rainier is a major area attraction. Once an active volcano, it is now capped with glacier snow year-round. In the national park at its base, you'll see mountain meadows, cascading waterfalls, a box canyon, and the clear mountain lakes. *Mount Baker* and *Mount St. Helens* (which erupted in 1980) are also nearby.

Snoqualmie Falls

Plan on visiting Snoqualmie Falls and stopping for brunch, lunch, or dinner at the Snoqualmie Falls Lodge, which was established on the edge of the falls in 1916. The food is good, old-fashioned, tasty home cooking—go when you're hungry. You'll need advance reservations, so plan ahead (888-2451).

Snoqualmie Falls is located about forty-five minutes southeast of Seattle. The 268-foot drop is 101 feet steeper than Niagara Falls.

Chateau Ste. Michelle (Woodinville)

On your way back from Snoqualmie Falls stop at Washington's largest winery. Free tours and samples are available. They also sell wine, of course. (I was surprised when visitors from Washington, DC, brought along some Chateau Ste. Michelle wine to dinner not knowing that I was from Seattle. They had first tried it while at a meeting in Seattle and it is now a favorite.) You'll drive back to Seattle over the only concrete floating pontoon bridge in the world.

Haviland Winery (Woodinville)

Across from the Ste. Michelle Winery is the Haviland Winery. Newly opened in 1987, this family operated winery has a unique, intimate appeal. The visitor center is located in a new building resembling a stately old Victorian manor house. If they are having a party there while you're in town, I'd suggest you join the fun!

You will find the magic of *The Ring* blends well with the magic of the Pacific Northwest. I still yearn for the smell of salt water and the breaktaking view of snowcapped mountain peaks through the masts of sailing ships. Seattle is a hard city to leave.

SPOLETO FESTIVAL OF THE ARTS IN CHARLESTON

▶ ─── ▶

GENERAL AMBIANCE ★ ★

SOCIAL CLIMATE ★ ★

ACTIVITIES ★ ★

FOR TRAVEL ARRANGEMENTS CONTACT:
Charleston Conventioneers
P. O. Box 29
Charleston, SC 29402
(800) 542-4455

▶ ─── ▶

I had been told that Charleston, South Carolina, was one of our most beautiful Southern cities. I was not, however, prepared for the timeless beauty of its large, well-restored Historic District and its Southern plantations with their spectacular gardens, located so near a flourishing modern city.

General Ambiance

Driving from the airport toward Charleston Harbor, it is the contrast between twentieth-century Charleston and historic Charleston that is so striking. As you cross the massive bridges that span the Ashley and Cooper rivers, the view changes from that of modern skyscrapers and nuclear submarines at the naval base, to that of pre-Revolutionary War cobblestoned streets, magnificent eighteenth-century homes, and horse-drawn carriages in the Historic District.

Social Climate

The pineapple is the symbol of hospitality, and it is no accident that this motif appears on everything in Charleston, from carved mantel-

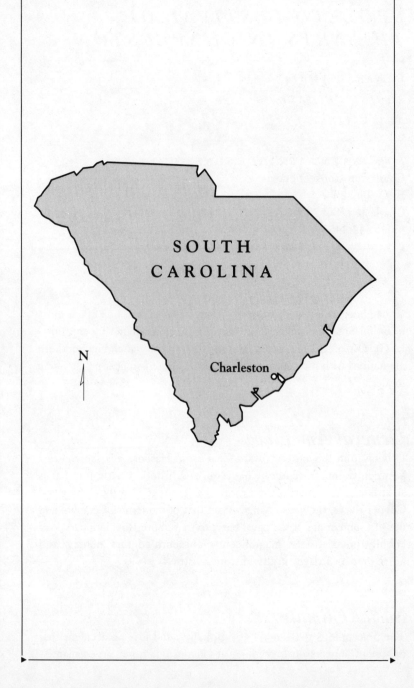

SOUTH
CAROLINA

N

Charleston

pieces to dinnerware. Charlestonians, the epitome of Southern hospitality and charm, are very gracious to their visitors. At first I thought the Historic District was working its magic on me; however, after visiting the outlying areas and greater Charleston, I realized that it was the people of Charleston: they are genuinely charming and eager to introduce the visitor to their culture, past and present.

I also found the dining and social atmosphere in the Historic District to be excellent for the woman traveling alone, because Charlestonians are particularly courteous and most anxious to please women. I was often asked if I would like to join another single person or a group of people for dinner and/or to walk with them to one of the Spoleto performances.

Activities

It is hard to believe that both contemporary and historic Charleston are thriving side by side so successfully in today's throwaway society. This is due in great part to the efforts of very active and organized preservation societies and to the people of Charleston, who are deeply committed to neighborhood conservation. As you can imagine, a city of such contrasts offers a wealth of vacation options.

You can stay at a countryside inn near one of the plantations or at a resort hotel on one of the barrier sea islands, taking sightseeing trips into greater Charleston or its Historic District. Or, you may choose to stay in Historic Charleston at a restored inn, taking day trips out to the barrier islands and plantations. Either way, the result is that you will have all the advantages of the old and the new within easy reach, as well as accessibility to the multitude of Spoleto activities.

Spoleto Festival U.S.A.

Spoleto, an annual event, is held in Charleston in late May and early June. This premier event of music, dance, drama, and opera, first held in Charleston in 1977, is the companion of an arts festival that has been held in Spoleto, Italy, since 1958. Both festivals owe their existence to and are under the artistic direction of Gian Carlo Menotti. Charleston has expanded the original Spoleto Festival by inviting the local and regional performing and visual arts community to participate in the Piccolo Festival. And in recent years, the Piccolo-Spoleto Festival has grown to include hundreds of visual and performing arts events and exhibits.

On my first visit, the Spoleto events included ballet performances by Baryshnikov and the National Ballet of Spain, jazz performances by the Ahmad Jamal Trio, Westminster Choir concerts, and Menotti's opera, *The Saint of Bleeker Street*; the local and regional Piccolo offerings included music selections from *Porgy and Bess* by the Charleston Choraliers, "Southern Comphort" performances with community performing groups, and concerts by the Festival Orchestra featuring the Charleston Symphony Singers.

The visual arts were represented by works from the private collections of members of the Festival Board (for example, works by Rubens, Degas, and Picasso) and by North Carolina Glass, which exhibits contemporary art glass by North Carolina artists.

Festival events and exhibits are held all over the Historic District and the surrounding Charleston area. I found it easy to purchase tickets at the box offices the day of the performances, although for very special events it would be wise to obtain tickets well in advance for your visit.

Planning Your Trip to Charleston

When to Go

Charleston has a temperate climate most of the year, so no matter when you choose to visit, there will be something interesting to do or see; most of its attractions are open year-round. In the spring, the azaleas and other flowers are in full bloom and everyone drives to the countryside plantations to see their magnificent displays in formal landscaped gardens. The Historic Charleston Foundation sponsors an annual Festival of Houses Tour in which more than eighty private homes, gardens, and historic churches are open to the public. In the fall of the year, the Preservation Society of Charleston sponsors candle-light tours of historic homes and gardens. Every September, the

Charleston Restaurant Association sponsors an international food festival and invites the public to sample the wares of their finest restaurants.

There is good reason to visit Charleston in the winter as well. An Antiques and Art Exposition, held in early November and during the Thanksgiving and Christmas holidays, is memorable with its special events and activities sponsored by the community, churches, museums, plantations, and hotels. Candlelight tours of historic homes and plantations, decorated for the holidays, are held during this time of the year. A Parade of Boats in Charleston Harbor is another annual winter event. Throughout December, local synagogues invite visitors to their annual Hanukkah Suppers, and there are many holiday concerts given by church groups and local orchestras.

What to Take

Though it will likely be quite warm during the daytime in Charleston, it can be a little chilly at night. You may want a light sweater, jacket, or shawl for when you go to dinner and the evening Spoleto performances. A number of better restaurants have a strict dinner dress code; if in doubt, call ahead to inquire about appropriate dress. You may want a nice dress or two to wear in the evenings, but casual clothing is just as acceptable in many of the restaurants, drinking establishments, and Spoleto events. (I'd avoid jeans, short shorts, or halter tops, however.)

Getting There

One of the real advantages of visiting major U.S. cities is the ease of arrival and departure. Delta Airlines has frequent flights into the Charleston airport every day. The airport is located about half an hour from downtown.

You can take a taxi from the airport for approximately $16 or you can take an airport limousine (really a van) for $7.

Getting Around

You won't need a rental car when you're in town. If you stay in the Historic District most events will be within walking distance. You can also take a cab or bus if you prefer not to walk.

You will, however, want to rent a car to drive to the plantations outside town. A two- or three-day car rental at the end of your trip will be plenty of time to add these side excursions to your itinerary.

Treasures to Purchase

Shopping in the Historic District is quite a commercialized affair. But it's fun to wander through the *Old City Market* with its specialty shops and open-air stalls where the locals come to sell produce, crafts, costume jewelry (lots of shells here), and flea market items. In the Market and on the street corners you will notice women weaving and selling sweet-water-grass baskets. As they weave, the older women teaching the younger women their almost-extinct art, you hear them speaking in their lovely Gullah, an English dialect that contains a mixture of elements from various African languages. The baskets they sell are expensive but worth the price, even if you buy just a small one (approximately $16) in which to keep your guest soaps. *King Street*, in the Historic District, has some of the finest antique shops and art galleries in the South. Their knowledgeable salespeople welcome both browsers and serious buyers interested in eighteenth- and nineteeth-century English furniture, porcelain, crystal chandeliers, and jewelry.

Charleston

Exploring Charleston

Once settled into your lodgings, your first stop should be the Visitor Information Center located at 85 Calhoun Street. The knowledgeable staff here can assist you in planning your stay. Charleston has so much to see that if you don't plan your time wisely, you could miss many points of interest. For instance, I had initially planned to spend only one or two days in the Historic District, but at the Visitor Center I learned it would actually take closer to a week to see all that the area had to offer!

One of the best ways to see the Historic District in capsulized form, before you begin intense exploration, is to take one of the many tours offered: walking tours, either guided (approximately $8) or self-guided using a map and cassette (approximately $7); self-guided bicycle tours with bike rental and map ($2 an hour or $10 a day); group carriage, trolley, or van tours ($6 to $10); or private horse-drawn carriage or private car (from $25).

As a special treat, consider taking the *Charleston Tea Party Walking Tour*. This tour begins with the group meeting first thing in the morning or afternoon in a lovely private garden for tea. After tea you tour Charleston's most historic residences, flowering courtyards, alleys, and interiors ($8).

Although a private tour has the advantage of the guide's undivided attention, a group tour offers the opportunity to meet people with whom you may plan another outing or dinner. After a tour you will better be able to decide which areas of town and which sights you are most interested in exploring further.

Safety. The Historic District of Charleston takes pride in its safety for visitors and residents. I walked alone at all times of day and evening, to and from my lodgings, without fear—even after dinner and an evening's entertainment! The main streets of the district are well lit and policemen on foot and horseback are plentiful. And there are plenty of joggers, morning and evening, so you are rarely "alone."

Historic Charleston. Charleston was founded in 1670 on a peninsula between the Ashley and Cooper rivers, on Charleston's magnificent natural harbor. The cobblestone streets of the early settlement (some of which are still in use today) were laid out according to a model brought from England. The original city was walled, fortifying it against land and sea invasion. While visiting the "old" city of Charleston, be sure to take a stroll along East Battery to *White Point Gardens* on the waterfront to see where the old cannons were mounted on the sea wall.

If time permits, make a trip out to the original *Charles Town Landing* where the first settlers arrived. Here you can walk ($3) or bicycle ($1 an hour) acres of landscaped gardens and lagoons, visit the special underground pavilion exhibits that tell the story of the early immigrants, and participate in a reenactment of colonial life.

You may also wish to visit some of the district's historic buildings, including the *Pink House*, built of West Indies coral stone during the Colonial era. It once stood in the red-light district where it operated as a pre–Revolutionary War tavern. The *Dock Street Theatre*, a restoration of the first theater in the U.S., is now used by local dramatics groups. Also on the "must see" list are the *Charleston Museum*, the oldest museum in the U.S., with its South Carolina collections, and the *Old Slave Mart Museum*, which is the oldest museum of Afro-American heritage in the U.S. (before the Civil War it was the office of a slave auctioneer).

Early Charlestonians had greater religious freedom than many people in the other original thirteen colonies. This is evidenced by the many synagogues and churches of various denominations in the Historic District. In fact, there were so many houses of worship that Charleston became known as the "holy city." *Congregation Beth Elohim* is the oldest synagogue in the United States and is considered to be one of the country's finest examples of Greek Revival architecture. *St. John's Lutheran Church* and *St. Mary's Roman Catholic Church* are mother churches. *St. Michael's Episcopal Church*, completed in 1761, is the oldest church in Charleston. These, and many other churches, have survived despite fires, earthquakes, hurricanes, and Civil War bombardment. The graveyards of these churches, many of which are open to the public, have their own stories to tell visitors to historic Charleston.

Take time to walk the residential neighborhoods of the Historic District. As you stroll leisurely past private residences, look into alleyways, courtyards, and piazzas full of fragrant blooming plants and trees (azaleas, magnolias, gardenias, crepe myrtle dripping with Spanish moss). Charlestonians don't seem to mind the intrusion as you discreetly peer over and through wrought-iron gates and fences at their fountains and statuary. Many of the wrought-iron fences were melted down for munitions during the Civil War, so a good number of the houses have beautiful stone walls instead.

Historic Homes

Charleston has a semitropical climate, and in pre-Revolutionary times, when the plantations became unbearably hot, the women and children moved to magnificent homes on the waterfront, in what is now historic Charleston. These homes were built with wide verandas facing the water so cool breezes could blow through great central hallways, cooling off the adjacent rooms whose windows were shuttered against the sun. A good number of houses were built in what is now known as the Charleston single-house style. These were a single-room wide and each floor had a veranda facing the water and private back porches that opened the rooms and allowed the breezes to blow through every room in the house.

Since early Charlestonians were taxed according to the number of doors in their homes, you won't find many doors leading onto their verandas. Instead, the windows on most floors slide up from the floor to the ceiling for access onto the veranda.

Many houses in the Historic District are open to the public, with admittance fees ranging from $3 to $5. There are a number of homes with special historic or architectural interest that I would suggest visiting. The Adam-style *Nathanial Russell House* has a flying circular staircase, attached only at the foot and at the top of the cantilevered stairs, which are unsupported from floor to ceiling. The Greek Revival–style *Edmonston-Alston House* contains beautiful period furniture, silver and china, as well as engravings and original documents of historic interest. You'll also want to see the English-style, pastel-colored double houses of *Rainbow Row*, and don't miss the *Heyward-Washington House*, which has the only restored eighteenth-century kitchen open to the public.

Charleston Harbor

No trip to historic Charleston would be complete without a tour of the Charleston Harbor, where significant sea victories occurred in both the Revolutionary and Civil wars. If you are staying in the Historic District, you can take the city bus or a taxi (approximately $2.50) to the City Marina, where you will have a choice of tours. The "Harbor of History Tour" aboard the *Charles Towne Princess*, is a 30-mile non-stop, two-and-a-quarter-hour yacht tour. If you are a history buff, you may prefer to take the two-and-a-quarter-hour *River Boat Rambler Ex-*

cursion Tour, which includes the harbor tour and a stop on *Fort Sumter National Monument*. During the Civil War, Fort Sumter was held by the Union troops, who refused the Confederates' demand to vacate the fort. On April 12, 1861, the Confederates fired on the federal troops—the first shot of the War Between the States. If you take a morning harbor tour you can stop for lunch at the *Marina Variety Store and Restaurant*, which serves modestly priced cold plates, sandwiches, and great noon fish and seafood platters for about $2.25 to $5.95. Very casual "wharf" or tour boat–type clothing is acceptable. (If you take an afternoon tour of the harbor, you may wish to have dinner here.) While waiting in their dining room, you will have a wonderful view of the South Carolina intercoastal waterway with beautiful water birds, including night herons and snowy egrets, fishing for *their* lunch!

Where to Stay in Charleston

Because the attractions are diverse and in many instances miles apart, the Historic District is an ideal, central location to stay. From here you can space your day trips between leisurely forays into the Historic District. Staying in town, rather than in the country or on an island, will give you greater opportunity to experience the varied cuisines of the region as well as the social life. And how nice to take a horse-drawn carriage back to the inn after dinner or the theater, rather than a taxi or rental car!

Historic Charleston has a variety of accommodations to suit every taste and pocketbook. There are many lovely B&Bs (bed and breakfasts) in and near the district, within walking distance of sights, shopping, dining, and social life. Most of the B&Bs and inns are restored historic buildings and have modern conveniences such as air conditioners, phones, and televisions. They are usually furnished with reproductions of period furniture, wallpapers, and accessories. Most B&Bs and inns range in price from $65 to $95 a night for a private room with bath. Some have rooms in the $50-a-night range, if you are willing to share a bath.

Meeting Street Inn, 173 Meeting Street. Conveniently located in the Historic District, you'll feel pampered when you stay in this pink West Indies single house–style inn. The rooms, each with a private porch off the back and a large veranda in front, are furnished in true Charleston low-country style with rice beds high off the floor, windows with inside shutters, and beautiful armoires instead of closets. A silver service breakfast, served either in your room or in the garden courtyard, includes good hot coffee, cheesecake or croissant, and juice. In the evening, the courtyard becomes the setting for twilight chamber music concerts while you sit at small wrought-iron tables and sip wine in the evening breeze, scented with the fragrance of blooming gardenias.

Two Meeting Street Inn, 2 Meeting Street, at the Battery. This beautifully preserved Queen Anne–style mansion has five elegantly furnished bedrooms—each with private bath—opening out onto a veranda facing the waterfront. Continental breakfast is served in the downstairs public rooms or on the patio. Sherry is served every afternoon from a sideboard in the dining room to guests who wish to meet each other or just sit and relax with a good book.

Sword Gate Inn, 111 Tradd Street. This inn was named for the distinctive iron gate on the property. It is a small, personal, charming establishment run by Walter Barton, who is a descendant of a judge who owned the property in 1878. The Sword Gate, located in the heart of the Historic District, has operated as an inn since 1952 and has six rooms with private baths. The erudite innkeeper offers full concierge service to his guests and presides at a wine-and-cheese gathering late every afternoon. Guests may sip wine in the magnificent Regency-style ballroom turned sitting room, or they may browse through the menus of the district's many dining establishments that are arranged on the dining room table. After you make your selection, Mr. Barton will make your reservations; he will offer advice on dress code and give explicit directions to the restaurant. Every morning a Charleston breakfast, with eggs to order, awaits the guests.

Mills House Hotel (single $76 to $92). If you wish to stay in a hotel, the Mills House, located at Meeting and Queen streets, is one of the finest that the Historic District has to offer. The Mills House is an elegantly restored hotel with period furnishings and provides all the amenities one would expect in such a luxurious establishment.

Where to Eat in Charleston

I strongly suggest that you have dinner at *Poogan's Porch* at least once during your stay in Charleston. Be sure to call a day or two in advance for reservations and inquire if they have a single table available on the "porch." I selected a wonderful Southern supper offered on their menu for $19.95. Dinner began with she-crab soup, low-country pâté, and then an entrée combination of shrimp Creole and cornmeal-encrusted fried catfish. (After that I barely had room for Poogan's outstanding bread pudding with bourbon sauce!) If your appetite is modest, order one of their low-country entrées or seafood specialties; they prepare especially fine Creole and Cajun dishes.

Tommy Condon's, located near the Old City Market, is a great place for entertainment—this Irish pub is so much fun, you'll hate to leave at closing time! The Irish folk singers warm the crowd up early with lovely Irish laments, bawdy folk songs, and sing-alongs. Tommy Condon's serves some good-looking appetizers of batter fried veggies, boiled spiced shrimp, and crab-stuffed mushrooms ($3.50 to $5.50). They also have a small supper menu with prices in the $5.95 to $11.95 range for fish, seafood, and meat dishes.

Another great place near the Old City Market is the *A. W. Shucks Oyster Bar and Restaurant*. It has a raw seafood bar and serves outstanding fish and seafood, fresh and locally caught. The price of an average lunch is $5.95, dinner entrées are priced from $7.95 to $10.95. (It's the only place I saw in the district where you could order fried oysters by the bucket!) Women dining alone are made especially welcome and the establishment will not tolerate unwelcome advances made to women by its male customers.

While I don't usually recommend places that don't serve regional or local fare, I feel compelled to mention *Papillon*, an Italian restaurant the likes of which you'd find in New York City. The variety of pastas, stuffed pies, pizzas, seafood, veal, chicken, and vegetarian dishes is unlimited (priced in the $7.95 to $9.95 range). If you are in the vicinity of the Old Market after a concert or the theater, stop by Papillon for their wonderful dessert coffees, Italian cheesecake, fine Italian ices, or gelato.

On Sunday plan to have an outstanding brunch in the *Barbados Room* at the *Mills House Hotel* (be sure to call ahead for reservations). Or, if you prefer, stop by the *Baker's Cafe*, which is a fine French pâtisserie. They specialize in outstanding breakfasts and lunches or you can buy a chocolate croissant or almond cream horn to munch on as you walk the Historic District. The Baker's Cafe is known for the famous Charleston black bottom tarts.

Around Charleston

The "low country" in the vicinity of Charleston was developed into prosperous rice plantations along the Ashley and Cooper rivers. To-day, these plantations are tourist attractions, truck farms, wildlife refuges, and prestigious condominium developments.

The Plantations

I cannot imagine a visit to Charleston without a trip to their grand plantations. If you take the River Road along the beautiful Ashley River, within about 20 miles of Charleston, you will reach the first of these magnificent places. *Drayton Hall* is a pre–Revolutionary War mansion of Georgian Palladian architecture that has been preserved in almost its original condition. When Northern troops were burning the plantations along the river, the owner of Drayton Hall sent a servant to tell them that everyone was ill with smallpox, thus saving this beautiful property. The house is unfurnished, allowing visitors to appreciate its magnificent handcrafted beauty.

You'll next come upon *Magnolia Plantation*, with its renowned landscaped floral gardens containing the largest collection of azaleas and camelias in America. If you are a nature lover, take the boardwalk through the cypress swamp or the walking trails to the wildlife observation tower and waterfowl refuge.

Middleton Place is perhaps the most interesting of the three because it is a working plantation. This was one of the less fortunate plantations burned by Sherman's troops, but what is left of the three-part house complex is still fascinating. The English country–style house is fully furnished with period furniture, pictures, wall hangings, and china and silver. The house is "dressed" for summer and for winter, depending upon the season, by the volunteers who staff and conduct the tours. During the warm months the floors are covered with rush mats, the curtains are of lightweight materials in light colors, and the beds are placed in the middle of the room with the headboards down to take advantage of the cross ventilation from the windows. During the cold months of the year, heavy brocade and velvet curtains hang at the windows, the four-poster beds are draped with warm fabrics, and woolen rugs cover the floors.

Its landscaped formal gardens, America's oldest, are a National Historic Landmark. It is suggested, and wisely so, that you allow two hours for a complete self-guided tour of the gardens, woodland paths, the butterfly ponds, flooded rice fields, the rice mill, stableyards (with many animals who are cared for by people on the property), and the antebellum slave cemetery. It will take *more* than two hours to tour the grounds if you stop to watch the blacksmith, potter, or weaver at work. (The weaver spins and weaves cloth from the wool sheared from the plantation's own sheep.)

Be sure to plan your visit to Middleton Place so that you will have time for lunch at the restaurant on the premises, which serves some of the finest plantation and low-country cuisine in the Charleston area. A typical lunch may include baked country ham, with a side of corn pudding ("freshly scraped from the cob that morning"), fresh asparagus hollandaise, Southern biscuits with homemade preserves and homemade vanilla custard ice cream with raspberry sauce (all for $12). If you visit the plantation later in the day, the restaurant is open for dinner and on Sundays they serve a brunch.

I also highly recommend arranging to stay overnight at the *Middleton Inn*, which is a country inn adjacent to the Middleton Place property. Their rooms overlook the beautiful Ashley River, whose banks are lined with live oaks dripping with Spanish moss. The spacious rooms have fireplaces, handcrafted furniture, and large marble bathrooms with oversize European-style tubs. The guests of the inn have free access to the plantation and its restaurant. Those who wish can even help with the chores, taking care of the farm animals first thing in the morning or at 4:00 in the afternoon. The inn has a heated pool and clay tennis courts. Arrangements can also be made for bicycles for touring or for horses from the Middleton Riding and Hunt Stables. Prices, depending upon the season, range from $75 to $95 a night.

Barrier Sea Islands

There are a number of barrier sea islands along Charleston County's 91 miles of coastline (some of these are located within a few minutes' drive of the city). But beware, not all the developed island resorts are open to the public; some are open only to guests registered at hotels on the island. Those open to the public include *Isle of Palms* with its *Wild Dunes Resort*, which has a top-rated tennis center; *Folly Island* with its public beach facility; and *Kiawah Island* with its public beach front at *Beachwalker Park* and its private *Kiawah Island Resort*.

You may enter the Kiawah Island Resort as a visitor, even though not registered as a guest, by checking in and signing out at the security gate. Guests and visitors to Kiawah Island have access to one of the most spectacular stretches of white sand beaches. The resort has a very fine golf course (with signs warning not to molest the alligators) and twenty-eight tennis courts with a pro on the premises and a matchmaking service for those single travelers who wish to play tennis. There is also a small shopping mall with specialty shops and restaurants with outdoor patio service. While on Kiawah, you may want to contact Island Tours and Transportation to arrange for a Jeep safari tour to explore marshlands and beachfronts unchanged since the Civil War. They will also arrange guided canoe trips on the salt marshes to learn about barrier island wildlife and ecology.

If you plan to stay on Kiawah Island I would suggest that you stay at the *Kiawah Island Inn*; its well-appointed rooms with breathtaking views are about $125 a night. Have dinner (beautiful menu featuring continental cuisine, $12 to $18) or Sunday brunch ($15.95) at the inn's *Jasmine Porch* dining room. You should be aware that this place has a strict dress code for dinner. For an evening of entertainment and dancing, stop at their *Topsider Lounge*, which is open to guests and visitors.

On your way back to Charleston be sure to stop and see the *Angel Oak* on *John's Island*. This tree, estimated to be more than 1,400 years old, is thought to be the oldest living thing east of the Mississippi. The tree, with a trunk measuring 25 feet and a limb spread of 160 feet, was a landmark to sailors and pirates. Angel Oak is only 6 miles south of Charleston, off Route 700, and well worth the trip.

As I regretfully bade goodbye to Charleston, promising to return again and again, I found myself in agreement with the tourist literature, which calls Charleston "America's Best Preserved Secret."

THE KENTUCKY DERBY

▶ ── ▶

GENERAL AMBIANCE	★ ★
SOCIAL CLIMATE	★ ★
ACTIVITIES	★ ★

FOR TOUR ARRANGEMENTS CONTACT:
T.V. Travel Agency
607 West Main Street, Suite 301
Louisville, KY 40202
(502) 589-4617

▶ ── ▶

*T*he Kentucky Derby, held the first Saturday in May, is indeed "the most exciting two minutes in sports." Since the first Derby in 1875, Churchill Downs Race Track in Louisville, Kentucky, has been its home. There is nothing quite like the thrill of seeing the world's most prestigious thoroughbreds and best-known jockeys come out onto the track ready to Run for the Roses while over 100,000 people join together to sing "My Old Kentucky Home."

General Ambiance

If I were just rating Churchill Downs alone I would give the setting three stars; however, much of your time here will be spent in the Louisville area. And while Louisville is a reasonably nice town with a more Southern flavor than its geographic location foretells, it's probably not a place I would choose to visit except at Derby time. Its potential for the future is, however, good. Louisville has begun to restore its historic sites and put large sums of money into attractive modern buildings. Its entrance into the vibrant city category, though, is still a number of years away.

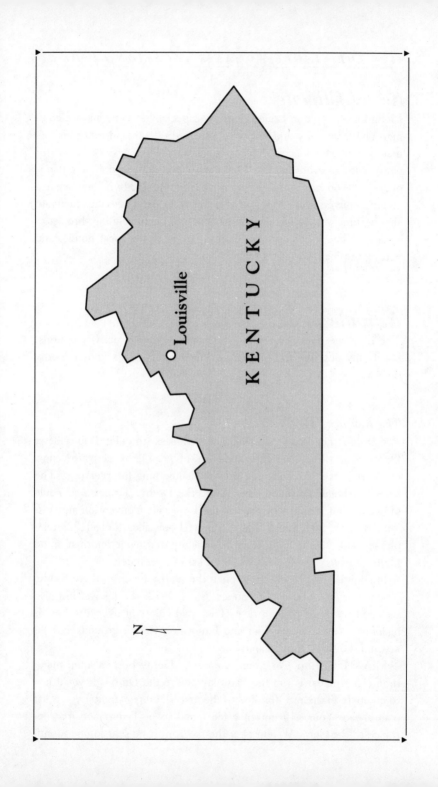

Social Climate

I found the people in Louisville to be especially friendly and welcoming. The hospitality and openness of the residents and other visitors makes it an easy place to meet people, and you're never at a loss for words with an event like the Derby on everyone's mind. The obvious opener, "Who are you betting on to win the Derby?" can begin a lengthy conversation. Many of the Derby Festival activities facilitate sharing time with other people without the overwhelming throngs of a crowd. The jazz concerts, Derby parties at the local hotels, and betting seminars are just a few examples.

Activities

The Kentucky Derby Festival offers a wide range of activity options. I will only describe the highlights. Much more awaits you at Derby time.

The Kentucky Derby Festival

You don't need to be a horse race enthusiast to enjoy Louisville at Derby time. The ever-expanding list of pre-Derby activities, now numbering over sixty events, provides something for everyone. The festivities begin a full ten days before the Derby. To get a schedule of events you should write or call the Louisville Convention and Visitors Bureau, 501 South Third Street, Louisville, KY 50202; telephone (800) 626-5646. They will be happy to provide information on Derby Festival activities as well as a list of area hotels.

In addition to a luncheon to open the Derby Festival, there will be baseball, rugby, and soccer games. Since 1972, the festival has also included the great balloon race. The vivid colors of over fifty hot air balloons rising from the Fair and Exposition Center grounds at 7:00 A.M. fill the skies above Louisville.

Mini Marathon. An annual Kentucky Derby Festival mini marathon (13.1 miles) is run the Saturday before the Derby. If you'd like to compete in the race (limited to the first 6,500 registrants) you must plan ahead. Your $10 entrance fee (good for a T-shirt and free entrance to the Chow Wagon after the race) must be sent in one month before the race. Check with the Convention and Visitors Bureau for the address from which to obtain an entry blank. Participants are also invited to attend a running wild spaghetti dinner and exposition the night before the race.

Great Steamboat Race. A ride on the *Belle of Louisville*, which leaves daily (except Mondays), is usually $5 for the 2:00 P.M. cruise and $8 for the evening dance cruise. However, if you want to be one of the 500 lucky passengers during the Great Steamboat Race you'll have to pay $1 per pound (a good reason to stick to a diet prior to your trip). You can save a place by calling (502) 582-2547. You'll race the *Delta Queen* from the start of the race at the Belvedere Riverfront Plaza at 4th Avenue and River Road down to 6 Mile Island and back. If you'd rather watch from shore, the *Flagship Restaurant* on the twenty-fifth floor of The Galt House offers an incredible view of the river below. Its location, next to the Belvedere Riverfront Plaza, the black tie service, and sumptuous menu make it an ideal place for dinner the day of the only annual sternwheeler races in America. Prices for entrées range from $16 to $27. Call (502) 589-5202 for reservations.

Boat Race Picnic. If you'd prefer a picnic-style lunch with folk music and a magician, the Watch Tower has an annual boat race party on their lawn. The cost is $20. Make your reservations early by calling (502) 896-2146. The menu includes Kentucky fried chicken, mint juleps, wine, and beer.

Puppet Shows. Puppeteers with marionettes and puppets perform throughout festival week in area schools, YMCAs, the Louisville Zoo, and area parks. A list of performances can be found in the local newspaper or by contacting the Kentucky Derby Festival Committee.

Cavalcade of Bands. The top high school marching bands of the area will hold your attention at the Derby Festival Cavalcade of Bands held at the Commonwealth Convention Center. The price of admission is the Derby Pegasus Pin sold throughout the city or at the door. Not only does your Pegasus Pin (the symbol of the flying horse) get you into this and other Kentucky Derby Festival events, it helps support the ten-day Derby Festival. Wear yours proudly, as most locals do. You may even win a car for your $1 donation.

Chow Wagon. The Pegasus Pin will also get you into the Chow Wagon. This very casual event reminds me of the Oktoberfest. Everyone is welcoming and glad to share the fun with another visitor.

Food, beer, soft drinks, and music in outdoor tents are the primary attractions. The entertainment—from 11:00 A.M. to 11:00 P.M. Saturday and 1:00 P.M. to 11:00 P.M. Sunday—includes bluegrass, country western, and contemporary bands. Top local talent, such as the Stone Mill Band, is featured. Don't miss Kentucky Burgoo, similar to a thick goulash soup except much spicier. The Chow Wagon has two locations: 8th and Jefferson streets and the Mall in St. Matthews.

Pegasus Parade. If you like parades, the Pegasus Parade is one of the better ones. It passes down Broadway and is followed by a free post-parade jazz concert on Broadway in Theatre Square at the entrance of the Brown Hotel. Nonalcoholic beverages and food are available. More potent drinks are, of course, available inside.

Hoofers Ball. If you are interested in something more formal, for $300 you can attend the very elegant Hoofers Ball at the newly restored and impressive Kentucky Derby Museum. It's held the Saturday before the Derby and begins with cocktails and hors d'oeuvres at 7:30 P.M. followed by dinner and dancing to the orchestra until 2:00 A.M. For reservations call (502) 637-1111.

Body Building Competition. A less formal event and one that's hard to beat for "people watchers" is the Body Building Competition. For $3 you can see the prejudging show, and for $7 to $12.50 the evening finals. This event, sanctioned by the National Physique Committee will feature men of the best form from lightweights to heavyweights.

Again, the above events are only the highlights. Be sure to check the local newspapers as well as the special Kentucky Derby Festival events brochures, available at your hotel or at the Visitors Bureau, for a complete listing of festival activities.

Preparing for Your Trip to the Kentucky Derby

Rates

The easiest way to secure your Derby ticket is to purchase a tour that includes it. You'll find the price of the tour is based on the type of Derby seat you want. T.V. Travel Agency in Louisville (telephone

[502] 589-4617) offers a three-night package (Thursday, Friday, and Saturday nights). Three nights at The Galt House, Oaks and Derby tickets, all transfers to the track, a cocktail party Thursday night, and breakfast Friday are included in their package. The price for double occupancy is $509 to $639 per person with an additional $150 single supplement charge. Like most hotel rooms at Derby time, the package is treated like a season ticket. Those who go this year have first option on renewing or upgrading their seats next year.

I strongly recommend the more expensive package with grandstand seats. Because you'll be in a box of six people, you'll have a ready-made group with whom to share race tips and the excitement of cashing a ticket. Even a $2 bet makes the race more exciting, especially if your choice is running up front. It's even more interesting if one of your group knows the racing histories of the horses; it doesn't hurt to have some background on which to base your bet.

Obtaining Your Derby Tickets

The Kentucky Derby is not an event you can decide to attend at the last minute. You must plan ahead, be persistent, and even a little creative. The key is securing your Oaks and Derby tickets. It used to be that you could get a ticket to the Oaks, a race for three-year-old fillies held the day before the Derby, on race day. It was an event the locals could attend and miss the throngs of tourists. Though it is still the race of choice for the locals, its popularity has grown greatly, and while ticket prices are still one half to one third that of the Derby, they are just as zealously sought.

There are a number of options for purchasing Derby tickets. Some tickets can be purchased at the gate. If you are lucky, you may be able to get the ticket you want through the local newspaper want ads, or you can write to Churchill Downs and get on a waiting list. Unfortunately, there is a long waiting list for all but general admission tickets, and you can usually expect it to be years before your ticket request is filled. You can also purchase a tour package that includes your hotel room and ticket.

General Admission. With a general admission ticket, which is always available at the gate, $20 for the Oaks and $30 on Derby day, you can attend the races as long as you don't mind being in the grandstand courtyard or in the infield. No seats are available and, unfortunately, your only view of the races will be on television monitors. The people who plan to watch from the grandstand courtyard often bring their own lawn chairs and picnic lunches. While some are in shorts and T-shirts, more are dressed for the occasion, much like the grandstand crowd with whom they mix. Located right next to the paddock, this is a great place to share the excitement of the crowd and watch the horses saddle up prior to each race if you can't get a better ticket. The owners usually walk their horses to the paddock and it's here that the trainers give the jockeys last-minute instructions as the owners look on. I especially enjoy the outfits, or should I say costumes, of the women. Their dresses and hats often appropriately match the colors of the silks of their horses.

The infield is the area inside the track. Here even the television monitors are few and far between. Most "infielders," college students in shorts and bathing suits, are more interested in the sunbathing and partying anyway. Members of the older infield crowd even brag about attending over fifteen Kentucky Derbys without seeing a race. A walk through the infield will give you a taste for that side of the Derby. It's an entirely different experience. While my visit to the infield was fun and everyone looked as if they were having a great time, it was a real relief to return to the comfort of the grandstand. There I could see ten full races and experience the excitement of watching the horses Run for the Roses.

Clubhouse Pass. For another $5 at the Oaks and $10 on Derby day, you can get into the Clubhouse. While the seats here are comfortable, you are inside and the only view of the track is on television monitors.

Grandstand. These tickets must be purchased in advance. Bench seats on the terrace or mezzanine provide a view of the track where the races end, and sometimes begin as well. The grandstand third-floor box seats have folding chairs with backs and provide a view of the whole track. While these tickets are advertised for sale in local newspapers prior to the races, on the "open market" you can expect to pay at least $60 for a grandstand ticket to the Oaks and over $200 for the Derby. This is a substantial markup on the actual cost of $20 for the Oaks and $60 for the Derby. If you can secure a ticket, the grandstand or even the mezzanine is much more comfortable for a full day at the races. Seats on the fourth and fifth floors, known as millionaires' row, provide the best view of the track and the celebrities attending. But these tickets are nearly impossible to obtain.

What to Take

By all means dress up and wear a hat to the Oaks and the Derby. Probably 75 percent of the women in the grandstand will be wearing hats, and you'll find anything goes, from the very stylish and elegant to those that resemble a horse's head or the spires of the Churchill Downs grandstand building. And don't bother carrying an extra box or hiding your hat on the plane trip to Louisville; the easiest and best way to get it to the Derby is to wear it. I often wear a hat when I fly just because it's helped me to meet some very interesting people. A hat, especially a very tasteful one, makes you stand out in a crowd. Besides, wearing a hat makes you look and feel dressed up and classy. So don't pack it away, wear it to the area as well as to the Derby.

The spring weather varies from year to year in Louisville, so check the weather forecast before leaving home. While it could be in the eighties during the day, it may cool down to light jacket or sweater weather at night. Nice slacks or a spring dress will be most appropriate for around the city day or night. You will also want more casual clothes for a few of the Derby Festival events.

Getting Around

There are no deals and no discounts on anything in Louisville, including rental cars, around Derby time. A car will cost you $45 for a day, $315 for a week, most with 100 free miles each day. However, you really don't need a car in town because most points of interest are centrally located. Bus service to the track is excellent, especially on Derby day when the buses run every ten minutes from downtown to the track entrance. The twenty-minute trip is a bargain at $4 each way. Cabs to the track are approximately $25 on Derby day ($10 to $12 at any other time).

Exploring Louisville

About ten years ago, Louisville recognized the importance of maintaining its heritage and began returning its historic buildings to their prior grandeur. The *Brown Hotel*, which sits at the end of 4th Street on Broadway, marks the beginning of the restored area in a most impressive fashion. Don't miss afternoon tea or drinks with a selection of pastries that are difficult to resist in the lobby between 3:00 P.M. and 6:00 P.M., Monday through Sunday. A pianist, who plays until 11:00 P.M., adds an extra touch to an already splendid setting. The area on 4th Avenue in front of the Brown is known as *Theatre Square*. The movie *The Kentucky Derby Show* plays there daily from 10:00 A.M. to 6:00 P.M. For $3 it provides a comprehensive review of the culture, people, beauty, and history of Kentucky—call (502) 585-4008 for further information.

The restoration continues down 4th Avenue, a pedestrian mall, past the restored *Seelbach Hotel* to the *Galleria*, an indoor shopping mall. If you forgot to bring a hat for Derby day, there are a number of shops here with good selections. The prices are modest.

The historic *Brenner House*, open for tours Monday through Wednesday from 10:30 A.M. to 3:30 P.M. and Friday and Saturday from 1:00 P.M. to 3:30 P.M., is nearby and well worth the $2 admission.

If you continue a few blocks farther you reach main street. Louisville has greatly expanded its ease of access to the performing arts with the completion of the relatively new *Kentucky Center for the Arts* on West Main Street between 5th and 6th avenues. Ballet, opera, and orchestral events can be seen here on a regular basis. For ticket information call (502) 584-7777. The *Actors Theatre* of Louisville, (502) 584-1205, also on West Main, and the *Macauley Theatre*, (502) 589-2727, on West Broadway, provide professional entertainment of superior quality. The *Derby Dinner Playhouse*, a theater-in-the-round just across the river in Indiana next to the Sheraton Lakeview, is also well worth a visit. A play with dinner will cost $14 to $19, or for $8 you can see the play at a matinee and enjoy a dessert. Call (812) 288-8281 for reservations.

The *Humana Building* across from the Kentucky Center for the Arts is by far the most spectacular building in Louisville. Designed by postmodernist architect Michael Graves, this building is striking in its emphasis on color and detail and unique with its dramatic waterfall on the street level.

Where to Stay in Louisville

I strongly recommend buying a Derby package that includes your room along with your Oaks and Derby tickets. All of the better hotels at Derby time sell "contracts," not rooms. A "contract" is for three nights—Thursday, Friday, and Saturday. Derby contracts for subsequent years are first offered for renewal to previous guests and are usually mailed between November and January. Recipients are then given thirty to sixty days to respond before the room is made available to individuals on a waiting list.

All of the hotels listed here provide courtesy transportation to and from the airport. At Derby time this service is worth $25 each way, the price of a cab. Courtesy phones to the hotels are available in the baggage claim area opposite baggage conveyors B and E at the newly remodeled Louisville airport.

The most exclusive and the most expensive hotels are the Seelbach and the Brown, elegantly restored older hotels on 4th Avenue in the midst of Louisville's restoration area. Both were very evasive about the price of a "contract" because "the price can vary." You can, however, expect to pay $750 and up for a three-night stay.

Seelbach Hotel, 500 4th Avenue; telephone (800) 585-3200. Originally built in 1905, the Seelbach reopened in 1982 after a $20 million restoration. It now has marble bathrooms and four-poster mahogany beds. It is an ideal setting for F. Scott Fitzgerald's *The Great Gatsby*.

Brown, Hilton Hotel, 339 West Broadway; telephone (800) 445-8667. Originally built in 1923 and reopened in 1985, this is one of the most decorative older hotels I have ever seen, and certainly my favorite in Louisville.

The Galt House, 4th Street and River Road; telephone (502) 589-5200. Another prime location and also available only by "contract," Galt House is on the river next to the Kentucky Center for the Arts. (This is the hotel included in the T.V. Travel Agency's Kentucky Derby package.) History has it that, while guests at the original Galt in 1864, Generals Grant and Sherman planned the strategy that led to the capture of Atlanta. It is now Kentucky's largest hotel.

Sheraton Lakeview, 505 Marriott Drive; telephone (812) 283-4411. Although an excellent choice, this hotel is not quite as conveniently located. It is approximately five minutes from town across the Ohio River in Indiana. The management has arranged continual Derby festivities at the hotel, however, so you really don't need to leave. When you check in you are provided with a two-page list of Derby week events, which include cocktail parties and evening Derby Handicapper's Seminars with complimentary tip sheets and racing forms along with instructions in reading them. All the male help are dressed in colorful jockey silks, and the women in Scarlet O'Hara tradition with full length, Southern belle gowns and parasols. In addition to an indoor pool, tennis and racquetball courts, and a live horse that boards in the lobby for Derby week, there is a 10-acre lake with twelve private floating villas ($250 a day), including one that can be floated into the center of the lake with boat service upon request. Their two bars and superb restaurant, the *Lords of London*, make this an excellent choice for a well-rounded trip to the Derby. Their "contract" is more reasonable, $325 for three nights. Additional nights are only $59 each. You have a much better chance of getting a contract for this property. The manager told me that anyone writing for a reservation ninety days prior to the Derby has a good chance of getting in, sixty days a fair chance, and thirty days a poor chance. Obtaining a contract for the Seelbach, the Brown, or Galt House will be much more difficult. They cater to their regulars and take care of "Churchill People"—owners, trainers, and their entourage.

How to Obtain a Contract. The manager of Galt House was quite candid and very helpful in suggesting how a single woman might increase her chances of getting a room at the Galt. He suggested you write on your company letterhead, regardless of your position. At the very least you should use tasteful, expensive stationery when requesting a room. The first letter should be sent as early as November, followed by a second in January. He also suggested a phone call to the manager after that to see how your reservation request is progressing. As a selling point for his hotel, he assured me they were selective about their guests and that a single woman traveling alone would not only feel safe and comfortable, but would likely find the other guests quite charming as well.

Where to Eat in Louisville

Most of the large hotels have both formal dining rooms and less formal cafes or grills that are excellent choices for lunch or dinner, depending on your appetite.

Graham's Cafe in the Brown has a classic sandwich served hot or cold and appropriately called The Brown for $7. This open-faced turkey, bacon, egg, and lettuce sandwich, topped with a special cheesy white sauce, is a traditional favorite from the days of the old Brown. They also have their own version of Derby pie, a deep-dish pecan ($2.95).

Kern's Kitchen has registered the name Derby-Pie, so any pie served as Derby-Pie will have been purchased from them for resale. The original Kern's Derby-Pie was first served at the Melrose Inn in Prospect, Kentucky, a quarter century ago. The Kern grandchildren still exclusively produce this classic chocolate nut pie, which is similar to pecan pie but much better.

For a light, inexpensive lunch of salad or quiche, try *The Old House Restaurant*, (502) 583-3643, or *The Bristol Bar and Grill*, (502) 583-3342, attached to the Kentucky Center for the Arts. *Alexanders*, (502) 583-1144, in the Galleria, is another informal place to stop for a drink or for lunch while shopping. They have a variety of snacks, sandwiches, seafood, and omelets for around $5. Alexander's serves the famous, original Derby-Pie. Don't miss it ($2.75).

The *King Fish Restaurant*, (502) 895-0544, at the end of 6th Street on the river, is housed in an old riverboat complete with a water-filled moat. While the riverside elevated freeway detracts from the view, you can still enjoy watching the barges float down the Ohio as you eat. This informal and inexpensive fish house offers little in quality. The food is primarily battered fried fish; however, it has a quaint old-fashioned cafeteria feel. It's a pleasant stop for an unhurried light lunch. You can get a complete meal for under $4.

The *Sixth Avenue Restaurant*, (502) 587-6644, on 6th Avenue just off Market, offers quality and history. This restaurant is located in what used to be the Seelbach Hotel. The Atrium dining room is in the now glass-enclosed courtyard of the old hotel. Ivy hanging off the windowsills onto the five-story old brick exterior walls on three sides of the atrium provides a unique setting for a relaxing formal dinner.

The classic American cuisine offers a variety of salads for $5 to $7 and entrées for $6 to $9 for lunch.

The four-star *Casa Crisanti*, (502) 584-4377, specializes in Northern Italian cuisine. While the service and ambiance are first class, so are the prices. *Hasenours*, (502) 451-5210, also formal, offers excellent German specialties along with a variety of seafood entrées. They have two dining rooms. The menu in the less formal atrium is more limited but so are the prices.

Louisville after Hours

In addition to the lounges at the large hotels, most of which have live entertainment during Derby week, and the Chow Wagon, Louisville has a variety of after-hour activities depending on your taste. Be sure to check the schedule of special events for the Derby Festival before deciding on your evening activities.

If none of them catch your fancy and you'd like to check out the down-home Kentucky cowboys, *Tomorrow's*, (502) 361-5496, is the place to go for live Western music and dancing. Wear your blue jeans, boots, and cowboy hat and you'll look like a regular, though you'll feel comfortable in any informal attire. The action doesn't pick up until after 11:00 p.m., so be patient. The crowd is friendly but not imposing (no cover).

If you are a real jazz fan and enjoy the black jazz mystique, *Joe's Palm Room*, (502) 581-1251, on 18th and Jefferson is the place to go. Joe's is an older establishment and a little run down, but it's well regarded by real jazz fans. Though not in the safest part of town, the music is great and it's comfortable inside (no cover).

For a rock music nightclub, you'll want to try *Flaherty's*, (502) 893-2563, at DuPont Road and Breckinridge Lane. It is a current "hot spot." *Rascals*, (502) 452-1031, on Newburg Road at I-264 in the Watterson Towers is another popular place to party, dance, and mingle until 4:00 a.m. The top forties are the rule at Rascals and *Corvettes*, (812) 283-4411, which is located in the Sheraton Lakeview Hotel. Although a little more subdued, the "fake money" poker games at Corvettes are a popular novelty and they fit in well with the Derby festivities.

Treasures to Purchase

The Louisville area is very proud of a local artist, Mary Alice Hadley, and her pottery, often decorated with prancing horses, smiling farmers, and cows. The Picasso influence is easy to spot on many of her pieces. Since her death twenty years ago, her pottery is highly prized and can be both expensive and difficult to locate for sale. There is, however, *Hadley Pottery Company* (1570 Story Avenue) in Louisville, which reproduces copies of the originals, and you can even purchase the less-than-perfect rejects at the factory (584-2171). *Kentucky Stoneware* is a similar, less expensive version.

In addition, many of the large hotels will have areas set aside where ladies from the community can sell local handcrafts. Reasonably priced, many of these are indeed very creative works of art.

Side Trips around Louisville

Horse Farms

While you do not need a car in town, you might want to rent one to drive either east or west on Highway 64. About an hour's drive east will take you to Lexington and a few of the over 1,200 thoroughbred farms in Kentucky. The most famous, such as *Calumet* and *Claiborne* (home of Secretariat) are located here. Calumet farms has bred more Derby winners—eight, including Citation (1948)—than any other farm. These horses live at a higher standard than many people, but then they also earn more!

Kentucky Horse Park

If you'd like to ride horses as well as watch them run, for $8 an hour you can do so at the Kentucky Horse Park, (606) 233-4303. To get there take Highway 64 east to Lexington, then Interstate 75 north to exit 120. It's hard to get lost with the signs directing you to the horse park. It is open daily from 10:00 A.M. to 5:00 P.M. and no reservations are taken. Hard hats are provided. You should wear long pants to avoid saddle burns and shoes with a heel that will keep your foot from sliding all the way through the stirrup. All the rides are in groups and are guided. You will spend part of your time riding the park trails and part of it in the rink where you can trot or canter as you desire. It's a beautiful 70-mile drive from Louisville and a wonderful way to spend the afternoon after driving through the thoroughbred farms.

Huber Winery

If you want to get into the rolling bluegrass hills go west on Highway 64. If you'd like, you can stop and tour the Huber Orchard and Winery just out of town. Call (812) 293-9463 to check the hours.

Wyandotte Caves

If you continue on Highway 64 approximately 20 miles, take the Corydon exit (#105), then 135 south one mile and turn left onto 62, you'll arrive at *Harrison-Crawford State Park*. The spectacular Wyandotte Caves located here offer two-hour tours daily except Monday at 8:00 A.M., 10:00 A.M., noon, 2:00 P.M., and 4:00 P.M.

After touring the caves, if you continue on 62 another 5 miles, you're in for the best home-cooked Kentucky fried chicken dinner you'll likely find. A couple leaving the *Overlook Restaurant* told me they drove 50 miles specifically for the dinner and they'll be back. Perched on a cliff above the horseshoe bend of the Ohio River, the view and barnwood paneling in the dining room add to the down-home ambiance. Home cooking at its best, hot biscuits with strawberry preserves, and lots of coffee accompany each meal. The Overlook Restaurant is open from 8:00 A.M. to 10:00 P.M. Monday through Saturday and till 9:00 P.M. on Sunday. Reservations are suggested on Sunday, though you can generally walk in and be seated during off-peak hours (telephone [812] 739-4264).

While you might go to the Derby without even knowing that the Preakness and the Belmont are the other two races included in the Triple Crown, don't be surprised if you're swept away by the enthusiasm and the infectious excitement of the track. You may even find that you, too, become one of "the regulars," renewing your contract each year for "the most exciting two minutes in sports."

Index

About the Author

Linda's passion for travel began as a child. She recalls being fascinated by her father's stories of his travels throughout Europe, the Far East, and South America. She had been to nearly every state in the Union before graduating from high school in Seattle. After graduating from nursing school at the University of Washington, also in Seattle, she moved to Germany, where she lived for three and a half years and once again traveled extensively, this time throughout Europe, the Middle East, and parts of Africa. She returned to the U.S. to attend the University of Minnesota, where she completed a Ph.D. in clinical psychology and personality research.

She currently resides in Minneapolis, and continues to travel at every opportunity. She prefers to visit countries and areas of countries not frequented by tourists. As a single woman, Linda primarily travels alone. Her travel experiences range from backpacking through Europe and sleeping on trains to taking luxurious cruises through the Panama Canal and down the Amazon River. She's camped on the African plains while on safari and ridden in 1920s-style luxury aboard the Orient Express.

When not traveling, Linda works as a research psychologist Minneapolis.